The
Cultural
Context

The Cultural Context

An Introduction to Cultural Anthropology

by
Robert Anderson

Department of Anthropology
University of Utah
Salt Lake City, Utah

Burgess Publishing Company
Minneapolis, Minnesota

Cover photo: Inca town of
Machu Picchu. (Courtesy
C. Melvin Aikens.)

Book and cover design by Dennis Tasa

Copyright © 1976 by Burgess Publishing Company
Printed in the United States of America
Library of Congress Catalog Card Number 75-16796
ISBN 0-8087-0126-6

10 9 8 7 6 5 4 3 2 1

For Alma, John, and Robert

Preface

Cultural anthropology, as a discipline within anthropology in general, provides us with information about human lifeways and some means of understanding them. I have tried in this introductory textbook to present sufficient material to think about, and a way to think about it. I hope it will be apparent that there is here a structure of ideas, consistently worked out and consistently applied to the behavior of peoples, to the end that the mode of anthropological thinking involved may be grasped and tried out on other peoples and applied to life about us.

Chapter One begins by sketching five societies, not because students in the Age of Television are unaware of the variety in the behavior of peoples, but because it is useful at the start to look at human communities as wholes, even if they cannot be exhaustively described in the space assigned. And they provide an opportunity to make a preliminary assortment of behaviors along the lines of our orientation. They are not a sample in the statistical sense, nor do they represent the evolutionary spectrum in its entirety.

The next three chapters lay the groundwork of principal terms, such as *culture, symboling, energy, system,* and their definitions and relations and examine other concepts of anthropology in historical perspective. They include basic terms in other orientations, related to the scholars who coined and defined them.

Succeeding chapters are grouped into parts that develop an evolutionary perspective on the three major aspects of culture—technology, social organization, and ideology (ideas and beliefs). (If the introductory course in anthropology does not provide an evolutionary context for understanding of events past and present, it is unlikely to be provided anywhere, to the detriment of the student's education.) Evolution is presented in easily grasped categories and rounded out by descriptions of the relevant segments of lifeways, but process (movement) takes precedence over static category. Where they fit best, there are brief discussions of hominid evolution, and of primate tool making, social organization, and communication, to underscore the precultural materials that were ensnared in culture's symboling process as the human brain came into being.

I wrote this book because I wanted to put together ideas I had encountered, invented, and developed in teaching undergraduate classes and graduate seminars, to rework them with new ethnographic and historical materials, and to make more effective the reach of this orienting framework. The work has a cultural focus, not a sociological or psychological one, and, so far as I have been able to make it, it is unitary and consistent in its presentation of the ideas I think important for the understanding of human behavior.

Culture, of course, is cultural anthropology's particular domain, and as a concept it is one of the most important in all of anthropology. I learned early on the unfortunate consequences for a student's thinking when culture is defined as an "abstraction," or as "ideas in the mind." Substitution of the notion of extraction leads to more concrete and productive thinking. It allows real human behavior and productions to stand clear for inspection. The thesis of this text is that the body of objects and events we extract from the whole field of our observation and call culture—objects and events we can see, hear, touch, taste, and smell—fit together as a structure and behave as a system, adapting to environments and evolving. So described, this dynamic and changing accumulation of human experience becomes a context against which varied human actions may be projected and find meaning. Meaning, then, is a place in a context, and grasping that place is an act of understanding.

The initiated will recognize the Whitean influence. However, I have departed from Leslie A. White's analysis in choosing to characterize culture as an open rather than a closed system, both in its general and specific aspects, and I believe I have pushed the notion of cultural system a bit farther than it has been pushed before now in anthropology. The student is asked to put the extracted cultural system up front, in a central position, and to cope progressively with the (at first) patently absurd idea that Homo sapiens may be viewed as an environment of culture. Note well: may be viewed as, not is. Habitat is construed as the other environment from which, as from our species, culture as a symboling-dependent open system captures and transforms materials and energies. This stance permits the use of the findings of ecologists on the one hand and on the other leaves open ended the question of the significance, if any, of biological variations of human populations.

It might be asked if such an objective view of human behavior—the construction of a system from human experience and its use to allocate and give meaning to ongoing events—tends to dehumanize our subject and humanity itself. To the contrary, it seems to me that with uniquely human behavior and productions in the forefront, we move correctively away from the excesses of some ethologists, students of comparative animal behavior, who view us as apes whose impulses prompt behaviors hardly different from those of our primate kin.

This text is intended for introductory courses in cultural anthropology a quarter or semester in length. There are sufficient numbers of ethnographic descriptions in it to back up the conceptual organization and to carry the story line, as it were, but assigned reading from the books recommended at the end of each chapter, or the instructor's other choices, can be integrated easily into the course. The book also could be useful as a focal text in general anthropology for innovative teachers who see culture as anthropology's principal concern and who will want to expand aspects of biological anthropology, prehistory, and linguistics under an orienting cultural-systems-and-environments model.

My first debt, gladly acknowledged, is to Leslie White, friend and mentor, whose work underlies the organization of this book and whose contributions to it go beyond the statements attributed to him. There are departures from his position, but perhaps the situation parallels what the editors of *Evolution and Culture,* also students of his, wrote of their own explorations in relation to White's work: There is "generic continuity . . . but some specific discontinuity" (Sahlins and Service 1960: 124).

I want to thank my colleagues Per Hage, Kristen Hawkes, John C. McCullough, Philip C. Hammond, and David E. Iannucci, and also Joseph Winter and Claudia and Michael Berry, for perspicacious comments on portions of the manuscript. With Kristen Hawkes, in particular, who read the whole work, I had a continuing dialog about the implications of the model and its consistent application. Responsibility for errors and dubious interpretations is, of course, my own.

Robert K. Dentan and Laurence Wylie kindly read and criticized the sketches of Semai and the villagers of "Peyrane," which were drawn from their engaging books, and they sent me photographs to illustrate them. I am indebted to both, as I am to the other anthropologists and friends who contributed photographs from their personal collections or put me in touch with sources. The credit lines are witness to their generosity, and I am greatly in their debt. Acknowledgment also must be made of the skilled photographic laboratory work of David G. Crompton of the University of Utah Archaeological Laboratory, of Per Hage's rendering of the chart of Shoshone bird classifications, and of the assistance of Maner L. Thorpe with the Yakut illustrations.

Thanks also are due Jack Kelso, consulting editor and friend, and the three editors at Burgess Publishing Company who successively were in charge of this project, James G. Baker, the late Alex Fraser, and Gerhard R. Brahms, as well as the members of the Burgess organization involved in its production, especially Ann Seivert and Dennis Tasa.

I also thank the students in my classes and seminars who over the years responded to and challenged portions of this orienting structure as it emerged. Finally, whatever clarity there is in the presentation was furthered by three other readers and critics, my wife and sons.

November, 1975

R. A.

Contents

Chapter Twelve Language as Cultural Mechanism and Content **297**

Chapter Thirteen Evolution in Ideas and Beliefs **313**

Part One
The Task
and Some
Approaches
to It

Chapter One
Five Lifeways

The geographer Isaiah Bowman once recalled a teaching tactic of the renowned earth scientist Nathaniel Southgate Shaler: "Shaler used to say to his geology students that he wanted no fuss made over rocks at the beginning. Just as we introduce a friend as 'Mr. Robinson,' so he wished at first to introduce granites, porphyries, and schists by simply showing 'how they looked.' His object was to get past the technicalities of analysis in the first instance and come at once to the marvels and delights of showing how varied and extraordinary are the bones of the earth and how rock types may be related to one another and to the vast and deep-seated mechanisms of an uneasy and evolving earth" (Bowman 1934: 11).

No less than rocks, surely, are the ways of humans varied and extraordinary, and knowing and understanding them is the privilege of the student of cultural anthropology. The introductions to the ways of humans which follow must be by their brevity partial and incomplete. They are, to use that overworked word, highlights of lifeways that point to some of the variety among humankind, and they are derived in each case largely from the work of a single observer who lived among the people described. Later we will prepare ourselves to relate these peoples to others and to the "vast and deep-seated mechanisms" that account for similarities and for differences among them.

3

The descriptions are cast in the present tense, but that does not mean that the artifacts and behaviors mentioned exist unchanged among these peoples today. Indeed, one of the lifeways has disappeared and a new one has enwrapped its carriers. But it is a convention in anthropology to employ the **ethnographic present**,[1] which represents the point in time at which the observer made the study and additionally a time in which the people still retained the practices we ourselves judge to be different and exotic compared with ours—not untouched but not destroyed by Euro-American domination.

The Eskimo of Coronation Gulf

We look first at the Coronation Gulf Eskimo, as they were in the second decade of this century, through the eyes of the Canadian anthropologist Diamond Jenness (1959), who spent two years with them and who was adopted into the family of the old hunter Ikpuck and his wife, Icehouse. They became known to anthropology as the Copper Eskimo because of their occasional use of fishhooks, chisels, and other implements beaten from native copper. Numbering no more than eight hundred at the time of Jenness's fieldwork, they were divided into about fourteen groups, shifting in composition, that frequented different localities.

January is the coldest, darkest, and stormiest month on Coronation Gulf, which lies between the Canadian Arctic coast and Victoria Island, one of the largest in the archipelago that stretches toward the Pole. The sun is below the horizon throughout January, and there are only five hours of twilight. Ice floes pack the sea and lock the gulfs and bays, and snow covers the land. The Eskimo are secure in their snow houses, which measure six feet from floor to domed ceiling and nine feet in diameter; a working and sleeping platform covered with caribou and musk-ox hides extends over half the floor space. To one side of the low door, which leads to an entrance tunnel, is set a half-saucer-shaped soapstone lamp in which a wick of cotton-grass seeds, floating in seal blubber, burns steadily with a low, smokeless flame. Above it hangs a

The snow houses of an Eskimo winter village are built near the sea, source of the all-important seal. Beside the dwellings are caches and skin boats, sleds and other gear. (Courtesy National Museums of Canada.)

[1]Boldface type indicates a glossary entry.

Adapted by permission of the publisher from *The people of the twilight*, by Diamond Jenness, Chicago: University of Chicago Press. Copyright 1928 by the Macmillan Company. © 1959 by the University of Chicago. All rights reserved.

stone cooking pot, and over all is a rack on which mittens and boots are drying.

The lamp is the center of Eskimo life and, one might say, of their universe. Eskimo families are camped in this seaside location because there are seals to be harpooned through holes in the winter ice, and only seals can provide sufficient oily blubber to maintain the lamps and the food energy required by the hunters and their families. If blizzards cover the seals' breathing holes and keep the hunters at home, hunger advances as bags of dried fish and blubber are depleted, and cold closes in as the lamps are extinguished. Killing of newborn infants and, less frequently, abandonment of the aged were not unknown in times past.

Yet this is the time of year when Coronation Gulf households are congregated in their maximum numbers, with twenty-five or more snow houses clustered at favored sealing grounds adjoining the mainland or islands in the ice-covered sea. There is usually a good supply of the sea mammals, unless, as in Eskimo belief, they are withheld by the sea goddess who controls the seals and storms. If that happens, she must be cajoled and threatened by the wonder-working **shamans**, who can send out spirits of men and animals to find her.

Seals are like birds and some land animals in that they have territories; theirs are beneath the surface of the sea. They emerge at half-hour intervals to breathe—anywhere perhaps when the water is open, but when the ice begins to form they break it for breathing holes that, protected by snow, are kept open through the winter. A trained Eskimo

Their dogsleds heavily loaded, Eskimo rest on a migration from one hunting ground to another near Cape Krusenstern, which is at the western end of Coronation Gulf. (Courtesy National Museums of Canada.)

A summer camp at the mouth of Coppermine River, which flows into Coronation Gulf. Even in the second decade of this century, when the photograph was made, the tents were a mixture of traditional and new. (Courtesy National Museums of Canada.)

Stripping the skin and blubber from a seal at a camp on Dolphin and Union Strait, west of Coronation Gulf in the Canadian Arctic. (Courtesy National Museums of Canada.)

Coronation Gulf Eskimo cut up a caribou near a lake on Victoria Island while the sled dogs wait for their portions. The people migrate north from the gulf during spring and summer. (Courtesy National Museums of Canada.)

Wielding spears, Eskimo fish behind a dam at the mouth of a stream near Bernard Harbor, on Dolphin and Union Strait. (Courtesy National Museums of Canada.)

dog scents a hole, and the hunter, scooping away the covering snow, lowers into it a slender bone that signals by its bobbing a seal's approach. The hunter, with all his might, drives a harpoon into the breathing seal and the struggling animal is pulled up by an attached line, the hole having been enlarged with an ice chisel. Three seals provide enough blubber to fuel a lamp for a month if it burns five or six hours a day.

Although they will dance whenever a few families are gathered and there is food enough to call for rejoicing, the Eskimo take especial advantage of the winter gatherings to attach a large dance house as a forecourt to one or more dwellings. Here, dancing and singing go on to the beat of a large tambourine drum for hours on end—interrupted only by the performances of the shamans, who in convulsive trances call upon their spirits to find the wandering souls of the sick, recover lost articles, predict the weather and fortunes of the food quest, and induce the sea goddess to yield her seals to the hunter's harpoon.

In April and May at Coronation Gulf the days lengthen gradually, until finally the sun begins to circle the horizon without setting. Some sealing continues as the animals appear on the ice, but the Eskimo turn now to intercept the caribou as they move north from their winter grounds on the barrens of the mainland and onto Victoria and other islands over the still-frozen sea. The first comers are lean from their long migration, and their coats, turning from winter white to brown, are perforated by the larvae of botflies. The caribou fatten on the lichens and mosses, but they will not be at their prime until July.

As a season of fishing and caribou hunting begins, Eskimo families move individually or in small clusters about the mainland and the larger islands. For nine or ten hours of each long day—and sometimes on expeditions lasting several days—Eskimo men are out with their fishing gear (lines, tangless hooks, lures, and three-pronged spears) and hunting weapons (bows and arrows formerly, rifles today). With the lakes and ponds slowly losing their ice covering, women, too, spend their days fishing. They carry their catches back to camp for boiling and drying, burdened further with bundles of willow, heather, and flowering dryad for the summer campfires. Dog-drawn sledges become useless as the snow melts; loads are carried on dog and human backs. Caribou skin tents and windbreaks replace snow houses. The dwarf willows show green tips, and duck, loon, and ptarmigan appear in large numbers.

Eskimo women, who sew the clothing for all, require seven caribou skins in order to outfit one adult in parka, breeches, and mittens; seal skin is preferred for boots. In addition to their clothing, and their tents and bags, the Eskimo derive from the caribou's hide straps and lines; from its bones and antlers they derive tools and weapons; from its back and leg sinews they derive cord and thread. Caribou meat, supplemented by fish and only rarely with the fat carcass of a bear, sustains the Eskimo through the days of light and is stored in caches to carry them into the sealing season. And, in fact, the half-digested moss in the stomach of the caribou is the only vegetable food available to Jenness's Copper Eskimo. When a hunting group has made a good kill, perhaps in a surrounding maneuver in which men, women, and chil-

An Eskimo woman and her adopted daughter peg out deerskins to dry. Men are the hunters; women process the skins and sew clothing. (Courtesy National Museums of Canada.)

Caribou meat dries on a rack in front of a summer tent on Victoria Island. The woman at left is cutting up a deer. This and preceding photographs were taken on expeditions of Diamond Jenness. (Courtesy National Museums of Canada.)

dren have taken part, they feast and idle for several days, gossiping, singing, playing games.

As September approaches, snow flurries, not unknown even in mid-summer, increase. Birds fly south, and as soon as the straits ice is strong enough to bear them the caribou cross to the mainland. Moving with the rear guard of the caribou, the Coronation Gulf Eskimo end their hunting and fishing, pick up their cached supplies of dried meat and fish, and collect as opportunity offers driftwood for spears, iron pyrite pebbles for striking fire, and the white seeds of the cotton-grass, which are used for tinder and lamp wicks. Burdened with their stores, the Eskimo return to their seaside wintering places, build their villages of snow houses again, and, as soon as it is possible, resume their seal hunting to replenish the supply of blubber for their lamps and bodies for the winter night.

The Cheyenne
of the Western Plains

In the mid-nineteenth century, a bison-hunting people who called themselves Tsistsistas and whom we know as Cheyenne roamed the

High Plains of the West between the North Platte and Arkansas rivers. Until the late eighteenth century they had been **maize** farmers, living in earth-lodge villages along the Missouri and on the margin of the woodlands west of the Great Lakes. Acquiring from the Spanish Southwest horses, which made the hunt more productive and attractive, and being under pressure from tribes who earlier than they had received guns from trading Europeans, they moved out into the Plains and became an equestrian hunting people. Many others did, too, from both east and west, and the Plains became a cauldron of peoples contesting for hunting territories and access to trading posts. The Cheyenne had allies, such as the Arapaho, who spoke a related language, and enemies, such as the Crow, Pawnee, and Shoshone, with whom they fought. In the span of less than a century, the Plains Indians developed distinctive lifeways based in part upon their pasts and the responses made to the new habitat and to each other, but lifeways with marked similarities. Then came the inexorable migrations of white Americans, the end of the Indians' principal resource, the bison, and wars which ended in the confinement of these native Americans to reservations—for the Cheyenne, in Montana and Oklahoma. Never more than three thousand in number, the Cheyenne declined in population during the time of war and the first decades of reservation life.

George Bird Grinnell (1923), guide, surveyor, nature writer, editor, and self-taught anthropologist, first met the people in 1890, only a decade after the disappearance of the bison herds and hardly more from the last wars, and he visited them intermittently over a period of thirty years. Government agents and missionaries had not yet succeeded, as they did partially and for a time, in suppressing the Cheyenne religion. It is the hunt, the raid, and their ceremonies that are among the memorable features of their lifeway on the Plains.

In the land shared by the Cheyenne and other hunters (we are back in the ethnographic present) a great rolling sea of grass stretches to the horizons. In stream valleys and hollows, cottonwood and willow cluster,

A Cheyenne camp on the Plains, photographed in 1870, when the classic equestrian hunter phrase of the culture was ending. The bison was the major resource for food and for materials, including the hides from which the women cut and sewed the commodious tipis. (Courtesy Smithsonian Institution National Anthropological Archives.)

Superb horsemen, like other Plains Indians, the Cheyenne used their horses in war and raid as well as in hunting and transport. These are Cheyenne warriors at a Sun Dance in 1892. Wars had ended for them about a decade before. (Courtesy Smithsonian Institution National Anthropological Archives.)

and pines grow on the ridges and hills. Summers are hot, interrupted by occasional showers; rainfall on the Plains varies from ten to twenty inches a year. Winters are cold, but the snow is not deep. In spring and early summer, when the grass is green, bison move in herds of a thousand or more; later, when it yellows and dries, they break into smaller herds, and in winter they shelter in the lee of the mountains (Forde 1950: 45-46). Cheyenne chase bison on horseback with lance, bow and arrow, and gun, individually and in small parties as well as in organized hunts with scores of mounted men surrounding a herd and stampeding it into a madly milling circle or driving it over a cliff. It is an adventurous and exciting pursuit.

As an impressionistic estimate, a band of a hundred Indians requires 400 pounds of meat a day, or 12,000 pounds a month; such a band in the Plains is well fed if six hunters each kill no more than two or three bison a month, not allowing for wastage and food for the dogs (Wissler 1941: 242, 245). The quota is not difficult to meet, and Cheyenne life in the mid-nineteenth century must be reckoned one of plenty. Bison meat is roasted and feasted upon, or it is sun dried and packed in skin bags to be reserved for leaner times. The bison provides coverings for the commodious conical lodges, warm robes, shields for war, lariats, and sewing sinews; tools are made from its bones. Also hunted are deer, elk, bear, beaver, and rabbit, as well as prairie chicken. It is from deerskins that men's war shirts and leggings, women's dresses, and moccasins are cut and sewn. Women prepare and fashion the skins; they also gather vegetable foods—prairie turnips, berries, bulbs, pods, and edible leaves. Maize and other garden products are procured in trade from friendly farming Indians.

As for war and raid, the reputation of this people is such that Grinnell entitled one of his chronicles *The Fighting Cheyennes* (1956). As we see them now in the ethnographic present, the Cheyenne fight to

The Task and Some Approaches to It

safeguard their hunting ranges and their access to trading posts and to steal horses and weapons. Sometimes the whole force of the tribe moves against a massed enemy, its Sacred Arrow bundle carried before it, but this happens less frequently than raids by small war parties on hostile encampments and their horse herds. Prepared by religious rituals that include purification in sweat lodges and ceremonial pipe smoking, and an evening of singing, dancing, and gift giving, groups set out, carrying their weapons, shields, extra moccasins, and provisions. They move in single file, on horse or afoot, a pipe carrier leading the way. In enemy territory scouts are sent ahead, and when a camp is located a plan is made. The aim is an undetected approach and a

Plenty Horses, a Cheyenne warrior, photographed near Okmulgee, Indian Territory, in 1875 by the pioneer Western photographer John K. Hillers. The people had divided into northern and southern segments in the first half of the nineteenth century. (Courtesy Smithsonian Institution National Anthropological Archives.)

11

Cheyenne women stake out bison hides, 1877. In addition to being used for tipi coverings, bison hides went into robes, war shields, lariats, and sinews for sewing; tools were made from bison bones. (Courtesy Smithsonian Institution National Anthropological Archives.)

surprise attack. Horses are cut loose and ridden or driven off. Hand-to-hand fighting is not inevitable, but if it occurs a warrior gains more prestige by striking a foe and leaving him unharmed than by killing him. If such strikes occur, the raiders' bodies and robes are blackened on the return journey as a sign of success, and the party charges into its home camp. Most able-bodied men belong to military societies, which, in addition to bearing the brunt of the fighting and raiding, serve as police during tribal encampments, on marches, and during the massed hunts.

Activities of war and the hunt are wrapped in ritual. The relationship of human and bison, as seen by the Cheyenne, is more than that of hunter and hunted. They are co-actors in a history stretching into a mythical past, a history in which supernatural forces often intervened and in which the bison was itself a supernatural figure and a spokesman for others. A bison skull rests in front of a medicine man's sweat lodge and centers the altar in tribal rituals; the bison is impersonated in dances, and it is believed that its numbers are magically increased by the performance. In dreams and visions the bison appears to men, directing them in techniques of healing or in the making of magical shields. Major ceremonials of the Cheyenne are the renewal rite for their four **Sacred Arrows**, which are expected to bring success in war and on the hunt; renewal of the **Sacred Hat**; the **Massaum** or Animal Dance, in which animals are impersonated; and the great Willow or Medicine Lodge, called the **Sun Dance** because of its similarity to a

The Task and Some Approaches to It

Dakota sun-gazing rite. These are performed during summer encampments within the great tribal circle of tipis.

Like all Plains Indians, the Cheyenne are engaged in the quest for guardian spirits, which are believed to respond in pity to the seekers' ordeals of self-torture and to make gifts of power-working songs and talents in war, in the hunt, and in curing. Highest of all supernaturals is Spider Above, or Wise One Above, who is flanked by spirits of the four quarters and many more, and whose opposite number is The One Underground. The spirits are appealed to with sacrifice and prayer and promises to undertake performances of the ceremonies.

The Cheyenne lifeway was, to credit the legends and tales handed down by the old, a richly satisfying one, but it was shattered, and only some of its parts survived and became merged into the new lifeway that succeeded it.

The Semai of Malaysia

"We do not get angry," say the Semai. "We do not hit people." And it is this characteristic of the Semai, this emphasis on nonviolence, that impresses outsiders who visit their land, in the opinion of their ethnographer Robert K. Dentan (1968). Even to prevent another from doing

Adapted by permission of the publisher from *The Semai, a nonviolent people of Malaya*, by Robert K. Dentan, New York: Holt, Rinehart and Winston. Copyright © 1968 by Holt, Rinehart and Winston, Inc.

Tying together the roof poles of a Semai multifamily house. The roof will be shingled with woven palm leaves and the walls covered with bamboo poles. (Courtesy Robert K. Dentan.)

An East Semai family, Telom River, 1962. (Courtesy Robert K. Dentan.)

Recreation among the gentle Semai. The woman is playing a two-stringed lute. (Courtesy Robert K. Dentan.)

East Semai rafts on the Telom River. The people are collecting drinking water. (Courtesy Robert K. Dentan.)

what that person wants to do or to deprive that person of a desired object is against the cultural grain among these people. To frustrate another, to make another unhappy is *punan*; it is **taboo** and exposes one to a legitimate demand, backed by public opinion, for apology and compensation. Having public opinion against one is a great embarrassment for a Semai; the Semai will make amends or, if so inclined, will move elsewhere. No wonder, then, that these Malaysians have no reputation as warriors. They will not attack, and if they are in danger they will flee.

The Semai live in the rugged and forested Main Range in the western part of Malaysia, a constitutional monarchy in the Commonwealth of Nations. When Professor and Ms. Dentan lived among them in 1962-63, these short-statured, brown-skinned Asians numbered about 12,700, dispersed in small settlements in clearings of the rain forest near the fast-flowing streams that fall from the mountain slopes.

A Semai settlement usually consists of one multifamily house, though some settlements have two or three. Each house has walls of bamboo poles and a pitched roof thickly shingled with woven palm leaves, the

The Task and Some Approaches to It

whole built sturdily for protection against elephants, tigers, and leopards, as well as wind and rain, and elevated as much as twenty feet off the ground. Inside, each family has a sleeping compartment set off by short walls (there is no privacy to speak of in Semai life). Running lengthwise through the house is a raised aisle on which rest the hearths and which is used for dancing and as a place for adolescents to sleep. There may also be smaller houses, more lightly built, for one or two families; however, in time of violent storms or when animals are about, people take shelter in a longhouse.

The houses of a settlement are within a five- or ten-minute walk of one another; it is about an hour's walk to the next settlement. The people of a single settlement or a cluster of them comprise a band, averaging forty-five individuals and not often exceeding one hundred. The band claims as its territory its settlement site and surrounding garden and forest land. Each band has a nominal headman; "nominal" is an important qualifier, because headmen can only persuade, not direct. There are some larger territorial groupings called *gu*; the people in each *gu* are distinguishable to some degree from those in other *gu* by custom and dialect. But the Semai as a whole have no political unity.

Only kin can be really trusted by a Semai, and kinship is restricted to the descendants of one's great-grandparents, those so related comprising what is called a *jeg*. All other people are *mai*, people not of one's "blood." This includes spouse and spouse's relatives, for one cannot marry someone in one's *jeg*, and mates, therefore, must be found outside of all but the largest settlements. There are no strict rules about where a couple lives after marriage; the pair tends to stay with the family of either the husband or wife alternately and at increasingly long intervals until final choice is made. Semai get lonely and are restive among *mai*, even when they are linked to them by marriage. A longhouse consists of related families, most often of brothers and their wives, or sisters and their husbands. What generation one is in and one's relative age within the generation are the principal considerations in labelling kin and behaving appropriately toward them; in general, a junior respects and defers to an elder.

Fields in which the Semai raise their main subsistence crops of dry rice, cassava or **manioc**, and maize or Indian corn are cut and burned either from the towering rain forest or from the second growth of trees and underbrush that has taken over in previously cleared and abandoned patches; clearings are made cooperatively, but each family has a patch set off by a line of felled logs. The piles of vegetation must dry for a month, and they are burned over twice just before onset of the heavy rains, the fire destroying the weeds and the ashes fertilizing the shallow jungle humus. At planting, women and girls, and sometimes men, drop rice seeds and manioc cuttings into holes that the men and boys have punched into the ground with digging sticks. Everything, in this kind of tropical farming, is planted in the same field together. Rice, when mature, is harvested with knives and carried to the settlement, where it is treaded, pounded in wooden mortars, and winnowed by repeated tossing in a basket. Food is cooked in metal pots procured in trade.

Supplementing the domesticated garden produce are wild roots and tubers, such as yams, and fruit, including the "foul-smelling but delicious" durian and the breadfruit. The Semai men hunt arboreal animals such as the gibbon and monkey with bamboo blowguns armed with poisoned darts. They also use a large variety of noose and spring traps in the hunt; the spear is used only defensively against large animals. The Semai also fish, with traps, baskets, lines, poisons, nets, and their bare hands. Chickens and dogs formerly were the only domesticated animals; more recently, ducks, goats, and cats have been acquired. The westernmost Semai, who live in or near Malay settlements near the coast and who have been changing in the direction of the Malay lifeway, have carabao (water buffalo) to help them in their more recently adopted wet rice farming, but the description we have extracted from Dentan's account is restricted to the dry-farming hill people.

We shall have occasion to touch on the ways in which the Semai have organized their thoughts and emotions about the world they see, hear, smell, touch, and taste. But we should not leave them, however temporarily, without noting their attitudes and behaviors, which they have in common with so many peoples of the kind anthropologists have studied, about sharing their worldly goods. Rice and manioc transported from the gardens, fish caught in the stream, fruit collected, or a pig caught in the forest are not consumed exclusively by the farmer, the collector, or the hunter and members of their own families, at the home hearth. "If one has only a little surplus over one's own immediate need, one shares it with one's nuclear family; if more, with people in one's house or neighboring houses; if a large amount, with all the people in one's settlement. One must also share with guests and with anyone who asks. Not to share is *punan*" (Dentan 1968: 49). And never a "Thank you," please; to say "Thank you" is rude, as rude as it is to refuse a request or to ask for more than a donor is able to give. And never a calculating of values to be matched in return at a later date, although eventually one is recompensed on another day when the other has something to share.

The Kalinga of the Philippines

"Ancestors of ours who built this (rice) field and from whom we inherited it, have pity on us. We are killing a pig . . . to 'end' your staying here. Do not come again.

"Our god, Kubanian, who is the Greatest . . ., drive those spirits away and make this soil furnish us good crops. Do not permit these spirits to come again, thou who art the greatest and supreme above all others" (Barton 1949: 18).

The setting is a terraced hillside in the mountains of northern Luzon in the Philippines; the time, within the first decades of this century. We may visualize as he speaks those words a Kalinga man accompanied by his wife, he in woven cotton breech clout and short jacket, she in knee-length wrapped skirt and like jacket, standing at the edge of a rice **padi**. They have brought a small pig as a sacrifice to induce the departure of ancestral ghosts believed to be lingering about. After the pig is

Adapted by permission of the publisher from *The Kalinga of northern Luzon, Philippines,* by Edward P. Dozier, New York: Holt, Rinehart and Winston. Copyright © 1967 by Holt, Rinehart and Winston, Inc.

The Task and Some Approaches to It

Village of Bugnay, on the southern border of Kalinga territory. Rice terraces climb the lower mountain slopes in the middle Chico River Valley. (By permission from *Mountain arbiters: The changing life of a Philippine hill people,* Edward P. Dozier, Tucson: University of Arizona Press, copyright 1966 by the University of Arizona Press.)

killed, the two depart for their home, first placing some rice, meat, and bananas on the padi embankment as they say, "This is the end of you. Eat and depart."

Kubanian, in Kalinga belief, is the great god, but there are also gods of thunder, lightning, the rainbow, and volcanoes; demons that bring depressed feelings, worry, bad luck, and illness; spirits, living in rocks, springs, and volcanoes, that can capture and eat human souls; and ghosts of the dead, *anitu,* who are feared and mistrusted (Barton 1949: 18-20).

The Kalinga, who live in the Mountain Province of Luzon, Republic of the Philippines, numbered about 24,500 when they were studied by the anthropologist Roy F. Barton in 1939. They had increased to 40,000 when they were visited twenty years later by Edward P. Dozier (an anthropologist reared, incidentally, in the Tewa Indian pueblo of Santa Clara in New Mexico). Their hamlets and villages of six to thirty houses (there are towns of up to 4,000 people in the southern part of their land, which Barton knew best) are surrounded by terraced and irrigated rice padis that climb upward from stream level. Farther off, dry rice, sweet potatoes, and sugarcane grow in fields that are cut and burned from the forest, which is allowed to grow back after two or three croppings. Although wealthy people build octagonal dwellings, most houses are rectangular or square single-roomed structures, walled with plaited bamboo or hewn planks, their pitched roofs thatched with reeds and grass and their mat floors raised three or four feet above the ground. Inside each house is a sand-filled box that serves as fireplace, some mats and chests, and little else, although each family has a store of treasured heirlooms—Chinese plates and jars, agate bead necklaces and chokers, and brass gongs.

Outside, men may be found lounging about, for their labor is equal to women's in importance but not so sustained. Women not only assist in the fields but take care of house and children, carry water and firewood, prepare meals, and pound and winnow rice. As Dozier (1967: 8-9) reported, "The rhythmic sound of pounding rice is heard from early in the morning until late in the evening. Virtually at any time during the day one may see the transporting of *palay* (unthreshed rice) in baskets on the balance pole by men or in baskets posed on the heads of women." Dogs, pigs, and chickens roam the village, and in the padis or wallowing in pools and mud puddles are carabao.

The core of a Kalinga household is a family, but of more importance than the family itself is membership in a broad circle of kin counted on both sides from great-grandparents through great-grandchildren; there one may find support in disputes, succor in trouble, assistance in rituals that accompany birth, marriage, sickness, and death. Within the areas called regions, four to seven miles across and embracing five hundred or more people, nearly everyone is a close or remote kinsperson, and most marriages take place within the region. In the south, an aristocratic class called *kadangyan* has been emerging, but for the most part the regional leaders, the *pangat,* rise to prominence by demonstrating talents in speaking, counseling, and arbitration. The Kalinga have a reputation as a touchy people, demanding compensation for injuries and insults; keeping peace by acting as a go-between and inducing compromise is a task of the *pangat.* There is a well-developed customary law which guides him.

Southern Kalinga raised dwelling. The walls are of plaited bamboo, and the pitched roof of reeds thatched with grass. (By permission from *Mountain arbiters: The changing life of a Philippine hill people,* Edward P. Dozier, Tucson: University of Arizona Press, copyright 1966 by the University of Arizona Press.)

The Task and Some Approaches to It

Footbridge of plaited bamboo spans the Saltan River and links two northern Kalinga hamlets. (By permission from *Mountain arbiters: The changing life of a Philippine hill people,* Edward P. Dozier, Tucson: University of Arizona Press, copyright 1966 by the University of Arizona Press.)

Until the beginning of this century, Kalinga in adjoining regions fought small pitched battles with each other and went on head-hunting expeditions. Killing enemies and taking heads brought prestige and the rank of *mongol,* brave warrior. These forays have all but ended (although head taking continued sporadically well into this century) through the device of the peace pact, initiated in each case by two respected men in hostile regions. Pacts are arrived at after an exchange of feasts and much talk, and they are renewed usually at yearly intervals; they are binding on all the people of a region. Travel and trade have been made safer and easier thereby.

A Kalinga faces a created world of gods, demons, and spirits which, in its hostility to him, resembles the social world outside the boundaries of the kin circle and region before the peace pacts were instituted. Nature is prodigal in yields of rice and other domesticated plants, of pigs and carabao, and of game from the occasional hunt (fishing is available but not important). But crops sometimes fail, and illness, death, and other misfortunes strike. Spirits bring the misfortunes, sometimes out of malice and sometimes because rituals and customary practices are ignored, and the spirits have to be appeased by offerings of pigs, chickens, sugarcane wine, and prayers. Illness calls for the rituals of a medium, almost always a woman, who chants and prays, strikes tones from a Chinese plate by means of a bamboo stick, and directs the sacrifice. Death of a parent or grandparent requires a year's

Five Lifeways

Kalinga mother and child and interior of house. Walls are of plaited bamboo. Fire is made on the sand bed, and over it household stores are kept. By permission from *Mountain arbiters: The changing life of a Philippine hill people,* Edward P. Dozier, Tucson: University of Arizona Press, copyright 1966 by the University of Arizona Press.)

Kalinga woman and children. In front of them are a mortar for pounding grain, a large rice bowl, and a carabao hide on which there is unthreshed rice. (By permission from *Mountain arbiters: The changing life of a Philippine hill people,* Edward P. Dozier, Tucson: University of Arizona Press, copyright 1966 by the University of Arizona Press.)

mourning period filled with dos and don'ts that ends with a feast and a dance—and all the while, ancestors and spirits watch lest something be omitted or misperformed.

But to dwell on their misfortunes and fears would put the Kalinga in faulty perspective. They were in the past and are now a rather happy people. Speaking of the tasks of daily life, Dozier (1967: 9) says that "all activities go on in an atmosphere of unrestrained chatter and laughter." They are as fond of music as they are of the art of speaking and employ flutes, harps, and percussion instruments made of bamboo. Particularly, in the past, they danced.

"A Kalinga dance used to be a beautiful thing to behold—the men lunging and retreating, while beating gongs suspended from human jawbones, and encircling the women, who, marking time without much locomotion, revolve in their places to face the warriors dancing around them. The Kalingas are fond of bright colors and, for the dance, thrust

The Task and Some Approaches to It

hibiscus blossoms or sunflowers through their punctured earlobes or wear them in their headbands. In the dance as it used to be, the women's dance skirts were adorned with platelets of silver, tin, or tinsel. More beautiful than the gay ornamentation, however, were the gracefully moving, sinuous, muscular bodies of the dancers and the streaming hair of both women and men. . ." (Barton 1949: 12).

The villagers of Peyrane

The community which Laurence Wylie (1974) pseudonymously called "Peyrane" lies about thirty-five miles east of the city of Avignon in the Department of Vaucluse, in that part of France known as Provence. Professor Wylie, an American student of the French language and civilization, was accompanied by his wife and two young sons during a year's residence in 1950-51, and he made later visits to keep in touch with far-reaching changes in progress. Perhaps no community in France or elsewhere has been more sympathetically yet objectively described than this one, by a scholar who merged himself, so far as it was possible for an outsider to do so, into the village life. He was a tolerated and respected student, the teacher of an English class in the school, and effectively the village photographer. He provides a good deal of history behind the Peyrane of 1950-51 and an account of following change, but, in keeping with the style of the preceding four sketches of lifeways, we shall fix upon just 1950-51 as our ethnographic present.

Adapted by permission of the author and publishers from *Village in the Vaucluse*, 3rd ed., by Laurence Wylie, Cambridge, Mass.: Harvard University Press. Copyright © 1957, 1964, 1974 by the President and Fellows of Harvard College.

Peyrane on its hilltop. Earlier in this century a nearly self-sufficient village of farmers and traders, it has become, like many others in France, a place for commuting city workers to live, a recreational resort, and a retirement haven. (Courtesy Laurence Wylie/Anthro-Photo.)

Five Lifeways

A resident of Peyrane walks in the village. The handsome old dwellings crowd one another, and their doorsteps obtrude on the stone-paved streets and squares. (Courtesy Laurence Wylie / Anthro-Photo.)

The Vaucluse is known for its sunny skies and the mistral, a cold, dry wind that blows fiercely from the northern mountains to the Mediterranean in scattered periods of up to a week or more, particularly in December, February, and March. The region as a whole has fertile soil and a relatively long growing season; irrigation water is available in its lower, western portion for the truck gardens that supply vegetables to European city markets but not in the more elevated fields about Peyrane.

Peyrane is one of the hilltop villages clustered along the sides of the twenty-five-mile-long Apt Basin, through which flows the little Calavon River, which is dry in summer and floods briefly in spring and fall. The population of the Peyrane "commune," the village and its farms, is only about seven hundred, half that of a century earlier. On its own hilltop, surrounded by red and yellow cliffs that fall sharply from it on three sides, Peyrane is a huddle of public and commercial buildings and individual houses and gardens that lie along half a dozen narrow, mean-

The Task and Some Approaches to It

dering streets. The old structures, of stone covered with stucco, are painted with red ochre and have red-tiled roofs, matching the brilliant colors of the cliffs and contrasting with green trees and blue skies.

At the approach to the village stands a war monument; nearby are a damp and bleak festival hall, converted from an old communal market, an aging and inadequate public school and its yard, and a post office. Farther on are the small town hall and a Roman Catholic church. Between and around them, fronting on the narrow streets and an occasional *place,* or square, are family homes, mostly two-storied and on the average twenty feet wide. The village boasts two cafés, a hotel with a restaurant, a bakery, two groceries, a butcher shop, a tailor shop, a beauty parlor, a smithy, the establishment of a dealer in wood, coal, and gasoline, and that of a dealer who buys farm products and markets them in the city and sells fertilizer and farm supplies. These provide about everything the community needs, although there is a sizable contingent from Peyrane at the Saturday morning market in the larger administrative and commercial town of Apt, four miles away.

For the most part, dwellings are old, many a century or more, and only two were constructed within the few decades before 1950-51. There is a housing shortage, but paradoxically a third of the houses are vacant; owners say government rent controls make it uneconomic for them to rent, and they would rather sell. Thus, it is hard for young marrieds to find a house. Few of the dwellings have running water, electricity, or toilets (there are three public ones), and the sewage system is rudimentary, drain pipes discharging over the edge of the cliffs. Peyranais, however, do not regard these limitations as in any way unusual.

Life in each dwelling centers in the *salle,* or principal room, tile-floored and rather bare but scrupulously neat and clean, which serves as living room, dining room, and kitchen, a place for entertaining neighbors and friends and holding family councils. The only heat, from a fireplace or wood stove, is here, as is the only artificial light, a shaded electric bulb hanging over the table. With the exception of new houses, like that of the *notaire* (who is at once recorder of deeds, banker, broker, and lawyer), there is an absence of luxuries such as central heating and electrical appliances that many Americans in city and country take for granted. There are, however, radios and sewing machines. Farm houses duplicate the village ones; they are more isolated and must be provided with a stout north wall and a roof secured by boulders in order to withstand the mistral. As Wylie writes (1974: 146), the family spends as much time in the sun as it can, but in winter ". . . the family is drawn about the fire in the *salle,* the core of the family's existence. It is inevitable that the English word *home* cannot be translated directly into French. The nearest equivalent in French is the word *foyer,* the hearth."

While life in Peyrane is hearth-centered, the principal public meeting place and recreation establishment is the café. It is a men's social club in this male-privileged society, an unofficial information bureau and gossip center. Women visit it only to make purchases; they have their recreation over coffee in their homes, in work-and-talk circles with friends, or during chats with store owners and their wives when marketing. In addition to purveying wine, the *cafetier* is licensed to sell the

A baptism procession. As the infant is carried from the church, its godfather throws small handfuls of one-franc pieces to the children, and the party of parents, godparents, and relatives makes its way through the village. (Courtesy Laurence Wylie / Anthro- Photo.)

Peyrane children and their school. Two hundred and fifty years old when this photograph was taken, and a school since 1833, the picturesque building has been replaced recently by a modern structure. (Courtesy Laurence Wylie / Anthro-Photo.)

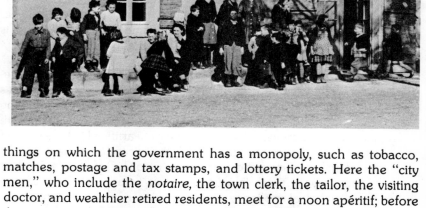

things on which the government has a monopoly, such as tobacco, matches, postage and tax stamps, and lottery tickets. Here the "city men," who include the *notaire*, the town clerk, the tailor, the visiting doctor, and wealthier retired residents, meet for a noon apéritif; before the evening meal, farmers, artisans, and workers from the nearby ochre mines gather for their wine and anise-flavored *pastis.* It is also the home base for a handful of poor adult males, The Lonely Ones, who live alone.

The *cafetier* promotes sales of his wares by sponsoring tournaments for *boule* players, who make use of the *place* across from the café. (*Boule* is a game played with cast bronze or steel balls in which the object is to throw the ball closest to a little wooden target called the "cork" and to thrust one's opponent's missiles away from it.) Profit also accrues from calls for wine by players of a card game, *belote.* And one evening a week the café is converted into a movie house by a visiting projectionist, who collects admission fees; once again, the *cafetier* sells wine.

Although the people say they enjoyed many traditional celebrations in better days before the world wars, the only important ones now are the Feast of Saint Michael, a fair held in September in honor of the

The Task and Some Approaches to It

village's patron saint; All Saints' Day and All Souls' Day in October; and Midnight Mass in the church at Christmas. Active organizations are the Volunteer Firemen, who hold a dinner on the day of their patron, Saint Barbara, and a Hunting Club, which tries to regulate the supply of game in the commune. There are also a number of cooperatives for grape growers and distillers and a successful tractor-and-plowing cooperative for farmers.

Livelihood of the Peyrane commune depends on the farms, vineyards, and orchards. There is little other activity save a few small ochre mines and the supporting tasks of artisans and shopkeepers. Of the ninety-two farms, all are capable of being run by family labor, with few hired hands; half are between twenty-five and fifty acres, a quarter of them having less land, and a quarter of them more. A farm is not a single, unitary entity but has scattered patches of small and irregular fields, an arrangement less the product of the hilly terrain than of the fragmentation in the long history of inheritance. Sixty percent of the farms are worked by the families owning them, the rest by renters and sharecroppers. These three groups do not delineate social classes, however, because a family may simultaneously own and rent from others portions of the land it works and a sharecropping family may have lived so long on a farm that it is highly respected and secure in the community. Peyrane farmers supply the commune and surrounding towns, but more importantly they ship wheat, asparagus, grapes, melons, tomatoes, cherries, wine, and other products to city markets in northern Europe. This commerce, and their need for certain manufactured goods, puts them in the grasp of rarely predictable economic forces.

The cost of living is high in Peyrane in relation to family incomes. In the village, practically everything—bread, oil, wine, and other staples, as well as clothing, fuel, recreation, and housing—must be paid for in francs. Professor Wylie calculated that the monthly market basket of a family of four costs $60 (this is mid-century, remember). And the average monthly income of a family from salaries, wages, and government subsidies is $60 to $70. How, then, do they live?

First of all, people exchange goods and services. The postman, for example, does errands on his rounds and receives gifts of eggs, cheese, or a bottle of wine. He is in addition the village electrician and plumber. The women contribute by keeping small gardens and rabbit hutches, sewing for their families and others, gathering baskets of berries and mushrooms, and collecting wood for fuel. Hunters contribute a meager bag of rabbits and small birds. Gifts come from relatives living on farms (the full-time farmers are more self-sufficient when it comes to food, but they are pressed for other necessities), and some village families raise vegetables and grapes on land they own or rent. Whenever possible, people take short-term jobs during the harvest. Even the ochre workers have gardens. The Peyranais may look fairly prosperous in their Sunday best, but they have to live frugally to make ends meet. As might be expected, there are very few motor cars—and they are used for work, not pleasure. Everything from tractors to radios and sewing machines is repaired and repaired again.

Difficulties are compounded in Peyrane by the fact that the population is skewed in its age distribution: more than 25 percent are over

sixty years old. The French lost heavily in two world wars, and many of the younger and more productive have gone to make a living in the cities. The elderly work as long as they can, but years inevitably take their toll in infirmity.

The French state is a constant presence with which the villagers of Peyrane would like to remain uninvolved, but of course they cannot. They have a love of *patrie,* of country, and a satisfaction in the achievements of France in the arts and other fields, inculcated in the home and in the government-controlled school that all must attend from ages four to fourteen, but an intense suspicion of the bureaucracy. The government is only one of the entities included under the frequently heard term *ils,* which means "they," others being corporations, newspapers, and the like. "Usually, however, it refers to the French Government in all its manifestations, for it is the Government which collects taxes, makes war, controls the wine production, and employs impersonal civil servants" (Wylie 1974: 206). Government family allowances, and sickness, unemployment, and old age benefits, do not temper the dislike; people complain of their insufficiency and of endless bureaucratic tangles.

Periodically, the Peyranais become involved in national and municipal election campaigns and divide themselves into moderates, Communists, and nonvoters. But local affairs, including choice of a council which appoints the mayor, are more important than programs promoted by outsiders. As an example, the local Communists divided themselves into factions at one time—not over political ideas but over the question as to whether it was proper to hunt rabbits with guns or ferrets. At bottom, the people of Peyrane have a disdain for politics and politicians. The quality they look for in a leader (who will be more tol-

The Task and Some Approaches to It

erated than followed) is that of being *serieux*—serious, solid, responsible, respectable, capable of minding his own business and not meddling in the business of others.

A description of Peyrane in the mid-1970s would not be the same as one for the early 1950s. True, the spectacular setting is unchanged, and so are a few of the village's structures. But there is a new and modern school, a luxury inn has been built, the restaurant has been enlarged and enjoys a wide reputation, and new dwellings have been constructed and old ones refurbished. A sewer system has been installed; there is an augmented water supply via canal from the Durrance River to make possible bathtubs, toilets, machines for washing clothes and dishes—and even swimming pools. Bottled gas, rather than the fireplaces, provides heat for cooking; television sets and refrigerators are commonplace, and the streets are often clogged with automobiles.

However, it is the composition of the population and the economic and other social relations of the people that have changed the most. With the progressive industrialization of France, villages like Peyrane are no longer the centers of the farm economy: they have become dormitory towns for city workers, second residences for middle and upper classes, and retirement havens, so that land values have increased enormously. Peyrane itself has attracted many artists and has become a popular resort town. As the village population relates directly to the cities, so do the farmers, none of whom now live in the village, relate to the city markets. Their concerns are with mechanization (the plow cooperative thrives and the number of privately owned machines grows) and with raising specialized crops for market demands.

Wylie has written: "The Peyranais no longer feel themselves to be—in fact no longer are—a unit functioning as autonomously as possible in defense against the Outside World; they have become an integral part of the world once staunchly resisted" (1974: 371). Despite the shift to a national perspective, however, the Peyranais retain a strong sense of family responsibility along with a "concomitant refusal to compromise [their] right to independence" (1974: 383).

Hunters of Arctic seal and grassland bison in North America, primitive and advanced cultivators in Malaysia and the Philippines, and villagers who share in the industrial civilization of France provide examples of the observed and experienced stuff of anthropology, which induces the questions the discipline asks and the materials for answering them. The five sketches are not intended to be a scientific sample of the world's societies either in time or space. They are only a small introduction to variety.

Professor Wylie wrote of his engaging villagers (1974: 13): "The real distinction of Peyrane is to be found not in its red cliffs but in the lives of the people who live in the town above the cliffs." Anthropology deals with distinctive lifeways. As presented here, the lifeways are not strictly comparable, because some facets of the whole were emphasized in one, ignored in another. We shall call them up again from time to time and supplement them when they are used as illustrations for topical matters; and we shall need to introduce ourselves to segments of other lifeways to grasp the evolution of human behavior.

Suggested Readings

The following readings and the ones that will be found at the end of each of the chapters are chosen for their appropriateness to the topics and peoples discussed. They include some sources used in this book and relevant supplementary materials. No more than the world's peoples do anthropology and allied disciplines speak in a single voice or embrace a single ideology, so do not be disconcerted by different perceptions and viewpoints. Availability of a paperback edition is indicated by an asterisk at the end of a reference.

Casagrande, Joseph B., ed. 1960. *In the company of man: Twenty portraits by anthropologists.* New York: Harper and Brothers.*

Dentan, Robert Knox. 1968. *The Semai.* New York: Holt, Rinehart and Winston.*

Dozier, Edward P. 1966. *Mountain arbiters: The changing life of a Philippine hill people.* Tucson: University of Arizona Press.

———. 1967. *The Kalinga of northern Luzon, Philippines.* New York: Holt, Rinehart and Winston.*

Forde, C. Daryll. 1950. *Habitat, economy and society.* London and New York: Methuen and Company and E. P. Dutton and Company.*

Golde, Peggy, ed. 1970. *Women in the field: Anthropological experiences.* Chicago: Aldine.

Gould, Richard A., ed. 1973. *Man's many ways.* New York: Harper and Row.*

Hoebel, E. Adamson. 1960. *The Cheyennes: Indians of the Great Plains.* New York: Holt, Rinehart and Winston.*

Jenness, Diamond. 1958. *The people of the twilight.* Chicago: University of Chicago Press, Phoenix Books.*

Marquis, Thomas B. 1931. *A warrior who fought Custer.* Minneapolis: Midwest Company. Lincoln: University of Nebraska Press, Bison Books.*

Service, Elman R. 1971. *Profiles in ethnology.* New York: Harper and Row.*

Wylie, Laurence. 1974. *Village in the Vaucluse.* 3rd ed. Cambridge, Mass.: Harvard University Press.*

Humankind's ways, then, are "varied and extraordinary." Humans make and wield stone knives, spears, digging sticks, spades and plows, and—peaceably and nonpeaceably—firearms and atomic devices. They live as hunters and collectors in refuge areas of the earth, as simple and advanced cultivators, as workers at power machines, and as technicians in the control rooms of intricate energy- and message-delivering systems. They are organized into households, bands, clans, villages, cities, nations, and international corporations. They worship their ancestors, or nature, or many gods or one—or none. They create works of art of many materials and in diverse traditions and speak a host of languages and dialects. How are similarities and differences in their behaviors and productions in different times and places to be accounted for, explained, understood? That is the basic problem and task of the discipline of cultural anthropology. Is there a direction to be discerned in the drama of humanity's fortunes (and misfortunes) as it has been played out so far? What are the conditions of change, including that kind of change called "progress"?

Anthropology is comprised of two main branches—biological, or physical, dealing with human biological evolution and variation, and cultural, dealing with traditions in human behavior and works. Within the latter branch are three principal subdisciplines—

Chapter Two
The Observed
World and Its
Cultural Aspect

29

anthropological linguistics, concerned with the history, structure, and working of language; archeology, charged with uncovering the remains and reconstructing the lifeways of the remote and recent past; and ethnology, whose task is the study of living cultures. There are other tags for facets of the ethnological quest: ethnography, for instance, based upon field study, with description as its center of gravity, and social anthropology, which tends to narrow its focus to social organization. That this book is subtitled *An Introduction to Cultural Anthropology* indicates that it will use primarily the nonbiological approach. But, since anthropology is the study of humans (*anthropos*, "man"; *logos*, "study"), some findings of biological anthropology will enter into the facts we present and the judgments we make.

If Alfred C. Haddon, a British anthropologist, was correct, the word *anthropology* was coined by Aristotle—in a rather negative context. Aristotle spoke of a high-minded Greek as *not* an anthropologist, *not* a gossip nor a talker about himself (Haddon 1934: 1). The term, in Latin and its derivatives, was tied to human biology and notions of "human nature" almost through the nineteenth century. But by the time of Edward Burnett Tylor, who wrote the first text in English with the title *Anthropology* (1881), it had come to include more than biology in its content, and culture, whose label has an independent history, was given its proper place. Yes, in a sense, an anthropologist is a gossip, if "himself" is expanded, to mean "humanity." And the anthropologist has claim to a well-rooted body of information and a philosophy and a many-faceted methodology behind his or her efforts to organize, understand, and use it.

How we understand:
Context and meaning

In the early days of educational television, the University of Pennsylvania Museum produced a program called "What in the World?" An unlabelled object, an artifact from the University Museum's collections— say part of a Polynesian canoe prow—was placed before a number of anthropologists. They were challenged to identify it, to state its provenience (its source or place of origin), its age, and its uses. Some informed guessing was involved. Each participant was a knowledgeable scholar, a specialist in one or more regions of the world who had stored up by observation and reading information about the things people made, what they were made from, and the styles in which they were made. Against this background of experience, the players oriented the object they were asked to identify. They established a **context**—a society, a culture, a region, a temporal period, or whatever—and placed the object within it. Thus they gave it **meaning**, and they helped their viewers gain **understanding**. We shall define *meaning*, then, as the place of a thing in a context; when we grasp the place of a thing in a context, we "understand" it.

However, we also want to know the meanings of things not quite like Polynesian canoe prows, and we seek out and fashion contexts for them in what might, at first glance, appear to be a quite different procedure. Take words, for instance. We learn the meaning of new and unfamiliar words by consulting a good dictionary, by asking someone

who knows, or by figuring it out by its place within surrounding words and sentences—again, context. When the word *provenience* appeared, it was linked with "source" or "point of origin," which was an appeal to common language experience—context. Words are concrete, perceptible objects. They themselves find meaning in real contexts and provide contexts for the meanings of other words and other things.

It is going to be our assumption that *every* word in *every* language points to or is involved with something real or points to a selection from or a composite of real things. It will not do to say that some words label imaginary things and let it go at that. Our notions of imaginary things no less than our most commonsense constructions of things in everyday life are compounded of sense impressions of some kind of real world "out there." Unicorns may never have existed in one piece in the sense that, say, donkeys or antelopes do, but their parts did, in the world of nature and humanity. The unicorn's creator, whoever it was (most actual inventors of most of the things in any cultural inventory are unknown), extracted bits and pieces from here and there and built that mythical beast. Its meaning for us (aside from James Thurber's use of it in his fable "The Unicorn in the Garden") lies in the mythology of which it came to be a part, and the culture in which the mythology rests provides the meaning for the mythology itself. So, although we might say that some contexts are concrete and immediately experienced and others are abstract, theoretical, or analytical, there is no unbridgeable gap between them. That is a particularly important point to keep in mind when we build orienting or analytical contexts with words.

The Observed World and Its Cultural Aspect

A key word in this discourse on the unicorn is **extraction**. Again, the creator of the beast extracted pieces from the experienced world of animals (whether this creator was awake or dreaming at the time is irrelevant at this point) and announced a thing never seen in one piece in heaven or on earth. But the pieces had been. And the word bound them together. So it is with a word like *red*. Some things, we say, are perceptibly red—iron ore, traffic signs, seven of the thirteen stripes in the flag of the United States. One part of our perception of these things, one quality, is labelled "red" or "redness," and there is extracted something that is stored in memory so that we are able to say of an object, "That is red."

It is preferable to say that red or redness is an extraction from the field of things we observe than to call it an abstraction. I base this statement of preference on experience in teaching and reading. There is something in the ordinary use of words that induces abstractions to float away from their hard underpinnings, whereas extractions are less likely to do so. I confess that the reason for this is unclear to me. But abstractions tend to assume an ethereal kind of existence severed from the things they were originally meant to point to, so ethereal, in fact, that first the reality of the abstraction is placed in doubt and then the things it was abstracted from. For the same reason, the word *manifestation* will be avoided: just what is manifesting what is often clouded.

There would be no need for this excursion if some books in anthropology that the inquiring student is likely to chance upon did not solemnly assure him or her early on that "culture is an abstraction" and then proceed to cast grave doubts upon its existence. The anthropologist Leslie A. White has often called attention to this aberration, most recently in *The Concept of Culture* (1973: 25-27).

It is a view underlying this book that the word *culture* labels a great many real and perceptible things and events, or parts or qualities of things and events (qualities extracted, as "redness" is extracted, from the real world). We are going to be concerned to some extent with how these things and qualities get there and more importantly with trying to explain the variations of them in time and place. If you *do* think of the word *culture* as an abstraction, remind yourself that it refers to real things extracted from the real world. *Culture* and other terms will be used to manage that world.

Unfortunately, we have not finished with abstracting confusions. We can make collections of knives, axes, hammers, awls. Knives cut, axes sever upon delivery of a blow, hammers are wielded in a like way but are blunt, and awls pierce. Each of these words is one or a set of extractions of shapes, behaviors, or uses of things. As a set, these things may be called *tools*. Is the word *tool* on a higher level of abstraction than *knife*? I think it preferable to say that *tool* has greater extension or extensibility, or, if you wish, generality, than *knife*. *Knife* refers to fewer things, *tool* to more. Some specific characteristics or qualities are ignored in words of greater extension, but nevertheless they point to characteristics or qualities observed or otherwise experienced in each individual object or component set. For instance, a tool is "an implement, especially one held in the hand, for performing or facilitating mechanical operations . . . " (*Random House Dictionary of the English Language,*

The Task and Some Approaches to It

Unabridged Edition, 1967).[1] So is a knife, an axe, a hammer, or an awl. All of this, again, may be so self-evident that it will cause impatience. But let the reader be warned that much ink has been spilled in anthropology on strictures about our inability to observe lineages or clans or societies whereas we can observe families. The fact that clans or societies are more "abstract" than families does not mean they don't exist.

Anthropological terms can be thought of as having greater or lesser, broader or narrower extension; they point to one, or a few, things or a great many. *My father* is quite specific (at least in our culture); *fathers* is of greater extension, *parents* more, *kin* still more. As the wry desk motto has it, "Eschew obfuscation." Or better, "Eschew exclusive preoccupation with abstractions."

Calling some things *culture*

The behaviors of and things made and used by the Peyranais, Kalinga, Semai, Cheyenne, and Eskimo were referred to as *lifeways* because this is a common, neutral, nontechnical term, appropriate for an introduction to anthropology's materials. We shall now substitute the word **culture**, a term of broad extension, a concept. **Concepts** we will take to mean basic and indispensable terms that select, point to, and collect real things (things that can be seen, heard, touched, tasted, or

[1]All further references to *Random House Dictionary* are to this edition.

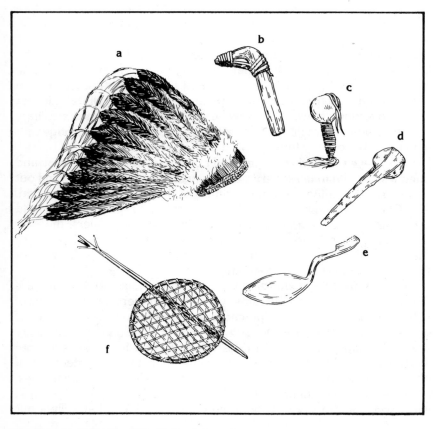

It is relatively easy to extract Plains artifacts from their whole setting: (a) war bonnet, (b) skin-scraping tool, (c) rawhide rattle, (d) stone-headed maul, (e) bone ladle, (f) game hoop and sticks. It is more difficult to extract and set apart human relationships, ideas, and beliefs, but they are no less real and extractable than the objects we call material.

The Observed World and Its Cultural Aspect

smelled) and draw boundaries around the collection. Appropriately used, concepts provide contexts for meaning and understanding.

Let us review some of the things the Cheyenne did and what they made and used and add some others to round out our field. Men among them hunted the bison from horseback with bow and lance, and the women skinned and butchered the kill and transported it to camp on a travois, a device consisting of two poles dragged by a horse. The Cheyenne man made and kept about him not only his hunting weapons but a knife, fire-making tools, and horse gear; he might also have a stone-headed war club and a gun, pipes and tobacco, and a bundle of magical charms. Women dug prairie roots with a digging stick, crushed berries, roots, and meat with a stone maul, dressed hides with stone and bone implements, sewed with sinews and bone awls, carried their babies on cradle boards, and made and set up the tipis. Theirs were the domestic duties of family and camp life; men were the hunters and defenders and also had major ceremonial duties.

Within each tipi lived a family. Three or four tipis comprised a camp of about fifteen people, all part of one big extended family and household—a man and his wife, their unmarried children, and their married daughters with their husbands and children. Terms these kinsfolk applied to each other were patterned somewhat differently from what the reader probably is accustomed to: a child called its own mother and her sisters *mother* and its own father and father's brothers (who usually lived in camps other than the child's) *father*; cousins in our sense were included under the terms *brother* and *sister*. Camps were grouped into **bands** of around three hundred people; the Cheyenne tribe in the period spoken of in Chapter One had ten bands. Only during the season of the spring and summer hunts and ceremonies did all or most of the camps and bands come together, pitching their tipis in a great circle open to the east. In fall the bands and camps scattered again, to wooded and sheltered areas, in preparation for the cold winter. Linking the people together were not only bonds of **kinship** but men's military societies, women's quilling and beading clubs, and a Chief's Lodge with a membership of forty-four honored men from all the bands.

The Cheyenne world was peopled not only with kin and friends and enemies but with many supernatural beings with whom they worked out relationships in minor and major rituals of the kind already described. The Cheyenne had a good deal of practical lore regarding herbs and other plants and several healing techniques. Some healers, the shamans, were thought to have supernatural power, derived, like that of the powerful hunters and fighters, from vigils in which the denizens of the sacred world appeared to them.

To make useful generalizations, the anthropologist would compare Cheyenne ways of living with other ways of other men, devising terms of sufficient extension to cover practices with greater and lesser degrees of similarities and differences. Our task right now is to set boundaries to what the term *culture* covers—and does not cover. So let us extract three kinds of things from the Cheyenne scene, making three categories of objects and events. The first will include the Cheyenne themselves, men, women, and children, who are tawny skinned, dark haired, and dark eyed, each of whom is born, eats, breathes, loves, hates, lives out his or her span, and dies—a population of human beings transmitting its biological traits genetically to offspring, a segment of the human race, of humankind. The second will include the natural world the Cheyenne can see, feel, hear, touch, walk upon, chase, eat, and shelter themselves from—rolling prairie and arching sky, clouds, rain, warming sun and cold wind, bison, antelope, prairie turnips, berry bushes, the distant mountains, and the pine-covered hills. And the third category, which is in between, will consist of Cheyenne ways, *what* the Cheyenne do, make, use, and think—tipi and travois, arrows and the manner in which they are released from the bow, behavior toward kin, the Sun Dance, belief in a Thunder Spirit, acts of reverence and petition, and much else. We do not include in this last category the Cheyenne themselves, as living bodies, but *what* they do and make, *extracted* from the whole, *analytically* set apart from biological *sapiens* and surrounding nature. To this category of objects and behaviors we give the name *culture* and, in this particular case, *Cheyenne culture.*

These three categories of things—humans, natural environment, and culture—comprise what we might call the total domain of the scientists who study humans and their behavior. Their separation and organization presents a **paradigm** (a pattern or model) within which disciplines choose their emphases, construct their working vocabularies, plot their strategies, assess relations between the parts, and build their **hypotheses** and **theories.** Biological anthropologists focus upon humans in a manner that emphasizes their genetically derived traits, their evolution, and their bodily variations. Evolution for humans, as for all animals, is considered in relation to the interactions of populations with natural environment and, in addition, for this special animal, the interaction of populations and culture. Thus, the biological anthropologist will regard culture as an environment of the human animal. But if a cultural anthropologist focuses upon culture the possibility arises for treating humans quite differently, as we shall see.

"Culture is what is learned"

Long before the eighteenth century, when a science dealing with culture began to take shape, hardy voyagers and overland travelers had observed with astonishment and reported lifeways different from those of their homelands. Speculations about reasons for the differences had been going on for centuries. These centered upon two parts of the paradigm mentioned, the human animal and environment, meaning by the latter the natural environment. The guesses were that people behaved differently in different places because of their different natures (they were inherently savage, or civil, or whatever) or because of the effects of the different geographical environments in which they lived (they were stimulated to work, or lulled into laziness, and so on). The first step toward shifting emphasis to the middle category of things, culture, took place during the period called the Enlightenment, when some social philosophers in Scotland, in England, and on the Continent saw clearly that behavioral differences between societies of humans rested upon their separate experiences and the continued social transmission of those experiences to successive generations (Harris 1968: 9-12). Thus, the differences were regarded as resting on *learned* behavior. One learned to be an Eskimo, a Hottentot, or a European.

From the Enlightenment to the present, most students of humanity have accepted learned behavior as identical with culture, or at least as a characteristic or criterion of it. That culture is social heritage is a central notion in anthropological definitions of culture from Edward Burnett Tylor's first definition, in 1871, onward into the present: "Culture or Civilization, taken in its wide ethnographic sense, is that complex whole which includes knowledge, belief, art, morals, law, custom, and any other capabilities and habits acquired by man as a member of society" (Tylor 1958, I: 1).

To say that culture is what is learned or acquired by humans as members of society is a start, but is that sufficient for us to understand many things we want to know? How did culture begin? How does it work? How do parts relate to parts? Tylor, of course, went farther than simple definition and proposed some answers to such questions, and other anthropologists have also pursued them. But to emphasize human learning is to shift focus from extracted things and behaviors themselves to the human-as-animal part of the paradigm, and we don't want to do that. (By *paradigm* here we mean our three-part model with humans, culture, and natural environment in it.)

An important point in this connection is that humans learn to play their roles in a community shaped and ordered by a particular culture in more than one way, in more than one kind of learning process. This may be illustrated within the simple framework that the anthropologist Morton Fried (1967: 5-7) found useful for his own purposes. Humans, like animals far down in the scale of complexity, learn *situationally*, in "the process by which an organism adopts or alters a behavioral response on the basis of experience." Humans and other animals are also capable of learning *socially*: "Social learning occurs when one organism, perceiving another encounter a stimulus and emit a response, acquires that response as part of its own behavioral repertory." But our species, *Homo sapiens*, alone (as far as we know) is also capable of learning in a third way, *symbolically*: "In *symbolic* learning the stimulus is not present but is represented by something else—by a symbol." (We shall have more to say about **symbols** and the symbolic process in relation to culture later, but here we remain with symboling as related to learning.) Fried then defines culture as "the totality of conventional behavioral responses acquired primarily by symbolic learning," pointing out that culture "includes very many socially learned traits" but is vitally dependent for its transmission upon a "system of symbolic learning."

It is apparent that people respond in all three ways to things present in the cultural system in which they live. To illustrate, we may borrow from another context the remark of the philosopher of science Abraham Kaplan (1964) about the "law of the hammer": "Give a child a hammer and it will find that everything needs hammering." The child discovers that a hammer makes a satisfactorily loud noise and finds pleasure in the play of its own muscles while lifting the heavy object. Thus, the child learns situationally to wield it. The child might also imitate its parent or an older sibling, thus learning socially. In all cul-

A Black Carib child learns situationally what can be done with a pail...

...and socially how to cooperate in carrying water home. But both kinds of learnings are reinforced by symbolic, oral instruction. (Courtesy Nancie L. Gonzalez.)

tures children learn socially to express themselves with subtle body postures and gestures. But neither the presence of the hammer (that wooden-handled, steel-headed, and clawed object), the uses to which it is put, nor the particular gestures and their meanings in a culture are accounted for adequately solely by reference to the way children learn about them.

Learning, then, is something that organisms do. Organisms also breathe, ingest food, and excrete wastes. Culture does none of these things, which make sense in biological contexts and not in cultural ones. We must look for other words to describe culture and its behaviors. Calling culture "what is learned" is a rough-and-ready way to point to our domain as a start, to separate it from **genetically** transmitted behaviors; but it is not sufficient to establish the cultural context. This is why the heading of this discussion appears inside quotation marks.

Customs, traditions, systems

Our task now is to choose and explain some words that can be applied to the ordering of humanity's ways, that will contribute to the building of the framework and provide a proper context for under-

The Observed World and Its Cultural Aspect

standing those ways. The three terms *custom*, *tradition*, and *system* are labels often employed by different varieties of anthropologists to fix upon the characteristics of human behaviors and artifacts. All three cover extracted things but emphasize different aspects of them.

Custom is a word that is serviceable only to a slightly greater degree than *learned behavior*, although both terms separate things that are not biologically inherited from those that are. It was among Cheyenne customs to hunt bison with lance, to erect tipis, to count coup on an enemy (strike him with the hand or a special stick), to dance in the Sun Dance, and, for brothers, to act respectfully and circumspectly toward sisters. It is among the customs of Americans of a given class today to eat prepared cereals or eggs and bacon at breakfast, to work at industrial or office machines, to drive automobiles and observe traffic signals (more or less), to salute the national flag carried in a parade, to go to church on Sabbath, and so on. Although now quite a banal and unexceptional tag, *custom* was highly useful in an earlier age in helping to lift humans' eyes from their own surroundings and in making comparisons between other people's and their own doings. Thus, Father Joseph François Lafitau, a French Jesuit, published in 1924 a book entitled *Moeurs des sauvages américains, comparées aux moeurs des premiers temps*, which may be translated *Customs of American Savages Compared*

Customs are culture. It is a Bedouin custom for a man to dismount before he shakes hands and converses with someone who is not riding. It is a sign of friendly intentions. (Courtesy Joseph Ginat.)

The Task and Some Approaches to It

with the Customs of Early Times. When a distinct discipline emerged and more thinking had been done about customs, they were given the appellation *culture traits,* and traits that appeared to have various kinds of immediately observable linkages between them were called *culture complexes.*

Custom is a neutral even if useful word. It might be said to have limited implications, in the sense that one may go from customs in almost any direction in the study of human behavior or go nowhere. Application of another word, **tradition**, however, says something additional about the things *custom* applies to. It is in effect the beginning of an explanation of the existence of customs at any given time. Where did customs come from? They came in part from the past; they are part of tradition. A time dimension opens up, and there is an invitation to explore the implications of the term. As the anthropologists A. L. Kroeber and Clyde Kluckhohn put it in a review of the culture concept, "... custom was given a time backbone in the form of 'tradition' or 'social heritage'" (1952: 35). The notion has become so important that it is one of the few things anthropologists agree they are studying or might study; that is, almost all of them accept this conceptualization, whatever else they say about their materials. According to David Kaplan (1965: 960), "... things and events are identified as cultural phe-

Custom and tradition are words synonymous with culture. Presentation of the Sun Dance is a Cheyenne Indian custom that is traditional. (Courtesy Peter J. Powell.)

Here the Sun Dance lodge covering the ritual objects have been removed, but the "thunderbird nest" atop the forked center pole remains. It carries symbolic sacrificial gifts to the supernaturals. (Courtesy Peter J. Powell.)

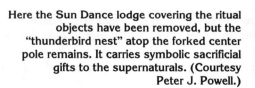

nomena principally by their traditional aspect. Or to put it in somewhat different terms, cultures are built up out of patterned and interrelated traditions—traditions in technology, social organization, and ideology."

The qualifiers, "patterned" and "interrelated," and the specification of "technology, social organization, and ideology" as traditions provide an opening into a conceptualization of culture even more useful than that of tradition by itself, just as tradition invites us to surmount the here and now of custom. For those words may be regarded as advance riders of the more powerful notion of **system**. They also point in the direction of another concept, *structure*, but inasmuch as we are going to subordinate that notion to the status of an aspect of systems we shall discuss it later and push on now to the system itself.

A simple definition of *system* is "a set of dynamically interrelated parts forming a whole," *dynamically* referring to movement. A clock, an internal combustion engine, and a donkey are all examples of systems—and so is a human being. Their parts work in relation to each other and to the whole. But systems can be found in unlikely places and may be constructed of parts that, on the face of it, are quite separate. Draw for yourself a vertical line representing a flagpole, and at a right angle to it draw a line representing the ground. Anywhere above and to the left of the pole, draw a circle to represent the sun. Your sun should make the flagpole cast a shadow on the ground, and you can discover the length of the shadow by ruling a line from the center of the sun circle to the ground, cutting the top of the symbolic pole. Now, if you draw other sun circles higher or lower in relation to the first, corresponding to imaginary positions of the sun in the sky, and project lines cutting the top of the flagpole in each case, you will arrive at other shadow lengths. As in nature, the higher the sun in the sky, the more acute is the angle at the apex of the triangle, the shorter is the shadow cast by the pole; the lower the sun in the sky, the longer the shadow. You have constructed a diagram or model of a system, a set of interrelated parts.

Culture also may be regarded as a system, its parts moving in relation to each other. It is, of course, of much greater complexity than the flagpole-and-sun system. We know less about it, and our predictions of relationships are much less accurate. But if terms of sufficient extension are used to label the parts of our model of the cultural system, useful **probabilistic statements** might be made about changes of the parts under different conditions. So, while viewing humanity's ways as customs and traditions represents an advance over simple description, reaching the point of speaking of particular cultures and of culture in general as systems enlarges the context, prompts the raising of new questions, and offers an additional tool for understanding.

A symboling-dependent system

Things in cultural systems are different in an important way from the things that are not included in them. They are symboling-dependent (White 1959: 6-8).

Like all useful concepts, the concept of symboling would point to observable objects, or qualities or motions, while bundling them together with a convenient tag. The term *symboling* points to the forming of associations or linkages of one thing and another that are of an unusual and arbitrary kind. One thing comes to stand for or represent another, as, say, the sound cluster of *cat* stands for a furry and engaging animal that dominates a human home in which it lives, or as the national flag, a cloth with a design on it, stands for a nation. A distinctive mark of such associations is that there is no evident biological or physical necessity or reason why that particular thing stands for another. A stool rather than a flag could stand for a nation, and among the nineteenth-century Ashanti of Ghana it did. *Neko* or *paka* could be made to stand for the small furry tyrant, and in Japanese and Swahili, respectively, they do.

There are two ends or **aspects** of the connecting and standing-for process called symboling. One is neurological, taking place in the human brain. This end is beyond the cultural anthropologist's pursuit. But at the other end the process and its results are open to inspection in linked objects and behaviors. People speak, and we can grasp the associations between words and things. They gesture, and we can discover the joining between the gesture and whatever it stands for. A Cheyenne warrior who placed his pipe upright on a bison chip indicated he was about to speak the truth about what he had seen or done; you may agree that the term *arbitrary* is well taken in this case. And the assertion that it would be hard to find any physical or biological necessity in the association of the two behaviors obviously is justified.

All of culture depends on this associational process. It is relatively easy to see in regard to language, religion, and philosophy, somewhat less so in parts of social organization, and perhaps least in technology; but everything in the cultural domain is symboling-dependent (White 1959: 6-7). Inspect your watch. Wheels, balance, spring, and hands are of metal, and the whole appears to be describable as a mere physical system. But what about the numbers on the face? Don't they stand for stages in the turning of the earth, the progress of the sun across the sky? And consider the crafting of the watch, the gathering and preparation of materials that went into it, the training of watchmakers. *Dependent* means just that: some objects and behaviors would not exist, or would not have the particular form or shape they do have, unless immediately or somewhere along the line of their coming into being they were hooked up in arbitrary associations with other objects and behaviors.

So far as we know, associations of that kind are not found outside of human behavior and things humans make. The natural growth of crystals, the turning of a sunflower in shifting light, or the hen's laying an egg do not exhibit that kind of linking behavior, which is to say that we do not need to describe them as symboling-dependent. Neither are symboling-dependent associations found in *all* human behavior or in *all* things humans make. We are talking about extracted culture, the things we have put into our system, not behavior that can be described satisfactorily in the language of, say, physics or biology. Fall from a height, blink your eyes at a lightning flash, or sneeze in a dust storm and you join company with any primate (the order of mammals to which all monkeys, apes, and humans belong), or indeed with any mammal.

An important characteristic of cultural systems that sets them off from noncultural systems, then, is symboling-dependency. It is symboling-dependent things that are related dynamically to each other within the system. New linkages of that sort are continually being made within it.

Transforming materials and energies

Whereas *symboling* is applicable only to cultural systems, the term **energy** is relevant to all systems. Symboling sets apart, energy cross-cuts and joins, in a manner of speaking. Just as symboling is a particular kind of association being made and maintained between things that comprise culture and just as our knowledge of the joinings comes by way of observation and our deductions made from observation, the concept *energy* also arises from observations and is a tag applied to those observations. It is a word of very broad extension.

In physics, *energy* means "the capacity to do work." Motion, light, heat, and electricity are familiar forms. It takes energy, we can say, to hunt, dance, make pottery, run an automobile, march in parades, go to war, send astronauts to the moon, or pray. In terms you should now be finding more congenial, the whole of culture and those segments of it we call cultures can be considered, if we wish, as organizations of energy. That is to say, all of those things and behaviors extracted from the total landscape and called culture, all of those things which are distinctive because they are hooked together by symboling, are in movement, perform work.

The term *energy* is not meant to point to a substance or to a single, unitary object or thing. It should not be thought of, either, as a kind of free-floating push. It is only a word that helps us to think about movements or displacements of every sort, whether in the physical world, in the domain of living things, or in culture. Perhaps because our commonsense conception of energy or power contains a hidden appeal to our muscular experiences of pushing and pulling, it is difficult to strip away the idea of pushing and subordinate it to a broader perspective, including energy in an extracted system such as culture.

Where does the energy of the cultural system, that is to say, its motions, come from? First, obviously, by way of human beings, who get it from the calories they burn, derived from the food they eat, *and* by way of energy-converting cultural devices such as water wheels, windmills, steam and internal combustion engines which burn fossil fuels, and atomic piles. In addition, there are the sources still important in much of the world but decreasingly so in industrialized societies—horses, dogs, donkeys, water buffalo, yaks, camels, and other domesticated burden-carrying and load-pulling animals.

That modern pioneer in cultural evolutionary studies, Leslie A. White, was the first to tie together the three concepts of *energy, symbol,* and *cultural systems* and to deploy them toward an understanding of distinctively human behaviors and artifacts and their variations in time and place. As he has phrased it, culture may be regarded as "an organization of energy transformations that is dependent on symboling" (1959: 38).

The Task and Some Approaches to It

In what sense does culture transform and organize energy? Plants transform solar energy into their own life processes, and animals eating the plants transform the energies the plants stored up into the motion and heat energy that is involved in *their* life activities. So do people. People eat, digest, excrete, breathe, reproduce, protect their young, seek shelter, and flee from or repel predators, as do other animals. The meaning of these activities so far as other animals are concerned can be understood in a biological context firmly and unequivocally—but among humans only up to a point. For instance, what it is deemed proper to eat, at what time and on what day and with whom, after what preparation and with what utensils, accompanied by what **etiquette** and **ritual** are all considerations shaped by accumulated culture. All animals eat, but only men and women (and only some men and women at that) breakfast, dine, and sup. Thus, eating among humans has a cultural aspect, its variations understandable by reference to the cultural system. Other motions which are energy organizations are also shaped by culture, having meaning with reference to culture. A man may raise his arm in greeting (a Roman centurion), or to stop a surge of motor cars (a traffic policeman), or to swear to tell the truth in a court hearing (but a Cheyenne placed his pipe on a buffalo chip to do that). The motion, the act of raising the arm in different cultural settings or contexts, may be spoken of in each case as a cultural act, an energy transformation and organization by culture.

Within complexes of symboling-dependent objects and acts, materials also are transformed and given new shapes, forms, properties, and meanings. Clay becomes pottery, reeds become baskets, trees become wood pulp and then newsprint, iron ore becomes rolled steel and then bridges. A stick becomes a root digger, a leader's staff, or a magician's wand. Only sticks grow in nature; they are transformed into other things in culture. Like the motions that shape and wield them, the new objects have a cultural aspect, they are explainable within a cultural context.

Putting things together

Referring to the figure on pp. 44-45, you will see that we are concerned with three extracted and conceptualized domains of things—*Homo sapiens*, culture, and natural environment—represented by the three labelled circles. They might be read as humanity, culture in general, and nature, although strictly speaking the content of all three circles is "natural" (there is nothing "unnatural" about human beings and their lifeways). To avoid that ambiguity, we can substitute the term *habitat* for *natural environment*. The two-directional arrows stand for interactions between the conceptualized entities, primarily exchanges of materials and energies but also effects of any sort of one upon the other. The overarching arrow between *sapiens* and habitat or natural environment points to direct interactions between them, but these we regard as more particularly among the concerns of biological anthropologists.

Our focus is the cultural circle. Within it we place all things we call culture which we have extracted from the world landscape, all objects and behaviors that are dependent upon the symboling process. It stands for the totality of culture everywhere, and it is tied to no particular time. The circumference of the circle may be called the symboling line, the

The Observed World and Its Cultural Aspect

Homo sapiens

Culture

Natural environment (Habitat)

Paradigm or model consisting of three extracted domains, or sets of extracted natural things or their properties. They are humankind in its physical and biological aspects, culture in general, and the rest of the world. The arrows represent interactions between them, primarily material and energy transformations. We may regard each of the three domains as a system if we wish and the totality as a system of which the three circles are parts. Our focus is upon the cultural domain.

boundary of culture. Within the *sapiens* circle we may visualize all human populations in their physical and biological aspects as possessing only physical and biological traits or characteristics. The habitat or natural environment circle contains all the rest of the natural world—lands, streams and seas, plants and nonhuman animals, soils, minerals and landforms, rain and wind, the sun and the planets. Neither biological and physical *sapiens* nor biological and physical habitat require the language of cultural anthropology for their description and understanding; they are *not* symboling-dependent. If any feature connected with them cannot be accounted for wholly in the language of biology or physics (or their subdivisions), it must be transferred to the cultural context to be understood.

Now we can see in fancy how culture works. Within their circle, cultural objects and behaviors interact with each other and form a system. The precultural or noncultural sources of their materials and energies are the domains of biological and physical *sapiens* on the one hand and nonhuman biological and physical habitat on the other. "Out there," in their own respective settings, they have characteristics and properties, forms and shapes. When they pass over the figurative symboling line into culture, they take on new properties and characteristics, new forms and shapes, deriving from their new associations and context.

As an example, a reed grows in marshy ground, reaching toward the sun and bending in the wind; it has properties such as resilience and tensile strength, color, consistency, and weight. A California Yurok Indian woman, say, cuts it and weaves it into a basket. It has crossed the symboling line into culture. Previously, it could be described in botanical or physical contexts, completely and satisfactorily, as a biological and physical thing. But baskets do not grow like crystals and reeds and do not behave like them. Baskets take shape in culture and move in many settings, and it requires the language of cultural anthropology to make an explanation of them. And it is the same with the motions of the Yurok basket maker's fingers. They are in part describable in mechanical and biological terms, but culturally, in their cultural aspect, they are basket-making motions. In our fancy, again, we can discern precultural, cultural, and postcultural contexts, so to speak. This particular basket will wear out and decay like the unplucked reed or it will be burned, and its materials and energy organization will be dissipated into nonculture, a fate reserved not alone for the mighty works of Shelley's Ozymandias, king of kings. But the cultural system will persist, making new baskets and monuments.

So we arrive at an orienting framework of *sapiens*, culture, and habitat which will provide the general context for our understanding of humanity's ways. Central to it is a conception of culture as a symboling-dependent, energy-transforming system of objects and behaviors which derives its raw materials and energies from *sapiens* and nature and which has striking effects upon both.

The uses of systems

The work of cultural anthropologists to make explanations for differences and similarities among lifeways cannot be done for them by scholars in other disciplines. What biologists find out about the cell and

The Task and Some Approaches to It

what physicists find out about atomic particles have no direct relevance to explanations of the presence of the Sun Dance lodge in one place and time and the presence of an Islamic mosque in another. Neither does philosophy, even the philosophy of science, have any relevance to anthropology so far as facts and discoveries are concerned. But, in another sense, what happens in other sciences and in their philosophies does have a bearing on the way anthropologists contrive explanations for the things and events they are interested in and on the way they try to clarify and test them. If workers in other fields find that their observations can be brought together and handled economically and productively by means of the construction of systems, for example, then similar operations might be tried out on particular kinds of human behavior. Substantially, the strategy is "heuristic"—indicating or pointing out, stimulating interest in a new path. We have not meant to say that culture *is* a system, or that cultures *are* systems, but only that human behaviors and artifacts may be regarded and conceptualized in this way.

The anthropologist Ronald Cohen, who does not define culture in the manner of this book, nevertheless discusses systems analysis in a paper entitled "Generalizations in Ethnology" and explains: "Let us begin by defining a system as a set of interrelated parts or units isolated to some degree from their context. . . . The system has, as one of its basic qualities, the idea that as a whole it does 'something' or a set of things . . . . It . . . produces effects, and it reacts or adjusts to the needs of its contextual environment. . ." (1970: 43). A psychologist, James G. Miller, writes, "Systems are bounded regions in space-time, involving energy interchange among their parts, which are associated in functional relationships and with their environments" (1956: 31). These formulations describe systems in general and specifically social or psychological systems, but they are probably applicable in either the general or the specific sense.

That the study of sets of things seen as systems may be a means of reintegrating and unifying the separate sciences into an understandable whole is one of the ideas behind the General Systems movement, of which one of the leading spokesmen is its founder, the biologist and philosopher Ludwig von Bertalanffy (1968). It has close relations with, but is not the same thing as, cybernetics, the study of governing mechanisms, associated with the mathematician Norbert Wiener (1948).

There are two kinds of systems, closed and open. The closed system may be likened to a sealed container of chemical reagents which interact with each other and reach a final state of equilibrium. What the final state is is determined by the things and quantities that went into the mix at the beginning; no materials or energies are imported afterward, and theoretically none escape. "A dynamical system is 'closed' if it neither receives nor yields energy (nor exchanges material with its surroundings)" (Wisdom 1956: 120). Our universe may be regarded as a closed system, but the parts within it, particularly the subsystems of living things, are open and behave quite differently. "An open system is one which is continually taking in something from its environment and giving out something to its environment, all the while maintaining its structure in the middle of this flow. All organization which comes under the category of life exhibits this character" (Boulding 1956: 33).

An important trait of the open system is that its "final state" is not like that of the closed system: it is not set by the initial conditions. As Bertalanffy puts it (1968: 40), in an open system ". . .the same final state may be reached from different initial conditions and in different ways." That is called the *principle of* **equifinality**. An implication for students of culture is that a culture can have reached whatever level it is at from different starting places and by various paths. Further, it is implied that two cultures which end up being similar at a particular point in time need not have had similar histories to get there.

Rather than reaching *fixed* final states, open systems reach states of equilibrium, which we call **adaptation**; if something changes, internally or externally, to jog that equilibrium, the system goes into action and redresses the balance. And the new, adapted state need not be exactly like the old condition before the imbalance occurred. Open systems have the capacity, in a manner of speaking, to exercise options, and to be changed in the course of adaptation. They can *evolve*, and that evolution is substantially open-ended.

This is a very brief introduction to some of the ideas that are a part of General Systems theory, but nonetheless I am sure you will see its applicability to the domain we have extracted and bounded and called culture. Up to the present, the most common model for culture (or, more usually, society) employed by anthropologists has been the animal organism, with its organs and organ systems all doing their specialized work and maintaining its life. The systems approach has greater extension and transcends it. Its principal idea is not that culture works like an organism (in some ways it does, some not) but that cultures *and* living things both behave as systems.

In summary, anthropology's goal is to understand and explain similarities and differences in the behavior of humans in different times and places. With understanding defined as the place of a thing in a context, we need to be clear about the contexts to which anthropology refers observations of its subject matter to achieve understanding; these major contexts are biological and cultural. At some length, we explained how we extract a domain such as culture from the world about us and distinguish it from the rest of the world by the characteristic of symboling-dependency.

In passing, we moved our concept of culture from the simple notion of custom to that of tradition, and then to that of an open system which extracts its materials and energies from humans and habitat.

In the next two chapters, we shall finish the construction of our orienting framework and then move on to an examination of technologies, social organizations, and ideologies and their evolution.

Suggested Readings

Bertalanffy, Ludwig von. 1968. *General system theory.* New York: George Braziller.*

Emery, F. E. 1969. *Systems thinking: Selected readings.* Baltimore: Penguin Books.*

Fried, Morton H. 1972. *The study of anthropology.* New York: Thomas Y. Crowell.*

Kroeber, A. L., and Clyde Kluckhohn. 1952. *Culture: A critical review of con-*

The Task and Some Approaches to It

cepts and definitions. Cambridge, Mass.: Papers of the Peabody Museum of American Archaeology and Ethnology 47, 1.*

Langer, Susanne K. 1948. *Philosophy in a new key: A study in the symbolism of reason, rite, and art.* New York: New American Library, Mentor Books.*

Tylor, Edward B. 1960. *Anthropology.* Abridged and with a foreword by Leslie A. White. Ann Arbor: University of Michigan Press, Ann Arbor Paperbacks.*

White, Leslie A. 1969. *The science of culture: A study of man and civilization.* New York: Farrar, Strauss and Giroux, Noonday Paperbacks.*

———, with Beth Dillingham. 1973. *The concept of culture.* Minneapolis: Burgess.*

Wolf, Eric R. 1964. *Anthropology.* Englewood Cliffs, N.J.: Prentice-Hall.

Chapter Three
Structure and Process in Culture

Clark Wissler, an American anthropologist known particularly for his researches among Plains Indians, proposed (1923: 75) that "the facts of culture may be comprehended under nine heads..., viz., Speech, Material Traits, Art, Mythology, Religion, Social Systems, Property, Government, and War." This "pattern, or skeleton," of culture, he said, pointed to a fundamental similarity in all cultures. There have been many such schemes before and after Wissler's. For example, George Peter Murdock (1945: 124) presented a list of some seventy-three items and, in organizing the Human Relations Area Files, an open-ended compendium of ethnographic information on hundreds of societies, set up over eighty major categories.

Cultural universals

The cultural things Wissler and Murdock were directing their attention to are known as *cultural universals*. It is important to understand that **universals** in culture are not matters of specific content (working boomerangs are rarely found outside aboriginal Australia and Melanesia, so they could hardly be called universals) but categories we construct to organize our observations. The categories are neither given in nature nor fixed. They depend upon the perspective and purposes of the classifier.

51

This appears to be recognized by everyone (Wissler said cultural facts "may be comprehended" under his categories, not that they must be). Nevertheless, one gets an uncomfortable feeling sometimes that the philosopher Plato, holding his eternal and fixed forms, lurks at the elbow of scholars, prompting them to hope that the real skeleton will emerge. Thus Murdock (1945: 125) goes on to say that "despite immense diversity in behavioristic detail, all cultures are constructed to a single fundamental plan—the 'universal culture pattern' as Wissler so aptly termed it."

We take the view that there is no "single fundamental plan." Wissler's ninth category, war, for instance, is a dubious one. Some anthropologists would point out that feud and raid might be characteristic of some societies upon which Wissler based his scheme, but not all cultures in any meaningful sense go to war. It may be doubted that even feud and raid apply to such peoples as the nonviolent Semai in the recent past. The problem is one of constructing categories of sufficient extension or generality to contain widely diverging practices, is it not?

Marvin Harris met the problem in his book *Culture, Man, and Nature* (1971: 143-46) by designating **ecology, social structure,** and **ideology** as universal components of culture. The plan was modified from that of the British social anthropologist A. R. Radcliffe-Brown (1952). Radcliffe-Brown, whose particular interest was social organization, had spoken of ecology, social structure, and mental characteristics of people as three adaptive aspects of the whole social system and had labelled only mental characteristics as culture. Harris retitled the latter "ideology" and put the three parts firmly into his total construct of culture, defined (following the "culture is what is learned" perspective) as "the learned patterns of thought and behavior characteristic of a population or society." These three components, then, are *his* universals, and his own explanatory operations, centering upon the ecological component, are consistent with that framework.

Leslie White (1959: 18-19) deals with components as universals, too—technological, sociological, ideological, and sentimental or attitudinal. These, he says, are suitable to a static view of culture, a simple enumeration of the kinds of things in it. When motion is involved, they are reducible to three aspects, which he presents in the organic analogy: "From a dynamic standpoint...technology, social organization, and philosophy are to be considered as *aspects* of any cultural system, or as kinds of behavior of the cultural system as an organic whole—as breathing, metabolizing, procreating, etc., are processes carried on by a biological organism as a whole." These three aspects—**technology**, social organization, and philosophy—we shall adopt as our universals, and we shall regard them as broadly descriptive of cultural structure, only substituting *ideology* for *philosophy*.

Aspects of culture

What are aspects? Consider mountains. Mountains are splendid things to contemplate—massive and ages old, always changing, although on the scale of nature their changes are hardly ever perceptible to the beholder. Even so, they change in appearance under sun and storm, snow and green vegetation, and the directions from which we

The Task and Some Approaches to It

A Black Carib wields an adze to gouge a log in the construction of a fishing canoe,...

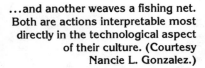

...and another weaves a fishing net. Both are actions interpretable most directly in the technological aspect of their culture. (Courtesy Nancie L. Gonzalez.)

look at them, the perspectives we take. Mountains and their parts present different aspects from north or south, east or west.

So with cultures. They may be looked at from different directions, from several perspectives. As just acknowledged, our choice of three perspectives is based upon White's theoretical work; whether they work in the context of open systems you may judge for yourself after we have proceeded into analysis of cultures. But the perspectives are also an historical growth, arising from the preliminary sortings by ethnographers of the things they observe. Ethnographers almost always describe the food quest, the tools and techniques by means of which it is carried on, and the means for storing, preserving, and preparing food, along with the type of clothing and sheltering and the weapons and strategies for defense and offense against enemies human and nonhuman. *Technology* is a good word for those objects and behaviors.

It is through the technological aspect of culture that the major part of the energy that moves and maintains the system is captured from environment and channeled into it. The notion of an energy-transforming system enables us to see that capturing energy that does not flow primarily through the **metabolic apparatus** of human actors is also an activity of culture, so that it is not only food calories, but wind and water, domesticated animals, wood, oil, coal, and the atom that culture exploits. Any devices for harnessing, burning, or cracking these sources, for storing, channeling, and delivering the resultant energies, must be coupled with food getting and sheltering.

From the second perspective, we look at culture in terms of **social relationships**. Relationships, concretely and empirically, are behaviors of people toward each other, individually and in groups. Men and women behave in describable ways as husbands and wives to each

Structure and Process in Culture

A ceremonial such as this dance of the Gourd
Society among present-day Cheyenne in
Montana can be thought of as a cluster of
social relationships. Men and women, old and
young, bound together by sentiment and
reciprocal actions move through the patterns
of the ritual, and the drummers, singers, and
spectators participate in prescribed ways. That
the Gourd Society is a recent revival of the old
Bowstring Society reminds us that many
relationing behaviors, though they are responses
to current conditions in the lifeway and its
environments, are rooted in the past.
(Courtesy Peter J. Powell.)

other and as fathers and mothers toward children—who behave in return as sons and daughters. Hunt leaders and shop foremen behave in
ways appropriate in a particular culture toward fellow hunters and
workers on an assembly line. The notion is implicit in a colloquy between a couple who have met in a cocktail bar, as portrayed by Mike
Nichols and Elaine May in one of their recorded night club acts. "I
think," says the young woman, "we're going to have a relationship."

Social organization also includes some behaviors toward things, as
when an Australian Aborigine is said to "own" his axe (have a property
relationship) or stockholders in our culture vote on management poli-
cies of a corporation and distribution of dividends. But interrelations of
people are always part of the chain of behavior. Owning, to the Australian Aborigine, almost always means widespread sharing of resources
and artifacts with others, while owning in our culture most often means
actively excluding others from access to them.

A young Cheyenne male turned his back or averted his face from his
wife's mother and did not address her directly, but rather through a

third person. That was Cheyenne son-in-law-to-mother-in-law behavior. "Spanish-American males greet one another by a stereotyped embrace, head over right shoulder of the partner, three pats on the back, head over reciprocal left shoulder, three more pats" (LaBarre 1949: 491). That is Spanish-American behavior between male friends-and-equals. Culture transforms energy organizations, such as turning the back or embracing, that any higher primate is capable of, into cultural behaviors—which is to say that it gives them an added dimension that is understandable in a cultural context. Often such behaviors are spoken of as "expressing" relationships. But we prefer to regard them *as* relationships, bundling them together and putting a tag on them. Are we deserting our extracted system of culture by involving human beings as we have? Decidedly not. We are looking at behaviors as such. They, not the humans, are the cultural things.

Not only the human animal's muscular behaviors but also movements inside of him or her are materials for culturally compounded, shaped, and interpreted relationships. A feeling of warmth, a heightened heart-beat, a nervous tingle at the base of the spine may enter into the behavior of men and women toward each other, a woman toward a child, a child toward a woman, or a person toward a flag while a military band is playing martial airs. Energy organizations, culturally viewed, may reach into the privacy of a person for their content. It is more difficult to establish **empirically** the presence of these sentiments than the presence of the easily observable muscular behaviors, but it is interesting that they are assumed to be there: the overt behaviors are said to stand for them, as for mother love or patriotism. If a man is saluting a flag, it is assumed he is experiencing an emotion. If he doesn't, the culture tells him, he ought to! But cultures vary a great deal in the degree to which sentiments (emotions, affects) are attached to overt behaviors. While it is a general expectation in our culture, for instance, that the recipient of a gift feel warmly toward a donor, in other cultures giving and receiving behavior is more matter-of-fact, without emotional involvement.

Customarily, ideas and beliefs are pointed to as the stuff of ideology, the third aspect of culture. Ideas and beliefs may be as focused as "fire burns" or as encompassing as the belief of the Dogon of Africa that the house of their paramount chief is a model of the universe (Griaule and Dieterlen 1954: 100). The heart of the matter is concepts, and we shall define ideology as the totality of concepts and their relations in a cultural system. Concepts have already been defined as basic and indispensable terms that select, point to, collect real things—things seen, heard, touched, tasted, or smelled—and draw boundaries around the collection (Chapter Two). Thus, they are bundles of **perceptions** with an attached word or other symbol. Organizations of concepts are found in proverbs, folklore, myths, codes of etiquette and law, technical manuals, religious and scientific doctrines and philosophies, and those assemblages that anthropologists bring back from the field—world views.

Aspect as a product of perspective can't be emphasized too strongly. Stone axes or automobiles do not have stenciled upon them "I am a piece of technology, and of technology alone." For instance, among the Yir Yiront, hunters of northern Australia (Sharp 1970), stone axes were made only by men and were owned by them, being loaned to women and children; thus axes entered into the relationships of the sexes and age levels. Materials for making them were lacking in Yir Yiront territory and were procured through a chain of trading partners, most exchanges taking place during corroborees, or celebrations that included initiations and totem rites. (Totems are plant and animal species and other things that stand in a special, mystical relationship with human social groups and are symbolic of such groups.) The axe itself was one of the totems of a Yir Yiront clan and was represented in ceremonies. It was also a symbol of masculinity. The stone axe and its movements, then, are not understandable wholly in a technological context among the Yir Yiront. Similarly in our culture, some kinds of automobiles are said to be prestige symbols and are driven (when new) primarily by people in certain social classes. When old, they are acquired by individuals with lower incomes and continue to impart prestige. In a naive context, a thing may be said to "be what it is"—axe or automobile. But understanding the thing and the behaviors around it may necessitate that we put it consciously into more than one context.

A situation in George Stewart's novel, *Earth Abides*, provides another example. The Americas were devastated by a sudden epidemic, but Stewart's hero, Isherwood, escaped it because he had been bitten by a snake while exploring the hills surrounding San Francisco and had been protected by its venom. He had picked up during his walk a geologist's hammer that had been lost. Gathering together a small band of survivors of the disaster, Isherwood managed to keep community life going. His geologist's hammer found many uses and became not only a survival tool but a sort of mark of Isherwood's leadership. When he died in extreme age, old Ish, as he was dubbed, had become a revered oracle. His hammer survived him, not as a utilitarian tool but as the central object of a shrine to which people appealed for spiritual guidance. Tool, leader's badge of authority, sacred object—the same geologist's hammer in technological, social, and ideological contexts: aspects of culture.

Structure in culture and cultures

At the highest level, the aspects of culture make up its **structure**. By *structure* we mean the parts of a whole and their arrangement. It is a definition broad enough to be applied to a brick wall, a cathedral, a triangle, a vertebrate skeleton, or culture viewed as technology, social organization, and ideology. This parallels our definition of system, up to a point, but note that the notion of dynamic interrelationships is essential to system but not to structure. *Structure* applies to the frozen moment, in a manner of speaking—simply to stipulated parts and the way they are arranged. We say "stipulated" because it reminds us that parts, like aspects, are decided upon and named by the arranger; a cake may be cut in more than one way. If you protest that a brick wall can hardly be described as more than its component bricks and mortar, consider that it also has a base and may have a pediment.

So far as the structure of culture as a whole is concerned, multiplication of parts is a risky undertaking in which one might end up with the more than eighty categories of the Human Relations Area Files and their many subdivisions. Classifications like that are useful for some purposes, such as tracing traits across cultures to compare them and make associations, but not for a manageable view of culture as structure. One might also say that the parts of culture as a totality are all of its segments, all of the separate cultures inside it. Conceivably, this might fit some purpose, but it would be equally unmanageable. It is better to extract a skeleton, not to settle for a jigsaw puzzle on a three-dimensional map. For that reason, we shall make do with the three main aspects—technology, social organization, ideology—as the parts of the total culture of humankind regarded structurally.

With respect to the structures of separate and distinguishable cultures, the situation is different. Aspects are still useful, but in order to describe and understand a particular culture satisfactorily it is necessary to separate it into more parts than three. Let us have recourse once more to our patient Cheyenne of the mid-nineteenth century for an example. There were in that culture tools and techniques which might be sorted into sets for hunting, gathering, preparing skins, and so on. There were nuclear and extended families, bands, a tribal camp circle, a Chiefs' Lodge and six military societies, women's craft societies or

The thatched wattle-and-daub house, the half-finished mortar, the canoe-shaped trough (back of the woman at left), the clothing of the people—all are understandable in a technological context. The relationships of the three adults and three children to each other and of the people to the things around them we refer to the social context. These are sedentary Guahibo Indians of Colombia. (Courtesy Nancy and Robert V. Morey.)

Structure and Process in Culture

guilds, a set of terms for kin and others in particular social positions and the behaviors adhering to them, organized raiding parties, women's work groups, and more. There were ideas and beliefs that might be grouped into sets dealing with the origin of the world and things in it, those clustering around shamanistic practices, or healing, or hunting magic, or world renewal ceremonies, or admonitions about the right way to behave. All of these parts (the list is not exhaustive, and things might be grouped quite differently) comprised Cheyenne cultural structure. A few of these are found in the contemporary American culture that Cheyenne share (nuclear families, for instance), but certainly not all, and the American culture today has parts (the maritime industry, a postal system) not found among nineteenth-century Cheyenne.

Statements about the structure of a particular culture, therefore, are likely to be in some measure different from those about another particular culture, although not entirely so. It depends both upon observable similarities and differences between the cultures and the extension or generality of the words we apply to the parts. Sometimes, in order to establish grounds for comparisons, we may wish to suppress or ignore a good deal of variation; at other times, for other purposes, we may wish to multiply parts. That is our privilege, provided we can make a case for it and communicate our reasons intelligibly to others. But *we* decide what the parts and their content shall be.

Conceptualizing movement: Cultural processes

"But the Earth does move," Galileo is supposed to have insisted after his recantation before the Inquisition in the seventeenth century. In the intellectual climate of his day, it was allowable to recognize that living things moved, that stones fell from heights and rivers flowed to the sea, but not that our planet moved: the Earth was fixed, and the heavenly bodies described circles around it. But movement and change throughout the universe have become a commonplace in thinking. Culture moves, too, and we call its movements **cultural processes**.

In everyday usage, the word *process* means "a continuous action, operation, or series of changes taking place in a definite manner" (*Random House Dictionary*), and that definition fits culture's movements well enough. Symboling is itself a process. It is enough to recall that it was described as a particular kind of linking of things and as such is a series of movements. **Cultural evolution** is a process, a transformation of cultural systems. But let us single out and define some particular kinds of symboling-dependent motions in relation to cultural systems and their environments represented by our diagrams, centering upon the processes of **discovery, invention,** and **diffusion, integration** and **enculturation,** and adaptation.

Discovery, invention, diffusion. Let us return to our Yurok basket maker to anchor the three processes of discovery, invention, and diffusion in the cultural system. She was introduced in order to illustrate the flow of materials and energies into culture and their transformation into objects and behaviors that called for new labels from our cultural vocabulary. We were concerned then with looking at culture from the top down, as it were, to grasp a relation of culture and its environments.

The Task and Some Approaches to It

The fact that the reed the Yurok woman plucked from the natural environment had properties such as resilience, tensile strength, color, consistency, and weight was *discovered* long before by unknown basket makers, house builders, and devisers of fish dams, either in Yurok culture or elsewhere. Putting the reed with appropriate properties to use in the form of baskets, houses, and fish dams was in each case, at some particular place and point in time, an *invention*. If knowledge of the reed's properties, the techniques of making the objects, and the particular forms and shapes given them had been passed on to the Yurok from some other culture, or moved from it to others, these would be instances of *diffusion*.

What discovers? The cultural system, from our point of view. What does it discover? Primarily, physical and biological characteristics of things that were, up to discovery time, in the system's environments but not taken account of in just that particular way by the culture, not attached to other cultural things, not launched into the stream of symboling-dependent things. Chunks of red ochre that once littered the ground or could be pried from a cliff face were perceived to have color, texture, and adhering properties, and came to be used in body ornamentation, a practice at least as old as the Neanderthals. Culture netted the ochre, made it, one might say, relevant, gave it new meaning. Discoverable properties of things are manifold, including not only color, texture, and tensile strength but that things are round and rollable, sharp and piercing, edible or inedible, permeable or impermeable, and so on.

Discoverable are the characteristics of a new terrain: it may be well watered and full of game. Environmental things have only to be wrapped up in the network of symboling-dependent objects and behaviors to become part of culture—that is, to take on a cultural aspect, explainable by reference to the remainder of the culture. You may compound your own examples from our culture to see if they conform. Banting's discovery of insulin hormone? Fleming's discovery of the bacteria-ingesting fungus *Penicillium*? European discovery of America or the Apollo crews' close-up discovery of the properties of the moon's surface?

It is easiest to think of discovery in the context of technology, and particularly in relation to the natural environment. But culture also discovers the properties and characteristics of human beings (Harvey's discovery of the circulation of the blood, Freud's of the importance of sex even in the sexually immature) and of itself (that culture transmits itself by nongenetic means has been an important discovery, and so has recognition that cultures of the present emerged from simpler forms).

While the facts that sharp stones cut and pierce and that stones can be fractured or chipped were discoveries, controlled chipping and flaking with the use of a bone or stick may be spoken of as an invention. So was the attachment of a stick or bone haft to the chipped and sharpened stone. Inventions are effective combinations of discoveries, the coupling of discoveries with older objects in the culture, and a compounding of joined things. To use a well-worn example, the combination of a boat and a steam engine (both cumulative inventions with long histories) resulted in a steamboat. That plants grow from seeds and that soil, sunlight, and water are necessary conditions for plant propagation and growth were old discoveries indeed; planting and cultivation with the use of a digging stick was an invention.

Discoveries and inventions, as it was suggested in relation to Yurok baskets, may travel from their points of origin and use to other places—or, taking account of our own emphasis, from one cultural system to another. For example, the properties of tobacco apparently were discovered in tropical America, and the practice of smoking spread north and south through aboriginal American Indian cultures, tubular and angular pipes being inventions added to the original modes of rolling cigars or stuffing the tobacco into reeds. Spaniards carried it to Europe, and they, the Portuguese, and the Arabs spread it to the shores of Africa, Asia, and the East Indies, whence it diffused inland. After it was introduced into Siberia by the Russians, tobacco moved across Bering Strait to the Alaskan Eskimo, who had not smoked previously (their neighbors to the south, the Northwest Coast peoples, chewed tobacco with lime from burned shells). This example of worldwide diffusion comes from Alfred Louis Kroeber's *Anthropology* (1948), which has many good examples of this bread-and-butter culture process, as well as of inventions.

Although diffusion is a kind of movement of culture that self-evidently takes place and although any given cultural assemblage has a large number of traits derived from diffusion, it has less interest than some other processes for those who take an ecological or adaptive approach to culture than it has for historians among anthropologists.

Integration and enculturation. Integration is another category of cultural motions, a label for the progressive fitting together of parts into a cultural whole. Ralph Linton, who wrote a book that had broad influence in American anthropology, *The Study of Man,* defined it as "mutual adjustment between cultural elements" (1936: 348). Alfred Louis Kroeber, dean of American anthropologists for many years, saw it as "accommodation of discrete parts, largely inflowing parts, into a more or less workable fit" (1948: 287). We would rather emphasize more sizeable parts of culture than Linton's "cultural elements" and put less stress than Kroeber on diffusion, but their basic ideas of adjustment and accommodation do point to a kind of movement within culture that calls for a label.

As with the notion of diffusion, the notion of integration is used more or less frequently and in various ways, depending on the orientation of a particular anthropologist. Social anthropologists in Great Britain and the United States have focused on the integration of social behaviors, and some American particularists (see Chapter Four) of whom Ruth Benedict (1946) is an example, emphasized psychological and ideological integration. Ecologists tend, I think, to transfer most of the content of integration to adaptation.

Integration is a many-sided process. For instance, in a well-integrated system change in one part, or a disturbance in the equilibrium of the whole, is likely to be followed up relatively quickly by changes in other parts which reestablish balance. If a system is more loosely integrated, the parts may have a lessened dependency and responsiveness to each other. There may also be a tendency for a well-integrated system to

The Task and Some Approaches to It

reduce variety or variation within its parts and for a looser one to have more variation (Anderson 1960). The notion has had attached to it concepts of modes, or kinds, and levels of integration as well. The point I want to make here is that the content of the idea is greater than that of simple accommodation or adjustment but that motion is at the base of it.

Inclusion of the next of our cultural processes, enculturation, within a section that began with a discussion of integration will strike some anthropologists as quixotic. It is done deliberately, not to annoy anthropologists but to emphasize once more that we are fastening our attention upon what culture does and looking for terms to label culture's actions. Culture transmits itself, establishes its continuity, by enwrapping human individuals and populations, by ordering and directing their behavior in a fashion that entitles us to say that the behavior takes on a cultural aspect and requires new words in order to be labelled. The process of this extension of control down the human generations to individuals born into a population and to individuals moving into the orbit of any given system from others we call *enculturation.*

The human infant, out there in the *Homo sapiens* environment of culture, is a helpless animal, dependent upon its elders for nurture for a longer time than in any other species. From its first days on, just what behaviors, appropriate sentiments, and physical things are involved in that nurturance derive from the symboling-dependent culture that surrounds it. Midway in its second year of life, when its capacity to enter into the neurological end of the symboling process matures, the infant comes even more firmly into the grip of culture, for then its behavior becomes programmed directly through language and other symboling-dependent means.

Enculturation is a process ordinarily thought of in relation to infants and children. Often it is phrased as "becoming Eskimo," or "becoming middle-class American," or simply "becoming human." But enculturation goes on with respect to adults, too, after it has gotten a good start in earlier years. If the point of view and the content of this book are new to you and your behavior is even slightly different henceforth because of this book, then enculturation has been operative. Thus, education is an aspect of enculturation. Of course, we would concede that there are psychological and sociological sides to the business of taking on new behaviors, but this is not a book about psychology or sociology. Therefore, we do not dwell on learning or socialization. At this point you might review the section entitled "Culture is what is learned," a title put into quotation marks because what it says and what it implies have only tangential bearing on the behavior of culture. It was asserted there that it is humans who learn. Culture enculturates.

Cultural evolution: General

Having been grounded in biology courses, students today are familiar with the term *evolution* in relation to living things, including our own species, *Homo sapiens.* For more than a century there has been little dispute within biological science that evolution has occurred. The question has rather been how, by what mechanisms and processes, it comes about. Two of the major mechanisms, of course, are **genetic mutation** and **natural selection**, clarification of the latter being the particular contribution of Charles Darwin in his *Origin of Species* in 1859. Recognition of evolution in culture came about before the principle was well established in the field of biology, and application of the idea to culture is by no means an analogy with biological evolution. The situation is precisely the same as in regard to the notion of system: evolution, like system, is applicable to all domains, nonliving, living, and cultural. And as in its independent application to biology, evolution in culture may be regarded in two aspects, general and specific, applied respectively to the whole of culture and to separable cultures (Sahlins and Service 1960: 12-44).

Nearly a hundred years ago, Edward Burnett Tylor said this about culture: "On the whole it appears that wherever there are found elaborate arts, abstruse knowledge, complex institutions, these are results of gradual development from an earlier, simpler, and ruder state of life. No stage of civilization comes into existence spontaneously, but grows or is developed out of the stage before it. This is the great principle that every scholar must lay firm hold of, if he intends to understand either the world he lives in or the history of the past" (1916: 20).

Tylor, one of the founding fathers of anthropology, was speaking at that point primarily of the kind of understanding arrived at in the context of general stages discerned and labelled in the whole sweeping course of culture, from its beginnings to the present. But that is only one side of **general evolution**. Tylor also was concerned with tracing the development of culture "along its many lines," by which he meant the separately singled out developments of language, writing, the "arts of life" (principally technology), the "arts of pleasure" (music, sculpture, painting, games, and so on), the "spirit-world" (religion), history and mythology, and society (titles of his chapters in *Anthropology*).

But there is still another way to look at general evolution, in addition to stages and lines. That is to try to grasp progressive change in culture as a whole by means of some single measurable factor. It need not be a factor whose changes have already in fact been measured with exactitude, nor need we demand that techniques be at hand now for precise calibration. More or less, greater or lesser, will serve, if such evaluations match up with observable cultural things and motions at many points. Such a criterion has been introduced already in connection with Leslie White's conception of culture as an energy-transforming system.

If we decide to view culture in broad perspective as such a system, with a past, a present, and (we hope) a future, we identify the objects and motions within culture as energy transformations or energy flow. The more parts and the more complicated the arrangements to contain them and link them together, the greater the energy flow and expenditure—that is, the more cultural work done. The story of culture from this perspective is one of progressively greater energy transformations. The world cultural system today extracts from environments and puts to work tremendously greater amounts of energy from more sources than it did in earlier times. In per capita terms, even though the energy in the cultural system is averaged over the four billion humans that culture encloses, it will be evident as soon as we begin to explore the ways

The Task and Some Approaches to It

From a general evolutionary point of view, hunting-and-gathering adaptations like that of the Paiute Indians of the American Southwest in the nineteenth century illustrate in some respects characteristics of culture as a whole before the domestication of plants and animals. The Paiute Indians subsisted on wild plants, seeds, roots, and fruit, and on hunting. The pinyon nut was a mainstay. (Courtesy Smithsonian Institution National Anthropological Archives.)

of the sparsely populated past that the mythical average person's share today is much greater than in the time when humanity lived only as hunters and gatherers or as simple farmers and herders.

White has formulated the relation of energy utilization and cultural development in terms of a law: "Culture advances as the amount of energy harnessed per capita per year increases, or as the efficiency or economy of the means of controlling energy is increased, or both" (1959: 56). Other relational statements are that "culture advances as the amount of human need-serving goods and services produced per unit of human labor increases" and that "culture advances as the proportion of nonhuman energy to human energy increases" (1959: 47).

Among recent criticisms of the first statement, White's energy law of cultural development, is Harris's (1968: 649-51) that it does not specify covariance (uniformly related changes) among parts of culture with enough exactitude so that it can be tested and verified. It should be elaborated, he thinks, into specific and manageable relationship statements so that both ends of a relationship can be measured. For instance, at what specified energy level does kinship, a social feature, extend to the boundaries of a community, or at what level can one predict that stratified marrying-in groups will arise? He grants, however, that the law, if viewed as a "metageneralization" (a broad statement standing behind others), points in the direction of materialist strategies for locating causes, the kind acceptable to science.

Another critic, Marshall Sahlins (1972: 6), suggests that per capita

Structure and Process in Culture

To the general evolutionist, adaptations like that of the Binumarien of highland New Guinea illustrate to some degree traits of culture after domestication of plants and animals—in spite of the great variations of cultures within that level. The garden is a tangle of taro, sweet potatoes, bananas, and maize. An instance of economy of effort in the photograph: Very big trees, difficult to cut up and burn, are left to form part of the fence constructed to keep out the pigs, which forage freely all day. (Courtesy Kristen Hawkes.)

measures are not appropriate for making comparisons between preagricultural and agricultural systems and that total measures for communities without regard to population should be substituted. Simple farming societies, he points out, may have larger populations that deliver energy, but the energy produced may average the same per head. More people make higher totals, but individually they produce about the same.

Whether modifications are required or not, I think White's generalization is one of the most useful and provocative in all of anthropology for the beginner who wants to grasp the big picture of cultural development. White had predecessors in recognizing the relevance of energy flow to the evaluation of cultures, and there were forerunners who saw the role of symboling in cultural accumulation, but as noted previously White appears to have been the first to link systems, energy transformation, and symboling-dependency in a clear way.

Referring again to the world cultural system and numbers of people who share, albeit unequally, its available energy, it is almost self-evident that our present four billion humans have been born and live largely as a result of the conditions that culture progressively set up. So in a sense culture contributed to the production of the billions of humans whose billions of motions are involved in energy transformations of the symboling-dependent system. And it is interesting that as culture has evolved it has, by and large, made humans work harder and longer. In the kind of culture represented by the aboriginal Australian hunters or South African Bushmen, the human producers have more leisure than their counterparts in industrialized cultures (Service 1971c: 9).

In the whole of culture, then, evolution may be looked at in terms of general stages, as changes in bounded parts or aspects considered in depth, or as progress along some basic scale such as energy transformation. In addition to energy transformation, two other overall measures of general evolution have been suggested—rising levels of social integration and increases in the all-around adaptability of culture, that is, the capacity of culture to be successful in many and varied habitats (Sahlins and Service 1960: 36-38). Rather than overload ourselves now, in this first introduction to general evolution, we will examine these measures later.

The evolutionary pioneers were not so fixed upon stages that they ignored the details of non-European cultures. Lewis Henry Morgan wrote a cultural study of the Iroquois Indians in 1851, "the first scientific account of an American Indian tribe," as a contemporary called it. Tylor and his contemporaries were also interested in particular cultures described by explorers, traders, missionaries, and military men; many works in the nineteenth century and before are rife with references to Tasmanians, Australians, Oceanians, Asians, Africans, and native Americans. Their orientation was largely, but not solely, in terms of evolutionary stages and lines; cultures were presented as examples within stages or were used as sources from which to extract materials to build up evolutionary sequences of different parts of the whole of culture, like the family, or political organization, or religion. There is nothing wrong with that, but interest has shifted today to another kind of evolutionary context in which there is closer attention to the ways particular cultures move and change. This is called **specific evolution**, and it is linked closely with the process called cultural adaptation.

Adaptation and specific evolution

Copper Eskimo culture, it is evident, was fitted to exploit its harsh northern environment, the Arctic coast, and the treeless hinterland, which has long, dark winters and short summers. There were devices and techniques for fishing and for sea-mammal and caribou hunting and for food preservation; there were snow igloos and skin tents, seal oil lamps, tailored fur clothing and sealskin boots, skin boats for water travel and dog-pulled sledges for land travel. The simple social organization, which included households, families, a sexual division of labor, hunting groups, winter villages, and a limited number of other features, was a flexible one that could meet seasonal changes in availability of food. A shamanistic religion involving belief in spiritual animal helpers was geared to the sometimes precarious hunting life.

But, when Copper Eskimo culture was first described by ethnographers, there was evidence of changes that belied isolation in the immediately preceding century. Iron kettles and tools, steel needles, a few guns were in use. More importantly, epidemics of Euro-Americans' diseases had killed large numbers of people, fighting among the Eskimo themselves and between them and dislocated neighbors had taken place, and some communities had shrunk and disappeared while the remaining ones probably were coalesced remnants of previously separate bands. Within the social organization, it is probable that old marriage rules and practices had been altered and that the **nuclear family** of husband, wife, and children was rather more isolated than previously. Presence of Hudson's Bay Company trading posts, which had contributed to the changes, was a harbinger of greater ones to come, for there were increasing inroads upon the subsistence economy by a market economy, in which the selling of furs procured the tools and utensils of the white Euro-American culture.

This reference to a particular, changing culture suggests that we must enlarge the content of our basic diagram (see the figure on pp. 44-45) to that found in the figure below in order to take account of an environment different from habitat and *sapiens*. That kind has been called the **superorganic** environment, comprised of impinging cultural systems (Harding 1960: 49). Eskimo culture did not invent the gun, and the shift to a partial market economy did not result from the aboriginal encounter with nature. Our Eskimo had responded to the presence of other Eskimo and to American Indians to the south of

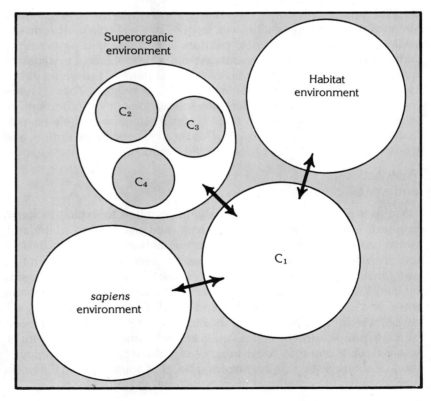

The superorganic environment of a cultural system (C_1) is comprised of all the cultures (C_2, C_3, C_4...) to which it adapts. The arrows indicate two-way interactions.

The Task and Some Approaches to It

them for a long time, but now their culture was altered in a far more substantial way in response to the European system with its trade and trade goods. It could not be a simple matter of substitution of the gun for the harpoon and bow and arrow, for possessing guns required that the Eskimo hunt fur-bearing animals and exchange their fur to obtain both guns and the powder and shot that needed to be replaced continually rather than use the guns to obtain only their own food and clothing.

The events described here can be understood in the context of the terms *adaptation* and *adaptive process*. *Adaptation* means that state of equilibrium or balance cultures tend to assume in relation to environments. *Adaptive process* refers to the movements of culture by which the state is maintained or is redressed in the event of imbalance resulting from environmental change or from internal shocks that disturb environmental relationships.

One of the obvious requirements for maintaining the adaptive state is that the energy intake of the cultural system from environments must equal or exceed its expenditure, for there is cultural work to be done. Not only is energy required for wielding tools and weapons (in the case of the Eskimo, harpoons and lances; in the case of the aboriginal Australians, spears, spear throwers, and digging sticks) but for the motions and behaviors that comprise social relationships and for those understandable in an ideological context. Successful adaptation means both adequate control of environments and a healthy condition of the environments so that they continue to afford the means for the culture to persist. *Adaptation* is a term of broader extension than other processes discussed so far (with the exception of evolution), because adaptations may consist of discovered, invented, and diffused technological knowledge and devices, organizational inventions and adjustments, invented and adopted ideological traits, and the ways knowledge and behaviors are transmitted within the culture. But remember that, although adapting is something a culture does, environments must be kept in view.

We noted before that when an open system such as a culture moves to meet imbalance resulting from disturbances within itself or the environment, the new state it arrives at may be different from the old one, new in content and in organization. Significant change of this sort is specific evolution. It is apparent that there is a close relationship between the adaptive process and evolution of cultures. The usual phrasing is that adaptation is the principal mechanism of evolution.

For example, the Cheyenne in the course of their own specific evolution changed from woodland hunters and fishermen to mixed horticulturists and prairie bison hunters, then abandoned farming to become equestrian bison hunters, and finally, after extinction of the bison and military defeat, became a reservation people, a partially integrated segment of the industrial culture of the United States. Their culture adapted successively to life in the woodland, to life among prairie rivers, and to life in the High Plains. It adjusted on the one hand to the pressures of firearm-equipped tribes to the east and the supply of horses coming from the southwest, and on the other to the westward-moving whites with their trading posts and military forces. It also responded to the competing cultural systems of other tribes.

Adaptations of parts of the culture in the evolutionary movement may be illustrated in several ways. Hoes made of bison scapulas were effective for cultivating maize gardens in the soft soil of the river bottoms, but only sharp digging sticks were useful for prying roots from the prairie sod when farming was abandoned. The earth lodge was practical for sedentary farmers, but the portable tipi was fitted for mobile hunters, who could neither carry the earth lodge along nor return to it, thereby affording a stationary target for raiding enemies. The **extended family** which had occupied the earth lodge remained together in the cluster of tipis we have called the camp, but new conditions produced some changes in the kinship system. Men's social clubs of the village days became primarily military societies in response to the culture's position in the fighting and raiding among mounted tribes pouring into the bison-covered Plains. All of these were adaptive changes occurring in the course of the specific evolution of Cheyenne culture.

But the particular kind of equilibrium state which may be reached for shorter or longer periods following disruptions need not be the same for all cultural systems starting from roughly the same original position. Witness the Missouri River neighbors of the Cheyenne, the Caddoan-speaking Arikara, who were farmers long before the Cheyenne moved from the woodlands, who stuck with their earth-lodge villages longer, and who only very briefly tried equestrian bison hunting. Then, devastated by disease and war in their vulnerable villages, they were dispersed among nearby reservation peoples (Holder 1970). The course of neither culture, viewed in an evolutionary way, coincides with the stages or the overall progress of culture, although both are part of the variously turbulent or placid stream from which general evolution is extracted. Cheyenne and Arikara varied from their own pasts and from each other, taking on different specializations.

As another example, the Uto-Aztecan-speaking Hopi Indians of the Southwest emerged as farmers from the seed-gathering and hunting Desert Culture that had become established more than 10,000 years ago, whereas many of their linguistic relatives, such as the Paiute, never did. In spite of immense buffeting by other peoples, Indian and white, the Hopi have succeeded in maintaining to the present time the substance of their horticultural adaptation. On the other hand, the Aztecs of Mexico, who shared a past much like the Paiute and earlier Hopi and spoke a language related to theirs, built a more complex civilization. The history of aboriginal North American culture presents this kind of branching picture, and so does that of any region or continent through time.

General evolutionary statements, then, direct attention to successive forms emerging in the whole of culture, each of which represents a kind of breakthrough to a new level of development, or they grasp the movement as a whole by an idea such as progressive energy transformation. Specific evolutionary statements relate to specific, delimited cultures set in their own natural and superorganic environments, making adaptive movements, reaching new states of equilibrium after they have been shaken by conditions or events occurring inside themselves or outside.

There is another term relating to evolution that you will encounter as you read your way into anthropology. That is **_multilinear evolution,_** which was a concern of the American anthropologist Julian H. Steward (1955). Steward did not regard evolution as a process with specific and general *aspects,* as we have been treating it here, but as "a special type of historical reconstruction or as a particular methodology or approach" to culture (1955: 27). He pointed out, for instance, that there have been parallels in the growth of civilizations based on irrigation in arid environments in the Old and New Worlds, and he centered his attention on finding explanations—including ecological ones—for the recurrence of particular kinds of culture traits and complexes in two or more such regional instances without generalizing his statements beyond them.

We do not find it useful to give **multilinear evolution** a separate status in this introduction. We shall regard it as specific evolution with an enlargement of boundaries from smaller cultural systems to regional ones, accompanied by cautious and specific comparisons between them that do not move to the general. Along with his rejection of the usefulness of general evolution (which he labelled "universal"), we should note that, in spite of the similarity of terms, Steward's multilinear evolution is quite unlike Tylor's auxiliary notion of the evolution of culture "along its many lines." Criticisms and appreciations of Steward's work are numerous (e.g., Dole 1973, Carneiro 1973, Harris 1968, and Manners 1964).

In this chapter we have been concerned with the skeleton of culture in general—the skeleton which is its structure, its parts, and their arrangement. The parts, like culture itself, must be extracted analytically from our observations and named according to some agreed-on criteria. For the whole of culture, we regard the three aspects of technology, social organization, and ideology as the basic parts (although we may devise others when we look at particular cultures). Technology is the most important and consequential aspect.

In a sense, we look at culture statically when we fix on its structure. Movements in culture are called processes, and they include discovery, invention, diffusion, integration, and enculturation, all of which we oriented and defined in relation to our diagram or model. The largest and most embracing process is evolution. Evolution itself has two aspects, which means it may be looked at in two ways: the general, in which the whole of culture is our concern, and the specific, in which the focus of attention is a particular culture going its own way, so to speak, adapting to its environment.

Suggested Readings

Harris, Marvin. 1971. *Culture, man, and nature.* Chapter 8, "Sociocultural systems and processes." New York: Thomas Y. Crowell.

Kaplan, David, and Robert A. Manners. 1972. *Culture theory.* Chapter 2, "Theoretical orientations." Englewood Cliffs, N.J.: Prentice-Hall.*

Kroeber, A. K. 1963. *Culture patterns and processes.* New York: Harcourt Brace Jovanovich.* (Excerpts from *Anthropology.* 1948. New York: Harcourt, Brace and Company.)

Linton, Ralph. 1936. *The study of man.* Chapter 19, "Diffusion," and Chapter 20, "Integration." New York: D. Appleton-Century.

Sahlins, Marshall D. 1964. "Culture and environment." In *Horizons of anthropology*. Sol Tax, ed. Chicago: Aldine.*

Steward, Julian H. 1955. *Theory of culture change: The methodology of multilinear evolution*. Urbana: University of Illinois Press.

White, Leslie A. 1959. *The evolution of culture: The development of civilization to the fall of Rome*. New York: McGraw-Hill.*

Williams, Thomas Rhys. 1972. *Introduction to socialization: Human culture transmitted*. St. Louis: C. V. Mosby.

Chapter Four
Ideas in the Anthropological Tradition

A cartoon image of the anthropologist as pith-helmeted adventurer (always white-skinned, of course), armed with camera, tape recorder, and note pad, who plays participant-observer in the rites of savages (a savage is a dark-skinned fellow with a bone pushed through his nasal septum), is an element of American popular culture. Like all cultural things, it has more implications than appear on the surface, including the flavor of racism.

A science of the primitive?

The view that anthropology is a "science of the primitive" has had some support in the discipline. For instance, a British social anthropologist, Ralph Piddington, defined the anthropological sciences as "the Study of Man, particularly primitive man," and cultural anthropology, combining prehistoric archeology and social anthropology, as concerned with "the cultures of primitive man" (1950: 2). He added, to drive a final nail, "The method of social anthropology is based upon field-work—the direct study of the beliefs and customs of primitive peoples" (1950: 10). To Piddington, anthropology could go so far as the techniques devised in the study of little whole-societies would permit, and no farther. In a manner of speaking, primitive societies were little wholes, and thus anthropology was a science of little

71

Biologically speaking, this Binumarien of highland New Guinea is simply a human variant and no more primitive than any other contemporary *Homo sapiens*. Some elements of the culture that prompts him to act might be called "primitive" on an objective scale. Warfare has been outlawed in his land, but antagonisms from old blood debts remain. This man, his face covered with ashes to show his readiness to fight, waits for an enemy. In deference to the law, he carries a club instead of the more lethal bow and arrow. (Courtesy Kristen Hawkes.)

wholes. The British have gone beyond this now, although they are still reluctant to breathe deeply of evolution.

Anthropology, of course, is not a sort of intellectual custodian of "the primitive"; its task is to account for similarities and differences in humanity's ways of behaving in different times and places—ideally, in all times and places. Primitive lifeways, however defined, are part of its materials, but anthropologists also try to cope with the complexities of industrial cultures and intermediate ones. And *primitive* is definable contextually. In relation to the concepts we have adopted to manage observations about human tools, behaviors, and ideas, we would say that a technology is **primitive** if it consists primarily of hand-wielded and human-muscle-powered devices, that social organization is primitive if it binds relatively small numbers of people into small communi-

The Task and Some Approaches to It

ties with kinship and locality as the dominant ties, and that an ideology is primitive if it is heavily freighted with supernaturalism.

The term *primitive* also connotes "original" or "early." In a strictly temporal sense, it is obvious that there are no primitive peoples and cultures in the world today. Each has an equally long history reaching back to the early and original beginnings all of us share. But we know quite a bit about those common beginnings, so that we can assert that stone tools of the Australian Aborigines and their techniques for making them are more like temporally early (although not the earliest) ones than they are like a steel axe, a pneumatic jack hammer, or a rolling mill. Or that their bands of twenty or thirty people are more like the probable organizations of **Neanderthals** and **Cro-Magnons** than they are like nation-states and their dependencies linked by mammoth corporations and the world market. Or that the ideology of the ceremonies for the magical increase in numbers of animals and plants are probably more like that behind late Ice Age fertility and hunting rites performed in caves decorated with polychrome paintings than it is like, say, contemporary biology, theoretical and applied. If we can't make these assumptions, we'll get nowhere.

The point is that Australian hunting-and-gathering technology achieved a stable adaptation to its environments and changed very slowly; the social organization was geared to the technology, and the ideology rationalized the social structure and the place of the whole culture in the surrounding world. If the technology is primitive, as defined, so in all likelihood is the rest of the culture in important respects, and we may project our observations of primitive social organization and ideology, as defined, back into the past. The alternative is to assume a Golden Age from which humankind has degenerated, a position that was fought over and destroyed in the eighteenth and nineteenth centuries. Another example of technological stability comes from Africa. "A hunting camp site of central Africa dated to 2340-2750 B.C. shows a technology which can be paralleled almost perfectly with similar items of Bushman culture in the general area today" (Vansina 1970: 166; drawing upon work of the archeologist Creighton Gabel). While it would not be warranted to project Bushman social organization back 4,000 years with respect to detail, we may do so with respect to the kind of social organization it is. Both the contemporary Bushman culture and its antecedents are, by our definitions and reasoning, primitive. Not the people, biologically. Our species has changed far less in 30,000 years than have segments of world culture.

There is another side to use of the term *primitive*, however. Circumstances have changed for native Australians, and few of them live in a primitive culture—only in a harsh and deprived one that is a segment of Australian national culture. They, like their neighbors in New Guinea and Papua, demonstrate their intellectual powers and nonprimitive learned skills when permitted to. They seek social recognition and political influence in the world as it is today. They resent, as who would not, being labelled by a word that in ordinary lay usage is an epithet having biological connotations. The situation is no less galling for native Americans whose lands are invaded each summer by anthropology students, some of whom still seek the exotic and "primitive" (Deloria

1969). To understand cultures neutrally, in evolutionary perspective, we need not dispense with the term, but we should not allow it to carry racist overtones or to be used as a political weapon.

Relativism, generalization, and tolerance

The problem of using a word like *primitive*, then, has several facets. Sometimes its use is justified, sometimes not; it is one of those matters that depends on perspective and orientation, which should always be made clear. The words *relativism* and *generalization* (or *relativistic* and *comparative*) represent two such perspectives in a technical sense. *Tolerance,* on the other hand, is not a technical word but stands for a mode of behavior that both relativists and generalists are well advised to adopt.

One of the most widely read books in anthropology in the English-speaking world is Ruth Benedict's *Patterns of Culture*, first published in 1934. It is an example of what has been called **relativism**, which questions the practicality and wisdom of attempting to explain or understand instances of cultural behavior out of the context of the particular culture in which they are found. It is Benedict's theme that the diversity of cultures is endless and that each culture has been integrated in a fashion that makes it incommensurable with others. Her labels for the kinds of integration she assumes for the cultures she describes are derived from philosophy and psychology.

That the term *relativist* has been preempted by this perspective is unfortunate; Benedict's perspective had better be called *particularist*, for all anthropologists (and by the nature of the process of understanding, all people) are relativists. The difference between anthropologists in this respect is not whether some understand by relating observations to conceptual categories and some do not but what kind of extractions they make, how they label them, and the extensibility of their categories. What size of universe, large or small, do they have in mind? If Zuni manipulation of prayer sticks, a Zuni's state of mind, and the ideas that cluster about the manipulation, for instance, are related only to the **Apollonian** style of integration (that is the term Benedict applies to Southwestern Pueblos), the referent is limited. If, on the other hand, the Zuni behaviors are related by means of broader concepts to religion or to the ideological aspect of culture in general, the referent is extensive. No thing is the *same* thing as another nor like it in all respects (this applies from one Zuni prayer stick to another, too), but it may resemble or not resemble another. Likeness and unlikeness, these repeat themselves in our perceptions, and we compound concepts of lesser or greater extension to manage them. To insist upon a limited frame of reference exclusively is to deny the possibility of a science of culture (or a science of anything).

A synonym for *particularistic* is *idiographic*, and its antonym is *nomothetic*. The goal of the anthropologist who takes a **nomothetic** stance is to discover regularities in the working out of cultural processes and in the appearance of similar structures in different cultural systems and finally to sum up the conditions under which they appear. The anthropologist tries, in other words, to construct laws, both general and

limited, which explain similarities and differences in cultural behaviors and objects. Observations which do not meet expectations prompted by the proposed laws are a challenge: and the nomothetic anthropologist sets to work to discover what special conditions may be operating and may cheerfully revise the laws if necessary.

One circumstance that has confused the matter of relativism and generalization in anthropology has been its linkage with ethical relativism and tolerance, which moves us into another area. Ethics are rules of conduct, guides to action. Ethical relativists (or particularists) tend to evaluate or make judgments about such rules and the conduct that pertains to them only in relation to the culture in which a particular rule is found. Nonrelativists (or nonparticularists) seek the basis for discovery or construction of general judgments or a universal ethic and have incurred the charge of **ethnocentrism**. Ethnocentrism is the setting up of one's own customs as a standard for evaluations, holding one's own customs superior and those of others inferior to the degree that they differ. This is a controversial area in which science, as science, has as yet offered no accepted guide to behavior. Science-related philosophy has made substantial suggestions, however; see for an example *operational ethics* (Rapoport 1954). There is an ethic related to scientific procedures and publication, and scientists as citizens have a general obligation to examine ethics and act ethically. Context is a tool that should help you think about the matter.

Generations of hunting and simple farming people have tolerated anthropologists and other persistent intruders into their communities. The study of lifeways ought to breed tolerance as well as understanding. These are semi-sedentary Guahibo Indians of Colombia who are being incorporated into the mainstream of culture generated by high-energy organizations. (Courtesy Nancy and Robert V. Morey.)

Ideas in the Anthropological Tradition

Tolerance may be regarded simply as the capacity to accommodate and to refrain from overt and hurtful judgments in relations with people, or, as the *Random House Dictionary* puts it, "a fair and objective attitude toward those whose opinions, practices, race, religion, nationality, etc., differ from one's own; freedom from bigotry." I believe anthropology as a whole contributes to tolerance, and a bigoted ethnographer would meet a signal lack of success in the field. Sir James Frazer, a nineteenth-century compiler of customs, who, "when asked if he had ever seen one of the primitive people about whose customs he had written so many volumes, tersely replied, 'God forbid!' " (Beattie 1964: 7), would have been a poor ethnographer, and his remark is quite out of keeping with a science of culture.

A look at anthropological history

History, like evolution, must be extracted from the flow of events, and as you well know extracted histories are different one from another. One that details the doings of kings, nobles, and cardinals is not like one telling a story in terms of common people, and there are political, social, economic, and intellectual histories, among others. But, it may be objected, history *is* (or *was*). No doubt, and real events in the past have had their chains of effects reaching to the present and perhaps to the future. The problem lies in the extraction and evaluation of events in such a way that an organized and useful story may be told. For history is also what has become fixed in that part of the ideological aspect of culture called "histories," and like its ideological mother it has been shaped by other parts of culture as well as by the events it has itself, in the narrow sense, responded to in the symboling process.

Histories have been shaped by social organization, for one thing. Polynesian chiefs had at their service genealogists who obligingly traced their patrons' noble descent from the gods, the result being a temporal framework that confused Oceanic history for anthropologists for a generation. Richard III, he of Bosworth Field, suffered from historians partial to his Tudor successors. And the technology of communication has had a hand: writing and printing altered history previously only committed to memory, with or without the aid of mnemonic devices like the Peruvian quipu, sets of knotted strings, or the Plains Indians' winter counts, in which a few symbols drawn upon animal skins recalled a sequence of events.

The writing of history may be looked at as of two kinds, **presentism** and **historicism**, as an historian of anthropology, George W. Stocking, Jr. (1968), puts it. Presentism he likens to what another historian, Herbert Butterfield, called "Whig" history: a study of the past for the sake of the present, in which things existing now are traced back through somewhat similar antecedents to show a progressive, forward movement "to produce a story which is the ratification if not the glorification of the present" (Stocking 1968: 3). Antecedents are taken out of their own contemporary contexts; the conditions that shaped them are scanted. Historicism, on the other hand, seeks first to understand events of the past in their immediate contexts. Probably the best of history being written today follows that procedure.

The Task and Some Approaches to It

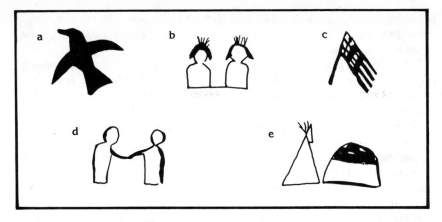

Plains Indian winter counts drawn on animal skins are one kind of mnemonic device representing a first stage—pictographic—in the development of writing, preceding rebus and alphabetic forms. The Dakota pictographs here are interpreted as follows: (a) the cold winter in which many crows froze to death, (b) two Mandans (identified by their hair arrangement) are killed by Minneconjous; (c) the first United States flag brought by troops; (d) Dakota and Mandan make peace (the emissaries swam to the middle of the Missouri River and shook hands); (e) Dakota and Arikara (tipi and earth lodge) camped together in peace. The years have been identified as 1788-89 through 1792-93. (After *Pictographs of the North American Indians,* Garrick Mallery, Washington, D.C.: Smithsonian Institution, Bureau of Ethnology, Fourth Annual Report, 1886.)

Anthropological history, and particularly the history of ethnological theory, has been written, like older political history, principally around leading figures and the schools they founded and led. Schools may be likened to dynasties; Leslie White (1966) has compared them with cults. Much of the history written about them has been of the Whig variety, although there has been some effort to understand them in relation to their contemporary settings. I confess to a misgiving about presenting the schools in the way it is done here, but we do not have time or space for a longer excursion, and some reference points are needed for the anthropologists and doctrines mentioned.

After a period of theoretical beginnings during the Enlightenment of the eighteenth century, the first recognizable school of anthropology to emerge was the classical evolutionary in the second half of the nineteenth century, represented most notably by Edward Burnett Tylor in England and Lewis Henry Morgan in the United States. Its principal orientation was toward general evolution, by means of which it brought some order into the growing body of information about human societies, past and contemporary. About the turn of the century, there were two ideological turns against evolutionism that took two directions—historical and structural-functional. Definitions of these terms in relation to ethnological theory will be looked at in a following section.

On the continent, the historical approach was represented by the German-Austrian school of Fritz Graebner and Father Wilhelm Schmidt, with whom are identified the idea of culture circles, complexes of traits that were held to have migrated widely from their points of origin on the Eurasiatic continent, and culture strata, or layers, which were seen as overlays of more recently diffused complexes upon earlier ones in specific places. In England, there was a short-lived and inconsequential "heliocentric" diffusionist school of the anatomist-turned-ethnologist G. Elliot Smith and his followers W. G. Perry and W. H. R. Rivers, which derived civilization wherever substantially found from Egypt. The term *heliocentric* relates to an element in the Egyptian complex, sun worship. In North America, the leading proponent of historical anthropology was Franz Boas, German-trained physicist and geographer who turned to anthropology after an expedition among the Central Eskimo. At Columbia University he trained many of the last generation of American anthropologists, including the influential and

Ideas in the Anthropological Tradition

scholarly Alfred Louis Kroeber and Robert H. Lowie. The term *particularist* is tending to replace *historical* in retrospective reviews of the Boas school.

The structural-functional turn away from evolutionism is usually identified with Bronislaw Malinowski and Alfred Reginald Radcliffe-Brown. Malinowski, trained as a physicist in Poland, became a British citizen and London School of Economics anthropologist after his three years of field work in the Trobriand Islands near New Guinea. Radcliffe-Brown was ethnographer of the Andaman Islanders and western Australian Aborigines, and his earliest academic home was Cambridge University. "R-B," as he was called by British colleagues, regarded himself as being rooted in the French sociological school of Emile Durkheim and Marcel Mauss, from which also stems Claude Lévi-Strauss, contemporary exponent of idealistic "structuralism."

Within the last three decades in the United States, there have been several movements, with some overlap between them. As summarized by Marvin Harris (1968), who wrote the first general history of anthropological theory (primarily that of the English-speaking world) since Robert H. Lowie's (1937), they include personality and culture studies, statistical handling of sociocultural facts, a linguistics-allied method for eliciting categories from informants, and ecology. A pioneer and important contributor in the last-named movement was Julian H. Steward (1955).

In Leslie White's view, there can be discerned in anthropology's history a struggle to establish and vindicate the evolutionary approach on the one hand and on the other the recognition of culture as a domain in its own right, to be explained by **culturological**, rather than by sociological or psychological, means (1949, 1966). Harris does not agree that evolution and the superorganic have been central issues. To him, the history of ethnological theory presents the varying fortunes of what he terms the principle of "technoenvironmental and technoeconomic determinism" and a research strategy that "assigns priority to the study of the material conditions of sociocultural life" (1968: 4). There is no difference between the two writers about the importance of being a materialist; the gap comes in Harris's relegation of general evolution to a metaphysic, removed from the workaday world of the anthropologist. But both, it seems to me, are primarily Whig or presentist history, although not too much the worse for it.

History and historians

There is, then, more than one way in which a story can be told. But there is a meaning of the term *history* itself as an analytical tool, as an approach to the world, that it is important we grasp. It is like evolution in one respect and, in another, not.

From the time of Aristotle, Greek philosopher of the fourth century B.C., history has been described as concerned with the specific and singular rather than the general, with the uniqueness of events and the differences between them rather than with their "universal" qualities or with characteristics that link them to other events (Nagel 1952: 162). Historians, like evolutionists, make generalizations, but theirs are "descriptive generalizations" (the phrase is Kroeber's) that manage to keep and impart the individuality and flavor of the real events they cover, and the generalizations or summings-up are themselves specific, singular, unique. The Age of Elizabeth I and the Crusades are examples. An historical generalization about one or the other would be a concise story about it, and of course it would fit only one set of events, not any other. In this kind of summing-up, history is like cultural geography: history is geography standing up, and geography is history lying down. The Mississippi Valley and the Great Plains are as unmistakably specific and singular as the Age of Elizabeth I and the Crusades, although the geographer's time scale is flattened.

Concern with time also is a mark of the historian's craft and of history as a kind of study. It is considered important to locate events in some kind of calendar. Leslie A. White, who puts history squarely in the set of approaches available to all scientists, specifies concern with uniqueness *and* time or temporality as its distinguishing characteristics. " 'History' is that way of sciencing in which events are dealt with in terms of their temporal relationships alone. Each event is unique" (1949: 8; also cf. 1945).

Historians, then, tell stories that incorporate and make reference to particular people, places, events, and dates, and they generalize with the use of summings-up or categories that cannot be separated from those *particular* things they incorporate. And they refer to no other ones. One could not displace the term *Crusades* to the American continent or to the nineteenth century. However, they explain as well as narrate. Their explanation of a state of affairs at a given time would involve reference to antecedent or prior states of affairs (the "initial conditions") and the events in between.

Of course, choices must be made about the events that are involved in an explanation. "Clearly, the mere listing of a series of events preceding the given item cannot qualify as an explanation; temporal pre-

The morning after a Binumarien intervillage feast in the New Guinea highlands. The anthropologist as ethnographer shares the particularistic interest of the cultural geographer and historian in describing the scene and relating it to its surroundings and preceding events. But as ethnologist, he or she is more inclined to try to relate the observations to lawlike generalizations. (Courtesy Kristen Hawkes.)

cedence does not in itself make an event relevant to the genesis of the item under consideration" (Hempel 1959: 282). Events must be weighted, and weighting is a matter of judgment. It is an advantage if selective weightings can be made against a set of principles or laws that comprise a theory about human social or cultural behavior.

However, in general, historians have not been interested in constructing laws of human behavior on their own, and they draw upon principles and laws of other disciplines. As two students of history put it (Joynt and Rescher 1961: 154), " . . . the very way in which history concerns itself with the past is quite different from that of the 'historical' sciences. The historian is interested in the particular facts regarding the past *for themselves,* and not in an instrumental role as data for laws. Indeed, unlike the researcher in 'historical' science, the historian is not a *producer* of general laws, but a *consumer* of them. His position *vis-a-vis* the sciences is essentially parasitic. The generalizations provided by anthropology, sociology, psychology, etc., are used by the historian in the interests of his mission of facilitating our understanding of the past" (italics in the original).

But in addition to lack of interest as an explanation for the absence of nomothetic statements there is the brute fact that there can be no such statements if history is only "descriptive generalization." A science of uniquenesses or particulars is a contradiction of terms. If a scholar does make general and lawlike explanations, he or she is doing more than history—as history is defined here. However, the historian's craft is by no means to be depreciated. The narratives that historians painstakingly construct from documents may uncover problems and raise questions that more theoretically minded social scientists can attack systematically. In the complex world into which anthropology is moving, let's work in tandem with historians.

The meanings of *function*

The term **function** derives its usual meanings in anthropology in the context of British social anthropology. As an idea, it is older than that school, of course, and many others use it, but it became particularly prominent there. The recurrent theme of **functionalism** is that societies are like living organisms in which each part and activity is more or less indispensable to the whole and it is an anthropologist's business to demonstrate the "function" of the activities and parts. To Radcliffe-Brown, for instance, "the *function* of any recurrent activity, such as the punishment of a crime, or a funeral ceremony, is the part it plays in the social life as a whole and therefore the contribution it makes to the maintenance of structural continuity" (1952: 180). So the function of a burial is not only that it puts away a disturbing corpse: the ceremony brings together members of the group to which the deceased belonged and reinforces their solidarity.

Human behaviors, by this view, are not fragments for which functions are to be found individually but are always more or less closely integrated within institutions, and institutions with the whole. For example, in an essay entitled "The Mother's Brother in South Africa," in his *Structure and Function in Primitive Society* (1952), "R-B" explains the privileged and familiar behavior of an African BaThonga nephew to his

Like this Middle Eastern donkey, the ambiguous word *function* carries a heavy load in anthropology. It refers to "maintenance of structural continuity," to "satisfaction of needs," and to "variable relationships." The donkey itself is a "functional alternative" to a tractor or to human backs. (Courtesy Joseph Ginat.)

maternal uncle (as when he seizes a meal prepared for his uncle and eats it) by relating it first to segmentation of the society into descent lines and then to the differential behavior toward father and father's line (obedience and respect) and mother and her father's line (warmth and succorance) arising from relations within the family. A boy, he says, tends to regard his mother's brother as a male mother and tenders him the same affection as he does his own mother, because uncle is a member of mother's lineage. Compounded with that is the license and privilege he can have with a member of his own sex; he would feel affection for his mother but would be under some cross-sex restraint toward her. This restraint would be lifted in relation to his uncle, for whom he already feels affection as a male mother. This behavior does not end with purely secular relations but extends to the gods of the mother's lineage (the boy may seize a part of a sacrifice made to them and run away with it) though not to those of his father's group (whom he must worship in high respect). Thus, the behavior has ramifying relations. The important thing is that it serves to maintain the social structure represented by lineages.

While Radcliffe-Brown's starting point was a social system, Malinowski's was human physiological needs, which gave rise to and were satisfied by institutions. "For function cannot be defined in any other way than the satisfaction of a need by an activity in which human beings cooperate, use artifacts, and consume goods" (Malinowski 1960: 39). The needs he spoke of as basic were nutrition, reproduction, safety, relaxation, and so on (1939: 942). They were matched by "derived needs," or cultural responses, such as "commissariat" to nutrition, marriage and family to reproduction, "domicile and dress" to bodily comforts, and "protection and defense" to safety. As the individual's needs must be satisfied in order for life to go on, so must derived needs be satisfied for a culture to persist. It appears that to Malinowski "form" (that is, the *way* in which any need was satisfied) was determined by function.

There exists a large stock of criticisms of the logic and substance of functionalism (examples are Hempel 1959, Goldstein 1957, Harris 1968, and Jarvie 1969, 1973), but I will mention only one point, that of **functional alternatives**. A need, it is obvious, can be satisfied in more than one way, and several varieties of a general kind of activity can contribute to maintenance of a structure. If hunting and gathering satisfy the need for food in one culture, horticulture or herding may satisfy it in others. If troublemakers in one society are labelled as witches and killed, in another they are imprisoned or sent to a psychiatrist. Needs for safety, and protection and defense, are being satisfied here, and no doubt the measures society takes to dispose of or correct troublemakers can be said to contribute to the persistence of the society. But in what sense is the content of the behavior, different in each case, determined by the function, the same in each case? And do we add to our understanding of variations when we point out that they all have the same function, that they all contribute to social continuity?

In the context of functionalism, then, *function* has special meanings. But evolutionists use it, too. White, for instance, speaks of it as a kind of relationship, one that is moving or fluid and that is wholly spatial (think of a flat plane) and nontemporal in character. "When the spatial relationships uniting a number of events, or material objects, are regarded as variable, then we speak of *function*" (1949: 9). This might be called a quasi-mathematical notion of function; relationships (distances, correlations, or whatever) might be measured or quantified, but this is not followed through. Carneiro in a similar vein relates function to systems. "We may define a *system* as a set of structurally and functionally related elements articulated into a working whole" (1960: 146).

To my mild surprise, I found little or no need for the term *function* when I began to think about human behavior in relation to the orienting model outlined in the preceding two chapters. Cultural motions can be labelled by process terms of greater or lesser extension, and they carry neither the disability of the connotations of the functionalist school nor the limitations of nontemporality. If one were to stick with the diagram of flagpole, sun, and shadow as wholly representative of a cultural system, then functional relationships might suffice. Not so with culture, which is transformed as it moves through time. Discovery, invention, and diffusion can't be hung on a flagpole. They can be on our three-circle model of a cultural system and its environments.

There is one further disability of *function*, although it arises from language usage rather than being inherent. That is, it is easy to slide from saying "the function is..." to "the function is *to*...." That introduces the idea of "purpose," which may have its place, or places, but this is not one of them.

I also concluded that the word *institution*, which Malinowski defined as "functional isolates"—"units which contain natural limits of coordination and correlation" and "organized systems of human activity"

The Task and Some Approaches to It

(1960: 158, 160), is not indispensable. Aspects, subsystems, and other notions are adequate, without carrying the special meanings of functional analysis. It is interesting that in a book in sociology that applies systems ideas, the concept of institution is found wanting: "While one of the most heavily utilized terms in the field, it has only the vaguest of referents" (Buckley 1967: 161).

Middle-ground organizing devices

In one of the vignettes that enliven his classic work, *The Cheyenne Indians* (1923), George Bird Grinnell describes the "incidents of a day" in a chapter he entitles "Village Life." He relates how, in the setting of the summer camp, women before sunrise kindled fires and carried water from the nearby stream and, when the light spread in the eastern sky and men and boys had dashed out for their morning plunge, they prepared the morning meal. Youths drove horses in from the hills, tethered selected animals near the tipis for use in emergency, and drove to pasture the others that had been kept in camp during the night. After the morning repast and the calling out of news and of orders of the chiefs by a crier who circled the camp on horseback, men saddled up and set out to hunt, some women began their skin working and tipi making, and others set out in parties to gather firewood and dig prairie roots. Men who did not go out hunting that day lounged about, gossiping and working at their own crafts. In late afternoon, men's hunting parties and women's foraging groups came in. The evening meal was prepared while children scurried about carrying invitations to guests. As night fell, stories were told around the fires; the sounds of social dances, gambling songs, and doctors' chants rose into the air. Then the fires smouldered, and the camp fell silent.

For every culture, an account of the round of an ordinary day might be constructed. It would be different in different seasons, it would be interrupted by unusual or by recurrently scheduled events such as ceremonies, and it would change over the years. But there is a regularity and order in daily life that we all recognize—for our own society as well as for others.

So it is with the seasonal or annual round. From summer and early fall encampments, with their collective hunts, great ceremonials, and offensive and defensive forays, the Cheyenne bands and camps moved separately to late fall and winter bases to subsist on the scattered game, hunt for fur-bearing animals, and shelter the horses near the wooded hills. The Eskimo round focused on the catching of sea mammals in fall and winter and of inland caribou in summer and entailed adaptive adjustments in habitations, varying population concentration, and hence some shift in social organization, taboos, and other rules and behaviors.

There are other repetitive sequences of human behavior shaped by different cultures—progressions through their life spans by individuals and groups, called the *life cycle*, and the formation, growth, and transformation or breakup of domestic or residential clusters. Descriptive summaries of such sequences of behavior will be termed *middle-ground* organizations. They all relate to the idea of **cultural pattern**, which is possibly the most popular and pervasive one in all of cultural anthropology.

The term *patterns* usually refers to sets of recurrent, traditional customs and their arrangement. They are complexes whose component items hang together in a recognizable way. Consider this example. Among the Kalinga in former times, head hunting involved the setting out of small groups of men, armed with spears, axes, and shields, who crept into enemy territory and struck at isolated individuals, particularly women, the elderly, and the infirm. The victim's head, and perhaps fingers, were cut off, and the party hastened homeward, where fellow villagers kept watch to help repel pursuers. Approaching the village, the head takers yelled piercingly and were answered by staccato calls of women, and there was a triumphant entry. A flower-lined bamboo basket was made for the severed head, and it was placed near the village shrine. A feast and a ceremony called *sagang* followed, during which the head was transferred to rocks atop the shrine and back to its receptacle. Later, the head was boiled, and bits of bone were distributed as trophies to the warriors (Dozier 1967: 71-73). This in brief was the pattern of head hunting among the Kalinga.

Among ourselves and all people we may speak of patterns of working, eating, sleeping, giving and receiving, greeting, rejoicing, playing, fighting, marrying, child rearing, and what not. The concept of patterns is fluid and can be applied to minor things like waving goodbye or tipping the hat or to major segments of culture, whole cultures, or even broader traditions. At the more inclusive end of the spectrum, patterns often become "configurations." There is no agreed-on classification. Kroeber tried his hand at labelling different kinds—universal (like plow agriculture, monotheism, and the alphabet), total-culture, and style patterns (1948)—and wrote a weighty but inconclusive book, *Configurations of Culture Growth* (1944), in which he examined patterns of growth and decline in philosophy, science, sculpture, painting, drama, literature, music, and so on. In a recent text, the anthropologist Thomas R. Williams treats patterns as being composed of "culture trait complexes," his subsystem of social relations, for instance, being comprised of twenty-four "major patterns," such as kinship, law, sickness and health, and stages of life from infancy to old age (1972: 195-96). The notion has a longish history and varying extensions.

One of the family of pattern notions is the **culture area** concept. It draws a line around a cluster of cultures which are in many respects like each other and different as a group with respect to those outside. As defined by Harold E. Driver, a leader in distribution studies and a methodologist, "A culture area is a geographical area occupied by a number of peoples whose cultures show a significant degree of similarity with each other and at the same time a significant degree of dissimilarity with the cultures of the peoples of other such areas" (1961: 12). As Driver notes, *significant* indicates that constructing areas is a statistical problem, but most of the time only familiarity with the cultures, and intuition, enter into their delineation. It was familiarity with culture area patterns that helped "What in the World?" panelists identify the provenience of artifacts presented to them in their television appearances.

The culture area device is associated prominently with Clark Wiss-

The Task and Some Approaches to It

ler (1950), who had a sort of "Eureka!" moment at the American Museum of Natural History in New York, where he was arranging exhibits of Indian artifacts (Mayhall 1962: 62). Previously, items such as bows and arrows, or clothing, or shelters, had been arranged by categories, the items in each display being drawn from widely ranging areas. Wissler saw that striking clusters of traits, clusters whose items hung together, were characteristic of specific geographical regions both in their type and their design. For instance, lances, bows and arrows and quivers, shields, fringed skin clothing, beaded moccasins, geometrically decorated rawhide boxes or parfleches, bone tools for preparing bison hides, and so on, came from the Great Plains. On the other hand, not tipis but bark longhouses and not rawhide boxes but bark containers were characteristic of the Northeast Woodlands. So he arranged objects that came from a given region in a particular display of their own. He no doubt had in mind earlier publications like those of Otis T. Mason, a specialist in Indian technology, in which a number of "ethnic environments" (1907) had been discussed. And the concept had been anticipated by the German evolutionist Adolf Bastian (Lowie 1937: 36-37) and others. But Wissler developed the notion of culture area, which was particularly congenial to the emerging historical or particularist school in the United States.

Wissler's ten North American culture areas (Plains, Plateau, California, North Pacific Coast, Eskimo, Mackenzie, Eastern, Southeastern, Southwestern, and Nahua or Mexican) were rearranged into six areas, subdivided into eighty-four subareas or components, by Kroeber (1947), and Driver (1961) delineated seventeen areas. The variation between their groupings illustrates the problem of drawing boundaries, for cultures change in appearance in a gradient fashion across the landscape, and only rarely is there a radical break between them. As Driver says, "The boundaries of culture areas ... are generally the lines at which two ways of life are in balance, and only occasionally represent an abrupt change" (1961: 14).

While Wissler spoke of culture centers, represented by typical tribes within an area whose cultures contained all of the diagnostic traits and a minimum of those characteristic of other areas, and sensed the significance of this as a way to bring a time element into a quite static picture, Kroeber carried the idea a bit farther with his notion of "climax." Climax is taken to be the point in time at which the highest known development in an area has taken place; in relation to it the "culture center" is "the district of greatest cultural productivity and richness" (1947: 5). They are the time and space (or place) sides of the same phenomenon. A center has a climactic point in time. Given center and climax, one then posits that invented traits flow outward from the center to neighboring cultures and beyond and influence the course of culture history.

Culture area maps have their uses, particularly for introducing anthropology students to the cultural lay of the land. But there is a delusory side to them. While an ordinary map of the geographical features of a continent presents a picture at one point in time, a cultural map doesn't. Culture may change faster than the rest of nature. For instance, a cultural map with an area representing the Plains with classical equestrian bison hunters dominating them, if it were true to time, would show much of the Eastern Woodlands swept all but clear of native cultures and the California Indians in scattered enclaves. Thus the usual culture area map is a composite of time segments as well as areal segments.

You will discern that the culture area concept is a particularistic device, like the historian's Age of Elizabeth I and the geographer's Mississippi Valley. It brings some order into observations, as do other patterns, styles, and configurations, and it may prompt questions without answering them. For instance, it might be asked why there is some congruence between culture patterns and geographical regions, and an

A pattern: Native food areas in the New World. In this scheme, Wissler extracted dominant food resources exploited and used them to label eight areas on two continents. When he took other culture traits into consideration, however, he came up with ten culture areas for the North American continent alone—as can be seen on the next map. (After Wissler 1950.)

The Task and Some Approaches to It

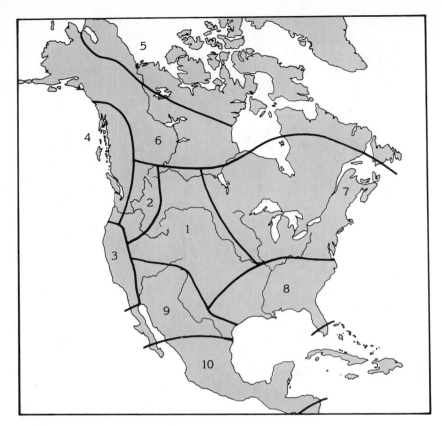

Wissler's ten North American culture areas: (1) Plains; (2) Plateau; (3) California; (4) North Pacific Coast; (5) Eskimo; (6) Mackenzie; (7) Eastern; (8) Southeastern; (9) Southwestern; (10) Nahua. (After Wissler 1950.)

ecological study might begin. It is not inevitable that such a direction of research would be taken, however; indeed, the American particularists put more stress on diffusion than adaptation in their treatment of culture areas.

More on cultural systems behavior

After this foray into anthropological history and a look at concepts tangent to our orienting framework, we return to the main task, interrupted at the end of Chapter Three. In the last decade and a half there have been some clarifications of culture processes that are aids to an understanding of evolution. They relate to stability and kinds of change and what lies back of them, and they go along with the central idea of system.

Recall that adaptation was described both as a steady or equilibrium state of a cultural system or as a set of movements that a culture makes to maintain its equilibrium or to restore it when it has been jogged by internal or external (environmental) events. Equilibrium is a state of rest, but of course rest does not mean a static or frozen condition; something is always going on. In physics, rest is regarded as a kind of motion in itself. Like a physical body, according to the "principle of stabilization" described by Thomas G. Harding (1960: 54), "A culture at rest tends to remain at rest." A corollary: "When acted upon by external forces a culture will, if necessary, undergo specific changes only to the

Ideas in the Anthropological Tradition

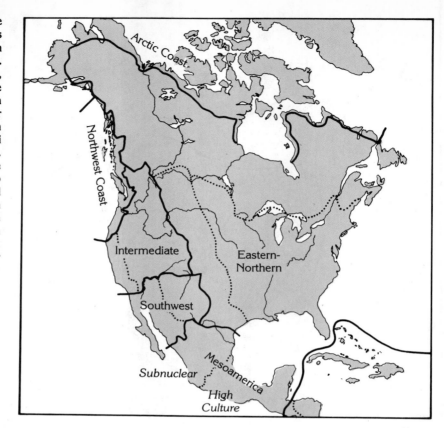

Kroeber reduced the number of major areas of native culture in North America to five. Within Mesoamerica, however, he distinguished High Culture and Subnuclear subareas, and within the Southwest Anasazi and Hohokam spheres. The Intermediate he divided into California and Intermountain subareas, and the huge Northern-Eastern into Eastern, Northern, and Plains. (After Kroeber 1948.)

extent and with the effect of *preserving* unchanged its fundamental structure and character."

Harding illustrates ethnographically with the Yakut, a Turkic-speaking tribe of northeastern Siberia who once lived in Central Asia. Although in contact with well-adapted reindeer breeders in the north and agriculturalists in the south, the Yakut clung to the breeding of horses and cattle in a northern environment hardly suited to it. They

Once dwellers on the Central Asiatic steppe, the Yakut carried on the breeding of horses and cattle in the Siberian forest. Here a Yakut man and woman ride a bullock harnessed to a sled. (After *Narody Sibiri*, M. G. Levin and L. P. Potapov, eds., Moscow and Leningrad: Academy of Science of the Union of Soviet Socialist Republics, 1956.)

The Task and Some Approaches to It

Horses in a Siberian winter pasture paw through the snow to reach forage. The Yakut were hard pressed to provide hay for the animals and built earth huts for them. (After *Istoriya Yakutskoĭ ASSR*, Tom. II, Moscow and Leningrad: Academy of Science of the Union of Soviet Socialist Republics, 1957.)

made some adjustments to this environment at enormous expense in labor in relation to return. The Yakut built earth huts for the animals, spent summers making great quantities of hay, and even tried to feed their horses meat and fish. The economic and social structure based upon cattle and horse raising was maintained, but, says Harding, borrowing a phrase the archeologist Robert Braidwood applied to European foragers and hunters following the glacial age, "they changed just enough so they would not have to change..." (1960: 55).

The term *involution* has been applied to cultural motions of this kind: "Cultural involution is a form of innovation that attempts to preserve an extant structure, solving its new problems by 'fixing it up'" (Service 1971a: 12). Robert L. Carneiro, in more general terms, has spoken of the phenomenon as "state-restoring." "A state-restoring change is one by means of which the system reestablishes a previous condition of balance or equilibrium which has been temporarily disturbed" (1960: 147, n.). It contrasts with the kind of change called "revolution" by Service (1971a: 13) and "state-transforming" by

Yakut summer dwelling of birch bark and a yurt, or winter house, hexagonal in shape and with a conical roof. Both had interior fireplaces. (After *Istoriya Yakutskoĭ ASSR*, Tom. II, Moscow and Leningrad: Academy of Science of the Union of Soviet Socialist Republics, 1957.)

Yakut men and women were clad in fur outfits. The horned cap of the male is characteristic headgear. (After *Istoriya Yakutskoĭ ASSR,* Tom. II, Moscow and Leningrad: Academy of Science of the Union of Soviet Socialist Republics, 1957.)

Carneiro (1960: 147 n.). Adaptation, then, has a conservative aspect as well as a creative one.

Putting the stability principle like this prompts a word of caution. As it stands, it might be assumed that culture, like a self-conscious individual person, has some kind of purpose in mind. We do not mean that. We just say that observations of some cultures have suggested the generalization that often they maintain their basic structures in spite of severe blows from the environment or that more often than not they hang together and neither disintegrate nor radically reconstitute after they have been jarred out of equilibrium—although those alternatives can happen, too.

A second principle has been called by David Kaplan the *Law of Cultural Dominance.* "It may be stated this way: that cultural system which more effectively exploits the energy resources of a given environment will tend to spread in that environment at the expense of less effective systems. . . . Put another way, the law states that a cultural system will tend to be found precisely in those environments in which it yields a higher energy return per unit of human labor than any alternative system available" (1960: 75-76).

As illustration, recall that the Cheyenne have been woodland hunters and fishermen, mixed horticulturalists and bison hunters on the prairie, mounted, nomadic bison hunters and fighters on the High Plains, and finally a segment of an industry-based America. Their fortunes were described in Chapter Three as the specific evolution of a cultural system which adapted to successively different natural environments and other cultures. The principle (or law) of **cultural domi-**

nance adds another context from which we can interpret the changes that took place. To build it up, we have to refer to the successive adaptive states as cultural types, or kinds.

In their earth-lodge villages and with their maize, squash, and bean gardens in the river bottoms, the Cheyenne led a fairly comfortable and secure life. In addition to their crops, they had as a resource the bison, which they hunted on foot. The mixed horticultural-hunting type of culture, which the Cheyenne shared with the Arikara, Pawnee, and other riverine farmers, was dominant on the prairies and in extensions into the Plains because, given its technology and associated social organization, and no more, it exploited in the most efficient way possible the energy resources of the land. So long as horses were absent, the horticulturalists were in relatively little danger from the small groups of hunters adjacent to them. This farming lifeway had pushed up the rivers of the West, and it held its own for long periods of time.

But the horse, and later the gun, as elements in Plains technology, changed that. Mounted hunters were able to exploit the hordes of bison with great efficiency—to catch them, to transport meat and hides, and to engage readily in the trade in bison robes and horses opened by still another cultural type which was encroaching (the advanced agricultural and commercial culture of the Euro-Americans). This was the heyday of the Plains culture, of the classical type of mounted hunters, to which we have referred; it lasted little more than a century, but in its time it was dominant on the Plains. The culturally extracted and organized energy of the horse and bison enabled it to overcome that of the sedentary farmers or to put them into such a hazardous position that they transformed themselves into mounted hunters and abandoned their fields. Thus the dominant type spread.

The oncoming advanced farmers and men of commerce, representing a still stronger type, a higher-energy culture, exterminated the principal resource of the Plains Indians, the bison, defeated the Indians

Specific evolution of Cheyenne culture, looked at as a bounded system, has depended heavily on the superorganic environment around it. This is part of a Northern Cheyenne community in Montana today. (Courtesy William Manning, Northern Cheyenne Research Project.)

An older Cheyenne house in winter. Motor cars are as much a part of the scene as they are in the rest of the rural and urban United States. (Courtesy William Manning, Northern Cheyenne Research Project.)

militarily, and forcibly incorporated their remnants into the American system. From a humanitarian point of view, the result was deplorable, and its effects for the mounted hunters continue to this day—but it was all but unavoidable. For the emerging industrial culture could exploit not only the grass, with cattle rather than with wild bison, and the soil, with mechanized farming rather than with hoes, but the coal and shale beds and oil fields, the flowing streams, with dams and hydroelectric plants, and the radioactive minerals deep in the rocks.

As Kaplan puts it (1960: 73), "The course of cultural evolution has ... been marked by a succession of types each of which has embodied more varied and effective energy-capturing devices and consequently has tended to spread at the expense of its less fortunately endowed predecessors .... Each successive higher culture type has tended to spread farther and faster than previous types until in our own day we find that Western Culture is not only extending its dominance over much of this planet, but is attempting to extend it into outer space as well."

One result of dominance is convergence, or increase in similarity of cultures, over large expanses of territory. Specific evolution usually is creative of differences as cultures adapt to their own environments. But dominant cultures are like higher forms in the world of living things, in that they show "increased adaptability to environmental variety" (Kaplan 1960: 69). They flow into and exploit many environments, and in so doing they destroy or alter cultures already in them in the direction of the dominant kind. Low-energy cultures do not have the same capacity. While, for instance, Eskimo culture, as an instance of low-energy type, is superbly adapted to its Arctic environment, as is that of the Semai to its jungle habitat, neither would be viable out of its milieu. Western industrial culture, on the other hand, exploits the sea life and the oil of the Arctic and the rubber of Malaysia—as well as the human populations there—in its own maintenance and extension.

92   The Task and Some Approaches to It

There is, however, one respect in which the *relatively* weak may inherit the earth. They sometimes leapfrog over the stronger. This comfort for some of the underprivileged, so to speak, rests upon another principle. It is what Elman R. Service (1960, 1971a) has called "evolutionary potential." Although he reduced its status from "law" to guiding principle in the later presentation, we give it in its original form: "The more specialized and adapted a form in a given evolutionary stage, the smaller is its potential for passing to the next stage." Or "Specific evolutionary progress is inversely related to general evolutionary potential" (1960: 97).

It means that after a culture has adapted successfully to its environments and becomes stabilized, it may maintain the adaptation by intensifying its efforts along its own specialized line; it may concentrate upon a particular food or energy source. When that happens, it is less likely than a not so specialized—that is, a generalized—culture to break new ground to a higher energy level and a new cultural type. Among Service's provocative examples is the shifting of dominance from Babylon and Egypt to Greece, to Rome, to the Arabs, and then to northern Europe and North America, and another is the discontinuities in the evolution of pre-Columbian Mesoamerican cultures. Each, in a sense, paid a penalty for success when it was overtaken and surpassed by poorer and more generalized contemporaries.

The principles of stability (Harding), dominance (Kaplan), and potential (Service) are examples of efforts to understand more clearly than before different states of cultural systems and how and at what rates they change. They have not been converted to measures, but we may have some confidence that someday they will. Even as they stand, they are an improvement over an older inclination simply to take for granted that cultures or cultural patterns are always changing or that traits flow outward from cultural centers.

Methodological superorganicism

If you reflect on cultural process terms of broad extension, such as *adaptation* and the movements toward *stability* and *dominance*, it may strike you that they tend to subordinate and leave flesh and blood men and women out of the picture. If you have not been bothered by this, it is probably because you have grasped the point that attention has, for our purposes, been shifted to extracted behaviors of humans and the things they have made. These extractions are intended to provide a context for understanding why Eskimo, Cheyenne, and middle-class Americans behave (or, more accurately, behaved) differently one from another. The people live; they have not gone away. But once *extracted* culture has been picked to pieces and put together again, once a sufficiently detailed orienting framework has been established, the *observed* behavior of real people may be cast against it and understood better than if we had never stopped embracing individuals.

A view that is common sense in Western culture is that humans individually and in societies cope with the world in order to survive. They accomplish this by inventing and using tools, by organizing themselves more or less effectively for cooperative effort, and by building a stock of knowledge and beliefs. But why have they coped and why do they cope in such different ways? In a sense, coping of itself tells us no more than learning of itself in a realistic search for reasons for variations.

One answer to that question we alluded to briefly before: as humans have different environments to cope with, the environments themselves provide the answer to the different outcomes. In extreme form, this produces the doctrine of **geographical determinism**; so far as I know, no geographers or anthropologists follow it today, and few have in the past. The succession over time of different lifeways in the same regions, different contemporary lifeways in similar environments, and lifeways similar in many respects spread over different environments are facts not accounted for by habitats alone.

Shifting the focus back to humans, psychologically minded anthropologists tend to view much of behavior as an expression or projection of individual human desires, impulses, and needs. Sociologically minded anthropologists tend to put first human aggregates, populations, and groups and then interpret behavior in terms of bodily bumpings-together and accommodations, so to speak. Social interaction, social process, social relations are the primary interest. That desires and needs are conditioned, and that social interactions are shaped in a surrounding world that includes technology, everyone seems to grant. But it is difficult indeed to account for accumulation and variation in technology from those two positions, which is perhaps one of the reasons many social scientists tend to restrict culture to "shared values" or "shared expectations," leaving technology as a given factor, off by itself.

Now, in basic and important respects, humans are similar the world over and have been for many millennia. We walk erect; at the ends of our free-wheeling forelimbs are five-fingered hands with opposable thumbs which are efficient for grasping and handling things. Our brains, relatively and absolutely larger than those of our primate relatives, continue to grow after birth, and in them lies the biological base for our symboling capacities, including the capacity for language. We are large animals, in relation to most of land life; we grow slowly, but with a burst before puberty; born helpless, we are dependent for nurturance for a longer period than other animals. Through our eyes we have binocular vision and depth perception, and we tend to depend on sight more than on our other senses. Our sex lives are distinctive, females being capable of engaging in sex throughout the year rather than only periodically. We are all social animals. These and a few other traits are ones called attention to by biological anthropologists as marking our species and its present single variety, *Homo sapiens sapiens*.

Having basic traits in common, then, we humans might be expected to have roughly the same desires, impulses, and needs, and since our bodies are basically alike we ought to produce the same kinds of groups and relationships by our interpersonal bumpings and accommodations wherever we are. Obviously we don't. Even our families, in which the dependent young are nurtured and in which humans find sexual satisfactions, have different forms in different places and at different times. We can find no biological differences to account for different kinds of families and a host of other behavioral dissimilarities between human populations. That is not to say that human populations may not look

The Task and Some Approaches to It

different one from another, have different skin colors and bodily proportions, for instance. But we have no evidence that such differences are other than trivial in behavioral outcomes. As Leslie White has remarked, "Few people would wish to argue that the physical type of the Chinese disposes them to eat with chopsticks or to write with a brush rather than a pen" (1959: 11).

We ought not, of course, close the door on a possibility that significant differences *might* be discovered at some future time and that they *might* be related to cultural differences. But from what we know now, we are justified in regarding humankind as a constant when we make *explanations* of those differences. And it is a working principle in science that variables are not explained by appeals to factors we have good reason to regard as constants. Recall again our early example of a system, comprised of the sun, a flagpole, and its shadow. If asked to account for the length of the shadow cast on the ground at different times, we answer that it depends upon the angle at which the sun's rays strike the pole. Given this particular system, the sun's position in the sky and the length of the shadow are variables and the height of the pole is a constant. In explanations of cultural differences, such as use of a brush by Chinese and a pen by Europeans, the people themselves in their biological aspect are regarded as the constant and the writing practices and other cultural traits are variables. We look at other variable features in the respective cultures, past and present, to explain that particular variable.

That is the basis of a strategy in cultural anthropology that has been around for a long time, whether it has been put to work explicitly or implicitly. David Kaplan, to whom reference was made earlier in con-

Japanese village. A local artist can be seen at work at his easel in right foreground. Problems relating to the history of Japan, its farming and industry, its social organization, ideology, and art we can treat in cultural terms without dwelling on motives, drives, and psychological dispositions of individuals. That is the principle of methodological superorganicism. (Courtesy C. Melvin Aikens.)

nection with traditions and the dominance principle, has aptly, if intimi-datingly, called it the principle of **methodological superorganicism.** It is the position that "cultural events can be explained in terms of other cultural events, and that the motives, drives, and psychological disposi-tions of individuals are not relevant to answering certain cultural ques-tions" (1965: 972). Motives, drives, and psychological dispositions are regarded as constants, in other words. The *superorganic* may also be understood as referring to the circumstance that objects and events are extracted (methodologically) from their physical and biological setting and looked at in their cultural aspect. *Superorganic* and *cultural* are the same.

In one respect only need constants be taken account of: they set limits to the behavior of a system in which they are incorporated or of whose environment they are a part. There is a limit to the length of shadow the flagpole in our example will cast. It is not clear yet what the human limitations on culture are, nor at just what point environ-mental constants will box in the totality of culture.

Is the rule unalterable?

Methodological superorganicism represents a very common working principle or rule in cultural anthropology. It will remain so as long as it is useful, which is to say as long as the results obtained by its use are satisfactory and as long as it does not get in the way of equally useful alternatives. But like any other principle, it need not be regarded as immutable. Let me give an example that suggests some limitations of it.

As Marvin Harris has pointed out (1968), one long-standing opinion on why the Chinese do not milk the cows and buffalo they have, and in fact abhor milk, is that this is simply a mismanagement of resources prompted by an arbitrary, irrational, and capricious culture trait. However, quoting a colleague who studied a Chinese village, Harris notes that "there weren't any worth milking" (1968: 368), because they were bred to be lean work animals—not milk or meat producers. In turn, this is understandable, because the land is devoted to intensive rice agriculture, not pasture, and because pigs, which are more efficient scavengers than cattle, provide the meat. There is firm ecological un-derpinning for raising draft animals, not milkers. "Indeed, it could well be argued that the national 'aversion' to cow's milk among the Chinese points to a 'rational' adjustment between food tastes and China's basic mode of food production" (1968: 368). That is, attitudes follow tech-nological and social circumstances.

Although the first explanation (that aversion to milk is an arbitrary and capricious trait) is faulty and the second (that it is a response to economic realities) is satisfactory, both are cultural explanations. Neither involves human biological factors. Thus the rule of methodo-logical superorganicism has been applied implicitly. More recently, however, Harris (1972) has explored the matter further and suggests that a biological factor might well be introduced into an explanation. It runs like this: Metabolizing of lactose in milk requires that it be con-verted into a simpler sugar, and this is done by an enzyme called lac-tase, which is found in the lining of the small intestine. If the lactase level is sufficiently high, the milk is digested; if it is not, the milk drinker becomes bloated and gets diarrhea. Infants in all populations produce enough lactase to cope with the lactose in milk, but apparently in some groups (as in Chinese studied on Taiwan) adults don't have a sufficiency of it. The result, instead of well-fed comfort, is a stomachache.

So a variable biological factor has been introduced, and an explanation of *its* origin can take two directions. One is that the difference between lactase-deficient Chinese and lactase-sufficient Europeans is a genetic trait, possibly selected among the latter by long exposure to milk drinking. Those who couldn't produce lactase died off, leaving the lactase producers to reproduce their kind. The other suggested explanation is that the human body, which has the potential of acting adequately in infancy, will continue to produce lactase at a sufficient level if milk intake can be continued during the transition from infancy to adulthood. If there is only enough milk available in the culture for infants (from their mothers, or a scant supply from animals) and post-infants are denied it, then adults won't continue to have the capacity to maintain a high lactase level. Thus, they will get stomachaches if they drink milk and so tend to avoid it. Both explanations in their biological aspect are still conjectural, but Harris's conclusion about the trait of milk rejection is this: "It now seems assured that this trait, like other seemingly arbitrary cultural preferences, is determined by definite interactive processes that link culture, man, and nature into an intelligible system" (1972: 13).

Patently, explanation for an aversion to milk in some populations (and a fondness for it in others) involves both biological and cultural factors. If the hypothesis about a genetic factor were correct, we would still have to take account of the long histories of European and Chinese technologies and economies that provided the selection factors for milk tolerators and milk rejectors. If the other hypothesis, about the bridging between infants and adults who had the capacity to keep up lactase levels, proved out, then intensive rice agriculture among the Chinese, which inhibited raising of milk cattle, and European mixed farming, which provided a milk supply, would be other relevant considerations.

The explanations, it is apparent, are accommodated by an orienting model of a cultural system interacting with its human and habitat environments. Europeans and Chinese probably are not alike in regard to lactase levels in adults, and so the *sapiens* environments of the two cultures are not the same. Thus, the cultural outcomes of interactions between the cultural systems and the human environments are not the same. True, culture altered the humans in the course of millenia, but they are now what they are, even if culture did the altering. Involving human traits sometimes adds a dimension to explanation of cultural ones. There probably are other situations in which attention paid to the character of the human environment as well as to habitat would make clearer the dynamics of cultural systems and would help explain the presence of culture traits that motivate humans to act. So, while we need not surrender the primacy of culture in making explanations, it is unwise to rule in advance that human environment must be neutered in *every* case by the rule of methodological superorganicism. We can disregard individual, but possibly not populational, differences.

Explanation and cause

Explanation and *cause* represent the last major ideas we need to round out our approach to humanity's ways. They are closely related to the set with which we began in Chapter Two—meaning and understanding—and perhaps they can be made clear by our taking the same tack as we did with those words, when we started with the "What in the World?" panelists finding meanings for artifacts. What are we doing when we *explain*, and what do we mean by *cause*?

The Semai fear being out in a "hot rain" that falls from a cloudless sky because, they say, it is likely to result in fever or jaundice (Dentan 1968: 20). A skeptic would want to test whether the events are associated by making careful and repeated observations of "hot rain" and the incidence of illnesses following exposure to it, and he or she might, if the reluctance of the Semai could be overcome, induce them to remain outside and check the consequences. The skeptic would be taking the stance known as *operationalism*, which calls for two procedures, controlled observation and manipulation, to establish the "truth" or "reality value" of any assertion.

The operationalist philosopher and mathematical biologist Anatol Rapoport puts it lucidly: "To explain an event . . . is to point out its connection with another event or with a class of events. The connection may be in repeated observations of the two events together or in our ability to affect one event by manipulating the other. Such connections are rooted in our experience" (1954: 65).

Semai also involve analogies in their explanations (making an analogy means pointing out partial similarities in the features of objects or events). Up to a point, this is acceptable to operationalists, who call it the *postulational method.* For instance, Semai have a word, *patud,* derived from a Malay word meaning "fitting, fair, proper, right." In the contexts in which they use it, it appears "the Semai do feel that there is a way things should be, a natural order . . . " (Dentan 1968: 13). There are natural orders in the way things should be eaten and in the weather, and both may be disturbed. It is proper to eat at one meal only food belonging to one category of edibles; mixing food from different categories "is mixing up the natural order, an impious violation of the nature of the world. Therefore eating or cooking foods from different categories is going to bring on some further reverberation in the natural order" (Dentan 1968: 36). Upsets might be baldness or pains in the back for an individual—or a thundersquall. They are events matched by analogy—in this case, all breaches in the natural order of things. In operational terms: ". . . there are . . . connections perceived among events which may or may not be rooted in experience. These are the connections of analogy. Two events are thought to be causally connected, because two other events which somehow resemble them have been observed or thought to be causally connected" (Rapoport 1954: 65).

Observe the appearance of the term *causally* in that definition of postulational explanation. Connections we make between events, either directly by observation and manipulation or indirectly by analogy, are regarded as *causal* connections. Explanation and cause are two sides of the same operation.

The Task and Some Approaches to It

Postulational explanations carry an obligation, however. They can be regarded as logically valid if they are consistent with their premises, but whether they can be called true depends on other criteria, particularly the making of predictions from them and the observation of whether or not the predicted events occur. The Semai explanations of illness and natural disasters may be valid, given Semai premises, but they would probably fail the rigid tests of the operationalists for truth.

There is another aspect of postulational explanation and causality that should be noted. That is the aspect in which an unusual or puzzling event, one that we haven't encountered before, is explained by reference to something usual and familiar. To use an example of Professor Rapoport, we would accept as an explanation for a lot of people running in the same direction down a city street the information that there is a fire there. Here is the way he puts it (1954: 61):

"Qu. Why are all those people running in the same direction?

"A. There is a fire down the street.

"Contained in the question is an observation of an *unusual* event. Ordinarily the people in a city street do not all run in the same direction. But we have observed that people tend to run toward a fire. The fire is taken to be the cause of the running. The unusual event (people running in the same direction) becomes through the explanation a usual one (people running toward a fire)."

Discussions in this chapter on the subject of cultural systems behavior can be turned into questions and answered in the same fashion. Why did the Yakut continue to breed horses and cattle in a harsh northern environment and maintain their old cultural structure? Because, when acted upon by external forces, a culture will, if necessary, undergo changes, but only to the extent and with the effect of preserving unchanged its fundamental structure. Yakut stability first appears as an unusual event. The stability principle, however, asserts that it really is not unusual, because other cultures have been observed to behave that way under certain circumstances.

Why did the mounted Plains Indians overcome the sedentary farmers? Because the culture of the mounted hunters was dominant. Why was it dominant? Because it exploited the energy resources of the Plains more efficiently than other cultures. The dominance principle is based on several observed events or cases. It represents events familiar to a specific evolutionist, so it is used to explain a new event, the overcoming of sedentary farmers by mounted hunters, initially considered unusual.

Answers like that have something of the circular and tautological about them, but they are not so in the context of the explanatory system we have chosen. We must start somewhere, and our starting point is that culture is to be regarded as an open system. Like all such systems, we assume that it is energy transforming, that it has boundaries (it consists only of symboling-dependent objects and events), and that it adapts to its environments. Dominance and stability are kinds of adaptation observed in cultural systems and given those names. The open system serves as a model, a representation of culture, and models at the very least help us to think of questions and suggest answers to them. Whether they are true and useful answers depends on whether predictions based on them work out in the real world.

If cause is to be regarded as related to explanations, we can give a variety of names to causes, depending on the way explanations are made. For instance, Ronald Cohen (1970: 33-44) presents four models of explanation found in anthropology—descriptive, associational, functional, and systems analysis, so we might speak of causes under the same labels. John C. Harsanyi (1968: 90) categorizes models and explanation as static and dynamic, depending on whether the variables being scrutinized all belong to one time period or whether some are found in an earlier period. Thus, we would say there are static and dynamic causes, but only in the context of that set. Leslie A. White (1945) says that there are historical, structural-functional, and evolutionary explanations, so that we might entertain the notion that there are three contexts in which we may define cause.

My intention in marshalling these formulations is to emphasize that cause had better not be regarded as a mysterious push or pull, or a compulsive necessity of some kind. It is an understanding derived from the explanations we make, a relation assumed between two events in order to explain one in terms of the other. To the operationalist, any causal explanation is acceptable if it is parsimonious (economical) and lends itself to manipulative or predictive trial.

From the scientific revolution in the seventeenth century until the twentieth, cause and explanation were phrased in terms of certainties or absolutes, and there was a striving for invariant laws, laws admitting no exception. That has changed. The circumstances of the change have a fascinating history which you might pursue in books such as *The Common Sense of Science* by Jacob Bronowski. Predictions deduced or derived from explanatory or causal assertions and intended to verify or disprove them are always phrased now in terms of chance, as probabilities. The goal is to reduce uncertainty about the future as much as we can, but the world as we observe it does not lend itself to utter certainty about the outcome of anything. We are satisfied with much less.

In this last of our introductory chapters, after an examination of the terms *primitive, idiographic,* and *nomothetic,* all relevant to our pursuit of cultural understanding, we delved into the history of anthropological theory in order to orient words such as *history, evolution,* and *function.* History, it is important to remember, is a temporal and more particularizing approach, and evolution is a temporal and more generalizing one. Other anthropological terms introduced in this vocabulary-exploring exercise included the set we called *middle-ground organizing devices—daily and annual rounds, life cycles,* and *patterns,* the last of which includes within itself the notion of *culture areas.*

We then returned to an examination of the adaptive behavior of cultural systems and explained the principles of *stabilization, dominance,* and *evolutionary potential.* Because it represents a strategy used by many, perhaps most, anthropologists, we explored the principle of *methodological superorganicism* and suggested there may be situations in which its use can be modified. Our orienting model does not make its use indispensable.

Finally, we took up those basic ideas *explanation* and *cause* from an operationalist point of view and suggested that while ordinary Semai and Western scientific philosophers employ similar logical operations the latter try to establish the "truth value" of explanatory statements with more rigor.

We shall encounter some other descriptive and analytical terms in our exploration of the aspects of culture, but I hope that you now have in hand an orienting framework and ideas related to it that will help you understand the variety of human lifeways.

Suggested Readings

Benedict, Ruth. 1946. *Patterns of culture.* New York: Penguin Books.*

Bohannan, Paul, and Mark Glazer, eds. 1973. *High points in anthropology.* New York: Alfred A. Knopf.*

Broce, Gerald. 1973. *History of anthropology.* Minneapolis: Burgess.*

Bronowski, J. n.d. *The common sense of science.* New York: Random House, Vintage Books.*

Harris, Marvin. 1974. *Cows, pigs, wars and witches: The riddles of culture.* New York: Random House, Vintage Books.*

Hymes, Dell, ed. 1974. *Reinventing anthropology.* New York: Random House, Vintage Books.*

Jarvie, I. C. 1973. *Functionalism.* Minneapolis: Burgess.*

Kaplan, David. 1968. "The superorganic: Science or metaphysics?" *American Anthropologist* 67: 958-76. Reprinted in Robert A. Manners and David Kaplan, eds., *Theory in anthropology: A sourcebook.* Chicago: Aldine.

Montagu, M. F. Ashley, ed. 1968. *Culture, man's adaptive dimension.* London, England: Oxford University Press.*

Sahlins, Marshall D., and Elman R. Service, eds. 1960. *Evolution and culture.* Ann Arbor: University of Michigan Press.

Steward, Julian H. 1963. *Theory of culture change: The methodology of multilinear evolution.* Urbana: University of Illinois Press.*

Stocking, George W., Jr. 1968. *Race, culture, and evolution: Essays in the history of anthropology.* New York: Free Press.*

Sturtevant, William C. 1968. "Anthropology, history, and ethnohistory." In *Introduction to cultural anthropology: Essays in the scope and methods of the science of man.* James A. Clifton, ed. Boston: Houghton Mifflin.

Vayda, Andrew P., and Roy A. Rappaport. 1968. "Ecology: Cultural and non-cultural." In *Introduction to cultural anthropology: Essays in the scope and methods of the science of man.* James A. Clifton, ed. Boston: Houghton Mifflin.

White, Leslie A. 1945. "History, evolutionism, and functionalism: Three types of interpretation of culture." *Southwestern Journal of Anthropology* 1: 221-48.

Part Two
Culture in Its
Technological
Aspect

There probably are only two radically different positions in anthropology from which to make explanations: "people do" and "culture does." The first has the advantage of support from common sense, while the second, if taken without an explanation of what the two-word sentence means, is absurd. Actually, both positions depend initially upon "people do." One remains there, however elaborate the succeeding explanatory operations, while the other takes a leap. The rationale for the leap is as absurdly simple as it is absurdly uncommon, and you are familiar with it. Let's check it over.

Thinking about technology

Much of the behavior of any human animal, although not all human behavior by any means, takes on meaning for us and becomes understandable by reference to the body of cultural things that surrounds humans. We assume that those things motivate a person to behave as he or she does. We have to go on and arrange the motivating things in an intelligible order so that we can make a study of them and conclude which are of greater and lesser importance, which probably came first and which, in the long run, followed. The means we have chosen to accomplish this is an extracted system. Within such a system, we can locate things that motivate the

Chapter Five
Hunting-
Gathering
Technologies,
Past and Present

105

doer, discover their relations with other things, and check those relationships in other cultures. Thus we arrive at some explanation of *why* what is there *is* there, and we can say we know the cause of the behavior because cause is related to our explanation. To take the stance that "culture does," then, is only a detour over which we return finally to "people do," armed with additional understandings.

This review is appropriate as we take up culture's technological aspect, because tools and the associated techniques of their use (or techniques and their associated tools, if you will) lend themselves readily to a "people do" position, and it takes a conscious and vigorous effort to go beyond it to "culture does"—for the purpose mentioned previously. Take some common definitions of *tool* and *technique*. A tool is "an implement, especially one held in the hand, for performing or facilitating mechanical operations, as a hammer, saw, file, etc.," and a technique is a "technical skill," "the ability to apply procedures and methods so as to effect a desired result" (*Random House Dictionary*). Manual manipulation is welded into the meanings of the two words as given. People do—to effect a result they desire.

Robert F. G. Spier, an anthropologist with a particular interest in technology, writes appropriately in this vein: "The tool serves as an extender of the human body, more specifically the hand and arm. It strengthens the grasp, protects the hand, magnifies the blow, increases precision of movement, and does many other things relevant to manipulation. More broadly defined, the tool aids the senses, largely through increasing their acuity and discrimination (e.g., a micrometer caliper). Generally, earlier tools are not sense-extending, a refinement which has come in the past five centuries" (1970: 21). Fair enough. People are central, people do; tools extend their ability to do.

As part of an extracted cultural system, symboling-dependent and energy transforming, tools and techniques are looked at from a different direction. Within the technological aspect of culture, they are mechanisms by which energies and materials are extracted from environments and transformed into cultural motions and things, an idea introduced early on. The technological aspect as a whole is defined both by the tasks it performs and its special relationship with culture's habitat environment. By definition, technology does in fact, with varying degrees of efficiency and economy, supply subsistence, shelter, and defense for the human populations it controls, and it cannot do this without a direct and continuing confrontation with habitat.

Like social organization (which converts a turning of the back into mother-in-law and son-in-law behavior) and ideology (which may make dreams into myths), technology, also, transforms human noncultural motions into cultural ones (as when finger twiddling becomes a basket-making technique), but technology's task of supplying subsistence, shelter, and defense demands extraction of energies and materials from habitat. Culture can set up patterns of human play and verbal and behavioral rituals without direct recourse to materials and energies from habitat in specific cases (provided it has fed biological humans beforehand), but in its technological aspect it must for the most part turn outward to the resources of the land. For there reside the materials and energies culture applies directly or channels indirectly through the

Culture in Its Technological Aspect

human bodies in its *sapiens* environment—from which it extracts them again.

There are two major aspects to the technological process, then—not only energy (and material) transformation but also the mechanical means for accomplishing it (White 1959: 53-57). So attention must be paid to the **efficiency** and **economy** of tools and techniques. How much energy a tool converts, transmits, delivers, or stores in relation to what it consumes or expends is a measure of its efficiency. And economy is measured by the units of energy required for the tool's production. These ideas are applicable to plants, animals, and humans as well, which is to say that plants, animals, and humans can be placed in a tool context. White (1959: 55-56) points out: "A plant of *Zea mays*, or Indian corn, is not only a certain amount of energy; it is also a means of controlling energy. A cow may be regarded as a means of producing milk, a milk-producing machine, that may be considered from the standpoint of efficiency and economy." So may a slave, and the slave's economy and efficiency may be compared with that of a machine tended by wage labor. (There is an interesting definition of *tool* that follows the one given above in my dictionary: "A person manipulated by another for his own ends; cat's paw." Figurative language, but a fetching example of humans in tool context, though the tool is in "people do" context.)

Typologies (classifications) based on a number of principles have been devised to manage the tool spectrum conceptually, the most common ones pointing to outline forms of tools, materials of which tools are made, uses of tools, and the places of tools in sequences of manufacturing, such as primary, secondary, and tertiary (Spier 1970: 22-23). Outline forms can be round, triangular, or linear, with or without projections or indentations, and smooth, serrated, straight, or sinuous. Sewing, hammering, cutting, scraping, piercing, rubbing, and turning are examples of uses. Materials include stone, metal, wood, fiber, and so on. Primary tools are those applied directly to work whose product is consumable, as a hammerstone which cracks a nutshell, and secondary tools are used to make others, particularly primary ones, as an antler tip applied with pressure to detach flakes from a stone knife. Tertiary tools make secondary ones, as a device for making tool bits for a machine lathe (Spier's example, 1970: 37).

Classifications are like the middle-ground organizations of cultural observations discussed in Chapter Four. They accomplish preliminary sortings, are useful for making comparisons, and raise questions, say, about the presence and absence, plenitude and scarcity of classes of tools in different cultural systems, their efficiency and economy, and their relations to social organization of work. Other middle-ground orderings combine classes with reference to cultural traditions, as **Oldowan** choppers, Levalloisian cores, and Upper Paleolithic blades, to be mentioned later in this chapter.

Techniques, as distinguished from tools, have to do with methods of manipulation of materials and application of energy. Thus, stone may be worked by percussion, pressure, grinding, and polishing, fibers by twisting, braiding, weaving, or felting, wood by cutting or burning. Baskets may be plaited, twined, and coiled, and pottery may be worked up from a lump of clay with the hands and a round stone, with clay coils, or with a potter's wheel. Such labelling of techniques and their arrangement in typologies have uses, and they will be invoked sparingly in ethnographic and archeological contexts later. But an organization of all of the things in the universe of culture into specialists' categories would result in a manual, not in an introduction to anthropological ideas.

Now let us round out the content of technology beyond tools and technology. Although we may, for simplicity's sake, think of the technological subsystem as centered upon tools and the techniques of their use, there are circumstances in which we may understand broader, supporting behaviors, as well as knowledge (which is conceptualized experience), by referring them to the technological context.

As White (1959: 55) remarks, "The social organization of the use of tools and machines is an important aspect of the technological process. Such things as division of labor, specialization, cooperation, systematization, and rationalization may affect the operation of the technological process very considerably, and with it the magnitude of the result produced." And no more than objects and behaviors are ideas to be locked into one matrix from which they cannot emerge and act elsewhere. What applied to old Isherwood's geologist's hammer and the stone axes of the Australians applies to bounded pieces of information or to concepts. They can be viewed in a technological context, too.

Accepting this does not make us a kind of sociologist who might put social interaction first and view technology as a consequence, nor a cultural idealist, who would assert that ideas, including plans, come first, that they are prior to object and action, that they are prime movers in the cultural process. For technologically relevant knowledge arises in the food, shelter, and defense quest, in matters dealing with the "material conditions of existence," accompanying the tools and techniques employed in those quests. But we must make an important stipulation about technological knowledge, ideas, or concepts. It must be demonstrated that the knowledge does realistically and in fact contribute directly to the extraction of materials and energies from habitat that the cultural system requires for its maintenance and growth. An indirect, remote, or roundabout contribution will not do. An operational test is required.

For example, among the Netsilik, who lived east of the Copper Eskimo on the Arctic coast of Canada, the skilled hunter knew well the lay of the land and the characteristics of ice floes, the habits of caribou and seal, and the capacities of his weapons. There were two kinds of shamans, one of whom called upon spirit helpers to discover the location of game and another who depended on his spirits to direct game toward the hunters (Balikci 1963: 386). Perhaps the beliefs and practices lessened the anxieties of the people and gave them some confidence in a hostile natural environment. But, without disrespect to the Netsilik (we have too many analogous practices in our own culture to be smug about it), we assert that no *tunraq*, as a guardian spirit was called, ever in fact sent a seal toward a hunter's harpoon or did the other things he was supposed to do—kill seals in the open sea, control thunder, or find lost implements and hunting weapons. Although shamanistic practices accompanied hunting, they do not qualify as behaviors understandable in a technological context. On the other hand, realistic knowledge of the lay of the land and sea and of the animals they held does qualify; it contributes directly and effectively to the capture of calories and other useful things.

Noncultural tool using and tool making

Before we proceed to look at varieties of technologies observed in the recent past, we need a temporal perspective on the human animal and his tools and some comparison between tools in cultural and noncultural contexts. They will be provided in this section and the next.

"Nothing comes from nothing" is one of those axioms that is part of naturalistic thinking. Miracles are inadmissible as explanations of events in science. Living things come from living things, and culture from culture. But within terrestrial time, life and culture had beginnings—life emerged from nonlife (but nonlife is something, not nothing) and culture from nonculture (and that is not nothing, either). Explanation of the emergence of living things is the concern of the biochemist, evolutionary biologist, and paleontologist, among others. The origin of culture is a problem for anthropologists, cultural and biological, and a number of specialists, such as primatologists, ethologists (students of comparative animal behavior), and neurologists. If symboling behavior is taken to be the foundation of culture, solution of the problem of origin is difficult but probably not impossible; just where and when symboling came about is still an open question, but progress is being made. We cannot observe the behavior of our remoter ancestors; what we have to work with is their anatomical remains and the things they used or made, on the one hand, and the behavior of contemporary animals who are related to us, on the other.

Among the latter is the chimpanzee. It is not a member of our immediate taxonomic (classificatory) family and hence not a **hominid**, but it shares membership with us in successive categories of increasing extension—the **hominoid** superfamily, anthropoid suborder, and primate order. In regard to direct lineal descent, or phylogeny, the ancestors of the chimpanzees and other apes parted company with our own closer ancestors early in the **Miocene** geological era, which ended about 12,000,000 years ago (Buettner-Janusch 1966: 121). Chimpanzees, like some other non-hominids, make and use crude tools for food getting and defense, but they have no culture as we define it in which their limited tool behavior finds meaning.

Although chimpanzees hurl stones in anger, they do not work the stone into tools; in particular, neither they nor any other animals outside of the hominid line have ever made stone tools with a cutting edge (Hulse 1971: 206). They have been observed to threaten enemies by uprooting saplings and thrashing about with them; it also appears they are prone to throw anything they can lay their hands on, including their own feces, but their aim is rather bad.

Now, a behavior which shows more foresight than the ones enumerated was observed by the British naturalist Jane van Lawick-Goodall (1967) among chimpanzees in the Gombe Reserve in Tanzania. To catch termites, a chimpanzee she called David Graybeard stripped a vine of leaves, chewed off a piece about a foot long, and inserted it into holes in a nest. Termites clinging to the extracted vine were licked off, and the tool was used again. Grass stems and sticks also were put to use in this way, not only by David but by a number of his fellows. The Gombe chimps also used spongy masses of leaves to soak up drinking water from hollows in fallen trees, and large leaves to wipe their hands and bodies.

Chimpanzees, then, can put two and two, or more accurately, one and one and one—themselves, a food or comfort goal, and a tool between them—together into a configuration or pattern. The learning is situational, and it spreads socially. The two learning processes are illustrated admirably by animals lower in the evolutionary scale than chimpanzees and hence even more distant from us, a colony of red-faced macaques (monkeys) observed by the zoologist Masao Kawai on the Japanese island of Koshima. In 1953, a female named Imo dipped a sand-covered sweet potato into water and washed it, discovering, perhaps, that it became more comfortably edible, although that is a guess. A month later, one of her playmates began washing potatoes; four months later, Imo's mother took up the practice. In four years there were fifteen potato washers, and at the end of ten years forty-two of the fifty-nine monkeys then in the troop had learned how to wash potatoes (Dröscher 1971: 191-92).

Symbolic learning? Enculturation? Only if it could be demonstrated that Imo had been heard telling her first pupil in some intelligible language, "Listen, take a potato and dip it into the water and scrub it, and it won't be so gritty," and if like advice had been heard passing from the initiated to the novices thereafter. Is that asking too much? I think not. So long as there is not present a structurally complex vocal language or any other clearly symbolic communication system, it is situational and social and not symboling-dependent learning that has taken place. Without the symboling process there is nothing we choose to call culture, and hence no enculturation.

Goodall remarked in her book that one anthropological definition of *sapiens* is that *sapiens* "starts at that stage of primate evolution when the creature begins to make tools to a regular pattern." Responding to her remark and to her observations among chimpanzees, Dr. L. S. B. Leakey, dean of African physical anthropologists, wrote, "I feel that scientists holding to this definition are faced with three choices: They must accept chimpanzees as man, by definition; they must redefine man; or they must redefine tools" (Van Lawick-Goodall 1967: 32). Leslie White had anticipated the options and redefined *sapiens*: *sapiens* is a symboling primate. In his view, tool using and making within a symboling-dependent legacy of conceptualized experience is patently different from that which prevails in a naked animal-tool-environment relationship (White 1949: 44-48). The new relationship and legacy apparently began within the narrower hominid line of hominoids and deep in the **Pleistocene** geological epoch.

Evolutionary perspective: The hominids

We are today in the geological epoch called the **Holocene** or Recent, which began about 10,000 years ago and represents only a short but continuing postscript to the long Pleistocene. Although the Pleistocene

The three grades or evolutionary levels in the family of the hominids— *Australopithecus, Homo erectus,* and *Homo sapiens.* Our species is represented here by the Cro-Magnon variety of the Upper Pleistocene. (After *Early man,* F. Clark Howell and the editors of Time-Life Books, New York: Time-Life Books, 1970.)

formerly was considered to have been 1,000,000 years long and concurrent with the glaciers that advanced and retreated four or more times over the northern hemisphere, some scientists in recent decades have pushed its beginnings to about 3,000,000 years ago. Customarily it is divided into three segments, Upper, Middle, and Lower, but some students now distinguish in addition a Basal Pleistocene (a term introduced by F. Clark Howell) which underlies the Lower (Butzer 1971: 46, 27). I have incorporated it into the figure on p. 112, which follows the prehistorian Jacques Bordaz (1970: 4) in fixing the approximate upper boundaries of the four segments, each of which ends with a major glaciation, at 500,000, 275,000, 100,000, and 10,000 years B.P. (before present). There were alternations of cold periods during glacial advances and warmer times when the glaciers receded; in consequence, plant cover in the northern hemisphere changed several times between subarctic tundra and subtropical forest.

Hunting-Gathering Technologies, Past and Present

There have been three grades or evolutionary levels of hominids—*Australopithecus*, *Homo erectus*, and *Homo sapiens*. Australopithecines, popularly called the African man-apes, were short-statured, upright, bipedal fellows with cranial capacities of less than 700 cubic centimeters. They are known from Basal and Lower Pleistocene in South and East Africa and the Indies, in strata that indicate temperate and subtropical environments. There is dispute as to whether a smaller form, on the one hand, and a larger, more robust form, on the other, should be classified as varieties or separate species and whether the first one was a meat eater and the second a vegetarian. Also, some would give a higher genus and species status to an early example, "**Homo habilis**," they judge as more progressive than the others.

In the lower Pleistocene, hominids evolved to the **Homo erectus** grade. *Homo erectus* populations, once known only through the remains of **Pithecanthropus** in Java and **Sinanthropus** in China, ranged through South, East, and North Africa, Europe, East Asia, and the

Temporal perspectives: Natural environment, culture, hominids. (After Bordaz 1970.)

Years before present	European (Alpine) glaciations	Geological divisions	Cultural (archeological) divisions	Hominid grades
10,000	Postglacial	Holocene (Recent)	Neolithic Mesolithic	
35,000	Würm	Upper Pleistocene	Upper Paleolithic	Homo sapiens sapiens
75,000 100,000	Interglacial		Middle Paleolithic	Homo sapiens neanderthalensis
200,000	Riss	Middle Pleistocene	Lower Paleolithic	
275,000	Interglacial			
	Mindel	Lower Pleistocene		
	Interglacial			Homo erectus
500,000	Günz		_____?_____	
	Interglacial	Basal Pleistocene		Australopithecus
	Donau and earlier glaciations			
3,000,000?	_____?_____	_____?_____		_____?_____

112   Culture in Its Technological Aspect

Indies, some of them living in environments with colder climates. They were rugged individuals, about the size of modern humans and not markedly different from them in their postcranial skeletons, but they had heavy ridges of bone across their brows, and they had big jaws and teeth (molars, however, were being reduced to modern range). The important thing about *Homo erectus* was the cranial capacity; at 800 to 1,200 cubic centimeters, it doubled the Australopithecine average and fell within the lower range of the capacity of our contemporaries (Brace 1967: 72).

With *Homo sapiens* of the Neanderthal variety, our immediate antecedent, who has been unjustly maligned as the cartoon cave man (Brace 1967: 87), we enter the Upper Pleistocene. Neanderthals were different from humans today only in their possession of a rugged face and a heavy, protruding jaw that accommodated large teeth; their cranial capacities equaled and sometimes exceeded those of modern humans. The wholly moderns, faces reduced to proportions we are familiar with, began to dominate the scene around 35,000 years ago; we call them, and ourselves, *Homo sapiens sapiens*.

Evolutionary perspective:
Tools and techniques

The *geological* Pleistocene was the setting for the *cultural* **Paleolithic** or Old Stone Age, itself divisible into Lower, Middle, and Upper (or Advanced) periods. There is ambiguity in tagging the entire Old Stone Age as cultural, because it is doubtful whether the earliest tools associated with it should be assigned to a cultural context. At any rate, whether or not the first period was a cultural one, each period can be characterized roughly by dominant stone tool forms and the technique of their manufacture (see the figure on p. 114). The Lower Paleolithic, which occupied the immense reach of time from about 2,000,000 years ago, deep in the Basal Pleistocene, to about 100,000 B.P., is associated first with *Australopithecus* and after about 500,000 B.P. with *Homo erectus*.

At the earliest archeological level of the famous Olduvai Gorge in northern Tanganyika, dated 1,500,000 to 2,000,000 B.P., L. S. B. Leakey uncovered rough stone choppers and flakes struck from river pebbles, semicircles of stones which he assumes delineate a "home base" of their makers, the smashed bones of animals, and Australopithecine (or "Homo habilis") skeletal remains. Choppers, "made by striking a few flakes from the side of a pebble in one or two directions," were made not only by Australopithecines but continued in use among the later *Homo erectus* people in Asia, Africa, and Europe and persisted in Asia among *Homo sapiens* populations nearly to the end of the Old Stone Age (Clark 1971: 35).

Was the Chopper and Flake industry, as it is called, part of culture in the Basal and Lower Pleistocene? The biological anthropologist John Buettner-Janusch is one of many inclined to give the man-apes the benefit of the doubt. "Once tools are found in the archeological record and fossil hominids are found associated with these tools, it is clear that the capacity for culture, culture itself, is already developed" (1966: 352). Brain size, he says, is less important as an indicator of culture. And another, Frederick S. Hulse, agrees: "Despite his small brain,

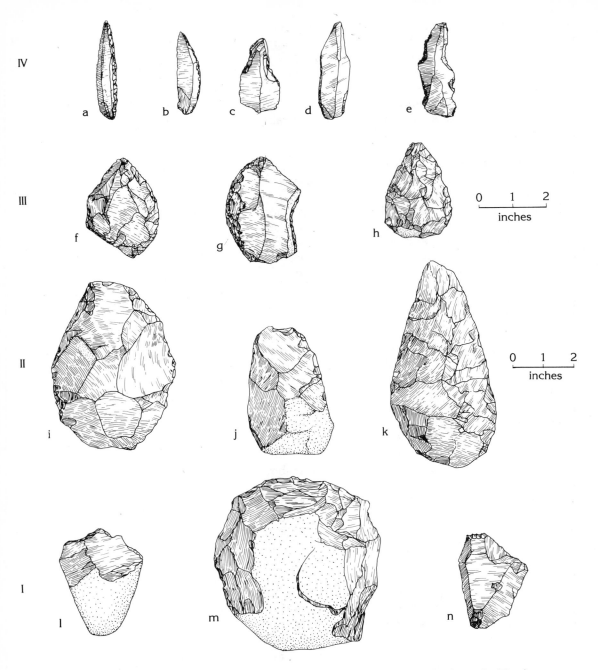

Evolution of stone tools in the Old Stone Age. I: (l) an Australopithecine pebble chopper, by our definition not part of symboling-dependent culture; (m, n) a chopper tool and a flake tool of the Lower Paleolithic, made by *Homo erectus* at Choukoutien. II: Acheulian and related Lower Paleolithic tools: (i, j, k) hand-axes from France, England, and Kenya. III: Mousterian, Middle Paleolithic, associated with Neanderthal: (f, g) side-scrapers; (h) hand-axe, from France. IV: Upper Paleolithic specialized tools: (a, b) knife points; (c, d) gravers; (e) strangulated blade or double "spoke-shave." (a-k after *Man the tool-maker,* Kenneth P. Oakley, Chicago: University of Chicago Press, 1957; l-n after Clark 1967.)

Australopithecus became capable, nearly 2,000,000 years ago, of creating a desired object for future use. Technology had come into existence" (1971: 209).

Another opinion is held by Phillip V. Tobias, who would exclude other Australopithecines from the category of culture builders but grant that status to the progressive "Homo habilis" (the majority of classifiers appear to put that form squarely with the others). He concludes that "... there is no convincing evidence that *Australopithecus* was a stone tool-maker according to a set, regular, and evolving pattern.... The evidence does however support the suggestion that *Australopithecus* was a tool-user, a tool-modifier and perhaps even an *ad hoc* tool-maker, but not a cultural tool-maker whose handiwork shows a progressive trend" (1965: 398).

We are, it appears, on stony ground; the matter is not closed, and it is best to keep an open mind on it. My own nonexpert and provisional preference is to withhold cultural status from the first chopper and flake tools, even though they became incorporated later into the cultural traditions of the bigger-brained *Homo erectus*. If the clever chimpanzees' tools can be understood in the context of mere situational and social learning, then it makes sense to demand more evidence of symboling behavior among the Australopithecines, even though those primates were brighter than chimps and even though their tools were more advanced.

Perhaps after further reading in the books of biological anthropologists and paleontologists you will want to challenge this arbitrary judgment and ask what evidence we would need to accept the Australopithecines as symboling primates. It would be evidence of behavior that could not be accounted for in physical or biological terms. I should think the evidence at the very least would relate to specialized tools, progressively refined and improved, and the continuing control of fire. This would connote a gluing together and accumulation of experience in the hominid line from which we might make tentative projections toward other parts of a human lifeway. In cultural anthropology, you see, we do not define humans merely biologically, as *Homo erectus* or *Homo sapiens*, but in relation to culture. It is not necessary to fix on some magical Rubicon across which the size of the brain must pass before it is considered capable of symboling (Geertz 1964), but the context provided by the lifeway of *Homo erectus*, as archeologists have reconstructed it, gives us more confidence than in the case of the Australopithecines that *erectus* achieved a symboling capacity.

The next important stone tool, the **Acheulian** biface or hand-axe, appears to have emerged from choppers and flakes in Olduvai Gorge and in northwestern Africa (Bordaz 1970: 20). It is usually pear shaped, but also circular and triangular, showing in the flaking along most of its edge a good deal of care and skill in its preparation; it is found with flakes struck from cores (the flakes themselves show evidence of having been used as tools) and with wide-edged cleavers which are more like earlier forms. Its makers were *Homo erectus* hunters of the Lower Paleolithic.

The context of the Acheulian hand-axe as it was used can be illustrated at the twin sites of Torralba and Ambrona in Spain, excavated by

F. Clark Howell. They were late spring and summer kill and butchering sites located on the stony slopes of a swampy, grassy valley which was probably on the seasonal migration route of big game animals. With the Mindel glacier still present in the north, the climate was cool and moist, and pines, grasses, and sedges flourished. The Torralbans apparently concentrated on bringing down elephants, perhaps driving the beasts onto boggy ground (occasional use of fire for this purpose is suggested), and dispatching them with spears, clubs, and heavy stones. But the quarry also included a primitive type of horse, deer, aurochs (or wild cattle), and steppe rhinoceros, as well as lions and wolves which preyed on the grass-eaters, smaller animals such as weasel, hare, mouse, and monkey, and a variety of waterfowl. In the excavated tool kit, flakes, particularly ones suited for scraping, predominated; bifacial forms included cleavers and hand-axes. Other items were the tips of elephant tusks and worked wood and bone. There were no identifiable home hearths, but there was much scattered charcoal and charred wood and bone, and there were rings of stones reminiscent of Olduvai; whether the last were shelters has not been established (Butzer 1971: 456-61).

We can accept the Torralban lifeway as a culture-dependent one, as we can that of the *Homo erectus* hunters of roughly the same period in the far-off caves of Chou-Kou-Tien in China. The size of the animals regularly slaughtered, the hunting techniques, the use of fire, and the variety of well-made tools imply stable, cooperating groups whose members were linked by human language. Let us assume, then, without labelling it an incontrovertible fact, that culture appeared first among *Homo erectus*. This does not rule out anticipatory stirrings among the man-apes nor close the door to reevaluation of the evidence.

The transition from Lower to Middle Paleolithic is marked by expansion in numbers and kinds of flake tools. They had been present all along, as by-products of chopper and hand-axe manufacture, and some Acheulian axe makers had improved their flaking by means of the so-called **Levallois** technique, which controlled the size and shape of the flakes struck from the flint block. The core that was left after all the flaking was itself a tool. Later, **Mousterian** flakers, who were Neanderthals, prepared the core in such a way that flakes could be struck from it until the core was practically used up; they then retouched or further worked on the edges of the flakes. A great variety of points, scrapers, and borers was made with the new technique (Bordaz 1970: 31, 39).

The Upper Paleolithic, in the context of flint knapping, is the age of blades. Blades are relatively long and thin flakes struck from cores and carefully prepared and trimmed indirectly, with blows of a stone, a bone, a piece of antler, or a wood hammer upon punches of antler or bone. Some blades were hafted. The increase in tool specialization evident in flint work is seen also in the rising number of bone and antler tools, made by cutting, scraping, and charring (Bordaz 1970: 51-65).

Let us put tools into a lifeway perspective again. About 10,000 years ago in late Würm times in the Kostenki-Borshevo region of the Don Valley of European Russia lived big-game hunters whose culture is representative of the Upper Paleolithic on the Eurasiatic continent. Other Upper Paleolithic peoples are more familiar to the reading public—the

Magdalenians of western Europe with their cave art and the Solutreans with their superb flint blades, for instance—but Kostenki appears to exemplify the good sturdy average of late Old Stone Age culture as it is described by the archeologist Richard G. Klein (1969: 213-30).

The Kostenkians, in groups of fifty or so, pitched their winter camps on small promontories above ravines near the river bank, good locations from which to attack game coming to water—mammoth, reindeer, wooly rhinoceros, wild horses, and cattle, moose, and other animals of late Pleistocene times. In other seasons, the Kostenkians probably followed the game to new pastures. Their shelters were tentlike or domed structures with wood or bone framework, covered with hides and earth, some of them only large enough for a single family, others of a long-house type that could house several families; within them were fire-places, as well as pits for storing food and gear. That the people clothed themselves in skins is an assumption that must be made for this cold climate, an assumption supported by the abundance of skin-working tools such as scrapers and bone awls. Their kit included blade and flake knives, scrapers, and borers, suitable for butchering, skinning, and piercing and for shaping bone and wood artifacts. Some points might have been fixed to throwing and thrusting spears, and other projectiles probably had only fire-hardened tips. Bone entered heavily into the inventory, not only in hunting and skinning tools and clothing fasteners but in what appears to be mattocks for digging pits. Some of the points appear suitable for arrows, which were in use at about the same time in the Ahrensburg culture near Hamburg, in the present day Federal Republic of Germany, but there is no other evidence of arrows here, and none for harpoons and bone gorges for catching fish. Perhaps the Kostenki people did not fish in winter—or did not fish at all.

As the inheritors of a legacy of diversified tools and efficient and economical techniques for making them, were the Kostenki people productive hunters? Apparently so. The excavators calculated the number of protein calories that might have been derived from animals whose skeletal remains were found in the sites' debris. The assumption was that a camp of fifty persons (twenty adults and thirty children) would require in this climate a total of 114,000 calories a day (an adult male 3,000, a female 2,400, and a child 2,000). Allocating the estimated calories produced among the members of such a hypothetical group, they deduced that one representative campsite probably was occupied for 5.5 months and the other for 7.8 months, which would cover the winter season. This would not take into account any meat dried and stored in the warmer season (probably minimal) or wild plant sources from which all living hunters, with the exception of the Eskimo, supplement their diet.

The detail crammed into this last leap of a third of a million years from Torralba to Kostenki (and it is still a sketchy minimum) possibly has made it hard going for you. Flint, bone, and wood are not intrinsically interesting to everyone. But a generalization about directional change to be discerned in tools and techniques over time can be related to energy expenditure and return, to efficiency and economy, in the technological aspect of culture. Bordaz (1970: 6) finds two trends in advances in stone implements: "First, there was an evolution in the forms and an increase in the number of implements, which were developed from a few generalized all-purpose tools and weapons to more specialized and better adapted ones. Second, there was an evolution in the mode of their manufacture. Man was learning to make better use of suitable raw material: he not only reduced waste but also developed new techniques which enabled him to utilize a greater variety of materials for the manufacture of stone weapons and tools." That a greater variety of material was used means that the properties of more materials were *discovered*. And new techniques mean *inventions*. There is an interplay between the two processes, as the quotation suggests.

What followed the hunting lifeway at the end of the Pleistocene was a set of adaptations to new environments of woodland, marsh, and desert, known collectively as the **Mesolithic** Age. It was the Mesolithic of the eastern Mediterranean that was transformed first into the **Neolithic**, which bears the principal connotation of farming lifeway rather than New Stone Age, so that will be our starting point when we take up temporal perspectives again. Now we will look at the hunting life in ethnographic contexts.

Survivors in the hunting adaptation

Hunting-and-gathering, farming-and-herding, and *industrial* or *machine* are terms of broad extension, comprising a typology of tools, techniques, and related knowledge for the whole of the technological aspect of culture. The terms are applicable both in specific and general perspectives. We have met the first among the Eskimo and Cheyenne of the recent past, and the differences between those specialized seal and caribou hunters and mounted pursuers of bison should lead us to expect much variation in hunting-and-gathering lifeways and in the tools and techniques by means of which they adapted to their habitats. Fishing also is included in this category, although not all hunters fish, and some fishermen have specialized. Similarly, mounted hunting is a specialization within the type.

In general evolutionary perspective, the three terms in the typology also represent a sequence of emergence and of discoveries and inventions, although obviously not all hunters became farmers, nor all farmers wielders of machine tools. And specific cultures reversed their courses, moving back into hunting after they had achieved farming; the Siriono of eastern Bolivia (Holmberg 1960) are one example among many; the Cheyenne are another.

Inasmuch as there were no technologies other than those of the hunters and gatherers up to 10,000 years ago, this lifeway accounts for 98 percent or more of culture's temporal span. And in regard to numbers of humans in the three lifeways, two anthropologists, Richard B. Lee and Irven DeVore (1968: 3), present a startling conclusion: "Of the estimated 80,000,000,000 men who have ever lived out their life span on earth, over 90 percent have lived as hunters and gatherers; about 6 percent have lived by agriculture and the remaining few percent have lived in industrial societies." This despite the fact, we might add, that in the Middle Old Stone Age, around 50,000 years ago, there were probably only one million human inhabitants of the earth (Clark

1967: 16) and on the eve of the Agricultural Revolution forty millennia later there were between five and ten million. Compared with hunting and gathering, then, agriculture has been but a brief episode in culture history, and industry little more than an eye blink, a chastening thought in our ecologically perilous time.

Hunters and gatherers live today, or have lived in the relatively recent past, in Canada and Alaska and the western United States; in South America on the Orinoco delta, in southern Venezuela and in Amazonia; in Africa, as represented not only by the Bushmen and the Congo Pygmies but also by groups in Angola, East Africa, and Ethiopia; in India, as specialized castes or tribes of hunters; in central Vietnam and northern Thailand; in the Andaman Islands and Malaya; and as remnant aboriginal groups in Australia (Murdock 1968: 15-20).

As noted in Chapter Four, no surviving primitive peoples pursue a way of life precisely as it was when all of our ancestors were hunters previous to 10,000 B.C. With expansion and increase in dominance of farming and herding, the ones who did not adopt those technologies were devastated by fighting, starvation, and disease or were pushed into environments where the new technologies could not follow and be productive. Murdock (1968: 13) estimates that by the time of Columbus they occupied probably only 15 percent of the earth's surface.

The Bushman
and Mbuti examples

Bushmen live in the Kalahari desert in Botswana and Namibia (South West Africa). Numbering about fifty-five thousand and now restricted to the desert and its fringes, these short-statured people with yellowish skin and peppercorn hair once occupied a third of Africa in the east and south before they were reduced in their numbers and pushed aside by cattle-breeding, Bantu-speaking Negroes advancing from the north and Dutch and English immigrants who settled in South Africa. Like the neighboring Hottentot, who adopted cattle raising, and the hunting Bergdama, they speak languages in the Khoisan or Click family, which are characterized by some peculiar consonants produced by implosion, or quick sucking action of the tongue against the teeth and roof and side of the mouth. We center on the !Kung (the exclamation point in *!Kung* represents one of those peculiar consonants, this one made with the tongue against the alveolar ridge back of the teeth), about four thousand in number, whose culture has been described by Lorna Marshall (1965) and Elizabeth Marshall Thomas (1959), who lived among them in the 1950s, and by Richard B. Lee (Lee and DeVore 1968: 30-48; Lee 1969).

The Kalahari is an elevated sandy basin whose vegetation consists of grass, bush, and scattered clumps of trees. It also supports many edible bulbs, tubers, roots, and drought-resistant plants with water-storage organs, and there are nuts, berries, seeds, fruits, leaves, and gums or resins to be harvested. Game animals include several species of big antelope, the buffalo, an occasional giraffe, and several smaller animals and birds. Tortoises, some lizards, snakes, ostrich eggs, grasshoppers, and termites are considered edible by the !Kung.

Women provide about two-thirds of the food. A woman goes out

Bushman girls digging roots. About two-thirds of the food among this Kalahari Desert people is provided by the women. (© 1976 by Laurence Marshall.)

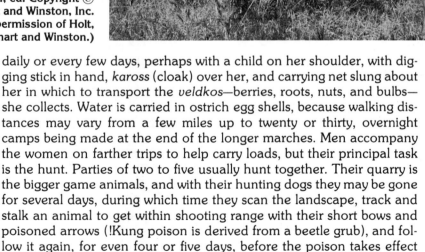

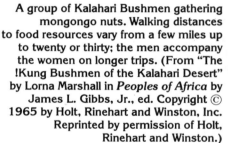

A group of Kalahari Bushmen gathering mongongo nuts. Walking distances to food resources vary from a few miles up to twenty or thirty; the men accompany the women on longer trips. (From "The !Kung Bushmen of the Kalahari Desert" by Lorna Marshall in *Peoples of Africa* by James L. Gibbs, Jr., ed. Copyright © 1965 by Holt, Rinehart and Winston, Inc. Reprinted by permission of Holt, Rinehart and Winston.)

daily or every few days, perhaps with a child on her shoulder, with digging stick in hand, *kaross* (cloak) over her, and carrying net slung about her in which to transport the *veldkos*—berries, roots, nuts, and bulbs—she collects. Water is carried in ostrich egg shells, because walking distances may vary from a few miles up to twenty or thirty, overnight camps being made at the end of the longer marches. Men accompany the women on farther trips to help carry loads, but their principal task is the hunt. Parties of two to five usually hunt together. Their quarry is the bigger game animals, and with their hunting dogs they may be gone for several days, during which time they scan the landscape, track and stalk an animal to get within shooting range with their short bows and poisoned arrows (!Kung poison is derived from a beetle grub), and follow it again, for even four or five days, before the poison takes effect and the animal dies.

The twenty-five to fifty people in a Bushman camp are sheltered in a circle of half a dozen domed huts, each about five feet high and made of interlaced branches dug into the ground and covered with bundles of grass. Most days are hot and nights cool; the Bushman wears only a skin breech cloth or an apron and at night depends upon the fire and a

Culture in Its Technological Aspect

kaross for warmth. Fire, of course, is a source of heat energy, and huts and cloaks conserve that energy. Meat is roasted, impaled on a stick, and *veldkos* is cooked in the coals and hot ashes of the family fire.

Bows, quivers, sticks for fire making, digging, carrying, and stirring, handles for knives and axes and spears, as well as bowls and spoons and mortars and pestles for pounding food, are made from wood. Knives, axes, and cooking pots are procured by trading of hides and ostrich shell beads to Bantu neighbors; bone and wood are still used for some knives and for spear and arrow points, although trade metal beaten out by the Bushmen has generally replaced them. Arrow shafts are made of bone and reed; cordage, from plant fiber and animal sinew; *kaross,* breech cloth, and apron, from hide; and small dippers and boxes, from tortoise shells. All in all, it is a brief but adequate inventory. The Bushman does not have much to carry when moving, and the Bushman can replace artifacts easily wherever camp is set up.

Water holes and *veldkos* areas center the range of the Bushman's food quest. In the 8,000 square miles of territory, occupied by a thousand people, where the Marshall expeditions spent most of their time,

Bushman male carrying his load on a carrying stick (on left shoulder). He has thrust his *assagai,* or spear (on right shoulder), under the stick to distribute the load over both shoulders. In addition to the skin bags and *assagai* he has with him his bow and quiver. (From "The !Kung Bushmen of the Kalahari Desert" by Lorna Marshall in *Peoples of Africa* by James L. Gibbs, Jr., ed. Copyright © 1965 by Holt, Rinehart and Winston, Inc. Reprinted by permission of Holt, Rinehart and Winston.)

Bushman band starting out on its march to a new camp. Water holes and areas of *veldkos* center the range of the food quest. (© 1976 by Laurence Marshall.)

there were only thirteen water holes: only three were permanent, four were dependable except in severe drought, and six supplied water in good years but disappeared in years that were dry.

How productive of energy is the Bushman system in relation to energy expenditure? Richard B. Lee (Lee and DeVore 1968: 30-48; Lee 1969) did research on that problem among 248 !Kung living in the Dobe area of northwestern Botswana. They were organized into fourteen camps around six water holes and exploited a range of 1,000 square miles, circumscribed by 20-mile radiuses from permanent water supplies. A census enumerated a larger number of Bushmen in the area, but Lee excluded from his study camp residents who worked part of the time for Bantu cattle raisers, as well as transients and emigrants, so that he had a bounded population consuming the vegetable foods and game it collected.

Lee's study of work performed and food consumed focused upon a representative camp of about thirty individuals who lived around one water hole. His weekly diary revealed that working adults labored only about two and one-half days out of seven on the food quest (figuring the average working day as about six hours) and still were able to support themselves and their dependents. Work done week by week varied directly with the distance from the water hole to available food sources, principally nuts of the mongongo tree, because, as food was eaten out close to camp, longer and increasingly arduous trips were required.

In terms of an Index of Subsistence Effort that Lee devised, representing the ratio of total days worked by the group's members to the total of individual daily rations consumed by all in the group, the Dobe Bushmen were well ahead of the game. The index for one of the weeks was .21, which meant a rate of 21 days of work for 100 man-days of consumption; in actual figures, 37 man-days of work provided 179 man-days of consumption. On another week, the people worked longer—77 man-days to provide 249 man-days of consumption, a rate of 31 work days per 100 consumption days, or an index of .31. Over three weeks, the index averaged to .23. "Since the non-productive members comprised 35 percent of the population," Lee writes, "another way of expressing the Index is to say that 65 percent of the people worked 36 percent of the time, and 35 percent of the people did no work at all" (1969: 67).

In addition to calculating the labor return in terms of man-days of consumption, Lee demonstrated that the diet of meat and mongongo nuts and other vegetable foods provided an average of 2,140 calories a day per person. This more than met the caloric requirement for males of 2,250 per day, for females of 1,750 per day, and for the most active segment of the group (both males and females around thirty years old) of 2,000 per day. It is evident that the Bushmen were adequately fueled, particularly if one takes into account that the young and the aged would eat less than the active thirty-year-olds. This, he believes, lays to rest the common belief that hunters live on the edge of disaster, even in an environment as demanding as the Kalahari.

Far to the north of the Bushmen, in the great Ituri rain forest in the northeastern part of the Republic of the Congo, another hunting-and-collecting technology thrives. There live some forty thousand Mbuti

Pygmies, who roam hunting areas within the 250,000-square-mile expanse of the dark forest, sharing its edges with Bantu- and Sudanese-speaking Negro farmers, with whom they have entered into a loose **symbiotic relationship**. In this relationship, which rests lightly on Mbuti shoulders, they have adopted the languages of the farmers and lost their own. They are living about as they did when the Egyptian Pharoah Nefrikare and his exploring commander, Herkouf, exchanged letters about them 4,500 years ago, in the opinion of their ethnographer, Colin M. Turnbull (1961, 1965).

The Mbuti stalk and kill animals as big as the elephant and buffalo, using short spears and poisoned arrows with fire-hardened points which are shot from wooden bows. Metal-tipped arrows and metal spear blades are also used today, but the Pygmies find their poisoned darts more efficient in the forest because they can kill with only a glancing and scratching impact, and it is difficult to aim for vital parts of animals in the obscuring vegetation. Metal has replaced stone (which they have forgotten how to work) in the machetes and axes which they use to cut saplings for their low, domed huts and to chop stores of

Annual round of the Dobe Bushmen. Note how the availability of water structures group movements. (By permission from *Man the hunter*, Richard B. Lee and Irven DeVore, eds., Chicago: Aldine, copyright 1965 by the Wenner-Gren Foundation for Anthropological Research, Inc.

	Jan.	Feb.	Mar.	April	May	June	July	Aug.	Sept.	Oct.	Nov.	Dec.
Season	Summer Rains			Autumn Dry			Winter Dry			Spring Dry	First Rains	
Availability of Water	Temporary summer pools everywhere			Large summer pools			Permanent waterholes only				Summer pools developing	
Group Moves	Widely dispersed at summer pools			At large summer pools			All population restricted to permanent waterholes				Moving out to summer pools	
Men's Subsistence Activities	1. Hunting with bow, arrows, and dogs (Year-round)											
	2.		Running down immatures				Trapping small game in snares			Running down newborn animals		
	3. Some gathering (Year-round)											
Women's Subsistence Activities	1. Gathering of mongongo nuts (Year-round)											
	2.		Fruits, berries, melons				Roots, bulbs resins			Roots, leafy greens		
Ritual Activities	Dancing, trance performances, and ritual curing (Year-round)											
						Boys' initiation*						
Relative Subsistence Hardship	Water-food distance minimal						Increasing distance from water to food				Water-food distance minimal	

*Held once every five years; none in 1963-64.
†New Year's: Bushmen join the celebrations of their missionized Bantu neighbors.

Hunting-Gathering Technologies, Past and Present

honey from trees. They continue to use sharp slivers of bamboo and reeds to skin game and thorny vines to scrape roots and vegetables. Their only garments are loin cloths beaten from the inner layers of tree bark, and their huts are covered with the leaves of mongongo trees.

There has been some specialization by the Mbuti groups called respectively the Net-Hunters and the Archers. Families of Net-Hunters, men, women, and children, work cooperatively, each family contributing a fiber net of up to three hundred feet in length which it attaches to the undergrowth and other family nets on either side until a great semicircle results. Men and boys stand at the nets, and the women and girls, closing in from a distance, beat the undergrowth and cry out to drive the game toward the nets to be speared. Hunting begins early in the morning and ends in early afternoon, when enough meat and vegetable food has been caught and gathered for a day or two. This mode of hunting is characteristic of Pygmy areas farthest from the farming settlements and government administrative posts and is probably a very old adaptation. The Archers are found where game is reduced near the settlements and net hunting is not so productive. A small group of Archers perch in trees along game trails, calling animals with imitative cries or waiting for them to pass and then shooting them with poisoned arrows. Once a year the Archers stage a cooperative hunt, but they corral the game with only a human semicircle, not with nets.

It appears there is never a shortage of game, at least in the forest depths, and a year-round succession of mushrooms, nuts, berries, fruits, honey, and roots is available, although meat is the principal resource. The Pygmies provide meat and forest materials such as saplings and leaves for the farming villagers to whom they are attached, and they get in return—or steal—spears, axes, machetes, knives, and cooking vessels. Mbuti are preeminently people of the forest whom the villagers dislike and fear, a situation which has given rise to interesting social organizational and ideological differences.

The anthropologist Marshall Sahlins (1972) has coined a phrase, "the original affluent society," to describe hunters and gatherers. To understand the aptness of it, we shall have to look at their social organizations and ideologies in addition to their technologies, and at alternative lifeways. But even at this point you have some evidence that it is truly descriptive. Contemporary hunters do not work particularly hard, save for short and exceptional periods, nor do they work continuously. Nature is not niggardly, at least not everywhere at the same time, and when food resources become scarce in one place by overuse or natural failure, hunters move to another place or find substitutes for their usual fare. It is not practicable for them to carry heavy loads of possessions, but such are not required in the lifeway; what is necessary can be carried, and a man or woman can replace most tools quickly from materials in the habitat. This, of course, applies to shelters, too. Privation is not unknown, but as we shall see when we explore social organization the hunters have an insurance system of sharing, so that those who might face want can rely on kin and neighbors.

In recent years, anthropologists have concluded that refugee hunters in harsher environments, like the Bushmen, or even those aboriginally in trying habitats, like the Eskimo, were not so bad off as ethnocentric Westerners first thought them to be. And the "advanced" or "specialized" folk, such as the fishing and sea-mammal-hunting Nootka, were not so exaggeratedly secure as first thought, although they, too, had a social insurance mechanism. The hunting-and-gathering technology (and the culture which rests on it) is capable of adapting to any environment in which there are exploitable plants and animals and of supporting adequately the populations that depend on it. In the past, it enjoyed habitats with richer resources and no doubt returned more for equal expenditure of human labor.

Specialized fishermen and sea-mammal hunters

The Nootka of the Northwest Coast of North America demonstrate the capacity of the hunting-and-gathering lifeway to accumulate tools and techniques when resources are relatively abundant, when they are of a kind that induces permanent and semipermanent settlement by the exploiters, and when goods need not be transported on human backs. The Nootka numbered about six thousand people in a dozen or so tribes and lived on the seaward side of Vancouver Island off the coast of Canada. They spoke a language in the Wakashan group, related to Algonkian, whose widespread tongues were spoken by simpler hunters and gatherers as well as farmers in North America. Our information comes from their ethnographer, Philip Drucker (1951), and refers mostly to a past state of affairs. The Nootka in the eighteenth and early nineteenth centuries were exploited and massacred by Spanish and British, devastated by smallpox and venereal disease, and drawn into the trade in otter skins and in commercial fishing and lumbering. However, the early technology can be visualized from observation of what remained in use and in the memories of the old.

Vancouver Island has a rugged coast, indented with sounds and inlets and studded with islets, rocks, and reefs. A hundred inches of rain fall

Nootka village of cedar-plank houses above Nootka Sound, Vancouver Island, after an extensive period of contact with Western culture. Captain Cook was in the vicinity in 1778. Note the painted crests or heraldic designs on the house at the right. (Courtesy National Museums of Canada.)

In hollowed-out cedar-log canoes, Northwest Coast Indians fished and hunted sea mammals. (Courtesy National Museums of Canada.)

in a year, the season from early fall to spring being particularly stormy; there is frost and some snow in the winter, but the climate is temperate. Behind the coast and beaches, slopes densely clad with conifers rise to mountain peaks. This "dark gloomy moss-covered world" (Drucker 1951: 8) under towering trees was the home of elk, deer, black bear, mountain lion, wolf, raccoon, otter, beaver, and other animals, but it was difficult of access and but little exploited. The sea and the water's edge provided most of the food—dog salmon and herring first, and whale, seal, sea lion, and porpoise next. Shellfish were collected on the beaches, ducks and geese were caught as they traversed the flyways, and berries and roots were gathered at the edge of the forest. Fish and sea mammals provided ample protein, but their fats had to make up for a low carbohydrate supply. Great numbers of fish caught during their runs were sun dried, or dried and smoked on racks, and packed in wooden boxes; some berries also were stored, as was salmon roe, which was collected on tree branches submerged offshore and stuffed into seal bladders.

The Nootka constructed gabled, cedar-plank houses, forty to one hundred feet long and thirty to forty-eight feet wide; permanent log frames were built at summer and winter village sites and fishing stations, and the removable planks for their sides were transported by canoe when the people moved during their yearly round. On warm days, men went nude and women wore only an apron of shredded cedar bark, but in winter and on cold and rainy days both sexes clothed themselves in bark fiber robes, rain capes, and conical hats.

A detailed examination of Nootka tools in the broad sense and the techniques for making and deploying them might well fill a volume; we will touch on some principal ones. Nootka carried their goods and hunted and fished in hollowed-out cedar-log canoes that ranged in length from forty-eight feet for freighting craft down through whaling and sealing craft, to fishing craft of twelve to eighteen feet. These craft were propelled with bladed wooden paddles. The tool kits of the carpenters who made the canoes, houses, and wooden boxes included arduously ground stone mauls, wooden wedges, stone and shell adzes, bone chisels and drills, grinders of sandstone, and sharkskin polishers. Boards were split from standing trees with wedge and maul, and canoe logs were cut, partially hollowed, and floated to the home beach.

Boxes were used not only for storage but for cooking; hot stones placed in them with cedar tongs brought liquid to a boil. Food also was broiled over coals, roasted in ashes, and steamed under mats. Fire was made with a simple wooden friction stick twirled between the hands. Nootka women were weavers, working with bark fibers suspended from frames; they also made by hand bags and baskets, including large ones that were supported by lines across the carrier's chest and forehead for carrying burdens.

Fishing and sea-hunting gear included fish traps (latticed traps were placed in tidal flats and cylindrical and conical ones were set in the rivers, both having dams or weirs to channel the fish into them), dip nets and rakes, hooks and lines, wooden harpoons with one to three foreshafts and two-barbed heads of bone, secured by a line to inflated animal hide floats. Sea-mammal hunting called for a good deal of coor-

dinated action, particularly when a whale, which might weigh up to thirty tons, was to be challenged by a few canoe crews.

With these devices, and with the concentration of fish and sea mammals in their seasons, the return on labor expended must have been considerable. However, Drucker reports (1951: 36-37), "While the food resources were rich, now and then periods of scarcity occurred. Ethnographers have stressed nature's prodigality to the peoples of the

Hunting-Gathering Technologies, Past and Present

Northwest Coast to the point that one is surprised by the thought that they should ever have suffered want. But occasionally a poor dog salmon or herring run, followed by an unusually stormy winter or spring, as the case might be, that prevented people from going out to fish for cod or halibut, quickly brought privation. Those were the times people walked the beaches looking for codfish heads spurned by seals and sea lions, and storm-killed herring and pilchard. They collected and ate the tiny mussels of the inner coves and bays and similar small mollusks disdained in normal times of the year. The spring of the year was perhaps more often a lean season than winter."

There has been a good deal of variation, then, in hunting-gathering-fishing technologies. Some represent adaptations of relative simplicity and others adaptations of relative complexity. As we shall see, either relative simplicity or complexity characterizes in some degree the social organizations that are associated with them. Specialized systems with higher energy inputs tend to spread initially at the expense of unspecialized, lower-energy systems; they become dominant in the habitats to which they are adapted. As noted in Chapter Four, however, the path of general evolutionary advance does not lead through the specialized hunters and fishermen to the promised land of domestication. In retrospect, relatively less specialized systems were the point of departure toward a higher technological level.

Suggested Readings

Balikci, Asen. 1970. *The Netsilik Eskimo.* Garden City, N.Y.: Natural History Press.*

Bordaz, Jacques. 1970. *Tools of the Old and New Stone Age.* Garden City, N.Y.: Natural History Press.*

Brace, C. Loring. 1967. *The stages of human evolution: Human and cultural origins.* Englewood Cliffs, N.J.: Prentice-Hall.*

Clark, Grahame. 1970. *The Stone Age hunters.* New York: McGraw-Hill.*

Coon, Carleton S. 1971. *The hunting peoples.* Boston: Little Brown and Company, An Atlantic Monthly Press Book.*

Drucker, Philip. 1965. *Cultures of the North Pacific Coast.* San Francisco: Chandler.*

Gould, Richard A. 1969. *Yiwara: Foragers of the Australian desert.* New York: Charles Scribner's Sons.*

Hewes, Gordon W. 1973. *The origin of man.* Minneapolis: Burgess.*

Klein, Richard G. 1969. *Man and culture in the late Pleistocene.* San Francisco: Chandler.

Lee, Richard B., and Irven DeVore, eds. 1968. *Man the hunter.* Chicago: Aldine.*

Nelson, Richard K. 1973. *Hunters of the northern forest: Designs for survival among the Alaskan Kutchin.* Chicago: University of Chicago Press.

Spier, Robert F. G. 1970. *From the hand of man: Primitive and preindustrial technologies.* Boston: Houghton Mifflin.*

———. 1973. *Material culture and technology.* Minneapolis: Burgess.*

Thomas, Elizabeth Marshall. 1959. *The harmless people.* New York: Alfred A. Knopf.*

Tunnell, Gary G. 1973. *Culture and biology: Becoming human.* Minneapolis: Burgess.*

Turnbull, Colin M. 1961. *The forest people.* New York: Simon and Schuster.*

Temporally, farming-and-herding technologies span less than 10,000 years of culture's 500,000-year course. In the time since the "food-producing revolution" began, to use a phrase popularized by the archeologist Gordon Childe, world population multiplied a hundred times, from roughly 7,500,000 to 750,000,000 on the eve of the Industrial Revolution in A.D. 1750 (Cipolla 1962: 98). Today the population approaches 4,000,000,000. Not all of this growth can be accounted for in a simplistic way by an increase in food supplies, but the potential for control of habitat represented by domestication of plants and animals was a necessary condition for the rise of high-energy systems and the production of more human beings. Although the time is approaching when strictly hunting-and-gathering cultures will be a thing of the past, we can hardly say the same for farming-and-herding technologies. They will be with us as long as humankind must eat or until we enter a science fiction world in which most of our food is synthesized in laboratories. Increasingly large segments of those technologies will be industrialized and the cultures they support will be incorporated into a world market system, but it is important that we grasp what they have been and what they are now if we are to understand cultural evolution.

Chapter Six
Expanded Energy Supply: Plant and Animal Domestication

129

The significance of
farming and herding

Some farming-and-herding systems produced no more energy per capita in relation to what humans put into them than did hunting-and-gathering systems, nor was subsistence always more secure; and there have been stable agricultural systems in which the accompanying human population increased very slowly if at all. But it was culture's conversion of plants and animals from their status as resources alone to an additional one as tools, controlled energy converters, that broke the limitations of the hunting lifeway. "The domestication of plants and animals was a way of laying hold of them as forces of nature, of directing and controlling them, of incorporating them into cultural systems" (White 1959: 46). Or, in the words of a zoologist, "in a very important sense...domestic animals (as well as plants) are a type of human artifact, since they exist in a form changed by man" (Reed 1959: 1,638, n. 7). Change did not come as a thunderclap after domestication; it was a slow process, and some segments of the total system changed hardly at all. But the world we see around us, however much is owed to the later Industrial Revolution, would not be as it is without the technological invention of domestication.

"Westerners have for long carried about with them a distinctly ethnocentric model of agriculture," writes the ecological anthropologist Robert McC. Netting (1971: 18). It is the model of European mixed farming found from Ireland to India which is characterized "by plow cultivation on clean-cropped winter-fallowed fields" combining "into the one cycle of subsistence and land, use of hard field grains, the grassland fodder or hay for hoofed animals, and the hoofed animals, which provide meat, milk, and other produce, including manure, hide, and wool" (Arensberg 1963: 84-85).

Widespread alternative farming adaptations are **swiddening, irrigated terracing**, and **hoe farming**. The first two, sometimes called, respectively, extensive and intensive farming, are confined today largely to the tropics. *Swiddening,* a term originating in northern English dialects, also called **slash-and-burn** and known by various local names such as *kaingin* in the Philippines and *milpa* in Central America, is carried on in secondary and primary forest: the cover is cut and burned, seed or cuttings are planted with simple tools such as digging stick and hoe in the ash-covered fields or gardens, and after one or more harvests the fields are surrendered to weeds and new forest growth for extended fallowing periods. Then the cycle begins again. A large labor force is not required, although hard work is involved. Shifting fields is a mark of swiddening, although this does not necessarily mean shifting habitation (Conklin 1969: 222, 230). Irrigation and terracing, most commonly but not only associated with wet rice cultivation, call for a high labor input in the construction of retaining walls and canals and preparation of the ground and for careful control of the water supply which brings nutrients to the growing plants. It is adaptable to deserts or rainy areas equally, and high and growing human population densities accompany it. Animal-drawn plows and cultivators are sometimes but not always used in this mode of farming. The third kind of alterna-

Culture in Its Technological Aspect

tive cultivation is hoe farming, in which the water supply may come from rains, flooding streams, or springs and which is carried on in fields more permanent than those of the swiddeners; labor input appears to be intermediate. Tools associated with the three alternative modes of farming—the digging stick, the hoe, and the animal-drawn plow—represent a tool progression of a sort, but obviously they are not the whole of the technologies involved.

It is conventional in anthropology to call plant cultivation with hand labor alone *horticulture* or *gardening* and that employing animal-drawn plows *agriculture*. Many anthropologists might agree with Paul Bohannan (1963: 216) that "the invention of the plow was undoubtedly one of the most important points of change in the history of the world, for it combined horticulture with the effective use of animals as a new source of energy that could be used in the acquisition of the necessities of life." But this would appear to be true primarily for European mixed farming and its antecedents and secondarily for Asiatic terrace irrigation. Mesoamerica and South America achieved civilizations without animal-drawn plows. At any rate, although we shall use the terms, there seems no overriding reason not to use the term *farming* to cover both horticulture and agriculture, and our ethnographic examples will be arranged under a three-fold classification—swidden, hoe, and irrigated terracing. For our purposes, a special taxonomy for uses of domesticated animals does not seem to be required, and we shall depend only on ethnographic contexts to orient them. So let us move on to an examination of farmers and herders.

New Guinean and Brazilian swidden farmers

In the rainy central highlands of New Guinea live the Maring-speaking Tsembaga, swidden farmers and pig raisers. When they were studied in 1962-63 by Roy A. Rappaport (1967a, 1971), some two hundred Tsembaga occupied 3.2 square miles of territory in the steep-walled and heavily forested valley of the Simbai River in the Bismarck Range. Taro and sweet potatoes are their most important crops, followed by yams, manioc, and bananas, all raised from cuttings set into holes punched into the ground with heavy digging sticks. They also raise beans, peas, maize, sugarcane, and leafy greens, all of which are fairly rich in plant proteins, somewhat jumbled together with the major crops in their gardens. At a given time, the Tsembaga have under cultivation some ninety acres, and nearly ten times that amount of land lies fallow under secondary forest; there is ample marginal land that can be cleared if needed, and during the year they were observed the people put forty-two new acres into production. Horticulture provides 99 percent by weight of the everyday diet. Some hunting and trapping is carried on, but it does not provide much food in relation to the requirements of the rather dense population.

Rappaport found a simple technology in its tool aspect—digging stick, steel axe, and machete, or bushknife, for gardening (stone tools were replaced only about 1950); bows and arrows, snares, deadfalls and pits for hunting; gourds and bamboo tubes for containers. Food is cooked directly on the fire and in earth ovens. Fighting with neighbors

Tsembaga fell the trees, cut away the underbrush, and burn the litter to begin a new garden on a hillside. The ash improves fertility. Fences are built to keep out the pigs, and the ground is weeded and burned over several times. (Courtesy Roy A. Rappaport.)

involves bows, spears, axes, and wooden shields. Some bark cloth is made, and fibers are woven into net bags, loin cloths, caps, and string aprons, the total of clothing unless we include ornamental waist and arm bands. The Tsembaga live in rectangular, gabled, pandanus-thatched houses (ranging in length from twenty to thirty-five feet and in breadth from seven to ten feet) which are sometimes grouped in villages around dance grounds and sometimes scattered.

To make their gardens, the Tsembaga first hack away the underbrush with machetes, cut down most of the trees, burn the debris after it has dried (ash improves the fertility of the soil), construct fences of logs and split rails to keep out wild and domesticated pigs, and weed the ground and burn it over several times again. After the crops are planted there is virtually continuous and selective weeding to be done. As the plants start to mature, harvesting begins and continues a little day by day, produce being carried to the houses up or down the slopes. A garden bears for between fourteen and twenty-eight months, after which it is surrendered to secondary forest growth and lies fallow for from eight to forty-five years.

Culture in Its Technological Aspect

Systems like that of the Tsembaga are keyed into stages of natural plant growth called *succession*. The forest trees and undergrowth are necessarily, although only partially, removed, and carefully cultivated food plants temporarily replace them. To the outsider, Tsembaga gardens are a tangle of growing things resembling the jungle itself. "A mat of sweet potato leaves covers the soil at ground level. The taro leaves project over this mat; the hibiscus, sugarcane and *pitpit* (a relative of sugarcane) stand higher still, and fronds of the banana spread out above the rest" (Rappaport 1971: 121). This ordering results in a garden that has maximum leaf exposure to sunlight, protects the soil, discourages insects, and provides alternative foods should one not yield well.

Tsembaga garden after about six months. Taro is maturing, sugarcane and *pitpit* have yet to reach full growth, and bananas, planted late in this garden, are small. Sweet potatoes are close to the ground and not visible in the tangle of plants. (Courtesy Roy A. Rappaport.)

A garden about one and one-half years after planting. Bananas grow in the background, and in front of them sugarcane is very tall. The taro is gone, but sweet potatoes remain on the ground. (Courtesy Roy A. Rappaport.)

Expanded Energy Supply: Plant and Animal Domestication

Pigs, fed primarily from sweet potato gardens, are not eaten by the Tsembaga as regular fare except on emergency and ritual-laden occasions such as sickness, injury, or death but are slaughtered at the end of ten-year cycles, at which time they have multiplied to such an extent that they become a burden on the gardeners. Eating of wild pigs does not have any ritual limitation, but overall their contribution to the Tsembaga diet is minimal.

Rappaport made a detailed study of calories expended in cultivation—clearing, fencing, weeding, planting, harvesting, transporting—in relation to crop yield in calories and concluded that the ratio of yield to labor was 16.5 for taro and yams and 15.9 for sweet potatoes. And that was during a festival year in which houses were clustered closer together than usual, so that the Tsembaga had to walk farther to their gardens. The infrequently eaten pigs were more important as a protein source than in regard to the total number of calories they provided.

Kuikuru men pack ears of maize into carrying baskets that will be supported by a tumpline across the forehead. Maize supplements their staple food, manioc. Two of the village's nine thatched dwellings are in background. (Courtesy Gertrude E. Dole.)

Kuikuru girl spins cotton into thread with a sustained spindle whose end rests on a pottery shard. Spinning and weaving is women's work, one important product being the hammock. (Courtesy Gertrude E. Dole.)

Culture in Its Technological Aspect

Counting gardens alone as calorie sources, men were provided 2,600 and women 2,200 calories a day, an adequate ration for these short-statured people in this climate. Marvin Harris (1971: 210) points out that a Tsembaga needs to work only 380 hours a year in cultivation. Only nine and one-half weeks a year, if one thinks of a Western forty-hours-per-week schedule! Activities such as food preparation are not included in the calculations, but patently the Tsembaga are not burdened in the food quest.

Another case in point is that of the Kuikuru, American Indian manioc farmers who dwell on a tributary of the Xingu river in central Brazil. There were 145 Kuikuru, living in one village of nine thatched houses, when Robert L. Carneiro (1961) studied them in 1953-54. They cleared their garden plots of trees and undergrowth with steel axes, machetes, and brushhooks (until about 1900 they used stone axes and the toothed lower jaws of the piranha), allowed the vegetation to dry, and then burned it off and planted the manioc cuttings in low, hoed-up mounds before the next rains began. The gardens were weeded by hand and hoe, and they were fenced to keep out peccaries, or wild pigs. As tubers were harvested, new cuttings were put in; after three staggered plantings of this sort a plot was abandoned and then reused after about twenty-five years. Each year about forty acres were surrendered and an equal number brought into cultivation.

At any given time the Kuikuru had about ninety-five acres of gardens that produced four to five tons of manioc tubers per acre per year; as many as 1,500 tubers were counted in one acre-and-a-half plot. Manioc accounted for 80 to 85 percent of the Kuikuru diet. At least half of the product was lost to peccaries and to leaf-cutter ants that carried away flour from the houses. Farmers anticipated the losses and planted enough to cover them. Carneiro estimated that an acre yielded no less than 2,000,000 calories a year (the salvaged half of the total). If 2,000,000 calories are multiplied by 95 (representing the number of acres in production) and apportioned among the 145 Kuikuru, we get the astonishing result that each man, woman, and child had available a daily intake of over 3,500 calories.

If that amount were eaten, a population of butterballs would result; efficiency can be maintained on 2,600 calories a day, by worldwide average, and, as a student of energy and society has suggested, "it is improbable that any population with a normal number of children would consume more than 3,000 Calories per day per capita without producing excessive fat, which actually reduces the capacity to work" (Cottrell 1955: 18). Evidence on human calorie needs in a climate more trying than that in which the Kuikuru live comes from a study made by William B. Kemp (1971) on a Baffin Island Eskimo community over a fifty-four-month period. The Baffin Islanders had a potential intake of 3,000 calories a day from sea mammals and store-bought food, "which was enough to sustain a level of activity well above the maintenance level" (Kemp 1971: 106). And that was with a mean winter temperature of thirty degrees below zero (Fahrenheit) and a strenuous hunting life among the males.

"The subsistence economy of the Kuikuru is one of abundance and reliability," Carneiro reports (1961: 48). "There never is a shortage of

Guahibo Indians in Colombia clear land for a garden. Swiddening, or slash-and-burn farming, is an adaptation to primary- and secondary-growth forest. It requires cutting and burning of trees and undergrowth, planting in the ash-laden soil, and frequent weeding before harvest. (Courtesy Nancy and Robert V. Morey.)

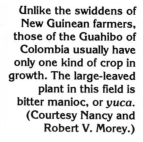

Unlike the swiddens of New Guinean farmers, those of the Guahibo of Colombia usually have only one kind of crop in growth. The large-leaved plant in this field is bitter manioc, or *yuca*. (Courtesy Nancy and Robert V. Morey.)

food, let alone any danger of starvation." Exploring the implications of Kuikuru affluence and how it is arrived at for South American tropical forest cultures in general, Carneiro came to several conclusions which upset conventional beliefs about swidden farmers. They do not have to move because of farming conditions that formerly were presumed to exhaust the land; the Kuikuru had lived near the same spot for nearly a century, and they had 13,500 acres of usable forest within a four-mile walk. Although the Kuikuru numbered only 145, their ethnographer estimates that a village of 2,000 could have been supported on a sedentary basis; some villages in Amazonia reached sizes of 1,000. Thus, swidden farmers are not limited to small communities. Although Kuikuru almost never actually produced a surplus of food over a year's requirements, they were technically capable of doing so. There is no truth to the belief that the culture did not rise to a higher level because the people lacked leisure for nonsubsistence activities. "At the present time a man spends only about three and a half hours a day on subsistence—two hours on horticulture, and one and a half hours on fishing. Of the remaining ten or twelve waking hours of the day the Kuikuru men spend a great deal of it dancing, wrestling, in some form of informal recreation, and in loafing" (Carneiro 1961: 49). And, a fact of importance for the cultural system, there is no significant loss of fertility in swidden lands that would cause their abandonment; it is simply easier, given the technology, to start a new garden in the forest than to cope with the increasing competition of weed plants and grasses.

Culture in Its Technological Aspect

Hoe farming
in Nigeria and Arizona

A culture that illustrates the tools and techniques of hoe farming and the progressively intensifying land use that often accompanies it is that of the Kofyar, who live on the southern flanks of the Jos Plateau in North Central Nigeria. The Kofyar, who were studied in 1960-62 and again in 1966-67 by Robert McC. Netting (1968), are not a politically organized tribe who give themselves an identifying name, but simply about seventy thousand people who occupy 200 square miles of hill and plains country and who are set off from their neighbors by small differences of dialect and custom. They speak a language in the Chad branch of the Afro-Asiatic family. The Kofyar hills in the past provided refuge from marauding and slave-raiding people; now the Kofyar are cultivating land southward out of the hills, although space for expansion is limited. The land enjoys fairly good soil and ample rain, an average of forty to sixty inches from April through October. Plants raised are grains—several millets, sorghum (also called guinea or kaffir corn), acha ("hungry rice," a relative of crab grass), maize, rice, and sesame seeds; roots and tubers—sweet potatoes, yams, coco yams (**taro**), and groundnuts; as well as beans, peas, pumpkins, okra, peppers, gourds, and more. Trees exploited include the oil palm and mango. Goats and

Grain, such as this late millet and acha, is placed to dry on racks in the homestead courtyard. The Kofyar established themselves in hill country refuges against marauders but are spreading to the level plains southward. (By permission from *Hill farmers of Nigeria: Cultural ecology of the Kofyar of the Jos Plateau,* Robert McC. Netting, Seattle: University of Washington Press, copyright 1968 by the University of Washington Press.)

The hoe-farming Kofyar of Nigeria raise grains, roots, tubers, and other domesticates and practice terracing, ridging, manuring, and crop rotation. Homesteads have mud-walled and thatched-roof dwellings, granaries, drying frames, and animal pens. (By permission from *Hill farmers of Nigeria: Cultural ecology of the Kofyar of the Jos Plateau,* Robert McC. Netting, Seattle: University of Washington Press, copyright 1968 by the University of Washington Press.)

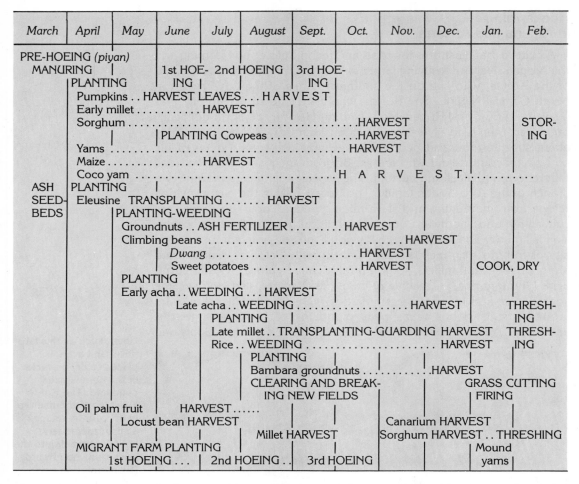

March	April	May	June	July	August	Sept.	Oct.	Nov.	Dec.	Jan.	Feb.

PRE-HOEING (*piyan*)
MANURING | 1st HOE- 2nd HOEING 3rd HOE-
|PLANTING ING | | ING
Pumpkins . . HARVEST LEAVES . . . H A R V E S T
Early millet . . . . HARVEST
Sorghum . . . . .HARVEST   STOR-ING
|PLANTING Cowpeas . . . . .HARVEST
Yams . . . . HARVEST
Maize . . . . HARVEST
Coco yam . . . . .H A R V E S T . . . .
ASH SEED-BEDS   PLANTING
Eleusine TRANSPLANTING . . . . . . HARVEST
|PLANTING-WEEDING |
Groundnuts . . ASH FERTILIZER . . . .' HARVEST
Climbing beans . . . . HARVEST
Dwang . . . . HARVEST
Sweet potatoes . . . . HARVEST   COOK, DRY
PLANTING | | |
Early acha . . WEEDING . . . HARVEST
Late acha . . WEEDING . . . . HARVEST   THRESH-ING
PLANTING | | |
Late millet . . TRANSPLANTING-GUARDING HARVEST THRESH-ING
Rice . . WEEDING . . . . HARVEST |ING
PLANTING |
Bambara groundnuts . . . . .HARVEST
CLEARING AND BREAK-ING NEW FIELDS   GRASS CUTTING FIRING
Oil palm fruit   HARVEST . . . . . .
Locust bean HARVEST   Canarium HARVEST
Millet HARVEST   Sorghum HARVEST . . THRESHING
MIGRANT FARM PLANTING   Mound yams
1st HOEING . . .   2nd HOEING . .   3rd HOEING

Farming calendar of the Kofyar, technological and economic base of the annual round. (By permission from *Hill farmers of Nigeria: Cultural ecology of the Kofyar of the Jos Plateau,* Robert McC. Netting, Seattle: University of Washington Press, copyright 1968 by the University of Washington Press.)

chickens, and lesser numbers of sheep, cows, and horses, are kept, the last three being regarded as indicators of wealth.

Kofyar tools, in the broad sense, are simple—short-handled iron hoes that can cut a deep furrow or skim the surface of the ground, narrow-bladed axes, old knife and spear blades for cutting grain, curved sickles for small grains and forage grass, tree trunk **mortars** and log **pestles**, grinding stones, winnowing trays, wooden bowls, coiled baskets, clay pots, calabashes, mud-walled granaries, and wooden drying frames.

The Kofyar hill farmers live in evenly dispersed family homesteads, each a round, mud-walled, and thatched-roof dwelling with its granaries drying frames, and animal pens, surrounded by intensively cultivated "homestead farms," whose fertility is replenished by compost from the goat pens and other animal manures. In addition the Kofyar practice extensive farming in swidden "bush fields" a thirty-minute walk distant which are fertilized only by ashes and by long periods of fallowing and in "migrant bush fields" in vacant plain land to the south which are several hours or a day distant. An impressive feature of Kofyar cultivation is the stepped terraces, which are faced with retaining walls, laid without mortar, a foot to six feet high, and which are constructed to deepen the soil, stabilize the ground on hills and slopes, and prevent

Culture in Its Technological Aspect

rapid runoff and erosion. The Kofyar further control runoff by heaping up the soil along rows of growing plants so that water is held in small, rectangular catch basins in the fields but does not inundate the plant roots. Most of this work is done on homestead farms, but where necessary the fallowed swiddens also are protected by low walls. The farmers display a remarkable knowledge of soils and what will grow best on

West African hoe farmers, Mossi of the Voltaic Republic. Women carry grain in from the fields. (Courtesy Herbert W. Butler.)

Mossi work party flailing millet. (Courtesy Herbert W. Butler.)

Communal winnowing of the millet grains after flailing. Mossi, Voltaic Republic. (Courtesy Herbert W. Butler.)

Expanded Energy Supply: Plant and Animal Domestication

them, and they shift to less demanding crops when fertility in a particular field declines.

"The hill Kofyar differ from many African farmers in that they have no period of the year when food is in very short supply. There is no annual 'hungry time'. . .in the hills, and older inhabitants can remember no time of scarcity that approached the severity of famine" (Netting 1968: 80-81). This, Netting points out, is due to their farming techniques (terracing, ridging, manuring, crop rotation), the variety of crops grown, and the different times they are planted (March to August) and mature (July to December). If one or more of the crops should fail, others are likely to succeed. By Netting's rough estimate, Kofyar farmers produce enough to supply one and one-half to two pounds of grain or two to two and one-half pounds of root crops per person per day (the daily mean food intake); their sorghum and acha porridge with its sauces made from greens, their millet beer, their groundnuts and beans (they eat little meat) supply proteins, minerals, and vitamins. While caloric estimates are not available, the comparable Sura people to the north have been found to have available 2,704 calories per person per day, and it is probable the Kofyar do better than that.

Terraced houses in Old Oraibi Pueblo, Arizona, photographed in the 1870s by John K. Hillers, pioneer Western photographer. The mesa-top town has been inhabited continuously since the twelfth century. Its culture was based upon maize, bean, and squash cultivation. (Courtesy Smithsonian Institution National Anthropological Archives.)

Culture in Its Technological Aspect

A different kind of hoe farming, in an arid land, and one which has not had a swiddening base, is that of the Hopi Indians of Arizona, who numbered about three thousand people living in eleven towns in 1940, the ethnographic present of the classical monograph about them written by Mischa Titiev (1944). The American Southwest is a dry plateau flanked by mountain peaks rising more than 11,000 feet in the east and cut by river canyons. The Hopi built their closely packed, multistoried houses of flat stone on three high, barren mesas and farmed the land below. One of the villages, Old Oraibi, which has been inhabited continuously since the twelfth century, housed about one thousand people at the beginning of the twentieth century, when it was the only settlement on the westernmost Third Mesa, but the population has since declined.

Hopi men cultivate maize, beans, and squash. Maize takes three to five months to mature, and much of the scanty rain falls too early or too late to water it. However, because of the lay of the land, most of the surface runoff is channeled in floods through the valleys, where the overflow is caught in dams and embankments, the underground seepage from the mountain slopes comes out in springs at the foot of the mesas, where it is retained in catch basins and led to irrigated gardens. Thus the Hopi capture both surface and underground sources for their corn fields, which are about an acre in size (Forde 1950).

The agricultural year begins in February, when weeds are trampled and removed by hand and with wooden weed cutters, hoes, and rakes; the ground is broken up with a bladed stick, and when planting begins near the end of April or later ten to twenty seeds of maize are dropped into widely spaced holes made with a digging stick. The clustered stalks make a bush growth; the soil around them is weeded and heaped up in basins, although it is not hilled. Beans and squash are grown in alternate rows with the corn, or in separate small fields. Maturing in September, the heads of corn are harvested, spread on housetops to

The northernmost of the Pueblos, Taos, New Mexico, also has terraced houses. The Rio Grande or eastern Pueblo culture, like that of the western Pueblo people such as the Hopi, was based upon cultivation of maize, beans, and squash, but irrigation was extensive. (Courtesy Jane Hawkins.)

dry, shelled, and ground into meal between stones—the mano and metate—by the women.

With drought an ever-present danger, the Hopi keep a year's supply of corn on hand; if in the past there was a bad stretch of two years or more, they had to fall back on wild plants such as juniper berries, pinyon nuts, mesquite beans, roots, and seeds. Game is scarce in the Southwest, although the Hopi had communal rabbit hunts in late autumn, catching the animals with flat-bladed throwing sticks and clubs. And they hunted deer, mountain sheep, and antelope with bow and arrow (the gun, of course, has long since replaced the bow). Domesticated sheep and cattle now have taken the place of wild game. It is interesting that sheep are not slaughtered routinely, but only before festivities (Titiev 1944).

Studies of calorie or energy production are not available for the period when Hopi farming was devoted wholly to subsistence, but it is worth noting that Titiev found, on the basis of a chart he kept for five adult married males for some 108 days from August into November, that they averaged 77 days of work at gardening, herding, house building, wood hauling, and miscellaneous activities. That would mean a day's work of varying length on 71 percent of the days for which records were kept—not up to the demands of the 5- or 6-day work week which we think of as standard in the Western world but more than that of the hunters we have looked at.

Wet rice farming:
Terracing and irrigation

The massive systems of terraces and canals of China, Japan, India, Southeast Asia, the Indies, and the Philippines that are part of the technology of wet rice cultivation present a sharp contrast to the fields and gardens of the hoe farmers and swiddeners. Terracing and irrigation is not confined to rice, for taro, which requires more water than the yam often found with it, is an old crop in Southeast Asia and is grown by this method throughout Melanesia and in Polynesia. The economic botanist Jacques Barrau among others believes that rice first appeared as a " 'desired weed'...in ditches of wet taro gardens in the tropical and continental part of the Indo-Pacific area, i.e., from India to Indo-China" (1968: 128) and that it is a later domesticate in irrigated fields first used for taro.

The pattern of cultivation of wet rice begins with seed beds in which the plants are allowed to grow until they are several inches tall. The soil of the padis must be prepared carefully—weeded, pulverized, and soaked to mud. When the rains begin, the seedlings are transplanted by hand, an arduous task for men, women, and children. "Once the seedlings are transplanted, however, there is little more to do except to keep the dikes in repair and to regulate the flow of water, for during most of the growing season the padis must be covered by a few inches of water so that only the upper stalks and leaves of the rice plant can be seen waving above the surface. Shortly before the rice ripens, the water is drained from the fields, and about a month later the rice is harvested" (Burling 1965: 30). One effect of the standing water is that it inhibits weed growth, although weeding must still be done.

142   Culture in Its Technological Aspect

It is human labor that is the most important factor in rice production, for the tools employed are simple—hoes, shovels, digging sticks, rakes, and baskets of various sorts for transporting and winnowing the grain. In some areas, domesticated animals such as water buffalo or carabao are used to trample the mud, and animal fertilizers are applied to the soil. The second factor is knowledge of the role of water and techniques for its control; it must be contained and drained, kept gently flowing if possible. Fertility of the padi is perpetually maintained by nutrients carried by water from the higher levels from which it falls. Citing a report that rice padis in the Philippines have been maintained in place for over 1,000 years, the ecologist Eugene P. Odum remarks that it is "a record of success that few agricultural systems in use today can claim" (Odum 1971: 103). The anthropologist Clifford Geertz observes that some areas in Java "reach extraordinary rural population densities of nearly two thousand persons per square kilometer without any significant decline in per-hectare rice production" (1969: 21). (A hectare is a metric area unit, the equivalent of 2.4711 acres.) He adds: "Given maintenance of irrigation facilities, a reasonable level of farming technique, and no autogenous changes in the physical setting, the *sawah* (as the Javanese call the rice terrace) seems virtually indestructible."

Productivity of this technology in one Chinese village has been calculated by Marvin Harris (1971: 203-16) on the basis of labor and yield studies made by Chih-i Chang and Fei Tsiao-t'ung. The village, Luts'un, had a population of about 700, with 418 adults taking part in cultivation of rice (75 percent of the total output) as well as soy beans, corn, manioc, and potatoes planted on the padi margins. Using a formula he

Terraced and irrigated fields in Japan. A scene between Nagano and Tokyo. Traditionally a labor-intensive mode of farming, irrigated terracing requires knowledge of the role of water and its control. It is associated with high population densities. (Courtesy C. Melvin Aikens.)

Expanded Energy Supply: Plant and Animal Domestication

devised which takes account of calories produced in a year, the number of producers, the hours they worked, and the calories they expended, Harris found that in rice production alone the net return, which he labels the "technoenvironmental efficiency," of the system, as given by the ratio of the product to the labor put into it, was 53.5. In other words, 53.5 calories were produced for every calorie expended. (In contrast, in terms of his formula, Bushman technoenvironmental efficiency was 9.6 and that of the Tsembaga 18.) The people of Luts'un, Harris points out, could not and did not consume by themselves that return on their labor. They required (on the basis of 2,500 calories per person per day) 638,000,000 calories in the course of a year, and they produced 3,788,000,000 (considering all crops, not just rice). In the advanced larger culture in which they lived, the energy was diverted into other parts of the whole system.

The Kalinga produce both wet rice on irrigated terraces and dry rice on swidden fields, supplementing it with sugarcane, sweet potatoes, and peas and adding protein from carabao, pig, fowl, dogs, and cattle. We do not have figures on hours of labor and amount of calories or energy produced, but the situation is in all likelihood comparable with that of the Chinese villagers. And lest we fragment the picture unnecessarily, we might remind ourselves that the materials and energies represented by houses and house building, the raising and sacrificing of pigs and chickens, the playing of gongs and flutes, the flowing dances, and the counseling of the pangats can be looked at as a system which draws upon domesticated and wild plants and animals and the biological capacities of the colorful Kalinga for its maintenance. Its technology is basic, for it is that part that confronts directly the source of all energies, the sun-activated world of nature. But it is not the only part or aspect, and we should not forget, in our search for understanding, the social organization and ideology that rest on it nor the superorganic environment of other cultures, of the Bontok and Ifugao, and beyond them the Republic of Indonesia, and beyond it the world system which is now relevant to the Kalinga (so relevant, in fact, that Barton was able to calculate market values of their possessions in pesos if not in the calories their technology produced).

African and Southwest Asian herders

As we do certain other modes of agriculture, Americans tend to view herding or pastoralism ethnocentrically, having in mind cattle ranches and dairy farms that produce meat and milk for market. Both stem from European mixed agriculture, which combines plow cultivation of hard grains on winter fallowed fields with the raising of hoofed animals for meat and milk, as well as for their manure, hides, and wool. "The food base of bread and milk and meat, which the Chinese say gives Europeans a distinctive stink, is. . .a common and distinctive Old World culture complex" (Arensberg 1963: 85). Other peoples may prefer porridge, milk, and blood, and, although they use animal hides, wool, and manure, the relationship of herding and farming is different than in the European system.

A major difference is stated succinctly by Rada and Neville Dyson-

Culture in Its Technological Aspect

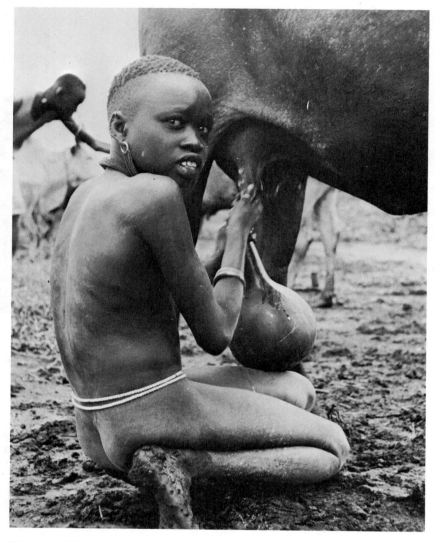

Nuer girl milking a cow. She collects the milk in a bottle-necked gourd. Milking is done by women, girls, and uninitiated boys, but driving the cattle is the work of the males. (Courtesy Pitt Rivers Museum, University of Oxford.)

Hudson (1969), one a biologist and the other an anthropologist, who studied several groups of African herders. Ranching and dairying involve the care of large numbers of animals by small numbers of workers whose aim is to convert vegetation into meat and milk for market. Subsistence pastoralism depends on the largest possible numbers of animals being raised on the available land so as to support *directly* the largest possible number of people. In subsistence herding, meat is used much less (animals are too valuable to slaughter regularly) than milk and blood from living animals. It is the base of a kind of cultural system that is often in equilibrium with its environments to a finely honed degree and reaches deep into African and Asian history.

An example of subsistence herding is provided by the Nuer, a Nilotic people of the Sudan, the subject of studies by the British social anthropologist E. E. Evans-Pritchard (1940, 1951, 1956), whose books are widely recognized classics. The Nuer, who comprise several tribes without a central organization, numbered about two hundred thousand

Nuer humped, long-horned cattle rest between the byres and huts of a homestead built on a mound. (Courtesy Pitt Rivers Museum, University of Oxford.)

when Evans-Pritchard lived among them for periods from 1930 to 1936 totaling about a year. They raise humped, long-horned cattle, which provide the major part of their subsistence, and some sheep and goats and cultivate sorghum (millet), a little maize, and a few beans. Fishing is important during part of the year, but hunting and the collecting of wild plants are minimal.

Nuerland is a nearly level plain cut by the White Nile and tributaries in the southern Sudan; part of the year it is covered with waist-high savannah grasses and during the other part by swamps resulting from the heavy rains (which begin at the end of May, have their maximum in July and August, and cease only in November) and by the flooding rivers. There is, then, a marked wet season from May to December and a dry one from December to May, the change coming quite suddenly.

During the rainy season, the Nuer live in villages consisting of **wattle-and-daub** houses and cattle byres (barns) placed on higher ground. The rainy season is gardening time. Gardens are cultivated for from five to ten years, after which, with movement of the village, they lie fallow; there is no deliberate manuring or rotation of crops; the hoe is the principal tool for preparing the ground and for weeding. Only enough grain is raised for current needs and to last, if eaten sparingly during the dry season, until the next harvest, the surplus being kept in grass and earthenware containers in the huts. It is eaten with milk as porridge and brewed into beer.

When the rain ends, the ground dries quickly, and water supplies near the village hillocks disappear. Nuer burn off the overcropped savannah near the villages and farther afield, because the grass that springs up after burning is more succulent than that which grows rank and tough in unburned savannah. The cattle are driven to temporary campsites on burned areas near available water pools, then back to the villages for a short time to eat the stalks of a second and last harvest,

Culture in Its Technological Aspect

August shower in Nuerland. In the rainy season, from May to November, the Nuer live in villages on elevated ground and tend their gardens. The principal farming implement is the hoe. (Courtesy Pitt Rivers Museum, University of Oxford.)

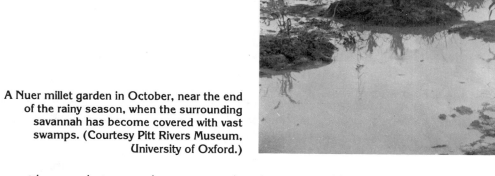

A Nuer millet garden in October, near the end of the rainy season, when the surrounding savannah has become covered with vast swamps. (Courtesy Pitt Rivers Museum, University of Oxford.)

and then, with several stops, to larger camps beside rivers and lakes, where they remain until June. In dry-season camps, men sleep behind wind screens and women in small beehive huts, and the cattle are protected from predators at night within thornbush **kraals**. Finally, boys and girls drive the cattle back to the wet-season villages, preceded by the oldsters, who have gone on about a month ahead to prepare the ground for sowing millet and maize. This is the transhumant round, the movement from winter to summer ranges and back again.

"It has been remarked," writes Evans-Pritchard (1940: 36), "that the Nuer might be called parasites of the cow, but it might be said with equal force that the cow is a parasite of the Nuer, whose lives are spent in ensuring its welfare. They build byres, kindle fires, and clean kraals for its comfort; move from villages to camps, from camp to camp, and

Expanded Energy Supply: Plant and Animal Domestication

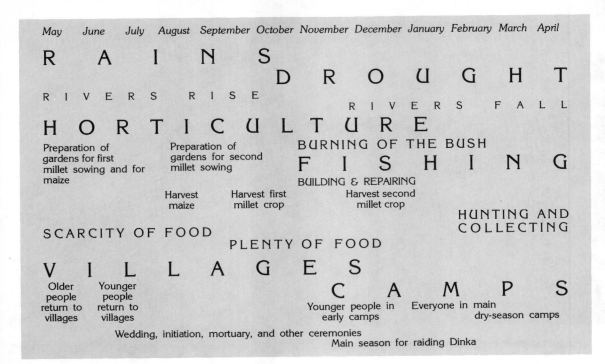

| May | June | July | August | September | October | November | December | January | February | March | April |

R A I N S   **D R O U G H T**

RIVERS RISE   RIVERS FALL

H O R T I C U L T U R E

Preparation of gardens for first millet sowing and for maize

Preparation of gardens for second millet sowing

BURNING OF THE BUSH

F I S H I N G

BUILDING & REPAIRING

Harvest maize   Harvest first millet crop   Harvest second millet crop

HUNTING AND COLLECTING

SCARCITY OF FOOD   PLENTY OF FOOD

V I L L A G E S

C A M P S

Older people return to villages   Younger people return to villages   Younger people in early camps   Everyone in main dry-season camps

Wedding, initiation, mortuary, and other ceremonies

Main season for raiding Dinka

Annual round of the Nuer, incorporating what Evans-Pritchard called "three planes of rhythm, physical, ecological, and social." (By permission from *The Nuer: A description of the modes of livelihood and political institutions of a Nilotic people*, E. E. Evans-Pritchard, Oxford: Clarendon Press, copyright 1940 by Clarendon Press.)

from camps back to villages, for its health; defy wild beasts for its protection; and fashion ornaments for its adornment. It lives a gentle, indolent, sluggish life thanks to the Nuer's devotion. In truth, the relationship is symbiotic; cattle and men sustain life by their reciprocal services to one another. . . ."

A Nuer cow is milked twice a day and yields four to five pints, not counting the calf's share; the two or three lactating cows in a homestead byre of about ten head provide about twelve pints, or a pint and a half per person in the average family group. The yield from perhaps five sheep and goats, which is minimal, is drunk by the small children and is not counted in the output calculation. Meat is eaten, but only that of cattle slaughtered for rituals (there are enough of these, however, to ensure a fair intake) or of those who die a natural death. "Nuer are very fond of meat, and declare that on the death of a cow, 'The eyes and the heart are sad, but the teeth and the stomach are glad.' 'A man's stomach prays to God, independently of his mind, for such gifts' " (Evans-Pritchard 1940: 26).

The Nuer, then, have a mixed subsistence derived from their cattle, from their gardens, and from fishing. While cattle are central to it, there cannot be complete dependence upon them, one reason being that the herds are often depleted by rinderpest, a fatal disease that entered Nuer territory about fifty years before Evans-Pritchard's fieldwork. On the other hand, because of the long dry season, they cannot depend upon cultivation, and in the floods of the wet season they cannot fish productively. As their ethnographer sees it, ecological relations "appear to be in a state of equilibrium. As long as present relations exist cattle husbandry, horticulture, and fishing can be pursued but cannot be improved. Man holds his own in the struggle but does not advance"

Culture in Its Technological Aspect

(Evans-Pritchard 1940: 92). The system, in terms of our orientation, has reached a stable stage in relation to its environments.

The same basic adaptation of a cultural system to a savannah environment through a mixed herding and agricultural technology, but with an interesting settlement variation, is illustrated by the Karimojong, a group of some sixty thousand people who occupy 4,000 square miles of semiarid plain in northeastern Uganda, the country south of the Sudan (Dyson-Hudson and Dyson-Hudson 1969). Rainfall there is more uncertain and localized than in Nuerland, and the herds are more mobile and are driven longer distances than among the Nuer.

Like the Nuer, the Karimojong maintain farming settlements where they grow sorghum and maize. Unlike Nuer villages, which are located on virtual islands and are occupied only during wet-season flooding, those of the Karimojong are permanent. Married women and their daughters cultivate cereals in fields around the settlements, subsisting on the grain and getting milk only when the cattle are close at hand or cheese when it is carried from the camps. There is always water at the villages, but grazing is sparse; men and herdboys move the cattle from camp to camp (one herd was driven fifty-five miles distant during a two-year period), living almost exclusively on milk and blood, rounded out with a little beer that women and girls bring them on short visits. Lactating cows yield about four pints of milk above the calves' share when grass is abundant and two pints when it is not; each man and boy drinks about two and a half pints of milk and a portion of blood each day. Again, Karimojong do not slaughter their animals except for ceremonies; they prefer to keep the whole herd as insurance against losses by disease, drought, and raid. Although they are minimally involved in markets, it is not profitable to sell cattle, because the return is not enough to provide much in the way of grain. As among the Nuer, grass is burned to improve its growth for cattle, and wells are dug occasionally to increase the water supply.

A statement by Evans-Pritchard (1940: 36) regarding Nuer adaptation—"...Nuer cattle husbandry could not in any important particular be improved in their present ecological relations..."—is seconded by the Dyson-Hudsons (1969: 11) for the Karimojong: "In the ecological system actually presented by the subsistence herding of the Karimojong it is hard to see how their rationality can be improved on."

Although they stand in contrast to these East African cattle herders in obvious ways, the specialized camel-breeding Bedouin of the northern Arabian peninsula also demonstrate the use of domesticated animals as resource and tool. The camel enables the Bedouin to exploit parts of the land that other technologies cannot and affords them the mobility and fighting strength (again, a mark of cultural energies and their deployment) that have given cultures like this domination over herders of sheep and goats, farmers, and town dwellers for 3,000 years (Sweet 1965a, 1965b). Their system and its environments are more complicated than the Africans', for this lifeway evolved adjacent to and in interaction with strong states based on farming and commerce, and the Bedouin depend on the townspeople for such things as grain, goats' hair cloth for their black tents, woven cotton and wool for clothing, and weapons and utensils, in return selling them surplus camels.

The camel-breeding Bedouin of Southwest Asian desert lands developed a lifeway symbiotic with that of the farmers and town dwellers. This man is a Bedouin of the Negev. (Courtesy Joseph Ginat.)

Thus, it is not a lifeway that is self-sufficient, but one in symbiotic relation with superorganic as well as natural environments.

During the season of scattered winter rains in northern Arabia, from October to May, camels can live on desert grasses and shrubs over wide areas of the tribal ranges, for with green vegetation they can go for as long as thirty days without water. In the summer dry season, the Bedouin must seek permanent water holes or watercourses, for although the camels can subsist on dried grass they must be watered every three days or so. Over the yearly round they are driven from pasture to pasture along a broad tribal migration path that averages 600 kilometers and may reach 800 from end to end. Pasturages are vacated before they are exhausted and take about two weeks to renew themselves. Grass in brackish swamps may be burned to provide better growth during the following rainy season. As the anthropologist Louise Sweet (1965a: 134) remarks, "The capacity of camels to tolerate extremes of heat and lack of water, to thrive on desert plants beyond the capacities of other domestic animals, and to cover great distances in the course of nomadic grazing supports Bedouin life in the outer ranges of the ecological niche of desert pastoralism."

The camel provides both milk and meat, although, as in the case of the African peoples, milk is more important. A female camel has her first offspring at six years of age, and then gives birth to one every other year. Young males are butchered for meat, but a milking camel, which has a lactating period of from eleven to fifteen months and, depending upon forage, yields from one to seven liters of milk a day (a liter is the equivalent of 1.0567 U.S. liquid quarts), is never butchered. Eight to ten camels support a tent of four or five people. A flexible system of camping units and tribal sections enables the Bedouin to split the herds when foraging conditions demand; an area well watered in one year may be barren the next. Game and edible wild plants are scarce in the Arabian desert; most important among the latter is the *samh* seed, which can be ground into flour.

Culture in Its Technological Aspect

Prelude to domestication

Where, when, and how did the farming-and-herding lifeway begin? There is no single such lifeway, judging from those just briefly sketched in their technological aspect. Domestication of plants and animals did not begin all in one place or at one time, and there is no particular reason to suppose that all farming-and-herding tools and techniques are lineal descendants of those found in the centers labelled as earliest by archeologists. In those areas, the earliest domesticators put to use the tools, techniques, and knowledge they had possessed for millennia to maintain and increase their food supply, and so possibly did others later. Nevertheless, what happened in Southwest Asia around 8000 B.C. and in China and Mesoamerica not long after is of importance because it underlay the rise of civilizations.

You will recall that the quarry of the hunters of Kostenki, at a time more than 10,000 years ago, was the big game of the late Pleistocene, particularly the mammoth, reindeer, wooly rhinoceros, and wild horse. European contemporaries, the Magdalenians, specialized in hunting reindeer; in Southwest Asia at the same time people of the Zagros mountains, in western Iran, sought the wild goat; and the Natufians of Syro-Palestine hunted the gazelle. The food supply of none of these Upper Paleolithic peoples was confined to the dominant game; they caught other animals and foraged for wild plants, but some specialization is the mark of their food quest.

Then the climates of Eurasia became generally warmer, and the Holocene or Neothermal epoch succeeded the Pleistocene. In the north, tundra and steppe gave way to forest and marsh, and the herds of big game animals retreated and disappeared, to be replaced by woodland fauna. On the north European plain, the cultures collectively termed Maglemosian (*maglemose* means "big bog" in Danish) illustrate adaptation to the new conditions in this "microlithic" period—so called because of the small flint flakes with which knives and projectiles

Four Bedouin of the Negev, one on horseback. In the summer dry season the Bedouin had to seek permanent water holes or watercourses for their stock and moved on a broad migration path from pasture to pasture. (Courtesy Joseph Ginat.)

were edged and tipped. Adze blades, held in wood and antler sleeves and fixed to wooden handles, were used to cut trees, hollow out dugout canoes, and shape paddles. Long wooden bows were the hunting weapon, their arrows barbed and tipped with microliths or made with a blunt head for shooting birds and small animals. Some tools, such as axes and club heads, were made of ground and polished stone. Now the subsistence quest was spread over a broad spectrum of resources— elk, red and roe deer, and auroch in the forest; fish and shellfish from the lakes and emerging beaches, the fish being caught in fiber nets equipped with bark floats and stone weights; and water plants, gathered from the bogs and lakes. Evidence of Maglemosian camps has been found from Ulster and eastern England, the north German plain, Denmark and south Sweden, and as far east as the Urals in Russia (Clark 1971: 79-83). Others of these "forest folk," as Gordon Childe called them, lived south of the Maglemosians in the country of sandy soils and scrub forests (the Tardenoisians) and in France and central Europe (the Azilians). In all likelihood, all had once been specialized hunters, and now they adapted to new environments and new demands.

Early centers of domestication

Southwest Asia. However, it was not the Europeans and other northerners who moved first from collecting and hunting to domestication, but Southwest Asians in "the region of the hilly flanks of rain-watered grasslands which build up to the high mountain ridges of Iran, Iraq, Turkey, Syria, and Palestine" (Braidwood 1967: 95). Domestication arose from antecedent cultures like the Natufian, itself dated around 8000 B.C.; Natufians hunted gazelles, but they also cut wild cereals with sickles made from microliths set into straight bone handles, and they ground the grain in pecked-out stone mortars with pestles. There is no clear sign of domestication of plants and animals over the whole region at this time, but the grains collected, particularly barley and wheat, and the animals hunted, especially goats and sheep, were the ones identified as being first under the control of farmers and herders. The site of Jarmo, dated around 6750 B.C., exemplifies an "era of primary village farming communities." It is a mound near present-day Kirkuk, in Iraq, on which were reared successive villages of twenty or more multi-roomed houses with packed mud walls set on rough stone foundations. With sickles set with obsidian (volcanic glass), the people of Jarmo reaped domesticated barley and two varieties of wheat, probably parched the grain in clay ovens, ground it in mortars and between grinding stones, and ate it as porridge from stone bowls. They had domesticated goats, sheep, and dogs and after a time raised pigs (Braidwood 1967: 118-21). A transition from hunting and gathering to farming and herding took place, then, in Southwest Asia 8,000 or more years ago. How did it come about?

The process, as the archeologist Kent V. Flannery (1969) sees it, in ecological terms involved a gradual transfer by humans of wild emmer wheat and barley from an "oak-pistachio woodland belt" that flanks the Zagros mountains of western Iran to the lower Assyrian steppe and as gradual a change in the relationship between humans and the wild sheep, goat, ox, and pig that they pursued. Biological changes in the

Culture in Its Technological Aspect

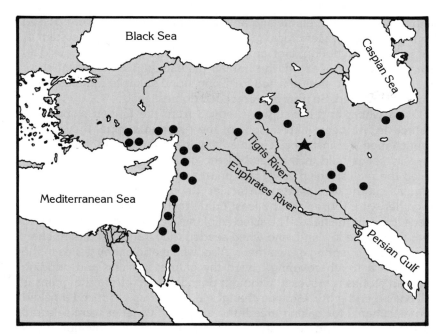

Sites that show a transition to farming are scattered at the edge of the upland regions of Southwest Asia, not in the Tigris-Euphrates plain itself. The location of Jarmo is indicated by a star. (After Braidwood 1975 and Clark 1971.)

wild plant and animal species, linked with mutations, **hybridization,** and altered selection pressures, accompanied their removal from earlier habitats to the new ones, changes which the botanist and zoologist can discern between wild and domestic species.

The well-watered woodland belt, its slopes covered with oak, maple, juniper, hawthorn, pistachio, and wild pear and hard-grained annual grasses such as wild emmer wheat, barley, and oats, has high alluvial valleys and alpine meadows. In general, however, it is too rugged for agriculture. There are warm and dry summers and cool and wet winters, and permanent streams flowing through it are fed by springs whose water sources are winter rains and mountain snows. Wild goats frequent the drier valleys. There the people hunted and gathered for millennia. The adjoining Assyrian steppe has hotter and drier summers, but winter rains cover fertile meadows with Bermuda and canary grass and wild narcissus, and the wide streams have farmable floodplains. Gazelle, wild asses, and cattle fed on the grasses, and carp and catfish swam in the rivers. It is an area which archeologists have found thickly sown with prehistoric farming villages similar to Jarmo. But originally wild wheat and barley did not grow on the steppe; their natural habitat was the rocky upland slopes. The food quest was made efficient when the plants were induced to grow on level ground and the animals were constrained and driven from pasture to pasture at different seasons.

The preagricultural Southwest Asians hunted and gathered over the whole region, not only in the woodland and on the steppe but also, with lesser returns, on the dry Mesopotamian alluvial plain (the later site of city civilizations) and on the edge of the Iranian high central plateau. They exploited virtually everything edible and useful. What they gathered and caught varied from place to place, and products of different local areas were carried out of their natural habitats and mixed together; furthermore, plants and animals in one local area were passed from group to adjacent local group in what Flannery calls a system of primitive redistribution. Not only food, but materials such as obsidian from Turkey, copper from the Iranian plateau, and natural asphalt or bitumen from the steppe (used for fixing stone flakes to handles) were thus redistributed. So transfers preceded domestication.

When wheat and barley were moved from the upland slopes and planted in the deep alluvial soils of the Assyrian steppe, they underwent change. For instance, it is an advantage in the wild for the plant to have its seeds held in the head of the grain by a brittle joining axis, called the rachis, which easily falls apart and disperses the seed. When humans cut the wild plants with sickles, the ones they were most likely to gather were those with the least brittle rachis, a rachis that held the seeds firmly in the head. The selected plants were the ones likely to find their way to the lowland, and when seeded they transmitted their characteristics to offspring grown there. Also, wheat and barley grains in the wild have a tough covering, called the glume; roasting and grinding between stones removes it, although porridge made from the grains is still coarse and gritty. Genetic changes in the plants produced a naked kernel, suitable for baking bread; the emerging varieties were selected by the planters and harvesters. Other mutations and hybridizations

Contemporary farming village in the foothills of the Samaria mountains. Building on high and rocky ground conserves the level land for crops. A mound of grain lies on the threshing floor in the foreground. (Courtesy Joseph Ginat.)

154

Culture in Its Technological Aspect

gave new high-yielding and free-threshing strains that were selected by the farmers and spread through the region at the expense of older ones. Oats, which had a wider range than wheat and barley in the wild, probably sprouted as weeds in the lowland fields and underwent changes. The point is that plants transferred from one zone to another in the primitive redistribution network met different selection pressures operating on naturally occurring mutations. As for planting itself, that is the least of problems in deciphering the domestication process. Humans for millennia had known that plants sprouted from seeds—where, when, in what seasons, and under what conditions (White 1959: 283). Duplicating and improving these conditions, for instance by seeding in watered places or by removing competitive grasses, were relatively simple.

Parallel processes occurred in animals. The hairy wild sheep, for instance, became a wooly one as humans, taking advantage of natural mutations (the actual mechanism of mutation was unknown to them, of course) selected animals with woolier pelts. The habits and habitats of the first animals domesticated—sheep, goat, ox, and pig—were well known to their hunters. And these species, as Charles A. Reed writes, "were already socially and psychologically preadapted to being tamed without loss of reproductive abilities." They had become accustomed to humans, and intractable animals were removed progressively from the herds, perhaps. Domestication took place when "the human culture milieu had evolved to a state of organization such that the animals could be controlled, and maintained generation after generation in a condition of dependence"—a condition provided by the sedentary communities of Southwest Asian farmers (Reed 1959: 1,636).

Yoked animals are driven over the stalks of grain on the hard-packed earth threshing floor. The practice probably began with plant and animal domestication several thousand years ago. (Courtesy Joseph Ginat.)

Expanded Energy Supply: Plant and Animal Domestication

The Americas. The American Indians could not domesticate wheat, barley, and oats, or sheep, goats, and cattle, for these resources were absent from their continents, but they brought into cultivation maize and **quinoa**, the "Irish" and sweet potato, manioc, sunflower, beans, and a host of other native plants in widely separated areas. Only in the Andes were there larger animals amenable to taming, the camel-related llama and alpaca, as well as the humble guinea pig. Turkeys, moscovy ducks, and dogs about completed the inventory. Maize was foremost as a source of energy for culture building. It is a plant with an impeccable American ancestry, originally a small-grained popcorn with kernels encased in pods or glumes. Its pollens have been detected in cores, dated back to 80,000 years, drilled into lake beds in Mexico. Evidence of the use of wild pod corn goes back to 7000 B.C. in the valley of Tehuacan on the mountain boundary between the states of Puebla and Oaxaca, where its evolution has been documented.

Richard S. MacNeish (1964a, 1964b) directed the excavation of twelve sites in Tehuacan valley which provide a story of the specific evolution of a segment of American Indian culture, literally from its grass roots, and before that to a time 12,000 years ago when extinct antelope and horse were hunted there. From about 10,000 to 7000 B.C., the Tehuacan people, using flaked stone projectile points and scrapers, and perhaps traps that have left no record, subsisted on jackrabbits, rats, birds, turtles, and wild plants, plus an occasional kill of large animals. Between 6700 and 5000 B.C., there was a marked shift toward dependence on wild plants, which included beans, amaranth, and chili peppers. Squash and avocado were domesticated. Pecked and ground grinding stones, mortars, and pestles appeared in large numbers, and choppers, useful for digging and mashing roots and plants, appeared among the older flake tools. In the phase called Coxcatlan culture, between 5000 and 3400 B.C., domesticates were augmented by maize, gourds, zapotes (a tree fruit), more species of beans, and chili peppers, and, as for tools, the characteristic American mano and metate (a hand

Location of earliest known farming in the Americas—the Tehuacan Valley in Mexico.

Tehuacan Valley

Where cultivation first
appeared in South
America—the north
central coast of Peru.

stone wielded upon a grinding slab) and hollowed out water jugs and
bowls were in use.

"It was in the phase following the Coxcatlan that the people of
Tehuacan made the fundamental shift. By about 3400 B.C., the food
provided by agriculture rose to about 30 percent of the total, domesti-

Expanded Energy Supply: Plant and Animal Domestication   **157**

cated animals (starting with the dog) made their appearance, and the people formed their first fixed settlements—small pit-house villages. By this stage (which we call the Abejas culture) they lived at a subsistence level that can be regarded as a foundation for the beginning of civiliza- ton" (MacNeish 1964a: 10).

It was a humble beginning, even so. For the first of the four phases of cultural development touched upon, it is estimated the Tehuacanos comprised only about three family groups of four to eight people who moved from wet- and dry-season camps in the food quest. Early in Cox- catlan times, with a broader inventory of tools and the first tentative control of food supply, they had increased by four times. At the end of the period, there was ten times the original population (MacNeish 1964b: 532-34). Not until after 1500 B.C. did the Tehuacanos be- come full-fledged agriculturalists, living in wattle-and-daub houses in villages of a hundred to three hundred people, with an estimated total population 150 times the original one (1964b: 534, 536).

We must not assume that civilization and its consequences in the Americas were played out on this small stage, although it may be the most meticulously documented one from its beginnings. Other areas in the highlands of Mexico and Central America also passed the threshold to major emphasis on cultivation around 1500 B.C. Maize appeared first on the north central coast of Peru around 2000 B.C., apparently derived from the north via a highland route. But there had been squash, cotton, and possibly bean farming among Peruvian fishermen before 3000 B.C., and between 2500 B.C. and about 1500 B.C. farming, based upon squash, lima and jack beans, chili peppers, avocados, and several other native plants, had become universal on the Peruvian coast. Major cultivated plants in ancient Peru, all of them American and most of them South American in origin, numbered about forty (Lanning 1967).

China. By 1500 B.C., north China was moving out of prehistory into history with the beginning of the Yin-Shang dynasties and the Bronze Age. When the village farming-and-herding cultures that underlay Yin- Shang began has not been established with certainty. There is a gap between blade- and microlith-using technologies of North Asian hunt- ers, gatherers, and fishermen and those of the cultivators, although Chinese archeologists have postulated an intervening Sheng-wen (cord-marked pottery) period (Chang 1965: 507-8; 1962: 178-79). It is known that as the glacial age ended and **Neothermal** conditions succeeded it, hunters and fishermen occupied the eastern fringes of the western north China highlands. It is generally agreed that farming began in a "north China nuclear area" in the great bend of the Hwang- ho or Yellow River, where the provinces of Honan, Shansi, and Shensi join; the culture is named Yang-shao (red pottery), and its dating is uncertain.

Yang-shao swidden farmers, wielding chipped, pecked, or ground stone axes, cut and burned the forest and cultivated millet and dry rice with hoes, spades, digging sticks, and weeding knives made of wood, antler, bone, stone, clay, and shell. Dogs and pigs, and possibly sheep, goats, and cattle, were domesticated. The first Chinese farmers raised silkworms and possibly cultivated hemp for fibers to spin and weave into fabrics; cooking pots, water and storage jars, bowls, and cups were

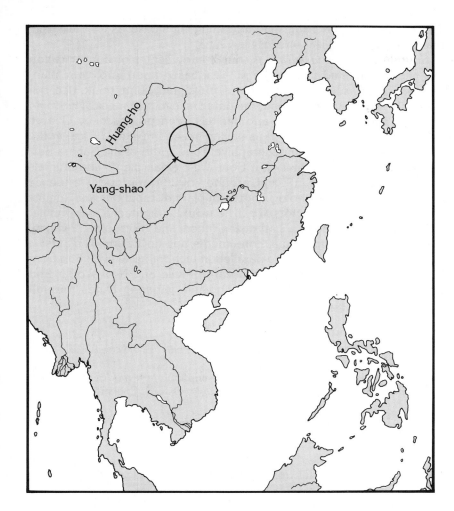

Cultivation in China began in the region of the Great Bend of the Huang-ho or Yellow River. The earliest farming culture is called Yang-shao.

made of fired clay. They used bow and arrow, harpoons, spears, and hooks to hunt and fish, although hunting and fishing only supplemented the domesticated food supply. Their villages, 650 to 1,000 feet in extent, consisted of a dozen or so round or rectangular dwellings, built partly underground, and some of them of a partitioned longhouse type (Chang 1962: 179-82). A significant thing about the Yang-shao villages in the nuclear area is that they were located between wooded highlands to the west and swampy lowlands to the east, a zone presenting the same kind of opportunities for interchange and redistribution of products we met with in Southwest Asia.

Yang-shao grew into the culture called Lung-shan (black pottery), in which millet was still the staple crop and dry rice continued to be harvested. But an additional cultigen (cultivated plant) appears in this culture—wheat. Cattle, sheep, and goats appeared to increase in importance, and to them was added the domesticated horse. Settlements remained in one place longer than in Yang-shao times, increased in size, and were surrounded by permanent earth walls. The Lung-shan culture spread east, north, and south, even to swampy areas, where earth mounds were heaped up to provide building sites (Chang 1962:

Expanded Energy Supply: Plant and Animal Domestication

182-86). It was on a Yang-shao and Lung-shan base, as we have said, that Bronze Age civilization arose in China.

Southeast Asia and Africa. A fourth early center of domestication has been postulated for Southeast Asia, based upon taro, yam, plantain, breadfruit, sugarcane, and citrus fruits, and, some think, rice, but there is no solid evidence about the time and circumstances of its origin (Burling 1965: 28-33). And another has been proposed by George Peter Murdock (1959: 64-70) as having arisen in Negro Africa, at the western end of the Sudan geographical zone south of the Sahara desert, at about the same time that Southwest Asian plants and animals were being established in Egypt, around 4500 B.C. Murdock's evidence is derived not from archeology, but from plant distributions and linguistic and other cultural factors. To it he would assign acha, pearl millet and sorghum, cow peas, a half dozen tubers and roots, okra, a variety of vine, ground, and tree fruits, condiments, and textile and oil plants.

All in all, there were striking parallels in technological evolution from hunting and gathering to agriculture in the Old and New Worlds and the social developments from hunting-and-gathering bands through states and empires which depended on it.

Suggested Readings

Burling, Robbins. 1965. *Hill farms and padi fields.* Englewood Cliffs, N.J.: Prentice-Hall.*

Evans-Pritchard, E. E. 1940. *The Nuer: A description of the modes of livelihood and political institutions of a Nilotic people.* Oxford, England: Clarendon Press.*

Fei, Hsiao-Tung. 1939. *Peasant life in China.* London, England: Kegan Paul, French, Trubner and Company.

Geertz, Clifford. 1963. *Agricultural involution: The process of ecological change in Indonesia.* Berkeley: University of California Press.*

Lanning, Edward P. 1967. *Peru before the Incas.* Englewood Cliffs, N.J.: Prentice-Hall.*

Marx, Emanuel. 1967. *Bedouin of the Negev.* Manchester, England: Manchester University Press.

Meggers, Betty J. 1971. *Amazonia: Man and culture in a counterfeit paradise.* Chicago: Aldine-Atherton.*

Netting, Robert McC. 1968. *Hill farmers of Nigeria: Cultural ecology of the Kofyar of the Jos Plateau.* Seattle: University of Washington Press.

———. 1971. *The ecological approach in cultural study.* Modular Publications. Reading, Mass.: Addison-Wesley.*

Sanders, William T., and Barbara J. Price. 1968. *Mesoamerica: The evolution of a civilization.* New York: Random House.*

Smith, Philip E. L. 1972. *The consequences of food production.* Modular Publications 31. Reading, Mass.: Addison-Wesley.*

Struever, Stuart, ed. 1971. *Prehistoric agriculture.* Garden City, N. Y.: Natural History Press.*

Titiev, Mischa. 1944. *Old Oraibi: A study of the Hopi Indians of Third Mesa.* Cambridge, Mass.: Peabody Museum of American Archaeology and Ethnology 22, 1.

Yang, Martin C. 1945. *A Chinese village, Taitou, Shantung Province.* New York: Columbia University Press.*

With a survey of hunting-and-gathering and farming technologies behind us, it will be useful to look at energy in its relation to physical and biological systems as well as cultural ones before we proceed to the other aspects of culture. Where does energy come from, and how is it transformed in its passage from one kind of system to another? Did domestication represent a true technological revolution in culture? Have its effects been dwarfed by energy developments in the last centuries? Is it justifiable to call technology the "prime mover" in cultural change?

Energy flow through living things

"Energy flows constantly into and out of the earth's surface environment" (Hubbert 1971: 61). Put so baldly in geophysical terms, energy seems remote from the wonder and variety of cultures. But it is relevant, as we know, to an understanding of the Chinese rice terrace, the Bedouin milk camel, the Nootka fish trap, or the Eskimo harpoon driven into a seal. These are interventions in the flow of energy, way stations with important cultural consequences. We have lifted some things and their behaviors out of the rest of nature and described them as symboling-dependent, but they are part and parcel of the

Chapter Seven
Energy Transformations and Technological Revolutions

161

total circulation of energy. As an ecologist puts it, "We, as human beings, should not forget that civilization is just one of the remarkable natural proliferations that are dependent on the continuous inflow of the concentrated energy of light radiation" (Odum 1971: 37).

Ethnographers' calculations of amounts of energy produced in specific cultures with hunting-and-gathering and farming-and-herding technologies employed the calorie as measuring unit. Although this unit is a customary and convenient shorthand, it should be understood that what is referred to is the "big" or capital *C* Calorie—the kilogram calorie or kilocalorie (kcal). It represents the amount of heat required to raise the temperature of one kilogram of water by one degree on the Celsius scale when the water is at fifteen degrees. Commonly used to quote the energy value of foods, it is by itself an adequate measure for energy production in most preindustrial cultures because practically all the energy put to work in them flows through living plants and animals and humans. It is applicable also in industrial cultures, despite their utilization of vast amounts of **inanimate energy** in addition to **animate energy**; it is convertible into other units of the metric system, and they can be converted into it.

Because nothing comes from nothing, as we noted in discussing human and cultural origins, *transformed* is a better word than *produced* when we are speaking of energy flow. Energy is neither created nor destroyed (this is the assertion of the familiar **first law of thermodynamics**)—only changed from one form to others and for the most part from more highly organized (less disorderly) to less highly organized (more disorderly) forms. With the exception of a small amount of heat rising from the earth's interior and the tides generated by the gravitational system of the earth, sun, and moon, all of the earth's energies are derived from solar radiation. The amount of solar radiation which strikes the earth varies from 200 to 220 kilocalories per square centimeter of surface per year in deserts, down through 120 to 160 in rain forests, to 70 in the polar regions (Gates 1971: 91). Practically all of that is either reflected, absorbed, and converted into heat or is used in evaporation, precipitation, and other processes of the water cycle. A minute fraction is captured by chlorophyll molecules in the leaves of plants, and this powers the process of photosynthesis—the building up of complex molecules from carbon dioxide in the atmosphere and water. Plants store solar energy primarily in the form of carbohydrates; some nonhuman animals eat plants and some eat other plant-eating animals; most humans eat animals and plants. This is a brief summary of the energy flow by which most human and cultural work gets done.

In this flow, a temporary and partial reversal of the usual order-to-disorder progression occurs. Living things produce energy of higher or increased order, or, as it is called, negative-disorder or negative-entropy. By the **second law of thermodynamics**, they cannot be 100 percent efficient in converting light energy into the potential energy of body stuff; at least some of it is dispersed as heat. By the same law, animals cannot convert all the potential energy of plants for their own uses. But as long as the sun provides radiant energy and chlorophyll molecules exist to capture it and synthesize materials into living bodies, energy will flow through living things. With regard to efficiency of conversion for our own species, the botanist David M. Gates (1971: 100) tells us "...man derives at best .01 percent of the incident solar energy through the food chain." In approximate terms, he says, a field of corn converts about 1 percent of the solar energy that falls onto it into vegetable tissue, a cow converts 10 percent of the corn's stored energy into cow, and humans use 10 percent of the cow's energy stored in meat. (Note, incidentally, that although the Nuer and Karimojong are not aware of the theoretical ramifications of energy theory, they act rationally in relation to the technology at their command by using the cow's renewable milk and blood rather than one harvest of meat. That is putting matter in "people do" terms. Culturally speaking, the system, given its technology, has moved to an efficient adaptive state by means of these practices.)

We can discern here a matter of consequence for cultural systems. If along the line culture can increase the amounts of energy that plants and animals convert and store and extract it more efficiently (that is, expend less energy in relation to the return), there will be more energy available to it for building more culture. That was the import of our discussion of farming and herding, of culture's intervention into energy flow, of control of animate energy sources. Our model of extracted culture helps us put Nuer cattle breeding and Chinese rice cultivation into a perspective relatable to biological and physical principles. Ecologists have done this already, in their own way, but the expanded model allows us to accommodate the principles to the whole of culture more satisfactorily.

In the course of describing energy extraction in several cultures, we made do with a variety of measures as they were suggested by ethnographers—hours and days worked by part of the population, estimated daily and annual Calorie production and consumption, and so on. We also referred to one try at an index of "technoenvironmental efficiency." I wish it had been possible to set down common measures, but they were not available. Ratios and indices are not easy to devise, and I don't think we have as yet an adequate and foolproof set of them. In particular, we lack a measure specifically directed to a "culture does" rather than a "people do" orientation, not to speak of specifically designed studies to put such a measure to the test. In its absence, one must fall back upon the comforting adage that has fortified anthropologists many times in the past: Our reach must exceed our grasp.

Was domestication a technological revolution?

In the course of cultural growth, change ordinarily proceeds slowly. It is characterized by the appearance of more of the same *kind* of thing that has gone before. Even though, for instance, the hunters of Kostenki had better and more varied tools than the earlier Torralbans, had a larger legacy of conceptualized knowledge about animals, and probably were better organized for hunting them, even though they operated efficiently enough to have possibly advanced, they remained hunters. But surely something happened between the Upper Old Stone Age and the rice-farming Kalinga and Chinese villagers that calls for recognition of more than mere quantitative change. There was qualitative change, a transformation that the Torralba-Kostenki succession did not accomplish.

Leslie White calls qualitative change "revolution." "Revolution is a *radical* transformation of a system, the substitution of one principle, or basis, of organization for another" (1959: 281). We usually think of revolutions as sudden or abrupt, like political revolutions. Time, as White pursues the argument, is relative, because preceding quantitative changes are a long time in ferment, and the working out of a revolution may take centuries. But in the end a revolution can be recognized because there has been substituted "one principle, or basis, of organization for another."

While cognizant that human muscle, fueled by the food people eat, powers most of the tools wielded both in hunting and in agricultural systems, White holds that the latter produced more energy more efficiently because of the special nature of domesticated plants and animals, a distinction we introduced in Chapter Six. They are tools as well as energy sources. "In cultivated plants and domestic animals we have both *energy* in definite magnitudes and *means* of harnessing and expending energy, and the two are inseparable" (1959: 55). Cultivated corn and domesticated cows, then, take on an aspect not present in wild forms, and this aspect can be phrased as introducing a new relationing principle between those domesticates and culture, a radical change. *Radical,* of course, refers to a change in the root or foundation of something. By definition, if nothing else, a revolution in the technological aspect of culture has begun.

Obviously, we can't rest on principle and definition alone. We have to decide whether domestication of plants and animals made a real difference in culture as a whole. There would be some doubt if we confined our farming-and-herding examples to the more primitive ones, but none at all if we look at the whole panorama of cultures up to the Industrial Revolution. It took less than 5,000 years for Bronze Age civilization to follow upon domestication in Southwest Asia and even less time in China. That outcome would not have arrived without agriculture and herding and could not have been sustained without them. Had domestication not occurred, it would be impossible to conceive of an Industrial Revolution.

A question related to domestication and its consequences is whether energy should be measured in terms of what each person produces on the average—as per capita production—or in terms of what specific cultures produce as a whole. I alluded in Chapter Three to White's energy law and Marshall Sahlins's criticism of White's phrasing of it. The law, you will recall, states that "culture advances as the amount of energy harnessed per capita per year increases, or as the efficiency or economy of the means of controlling energy is increased, or both" (1959: 56).

Sahlins questions the reference to "per capita." He points out (1972: 6) that per capita production of energy does not show an appreciable increase in simpler agricultural systems as compared with hunting-gathering ones; only the total amount, spread over larger numbers of people, increases. Inasmuch as practically all the energy produced and put to work in both hunting-gathering and farming-herding systems flows through human bodies and humans operate on roughly, say,

Culture in Its Technological Aspect

2,000 to 2,500 kilocalories per day, the per capita figure remains the same, whether one is a Dobe Bushman, a Tsembaga, a Kuikuru, a Kofyar, or a Javanese. However, as Sahlins puts it (1972: 6), "Neolithic societies in the main harness a *greater total amount of energy* than pre-agricultural communities, because of the greater number of energy-delivering humans sustained by domestication." In fine, agricultural societies *are* advanced over nonagricultural ones, but the basis for saying so is not per capita energy production but total-culture energy production.

In light of Sahlins's argument, I think the per capita measure may need to be reconsidered. It does not affect our orientation, and, indeed, the new measure fits neatly into it. As we have said, culture as a whole and in its several aspects harnesses and delivers energy, extending control over energy-delivering plants and animals *and* energy-delivering humans. As it increases the number of domesticates, it progressively increases the numbers of humans. *Analytically,* culture does, not people do. People are not *always* the best measure of culture. Humans themselves, in an analytical sense, are cultural tools, domesticated converters of energy, of the same order as plants and animals, *if* we look at culture solely in energy terms. Needless to say, they are much more than that, if looked at in other ways.

In summary, there is good reason to call domestication of plants and animals a revolution in technology. Domestication converted plants and animals into tools as well as energy sources—as culture had previously converted prehuman primates into cultural energy transformers and primate tools into cultural devices. Culture invented a set of converters of animate energy—domesticated plants and animals—which better sustained and increased the numbers of another set—humans.

Exploiting the fossil fuel storage bank

The energy stored in plants and animals over the earth is released by oxidation at about the same rate that the chlorophyll molecules replace it by capturing solar energy. When they cease to live, they are broken down by microorganisms of decay and continued oxidation, their materials are dispersed, and their energies are degraded into heat. But sometimes they are covered up under conditions that prevent complete oxidation and decay, as in swamps and bogs, and over long periods they are converted into hydrocarbons, the fossil fuels—coal, oil shale, petroleum, and natural gas. These have provided the principal energy capital of the Industrial Revolution, a finite capital created over 600,000,000 years but one that will have lasted us about 1,300 years in all, with 80 percent of it having been used up within a period of 300 years (Hubbert 1971: 61, 63). Fossil fuel is still being formed, but at a painfully slow rate compared with the demands of industry for inanimate energy sources.

Humans released, by burning, the energy stored in wood to heat and light their shelters, cook their food, harden their spear points, keep away nighttime predators, and surround game animals as far back as *Homo erectus* times. These were direct applications of inanimate power. Later humans floated burdens in streams, invented canoes and boats, used gravity to bring water to their irrigated fields, propelled their water craft with wind-powered sails, and harnessed water and wind to grind grain and pump water. Such controlled applications of inanimate energy added to the available store that powered cultural motions. But until the Industrial Revolution of the eighteenth century the bulk of energy that propelled symboling-dependent culture came from animate sources.

The burning of fossil fuels to heat water to steam and the burning of their explosive gases in closed cylinders to drive the pistons of internal combustion engines lifted power production to magnitudes that dwarfed the individual labors of human converters and their earlier animate and inanimate aids. It took much less time for the Industrial Revolution than for the Agricultural Revolution to establish itself, although its technology rested upon a long accumulation of discoveries and inventions such as metallurgy and other mechanical arts. James Watt's steam engines of the late eighteenth century only added improvements to earlier models that had been put together over a hundred-year period (Thirring 1962: 47-51).

Internal combustion engines bypass the burning of coal and oil to generate steam by applying the force of ignited gases directly to drive pistons and turbines (bladed or vaned rotors). Practicable ones were put to work in the second half of the nineteenth century. Only around 1885 were gasoline-fueled engines attached to vehicles (Thirring 1962: 180)—to the present sorrow of ecologists, for there are now more than 100,000,000 motor vehicles in the United States alone and they produce in excess of 17,000,000,000 horsepower (Summers 1971: 152).

Electrical energy came under cultural control after Michael Faraday worked out the principle of the dynamo, electromagnetic induction, in 1831, and Gramme produced the first motor in 1873 (Ubbelohde 1955: 67). Dynamos can be turned by energies originating in falling water, in wind, and in the atom, but fossil fuels have predominated in

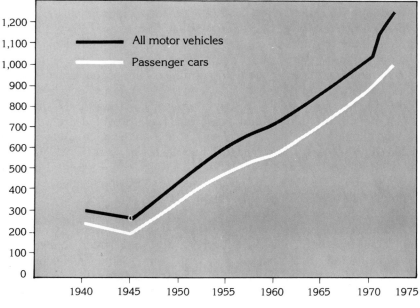

Moving goods and people with the internal combustion engine: Growth in billions of vehicle miles in the United States, 1940-72. (Reprinted from *Exploring energy choices* with permission of the Energy Policy Project of the Ford Foundation.)

Culture in Its Technological Aspect

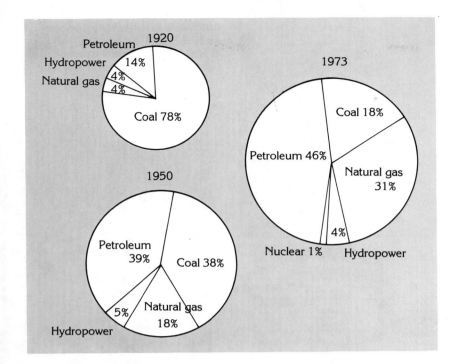

Sources of U.S. energy supply, 1920, 1950, 1973. (Reprinted from *Exploring energy choices* with permission of the Energy Policy Project of the Ford Foundation.)

the production of electricity. And they have predominated also in the production of other forms of energy. While wood was the dominant energy source until 1850, coal was providing 75 percent of inanimate power by 1910. Coal was overtaken by petroleum and natural gas in the next fifty years (Starr 1971: 41).

The increase in power delivered by inanimate energy converters has been enormous. For instance, early in the eighteenth century the working rate of overshot water wheels was 2-5 horsepower (hp), of good windmills 2-8 hp, and of stationary steam engines 7-100 hp (Ubbelohde 1955: 62). The figures can be read as 1.5-3.7 kilowatts (kW) for the water wheels, 1.5-6 kW for the windmills, and 5.2-74.5 kW for the steam engines. Where is the steam engine now? Kilowatts are no longer convenient measures and have been superseded by megawatts, 1,000,000 watt units. The largest steam-driven turbo-generator in the world when it was placed in operation in 1970 at a Tennessee Valley power plant to convert the energy of coal to steam to electricity had a capacity of 1,150 megawatts. The same building housed two smaller generators, each rated at 704 megawatts (Summers 1971: 149), altogether a mighty power concentration to perform work within the cultural system.

Or let us take per capita totals of energy consumption expressed in familiar kilocalories. By 1870, about a century and a half after the Industrial Revolution got underway, per capita daily consumption of energy in England, Germany, and the United States reached 70,000 kilocalories. By 1970 in the United States it had risen to 230,000 kilocalories per day for every man, woman, and child. And while hunting-gathering and agricultural technologies were not alike among themselves, differences were never so great as those produced by the Indus-

Energy Transformations and Technological Revolutions

167

Coal, oil, and natural gas, the fossil fuels, provided the principal energy capital of the Industrial Revolution. Here coal is being strip-mined with a mechanical shovel in Montana. (Courtesy William Manning, Northern Cheyenne Research Project.)

An oil refinery and tanks in Louisiana. Petroleum and natural gas overtook coal as the dominant energy source by 1960, and in 1973 they accounted for 77 percent of the U.S. energy supply being exploited. (Courtesy Exxon Company, U.S.A.)

Energy of fossil fuel is converted into mechanical energy. This diesel-powered earthmover carries about ten cubic yards of dirt pushed onto it by a bulldozer. (Courtesy Dennis Fassett.)

Light, too, is energy. With this 1,000-watt lamp technicians are simulating positions of the sun to calibrate angles on equipment placed on an Apollo spacecraft. (Courtesy Bendix Corporation.)

trial Revolution: the 30 percent of the world's people who lived in industrialized regions consumed 80 percent of the world's energy output. With 6 percent of the people, the U.S. consumed 35 percent of the energy (Cook 1971: 135).

A nuclear energy phase in technological evolution

The energy consumed in the United States in 1970 averaged out to 340,000,000 British thermal units (Btu's) for every man, woman, and child, a per capita equivalent of thirteen tons of coal or 2,700 gallons of gasoline. Of that energy, nearly 96 percent was derived from petroleum, natural gas, and coal, the fossil fuels; only .3 percent came from nuclear fuels (Summers 1971: 149). The radioactive elements and other energy sources will enter increasingly into power production as fossil fuels become depleted. Their use began less than a century ago, following the discovery of the radioactivity of uranium by Henri Becquerel in 1896 and the theoretical work of Ernest Rutherford, Albert Einstein, and other distinguished scientists and engineers. The social and political context of World War II and the cold war that came after it speeded its course, just as the economic and political consequences of the dwindling fossil fuel reserve have made exploitation of the atom and other sources an urgent matter.

The nuclear engine uses the heat produced when the unstable atomic nuclei of elements such as uranium rearrange themselves into more stable forms. The heat which is a product of the transformation is used to convert water into expansive steam to drive turbo-generators which in turn convert mechanical energy into electricity. Despite that similarity in utilization of heat, the difference in the sources from which energy is extracted represents a cultural invention of the first magnitude.

As you know, the first law of thermodynamics tells us that energy is neither created nor destroyed, that any of its forms, such as mechanical energy, represents a transformation from other forms. Energy is conserved; whatever disappears in one form appears in another. Einstein's special theory of relativity establishes the relationship between energy and matter. They are interconvertible, as are forms of energy. Einstein's simple formula, which the public unfortunately has come to associate only with the atomic bomb, is $E = mc^2$, where E represents energy (measured in tiny units called ergs), m the material mass (measured in grams, of which there are 453.6 in a pound), and c the speed of light. When mass is lost in an atomic explosion, it is converted into energy. What is the energy outcome? "A mass loss of one pound corresponds with an energy gain of about one million seven hundred thousand horse-power acting for one year" (Ubbelohde 1955: 66). From little masses, great energies flow.

Now, one could conceive of any material, from toothpaste to glue to sea water, yielding energies equivalent to its mass, but fortunately for culture and humans it is only the unstable heavy elements such as uranium that appear to have this dangerous potential. The engineering application of the formula involves unfreezing the uneasy nuclear equilibrium of uranium in a controlled way, speeding up or slowing down the nuc-

A reminder that a culture is not exclusive to a race, nor a race to a culture. An Eskimo in a parka...

...and another in the hard hat of construction and industrial workers employed on the Alaskan pipeline. (Courtesy Exxon Company, U.S.A.)

lear transformation, and collecting that part of the energy released as heat.

Not all the atoms of an element have the same atomic weight. Those with the same atomic number (that is, those having the same number of electrons rotating around the nucleus) but of different weights are called isotopes of an element. The fissionable or disruptible fuel used in most nuclear reactors so far is an isotope of uranium, uranium 235, a rather rare form in relation to all forms of the element, so that the outlook for continuing supplies would appear to be dim. However, some other forms of uranium can be made to absorb neutrons in a breeder reactor and thereby become transformed into fissionable material, actually producing more nuclear fuel than is consumed in the process. One such useful isotope is uranium 238, of which there are 99,283 atoms in each 100,000 atoms of natural uranium. One gram of it in a breeder reactor yields the heat equivalent of 2.7 metric tons of coal or 13.7 barrels of crude oil (Hubbert 1971: 67-68). And a future source of suitable nuclei for the fusion part of this process might be deuterium, or heavy hydrogen, which is plentiful in the oceans.

What is the outlook for this inanimate energy supply, which is replacing the earlier sources of the fuel revolution? Experts tell us it is reassuring for the reasonably long run (but perhaps no longer than 1,000 years under current rates of cultural growth) if fusion becomes practicable. Whether the earth's life can withstand the heat and radioactive pollution is, of course, another matter. But, overlooking the energy of stream flow, which still has a large potential, and the minor potentials of wind, bay-locked tides, and the heated waters of springs and geysers, the ultimate source of energy for culture and humanity might be the solar radiation that falls on the earth's deserts. It is directly converted solar energy, in the opinion of an engineering authority, that is "the only significant long range alternative to nuclear power" (Starr 1971: 43).

The "prime mover" question

Savagery, barbarism, and *civilization* are terms that were given clear meanings by the nineteenth-century evolutionary anthropologists. Morgan, for instance, distinguished three stages of savagery and three of barbarism based on presence or absence of given technological inventions and said civilization was what came after the phonetic alphabet and writing. As he is interpreted by Leslie White, his *Ancient Society* presents an extended theory, not wholly consistent in its working out but more than creditable for its day, with this implied assertion at its base: "Culture evolves as the technological means of exploiting the resources of nature are enlarged and improved" (White 1948: 150-51). The eighteenth-century European social philosophers also linked technology in their evolutionary stages, as evidenced by the terms *hunting, herding,* and *farming.*

The survey we have completed was presented in an evolutionary context. With its transformations of energy measurable in kilocalories or megawatts, technology evolves. We did not find that passage from hunting and gathering to farming and herding made an immediate and dramatic difference in production and consumption of kilocalories. Nevertheless, stages based on technology, and particularly the technology of subsistence, have a value for sorting out on a rough scale the kind of cultures traditionally studied by anthropologists. Industrial technologies produce energies of almost astronomical contrast, and anthropologists are only beginning to probe these in a substantive way.

Perhaps you should not be asked to judge yet whether other aspects of culture are so dependent upon technology and so responsive to its changes, either in the amounts of energy it produces or in the particular means employed to extract energy, that adaptive, and hence evolutionary, changes in them can be traced directly to prior technological change. Of course, I said in earlier pages that we could, but I based that judgment on logic associated with a model of cultural behavior. That judgment, however, does not close the matter. Let our minds, like our cultural system, be open.

The problem may be described as the search for a prime mover. That is an engineering term applied to what drives a machine—"The prime mover supplies the energy to be transformed" (Ubbelohde 1955: 34). In this sense, human beings, slave or free, and oxen, horses, and steam- or gas-driven pistons and turbines are prime movers. When Archimedes said that he could move the earth with a lever if he could find a firm balance point or fulcrum, he set himself up as a prime mover, the lever serving, as does a Kuikuru digging stick, to magnify the force he would exert. We might be stacking the deck if we left the argument at this point (or fulcrum?), because it is obvious that the prime movers mentioned supply movement and heat in culture, and by definition they would be assigned to technology because of its energy-extracting role. Ergo, technology is culture's prime mover. Although use of analogies is permissible, this one is not sufficiently exact and extensive: there is more to culture than energy sources and technological transformations, and we have still to link the "more" in culture to technology in a lineal way. Also, it is difficult to disentangle antecedents and consequences among the changes in particular cultures and to predict their course.

Elman R. Service holds that "there is no single magical formula that will predict the evolution of every society. The actual evolution of the culture of particular societies is an adaptive process whereby the society solves problems with respect to the natural and to the human-competitive environments [he means here impinging cultures, not *sapiens* environment in our sense—R.A.]. These environments are so diverse, the problems so numerous, and the solutions potentially so various that no single determinant can be equally powerful for all cases" (1968: 406). Evolutionary changes, he thinks, may be determined sometimes by technology but also sometimes by competition and conflict between individuals and between societies and by "consciously formed social and political schemes and plans" (1968: 408). He grants the rough utility in ascribing general stages of development in culture as a whole to technological inventions but wonders what further use there is for the formula in specific cultures.

Well, there is the problem, and what you decide the solution is depends on your knowing something about social organization and ideology and their observed relations with technologies in particular cultures.

You will have noticed that, although technologies were described as

Culture in Its Technological Aspect

consisting of the tools and techniques for subsistence, shelter, and defense (later expanded to accommodate naturalistic knowledge effectively and directly deployed in the context of these activities), discussion centered on subsistence technology. The technology of shelter was treated only briefly in systems based on animate energy sources and not at all in industrial ones, nor was the technology of defense mentioned more than cursorily anywhere. This was because they are mainly conservers and protectors rather than energy extractors and it seemed appropriate, given the time and space we have, to focus on the import of energies from habitat. That, after all, is the most important fact about the technological aspect of culture: it is at that point, or in that zone, that environmental energies move massively into the symboling-dependent sphere.

Our initial definition, pointing to subsistence, shelter, and defense, was a way to enter into ethnography as well as a means to grasp the position of technology in the cultural system. But just as we admitted technological knowledge into company with tools and techniques, so we cannot exclude from technology activities other than those three, such as the technology of communication. It is environmental energy conversion itself that is the crux of the matter. Its mechanisms and its magnitudes are what count in the long run.

Suggested Readings

Cottrell, Fred. 1955. *Energy and society: The relation between energy, social change, and economic development.* New York: McGraw-Hill.*

Singer, Charles, E. J. Holmyard, and A. R. Hall. 1957-65. *A history of technology.* 5 vols. New York: Oxford University Press.

Thirring, Hans. 1962. *Energy for man: From windmills to nuclear power.* New York: Harper and Row, Torchbooks.*

Ubbelohde, A. R. 1955. *Man and energy.* New York: George Braziller.

Watson, Richard A., and Patty Jo Watson. 1969. *Man and nature: An anthropological essay in human ecology.* New York: Harcourt, Brace and World.*

White, Leslie A. 1959. *The evolution of culture: The development of civilization to the fall of Rome.* New York: McGraw-Hill.*

White, Lynn, Jr. 1967. *Medieval technology and social change.* London, England: Oxford University Press.

Part Three
Human Social
Organization as
an Aspect of
Culture

In technology, representing culture's major confrontation with habitat, we looked at the means—hunting-and-gathering weapons and tools, fishing devices, domesticated plants and animals, inanimate energy converters—by which external sources were tapped and energy conducted into a symboling-dependent system. Now we make a partial shift inward to observe some of the interpersonal behaviors, individual and group, which go along with different kinds of technologies. Again there are two sides to our study. We want to get acquainted with some of the variety of human behavior in the world, past and present, and we want to bring some order into it and understand it.

Given technology's major contribution, we assume that movements in social organization are related to whatever technological capacities a system has, even though we can describe the relationships only loosely. The social organization of a hunting-gathering culture without food-storing techniques, like that of the Bushman, would act in one way if there were a decline in resources in the immediate habitat, and a specialized fishing system, like that of the Nootka, or a farming one, like that of the Kofyar, would act in others. And the social parts of those cultures, whatever they are, presumably have taken shape in relation to the technological

Chapter Eight
Diversity
and Adaptation
in Social
Organization

177

Groups, statuses, and rules are categories of extracted social behaviors. They can be applied to any aggregation of people, such as these Mossi, of the Voltaic Republic, who are drinking millet beer together after communal hoeing. (Courtesy Herbert W. Butler.)

capacities of the cultures over time. In sum, cultural behaviors in their social aspect may be looked at as adaptive responses of the cultural system to its environments that are consistent with its technological apparatus.

We can't assume that the social parts or their responses are always the most efficient ones possible for putting available energy to work, just as we couldn't assume that a technology operated at peak efficiency or was the best in a range of possibilities. There must be, nevertheless, a more or less efficient fit between the two.

Categories of cultural behaviors

How to categorize cultural behaviors usefully is one of our continuing problems. In technology, first of all, we used a set of broad extension terms—tools and techniques. The analog in social organization is a set—groups, statuses, and rules—which Elman R. Service (1971b) has deployed in the context of primitive culture and which is adaptable to advanced systems as well. I regard it as an analog to tools and techniques in part because these are rock-bottom things that can be shifted from one context to another depending on their tasks. A second set in technology was subsistence, shelter, and defense. This we match with economics, politics, and other major orientations of social behavior, a set we will leave open-ended; each is an aspect of what the social organization does, the tasks it performs. Finally, in technology there was an arrangement by evolutionary levels—hunting, gathering, and fishing; domestication; and inanimate fuel conversion. The categories we shall

Human Social Organization as an Aspect of Culture

adopt for social levels are those of Morton R. Fried (1967)—egalitarian, ranked, stratified, and state.

Any group, small or large, may be thought of empirically as an organized collection of people. (That we are concerned in extracted cultural systems only with social relationships does not take away our need to visualize backgrounds.) It may be marked or bounded by common residence or territory, as a household, village, or hunting band, or it may be a county or national state. Or it may be a dispersed group whose members are linked by kinship (as **clans**), religion (as cults or church memberships), economic ties (as modern corporations), or other characteristics. The term *group* is an elastic one that accommodates much variation, but it always connotes an organized aggregation. We know what we mean when we speak of the residents of Manhattan, Springfield, or Denver, the Michigan legislature or the Assembly of the United Nations, members of the Masonic lodge or Roman Catholic Church, or personnel of General Motors Corporation. Boundaries are always a problem, but nonetheless we can bound accurately enough for our purposes groups in primitive as well as in industrialized, stratified state societies.

Statuses, as Service (1971b: 11) defines them, are "named social positions which are assigned conventional attributes and roles that regulate or influence the conduct of interpersonal relations." Examples are father, daughter, elder, shaman, and the like or factory manager, traffic policeman, student, mayor, and millionaire. From a cultural systems point of view, statuses are named behavior bundles that are found, regularly and repetitively, in a culture, so it is a little redundant to add

Another set of analytical categories is derived from a look at aspects of social life in general. This Saint's Day fiesta in Xochitepec, Mexico, has economic, political, and religious aspects. (Courtesy Nancy and Robert V. Morey.)

Diversity and Adaptation in Social Organization

the notion of role as a separate thing to them. What a status does, its role or roles, is part of it by definition. However, we don't need to sweep aside everything when we redefine, and Service's definition is clear enough.

One connotation of the word *status* in everyday speech should be avoided. As a technical term in cultural analysis, *status* of itself does not point to ranking, to having or not having a higher position than others. Common laborer is no more nor less a status than physician, judge, or senator, although in some cultures (outside of revolutionary situations) it may have less prestige, authority, or power or may offer less economic reward, than the others.

Rules, which Service (1971b: 17-18) views as "ideological determinants of social behavior" and presents in their *Random House Dictionary* meaning of principles or regulations "governing conduct, action procedure, arrangement, etc.," he illustrates by reference to customary and prescribed practices such as the place of residence of a married pair with respect to their kin and the reckoning of descent.

So much, then, for groups, statuses, and rules, which we will regard as social parts, categorical universals in the social aspect of culture. If you read Service yourself, you will find that, for reasons of his own, he restricts social structure to groups and their arrangement, calls groups and statuses together social organization, and makes rules still another order of things. I am taking the liberty of calling all three of them structural parts.

As to the terms in the second set, we shall define *economics* as the social organization of production, distribution, and consumption of goods and services. The social parts of any culture may be looked at in relation to the ways they enter into and impinge upon those tasks of producing, distributing, and using up the product, and thus they become economic by definition. Up to a point, it is an inward look. But economics faces habitat via its connection with productive technology and faces superorganic environments when there is an interchange between the fruits of their respective technologies. *Political* we define as the social organization of power and authority (terms which will be discussed later) and find empirically as leading and following, commanding and yielding, in whatever degree. We will become acquainted first with some of the more important groups, statuses, and rules found in primitive cultures, because they perform both economic and political tasks—and others as well. They will be described in this chapter without particular economic or political emphasis.

With regard to process, social parts get invented (*invention* having the meaning given in Chapter Three) and grow in size and complexity. They also fission or segment, that is, break into two or more entities, and fuse, or merge two or more into one—as when one hunting band or farming village for whatever reason divides into two or more bands or villages or when separate ones cast their lot together permanently. A status segments when the tasks associated with it are separated from each other; if, for instance, ritual duties of household heads are taken over in major part by a religious specialist, a status segmentation has taken place. There will be an example of status fusion in our discussion of families and dyads.

When groups or statuses segment, integration is maintained by mechanisms such as kinship or by the addition of a new and distinguishable part, such as the Cheyenne Chiefs' Lodge and the military societies or the **redistributive chiefs** and **big men** among North Pacific Coast Indians and Melanesians, or, at higher levels, by market and state. Formation of all of these may be regarded as aspects of the major process, adaptation.

Since we are trying to build as simply as we can a particular orientation, we shall have to pass lightly over many detailed categories found in the literature about human social life. Without question, social anthropology has piled up the biggest body of observations, labels, and theories in the discipline as a whole. A good deal of the writing, moreover, is inviting and literate, partly because anthropologists from British universities have been prominent in doing it. But, as I mentioned in passing about specialized technological and archeological classifications, our intention is to present and apply some anthropological ideas in a consistent way, not to assemble a manual. We must be selective, even though the word *diversity* appears in the heading of this chapter.

Noncultural primate societies

Although the social organizations of other primates than ourselves are noncultural, as are their tool kits, they shed some light on what our immediate ancestors might have been like. What the anthropologists Sherwood L. Washburn and Irven DeVore (1961: 103) wrote about the Australopithecines more than a decade ago appears to be the consensus today: "Although these forms were bipedal and tool-making, there is little to suggest that their social life was very different from that of apes or monkeys."

Contemporary primate species vary in social behavior. It is impracticable to go into several variations in detail, but the baboon and chimpanzee will serve as contrasting examples in regard to **territoriality** and **dominance**, traits which often enter into discussions about hominids and lower primates. Baboons, ground-dwelling Old World monkeys, have in one or more of their species a hierarchy of dominance and subordination in small groups, and they defend definite feeding ranges. Chimpanzees, closer to the hominid line, have no permanent groups containing adults of both sexes and no strong dominance, and they do not defend closed territories.

The hamadryas baboon, a ground-dwelling Old World monkey, has a social organization that includes one-male groups to which females are attached and bands and sleeping troops. Here a male checks on his two females. (After Kummer 1971.)

The chimpanzee is a social animal, too, but its groups are highly variable, and its society, in contrast to that of the baboon, is open. This is a mature male in his usual sitting position. (After *Primate behavior: Field studies of monkeys and apes,* Irven DeVore, New York: Holt, Rinehart and Winston, 1965. [Copyright National Geographic Society.])

The hamadryas baboon, which lives on a dry, rolling grassland interspersed with acacia thorn trees and shrubs at the edge of the Danakil desert in Ethiopia, was studied by the zoologist Hans Kummer (1971). The baboon eats acacia leaves, flowers and beans, and grass and roots primarily but also insects and birds and occasionally the immature young of savannah animals. A band of around a hundred animals sleeps together on narrow ledges of a rocky cliff away from predators at night and during the day forages in loose formation in its own territory, which is aggressively defended by mature males against other groups although incursions into it are frequent. Several bands (as many as seven hundred animals) occupy separate portions of the cliff in uneasy truce, but each band in the bigger "sleeping troop," as it is called, sets out in the morning for its own range under the shifting lead of dominant males.

Internally, the band is structured into groups with one male, one to four females, and a few infants; attached loosely to it may be an immature male (20 percent of the animals are in that category) who is waiting a chance to appropriate an immature female and begin a group of his own and who warily avoids close contact with the male elder. Older males, who have a silvery mantle suggestive of the wigs worn in British courts of law, tolerate little philandering by their mates and bring them into line with a hard stare or a bite on the neck, and their females groom them faithfully. There appears to be a male inhibition against tampering with females attached to others, and given the watchful behavior of the male there is minimal interaction among female grown-ups, par-

Human Social Organization as an Aspect of Culture

ticularly between a female and any outside of her own one-male group. While female juveniles tend to remain with their mothers until they are kidnapped by a young male starting his own group, male juveniles form rough-and-tumble play groups that begin to form the dominance pattern of adults. There is, however, no rigid structure of dominance and submissiveness that runs from top to bottom in the multigroup band. There are several leaders who may successively start the band out on its foraging round and set the pace for the day, and these are the most aggressive defenders of the band.

In contrast, chimpanzees live in open societies in which wandering males, singly or in small groups, find companionship in many places with clusters of females and children. Vernon and Frances Reynolds (1965), who studied a population of sixty to eighty animals in eight square miles of the Budongo rain forest near Lake Albert in Uganda, found them subsisting mainly on tree fruit, supplemented by leaves, bark and stems, and insects. Unlike Jane Goodall's chimps in the Gombe Stream Reserve, the Budongos were not observed eating meat nor making tools. Ranging in size from two to thirty individuals, the groups "were constantly changing membership, splitting apart, meeting others and joining them congregating or dispersing" (1965: 396).

The largest congregations, of fifteen or more animals, occurred where food was plentiful in one spot; otherwise, the chimps usually travelled in threes and fours, or even as individuals. The small units were not necessarily "families," for the Reynoldses observed that they consisted variously of only adult males; only mothers and their young and occasionally other females; adults of both sexes, sometimes with adolescents but without child-carrying females; or, finally, a mixed bag of adult males, mothers with young, other females, and adolescents. The small groups joined others at the bonanza feeding places or while on a march to new sources, but it is impossible to label one or another as the building block of the society, as in the case of baboon one-male groups and foraging bands. What linked individuals in small groups, the Reynoldses concluded, was a variety of factors—"personality characteristics, or similar age, sex, status, or condition" or "familiarity through blood relationship," which is to say the ties between mothers and offspring and between siblings reared together (1965: 400). What brought the small groups together varied too—food concentrations, sex and grooming behavior, attraction by calls and by neighbors' drumming on tree trunks, use of customary paths and areas, and movements to new places impelled by decreasing food resources in the old. And finally the chimps showed little dominance and subordination behavior. "There was no evidence of a linear hierarchy of dominance among males or females; there were no observations of exclusive rights to receptive females; and there were no permanent leaders of groups" (1965: 415). Yielding to others took place on occasion, but quarrels and displays of threat or anger were few.

Were the Australopithecines socially like baboons or chimpanzees? Not exactly like either, but probably more like chimps. Up to about a decade ago, it was assumed that primate societies in general rested on attraction between adults of the two sexes, a hierarchy of dominance linked with male aggressiveness, and territorial behavior. The notion

Diversity and Adaptation in Social Organization

had emerged that the protohominids must have lived in male-dominated families, joined in territorial foraging and hunting bands. Discovery of the open societies of higher primates—chimpanzees, orangutans, and gorillas—with their variety of fluid groups and limited dominance just about ended that idea, so that it now persists only in best-selling popularizations of ethology and anthropology.

Reynolds (1972: 39-40) hypothesizes that our direct ancestors lived in open scavenging and hunting bands whose members, like the chimpanzees, had widely ramifying ties with those in other groups, a circumstance that made it possible to assemble sizeable numbers of males for cooperative hunting. The smallest relatively permanent unit was a matrifocal (mother-centered) one, a female and her offspring being linked with other mothers not as members of the harem of a dominant male but in friendly association. With females foraging plant foods for themselves and their young and the more mobile males turning to the hunt—perhaps transporting some of the kill to the females or calling them to the kill spot—a precultural division of labor was established. Attachment of the males to the matrifocal "families" came later, when, as the saying goes, father came home to stay. And significant territoriality among humans arose only with permanent settlement, probably with the coming of farming but perhaps earlier, in late Paleolithic times, when specialized hunters tended to stay in favored areas.

One of the outcomes of researches of the kind we have touched on has been that prehuman primate capacity for social learning has received more appreciative recognition than it had before, and unconditioned biological drives are held to explain less than had been assumed. But at their highest level the behaviors are just that—socially learned. To echo the challenge in our discussion of technology, we would accept a chimpanzee's avoidance of another as cultural if we could hear him say something like "I can't marry you, because you are my parallel cousin" or "Your father is a sorcerer." Just as it may incorporate a stone or wood tool wielded by emerging humans, culture may enmesh existing interactions or convert closed or open groups into cultural forms, so that they are transmitted through time in a manner in addition to and beyond that of situational and social learning. Humans are more than a product of one kind of learning, just as they are more than a product of genetic programming.

Bands and households of hunter-gatherers

A cultural system based on hunting and gathering will order the lives of a thousand humans, on the average, and the geographical areas over which hunting-and-gathering systems extend are thinly populated—one to twenty-five persons per hundred square miles and rarely more than one per square mile (Lee and DeVore 1968: 11). Their principal social groups are bands and households. They are egalitarians, but we may also speak of them as band societies.

Twenty to twenty-five people comprise a band, or local group; bands may join in aggregations of up to three hundred people during a part of the annual round under favorable conditions. Members are in continuing, although not necessarily daily, contact, and bands tend to become

Human Social Organization as an Aspect of Culture

associated with particular resource areas they exploit. Fieldwork in the last decade has shown that territories are remarkably open to visiting kin and friends, and households of one band may join another for varying periods. Bands tend to be exogamous, which is to say members marry outside of the band, and **residence rules** for the married pair are not rigid. They may be virilocal and patrilocal (males bring mates to live in their natal group and male children continue to live in father's group), uxorilocal and matrilocal (females bring mates to live in their natal group and female children continue to live in mother's group), or ambilocal (no significant preference). Descent rules are not important: kin are counted cognatically, or bilaterally, with mother's or father's side given equal weight, with no emphasis on descent through males or females (agnatic or patrilineal, or uterine or matrilineal). Inheritance rules are rudimentary, too. There are few personal possessions to inherit, and use rights on the land rest in the fluid group, not in individual statuses.

The ecological approach which characterizes study of band societies today was initiated by Julian H. Steward, whose article "The Economic and Social Basis of Primitive Bands" (1936) appeared in a volume honoring A. L. Kroeber. He classified bands on the basis of descent—patrilineal, composite (bilateral), and matrilineal—and related them to "exploitative patterns" toward natural resources. He was wrong about the prevalence of patrilineal descent among surviving hunters, but his work (cf. Steward 1955) is recognized as one of the bases of cultural ecology.

Bands is a useful general category, but increasingly today one finds in ethnographic accounts reference only to camps—simply the people found in camping places—so as not to assign any connotations of rigid organization. Their fluid state is accounted for first of all by the simplicity of the technology and the nature of the food supply—wild plants and animals. Although hunters and gatherers can be called affluent, resources vary with the seasons, calling for increasingly long trips from camp or a shift to a new base. There is no exclusive possession in our sense: hospitality and sharing are firmly rooted rules. Accumulation of goods, particularly of foodstuffs, is not practicable, and nature is the constantly available storehouse.

Shifting membership and elastic boundaries of bands are clearly adaptive in relation to habitat, given the technology. People may concentrate when and where a food resource is plentiful and disperse in smaller groups when it is not, thereby taking advantage of fewer and more scattered resources. This practice puts a minimum of strain on the self-renewing habitat, while ensuring that everyone is provided for. But alternating concentration and dispersion are adaptive to *sapiens* environment, too, in a way that has further beneficial effect on relations with habitat. We humans are often touchy and restive; we fret, quarrel, and harbor resentments, so that in a simple society without the kind of controls that appear later in social evolution, to move away from unpleasantness is a culturally enwrapped and appropriate response. As Richard B. Lee puts it, "In contrast to agricultural and urban peoples, hunters have a great deal of latitude to vote with their feet, to walk out of an unpleasant situation. And they do so, not when the food supply

Bushman household consisting of a man with two wives and their children. The woman on the man's left, his second wife, has mothered two boys, and the one to his right, his first wife, has three sons. (© 1976 by Laurence Marshall.)

is exhausted, but well before that point when only their patience is exhausted." Lee continues, "This mobility has a profound ecological adaptive significance. Fear and avoidance of conflict has the effect of keeping people apart. This perception of the threat of conflict functions to maintain group size and population density at a much lower level than could be supported by the food resources, if the population could be organized to use those resources more efficiently" (1972: 182-83).

Bands are comprised of **households**. The household is a small group (most often two or three adults and as many children) that occupies a shelter or two, prepares and consumes its food, cooperates in food getting and production of necessities, and has primary care of children. It is no more than the band a hard-shelled unit, for activities spill out of it, as when hunting involves males from several households or women cooperate in collecting materials for shelters. It can expand, break up, and reconstitute readily, responsive to phases in individual life cycles and economic and social demands, showing in some cultures regular development cycles of its own. It also is a generator of statuses,

because the capabilities of its members and the behaviors found in it give rise to distinctions such as household head and dependents.

Households, then, are the foremost of domestic groups, "those basic units which in preindustrial societies revolve around the hearth and the roof, the bed and the farm, that is, around the processes of production and reproduction, of shelter and consumption" (Goody 1972: 4). "Farm," of course, must be understood metaphorically in the case of hunters and gatherers. Households maintain their importance through the agricultural level, only in industrial cultures shrinking to sheltering and consumption units, with production and much of enculturation transferred to other groups.

Let us look at bands and households in some of the cultures whose technologies are familiar to us. Marshall's !Kung Bushmen (1965), numbered about a thousand in their region of 10,000 square miles. Living in the traditional hunting lifeway were twenty-seven bands, defined as "a group of families who live together, linked to one another and to the headman by kinship bonds" (1965: 267). Each band ranged

A large extended family household of !Kung Bushmen. The old father is on the right (facing the camera) and his three sons-in-law sit in the foreground. In the background are the old man's daughters and their children. (© 1976 by Laurence Marshall.)

Diversity and Adaptation in Social Organization

in size from twenty to sixty individuals. (Nine other groups were employed by non-Bushman herders and cultivators.) Marriages generally took place between bands. The vaguely defined territories centered around water holes and *veldkos* groves and patches to which the groups moved successively five or six times a year under the headman's direction. Although each of the eight families (small households) in the band Marshall lived with had its own hut and fire—"the visible symbol of home for a !Kung family" (1965: 256)—the fires were built so close together that people could easily talk or call to one another. A superhousehold, one might say, for the men hunted and women gathered *veldkos* together, meat was distributed to everyone, each family cooking its own, and women fed not only their own families but shared with other relatives and friends. Care of children and the aged, while centered at the family fire, also was widely shared.

Like the !Kung Bushman territory, that of the Ituri Pygmies is sparsely populated, and Pygmy households range widely. There are an estimated forty thousand Ituri Pygmies in all, and "each small hunting band, of anything from three to thirty families, may have several hundred square miles of forest territory, and if game is not in one part of that territory it is in another" (Turnbull 1965: 286). When fruit has been gathered and game has been frightened off by daily hunting, the camp moves ten or twenty miles to a new area. Households, as among the Bushmen, are small family units, but at the start of a hunt "men may eat at the household hearth just outside their hut, or in a group by themselves, the women placing food in the center of the group for everyone to share" (1965: 296). Each family claims the game that falls into its section of the hunting net, but it has a call on the kill from other sections if needed. Women's activities are organized along age lines, those of the same age helping each other to build huts, gather plant foods, and cook, and they freely turn over children to others to be looked after and suckled if they are called away. Families frequently visit kin in other camps, which eases the tensions aroused by quarrels at home, and gives adolescents an opportunity to seek mates. "It is rare indeed to find a hunting band, particularly among the net-hunters, that does not include at least one family unit that normally hunts with another band" (1965: 291). While the net-hunters segment during the honey collection season, the archers, who live in small groups most of the year, coalesce in the honey season, which coincides with the time of their cooperative hunt.

The band and household organization of the !Kung and Ituri Pygmies has been found to be characteristic also of some peoples in far different climatic circumstances. The eight hundred Eskimo occupying the region about Coronation Gulf two generations ago lived in fourteen or so named areas from which the local groups took their own names. During the summer, they hunted in groups that averaged twenty persons but ranged from five to fifty, largest numbers congregating for caribou drives and fish runs. In winter they converged into seven or eight scattered "villages" of igloos to hunt seals at their breathing holes (Damas 1969: 122). This maximum concentration of a hundred meant that some of the bands in whole or part joined with others at the winter sites. For the most part, Eskimo igloos were family size, although

Human Social Organization as an Aspect of Culture

a composite snow house might house two families—not necessarily kin, but having male heads who had set up a wife-exchange partnership. And there was communal eating: "Generally the practice at mealtime was for members of one snowhouse to entertain most of the other villagers in shifts, with each household taking a more or less regular turn in the cycle of entertaining" (Damas 1969: 127).

On the other side of the world, Cheyenne equestrian hunters and Nootka fishermen and whalers of a century ago suggest that even when the technology of the hunting level is more complex, when the populations are larger, and when new social forms intervene between household and the whole aggregate, people circulate and cooperate in ways that cross-cut important domestic groups.

Cheyenne families and attached relatives lived in tipis, and a cluster of tipis, or around twenty-five to thirty people, comprised a camp. Food was cooked at a central fire and was served at one place or carried to the lodges. Men and women cooperated in their respective tasks and shared their output; children were passed from relative to relative. Thus, the whole camp was in some respects a household. And as Grinnell (1923, I: 97) observed, "These camps wandered about from place to place, sometimes coalescing with another camp, occasionally losing families or individuals, who went off to visit temporarily, or perhaps, permanently to unite with other camps. Occasionally two of these camps met, remained together for many months, and then separated to go in different directions."

Everyone in a Nootka plank house cooperated and pooled resources under the direction of chiefs; each family had its own fireplace, at which food was prepared and dispensed, within the house. Chiefs who resided at the house corners were fairly permanent residents, but lower-ranking families moved freely. Drucker (1951: 279-80) reports: "One receives the impression that there was a continual stream of people, mostly of low rank, moving in and out of the houses. . . . A family noted as good workers, lucky and skillful hunters, or clever craftsmen would be courted to the extent of giving them economic and ceremonial rights, to entice them to associate themselves more permanently to his house."

Families and dyads

The family has been defined as "a social group characterized by common residence, economic cooperation, and reproduction" that includes "adults of both sexes, at least two of whom maintain a socially approved sexual relationship, and one or more children, own or adopted, of the sexually cohabiting adults." George Peter Murdock, who phrased that definition (1949: 1), held that the nuclear family ("a married man and woman with their offspring") is a universal group found either by itself or linked with others to form a polygamous family ("two or more nuclear families affiliated by plural marriages," by **polygamy**) or an extended one, formed "by joining the nuclear family of a married adult to that of his parents" (1949: 1-2).

There is reason today to doubt the universality of the nuclear (or elementary or conjugal) family. Let us look at major segments of three cultures in which neither it nor extended and polygamous families as

Diversity and Adaptation in Social Organization

Thatched-roof houses in a Black Carib community. (Courtesy Nancie L. Gonzalez.)

Kitchen of a Black Carib consanguineal household. (Courtesy Nancie L. Gonzalez.)

Craftsman making a fiber basket in a Black Carib consanguineal household. (Courtesy Nancie L. Gonzalez.)

defined are present. They all have households, but the households are not structured as families.

Of the Nayar caste in Kerala, southwestern India, in the eighteenth century, Kathleen Gough (1959: 28) writes, ". . .they had a kinship system in which the elementary family of father, mother and children was not institutionalized as a legal, productive, distributive, residential, socializing or consumption unit." Those tasks were in the main the concern of the *taravad,* a land- and house-holding matrilineal group that consisted of brothers and sisters, and the children and daughters' children of the sisters, but no resident fathers. Before puberty, a girl acquired a ritual husband; he neither lived in the *taravad* nor did he have any obligation toward the girl or the children she might bear later, nor did they toward him, with the exception of a duty to mourn him on

Human Social Organization as an Aspect of Culture

his death. After she reached childbearing age, the girl took a number of lovers or visiting husbands from a higher caste and from her own sub-caste outside of her lineage, and when she became pregnant one or more of them were selected to acknowledge paternity. His (or their) only obligation was to present gifts to the midwife, not to support mother and child, who were provided for in the mother's *taravad*. Thus, a Nayar child had both ritual and recognized biological fathers but at no time lived in a nuclear, polygamous, or extended family. Marriage there was, but it simply assured mother and children secure statuses in their own kin groups; it was not a preliminary to family formation.

Nancie L. Solien Gonzalez has described a community of Black Carib in Guatemala among whom nearly half (45.3 percent) of house-holds were of a type she calls "consanguineal"; that is, the resident adults in them were linked by "blood" and not marriage relationships. They included one or more women, plus children, without a resident male, or one or more women, plus children, plus a male "blood" rela-tive (Gonzalez 1969: 68). The nuclear family obviously was not present in those households, and without it there could be no compounding of polygamous and extended families. Black Caribs are a culturally and biologically mixed people descended from Negro slaves and Carib Indians who lived on St. Vincent's Island in the Lesser Antilles in the seventeenth and eighteenth centuries and who later migrated to the mainland. It might be protested that something like the nuclear family is present in other Black Carib households (54.7 percent) and in other

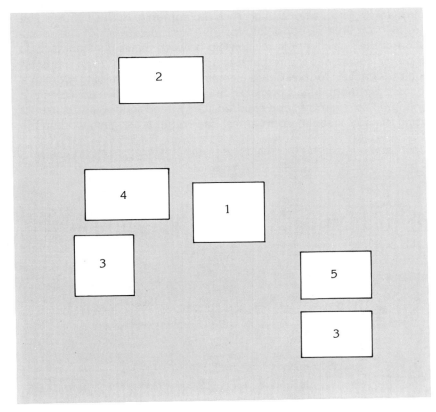

Diagram of five Black Carib households associated in a compound. Each household cooks and eats separately (in kitchens attached to the houses, not shown), but otherwise each helps the others. Household 3 occupies two houses. Four of the household heads are sisters, and their brother heads the fifth, as shown in the diagram at the top of p.192. (After Gonzalez 1969.)

Diversity and Adaptation in Social Organization

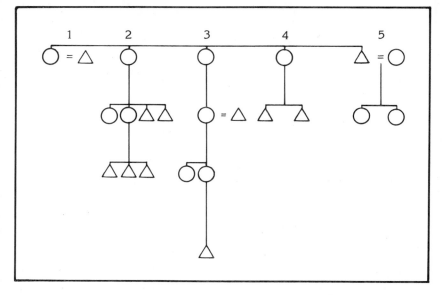

segments of the larger society of which the Caribs are part, but we can't expel from the system the statistically significant number of households lacking it. They are very much part of it.

Finally, the *kibbutz*, a kind of collective settlement established by pioneer immigrants in Israel, "has succeeded in eliminating most of the characteristics and functions of the traditional family. So says Melford Spiro (1970: 123), who studied such a community in the 1950s. "The parents have little responsibility for the physical care or for the socialization of their children; the relationship between mates does not include economic cooperation; and parents and children do not share a common residence." Couples share a combination bedroom-living room in a *kibbutz* apartment. Meals prepared in a communal kitchen are eaten in a communal dining room, and children, who attend schools and nurseries during the day, sleep in dormitories. Each adult is assigned work in the

Human Social Organization as an Aspect of Culture

kibbutz to which he or she is suited, and there is an ideology of share-and-share-alike that stems from the idealistic, socialist orientation of the pioneers. That there is a deep attachment between parents and children, who gather in the evenings for a period all look forward to, does not make the group a family in terms of the classical definition.

Now, ethnographers of the Bushmen, Mbuti, Eskimo, and Cheyenne, as well as those of the Nuer, Kuikuru, Hopi, Tsembaga, Kofyar—and, yes, the Bedouin camel drivers and Chinese villagers—all refer to families in those cultures. Among those groups there is variety in living arrangements and in the ways tasks are apportioned to their members and in their relations both among themselves and with outsiders. But the common definition of *family* ascribes to it characteristics that are viewed better as belonging to the domestic group in its household aspect. If we return the characteristics of common residence and economic coopera-

The dining room of a *kibbutz*. Food is prepared and served from a communal kitchen. The settlements continue the socialist ideals of Israeli pioneers. (Courtesy Joseph Ginat.)

Kibbutz play yard. Children attend school and nurseries during the day and sleep in their own dormitories. They are with their parents in the evening in the parents' bedroom-living room apartment. (Courtesy Joseph Ginat.)

Diversity and Adaptation in Social Organization

tion to the household, *family* loses some, although not all, of its old analytical importance.

Furthermore, by the older view, nuclear families are the building blocks of social structure, hard-shelled units that are compounded into larger ones. Richard N. Adams (1960) has proposed use of a device that at once opens them up and helps us account for different family forms in a framework of adaptation. It is the **dyad**, a set of two-way relationships which he applies to close domestic groups but which can be extended more broadly.

In the context of what ordinarily are called families, Adams notes that the primary units are the sexual dyad of a mature male and female (or conjugal dyad of husband and wife, if they are married), the mother-child dyad, and the father-child one. The first two involve biological events—copulation and birth—and the third depends on them but does not inevitably become recognized. Given the simple biological facts that males impregnate females and females give birth to children, there are two inescapable relationships—the sexual or conjugal one and the mother-child one. But the third, the father-child dyad, while it indubitably exists biologically, need not come effectively into being as a cultural relationship. The mother-child relationship is most likely to persist and become cultural because of the utter dependence of the human child for succorance on an adult, and this means, in most cases, its mother. But if mother and child are provided for economically by other means, father is dispensable—as among Nayar and some Black Carib households. While father has not been dispensed with in the Israeli *kibbutz*, even there he does not have economic responsibility. That responsibility is held by the whole *kibbutz*.

However, over the world's cultures, the three primary dyads are much more often than not linked in families, and Adams suggests an explanation that involves cultural adaptation. It runs like this: The first two dyads (sexual or conjugal and mother-child) ordinarily are not long-lasting enough in relation to the temporal span of a community to provide adequate stability and continuity for it. By identification of the status of "wife" with the status of "mother" (an instance of fusion) a firm link is set up between the two separate dyads, one of them of the same generation (wife-husband) and the other of two generations (mother-child). Ergo, a nuclear family (at least a family in form if not one that takes on all the tasks assumed in the definition) takes shape. "Seen from this point of view, the nuclear family becomes one combination that, if on nothing more than a random basis, must inevitably occur from time to time. It is the simplest way of joining the two dyads. . . . But while its occurrence is inevitable, its continuation is by no means inevitable because each of the dyads alone can also fulfill some functions, and there are, in addition, presumably other societal agents that can also fulfill them. The nuclear family therefore becomes only *one of the ways* the community maintains itself" (Adams 1960: 40-41, italics in original).

Other status pairs or dyads also come into being which may be viewed with primary reference to family or household or not, depending on the task at hand. They include siblings—brother-sister, brother-brother, and sister-sister—and other pairs beyond the three that Adams

Human Social Organization as an Aspect of Culture

suggested. In the matrilineal societies of such people as the Nayar, the Hopi, the Trobrianders (Malinowski's people), and the BaThonga of South Africa (referred to previously in relation to Radcliffe-Brown), the mother's brother-sister's son dyad is highly important, with mother's brother assuming some of the behaviors assigned to fathers in other cultures. Among the Cheyenne, the relationship of "friend" or "co-warrior" is noteworthy, as is the "partner" dyad among the Eskimo, both of them same-sex and non-kin pairs that culture uses to accomplish its work in the social aspect and that, as we shall see later, grade into the kind of groups called "associations."

Marriage has a place in a broader context than domestic groups, inasmuch as it joins not only individuals (statuses), families, and households but also larger aggregates. Relatives of the respective spouses *may* become in-laws (**affines** or **affinal kin**) to each other, either creating new bonds or reinforcing what bonds were already present. Lest we be led into thinking that marriages, whether or not they are made in heaven, establish heaven on earth, we should remind ourselves of people like the Semai, who feel secure only among "blood" relatives; all others are *mai*, and because one must marry one of them "marriage becomes a focus of anxiety" (Dentan 1968: 73). Or of the farming Lugbara of Uganda, who divide people with whom they have social relationships into *juru* and *o'dipi*. The terms are not easily translatable, but the Lugbaras' ethnographer, John Middleton (1965: 45), explains in part: "In the context of fighting, one fights with arrows against *juru* and not against *o'dipi*; in that of exogamy, one marries *juru* and not *o'dipi*." (Our people fight yours with arrows. Will you marry me?)

But it is precisely in that bridging of groups (kin and strangers, friends and foes) and strengthening of existing ties (mother's people, father's people) that **exogamy**, or marrying out, is so important in primitive cultures. Its other result is to make it possible to provide legitimate infant recruits to the groups.

Endogamy, the other side of the coin, is a requirement of marriage within a prescribed social distance. As White (1959: 107) puts it, "...the processes of exogamy and endogamy work hand in hand, the one to increase the size of group by extending the radius of the group of persons within which one may marry; the other, endogamy, operates to foster solidarity by preventing this radius from becoming too great."

While rules of exogamy and endogamy pertain to marriage, **incest** rules or taboos forbid sexual intercourse between particular statuses or between particular groups. They are by no means the same thing, for the work the two kinds of rules do is different though complementary. The one regulates external, intergroup relations, and the other primarily internal, intragroup relationships. The incest rule has the effect of avoiding and suppressing, by its forbidding of sexual intercourse, disruptive tensions and behaviors that might arise in and destroy culturally important human groups. It backs up and reinforces the exogamic rule, although the two do not coincide. It is not taking a serious matter lightly to compare the incest rule with the practice in primitive cultures of walking away from conflict. Both are positive means to manage and accommodate the sometimes recalcitrant biological material whose behavior culture channels and converts into workable forms.

How Morgan
diagrammed the terms
applied to
consanguineal kin in
the English system,
which is a descriptive
one. Lineal kin of Ego
(represented by the
big *I* in the center)
are kept separate from
Ego's collaterals. (From
Morgan 1871.)

What do kinship terms label?

Although we have disclaimed that anthropology is a "science of the primitive," the fact that it took preliterate cultures into its domain and for a century concentrated upon them resulted in a great accumulation of observations and theories of kinship. Wherever ethnographers went to live with the peoples from whom they learned, they had to take

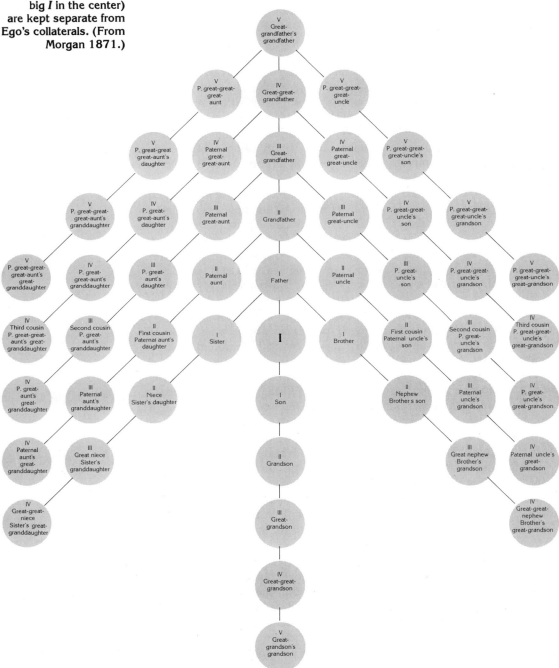

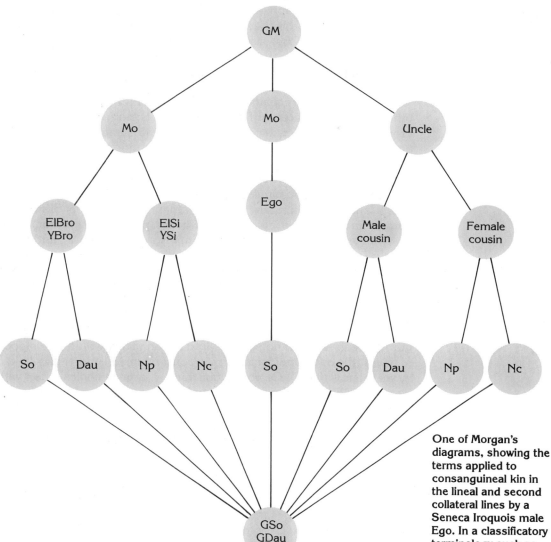

One of Morgan's diagrams, showing the terms applied to consanguineal kin in the lineal and second collateral lines by a Seneca Iroquois male Ego. In a classificatory terminology such as this, as Morgan pointed out, lineal and collateral kin are gathered in two generations above and below Ego. Abbreviations substituted for Morgan's terms in the five generations are: GM, grandmother; Mo, mother; ElBro and YBro, elder and younger brother; ElSi and YSi, elder and younger sister; So, son; Dau, daughter; Np, nephew; Nc, niece; GSo, grandson; and GDau, granddaughter. (From Morgan 1871.)

account of it. It appeared that the organization of groups and their relationships, and the duties, rights, and obligations of individuals, could in some measure be summed up in terms of kinship practices and rules. Moreover, the patterns of kin terms (called "terminologies" and "nomenclatures") were so different from those in Western societies that they demanded explanation.

Lewis Henry Morgan, founder of kinship studies as a scientific discipline, discovered a basic difference between terminologies of primitive and advanced societies and gave names to the two kinds, **classificatory kinship terminology** and **descriptive kinship terminology**. Like other discoverers, he began by perceiving differences and similarities in things, asked questions about them, and extended his observations. Among the Seneca Iroquois of New York, Morgan learned that the term *father* was applied not only to a person's progenitor but also to his progenitor's brothers, and *mother* not only to his biological mother but also to her sisters (a pattern already mentioned for the Cheyenne). Seneca terms *brother* and *sister* applied not only between children with the same parents (that is, siblings) but reciprocally between them and offspring of their mothers' sisters and fathers' brothers (the **parallel cousin** relationship). On the other hand, they applied other terms to children of fathers' sisters and mothers' brothers (their **cross-cousins**). Later, Morgan perceived the same pattern of terms among Ojibwa Indians in northern Michigan and found indications of it in writings about the Dakota and Creek (White 1964: xv).

Never one to shirk when his interest was aroused, Morgan made four field trips to western states and Canada to collect kin terms and sent letters and questionnaires to missionaries in the United States and abroad and to Indian agents, aided in his pursuit of information by Joseph Henry, first secretary of the Smithsonian Institution, and Lewis Cass, secretary of state (White 1957). A compilation of his results and his explanations for them were published in the massive volume *Systems of Consanguinity and Affinity of the Human Family* (1871).

Let's make a brief detour. If asked to define *kinship*, you in all probability would think first of a family cluster of father, mother, brothers and sisters, or sons and daughters, and beyond it uncles and aunts, cousins, grandparents and grandchildren, and so on. They would be "blood" relatives (the anthropological term is *consanguineal*) and in-laws linked by marriage (*affinal*). Or you might think of a genealogical chart with people, living and dead, connected consanguineally and affinally, representing in a sense a greatly extended family. Whether your point of reference is family or genealogy, I suspect you would hold that kinship terms label, in relation to a given person, other persons with positions in lines of biological descent.

Morgan held substantially the same position—that "they have to do with a people's recognition of their genealogical relationships and therefore describe to us the actual organization of the kinship order (or sometimes an anterior form of it)" (Service 1971a: 99). That is, things are arranged on the basis of real descent. As Morgan himself wrote, "Every system of consanguinity must be able to ascend and descend in the lineal line and through several degrees from any given person, and to specify the relationship of each to *Ego*; and also from the lineal, to enter the several collateral lines and follow and describe the collateral relatives through several generations. . . . In fine, a system of relationship, originating in necessity, is a domestic institution, which serves to organize a family by the bond of consanguinity" (1871: 11).

With Morgan's emphasis on the importance of descent line recognition in mind, we can understand his division of terminologies into two fundamental kinds. In our own and like societies, elementary family terms such as *father* and *son* are applied by a focal individual (**Ego** is what Morgan and other anthropologists call him or her) only to persons in his or her direct line of **descendants** and **ascendants**. To **collateral relatives**, persons in collateral lines (illustrated by father's brother's or grandfather's brother's lines), are applied terms which are either new ones, such as *cousin* or *nephew*, or combinations of the primary ones, such as *sister's son* or *grandfather's brother*. Primary terms generally are not found outside Ego's line, nor are nonprimary or combination terms applied to members of his or her line. These are the principles of descriptive terminology.

What we have set down previously about the Seneca pattern runs counter to those principles, and terminologies like that of the Seneca are *classificatory*. *Mother* and *father*, for instance, are terms applied not only to Ego's direct antecedents but to their like-sex siblings as well. *Brother* and *sister* are extended to offspring of Ego's classificatory *mothers* and *fathers*. (We shall raise a question about the word *extended* a bit later on, but using it does no harm here.) At those points, lineals and collaterals are joined by primary terms, and any such joinings are enough to reveal the classificatory tendency. And note a characteristic of Seneca terminology that is found in a large proportion of primitive cultures: relatives are *all* gathered together at grandparents' and grandchildren's levels. Socially, *you* have only two grandfathers and two grandmothers. Beyond that you have paternal and maternal great uncles and great aunts. In the same way, only the children of your own children will be your grandchildren—not the children of your nephews and nieces. As Morgan (1871: 13) pointed out, classificatory kinship tends to "prevent dispersion of the blood" and lets no consanguines escape, while the descriptive kind encourages divergence of lines and (he didn't put it this way) lets relatives beyond a certain point go hang.

In that last observation lies the evolutionary significance of Morgan's discovery. The patterns of kin terms reflect the importance of kinship in primitive cultures and the decreased importance of it in advanced ones. It was Morgan's idea that at a certain level of development, property and territory come to the fore as organizational principles. With respect to property, at least, he was wholly correct. However, when it came to explaining the several varieties of the two types of kinship, Morgan relied principally upon tying them with forms of marriage in an evolutionary scheme, an hypothesis that has been discarded.

We are at one of those places in our study in which you may feel you are being put through a wringer, but kinship is not an easy subject. You might have a feeling of being let down when I tell you now that, although Morgan was right about some things, his judgment as to what kinship terms label is today partially inoperative. We will mention only two authorities who contributed to clarification of the matter.

Radcliffe-Brown held that kinship terms are not labels for genealogical positions arrived at by counting up and down descent lines, but "terms . . . used in address and reference as denotative of social positions relevant to interpersonal conduct" (Service 1971a: 99). In R-B's words (1952: 52-53), a kinship system "is in the first place a system of dyadic relations between person and person in a community, the behaviour of any two persons in any of these relations being regulated in some way, and to a greater or lesser extent, by social usage." Terms, then, label observable behaviors, and terms, behaviors, groups, and ideas all together comprise a system. Although Radcliffe-Brown disagreed with Morgan on just what kinship terms point to, he was very much like him in seeing the family as the fountain of kinship and its terminologies. "The unit of structure from which a kinship system is

A male Trobriander applies the term *tama* to all males and *tabu* to all females in his father's matrilineage. The *tamas*, then, include his own father, but the term can hardly be translated "father" in our sense. (After George H. Fathauer, in *Matrilineal kinship*, David M. Schneider and Kathleen Gough, eds., Berkeley: University of California Press, 1961.)

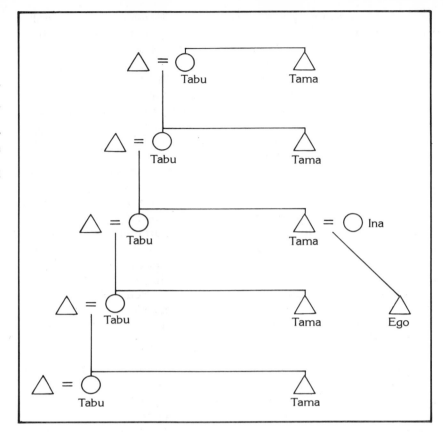

built up is the group which I call an 'elementary family,' consisting of a man and his wife and their child or children, whether they are living together or not, . . .[and] interlocking of elementary families creates a network of what I shall call, for lack of any better term, genealogical relations, spreading out indefinitely" (Radcliffe-Brown 1952: 51-52).

Another step was taken by the British anthropologist A. M. Hocart, who took issue with the notion that the "meaning" of a primary kinship term takes shape in the confines of a family and then flows outward as the term is "extended" to widening circles of kin. Rather, said Hocart, we should look for the use of the term in total context and define it in relation to the bigger context instead of in the narrow family one. Only then will we be prepared to translate kinship terms accurately and understand them.

He approached the matter by showing how ethnographers in Melanesia had fallen into error in trying to define the term *tama*. "The person most commonly called *tama* in Melanesia, the one most in evidence, is a man's father. He is the one who will be named if you ask, 'Who is your *tama*?' So *tama* has been duly set down as 'father'. . . .It was soon noticed, however, that other men besides the father are called *tama*. By all rules the first translation should have been dropped, and a new one found to cover all the different *tamas,* and thus express the essence of *tama*-ship. Unfortunately, no single word can do so, and it has remained in the literature of the South Seas as 'father,' with the proviso that it is

Human Social Organization as an Aspect of Culture

'extended' to cover father's brother, father's father's brother's sons, and so on. Ever since we have been racking our brains to explain how Melanesians call their uncles, and even remote cousins, 'fathers' " (Hocart 1972:223).

Going specifically to the Fijian system as an example, what *tama* means, said Hocart, is not "father" at all but "all males of the previous generation on the father's side," for among the Fijian hill tribes generations and "sides"—father's and mother's—are of key importance. Terms, then, label segments of kin as a whole. They "do not express consanguinity, as we have unfortunately been accustomed by Morgan to believe, but they fix the place of any relative according to generation and side" (Hocart 1972:224).

Do we, then, follow Morgan, Radcliffe-Brown, or Hocart to find the meaning of kinship terms? All the contributions are relevant. Morgan overemphasized "blood" relationships, but on the other hand it would be carrying things too far to say that descent has nothing to do at all with assigning names to *some* kin. Being born and having parents is one observed fact that culture interprets and makes use of, but not necessarily in a uniform way. Radcliffe-Brown's insistence that kin terms label relationships and relationships involve observable behavior is all to the good. These we can extract and put into our cultural system. But the worm's eye view of "extensions" that he shared with Morgan is needlessly confining and distracts attention from the whole and the working of the larger parts. Hocart's emphasis on big categories and translation of kin terms in relation to them overcomes that handicap. On the other hand, although his translation of terms is superior, we should not let ourselves ignore the *behavior* attached to generations and sides. (Hocart would not disagree, although in the work cited he focused on translation.)

Let me illustrate with the mother's brother-sister's son relationship among the Hopi. Mother's brother, not father, is a boy's disciplinarian, albeit a congenial one; he is a man of authority in the boy's household, **lineage**, and clan, transmitter at once of technical, social, and sacred lore, principal supervisor of his upbringing (Titiev 1944:25-26). The content of the relationship has grown out of household, village, and intervillage life, responsive to work, land ownership, residence, custodianship of rituals and sacred objects, and a host of other rights and obligations. Perhaps the relationship might be translated, in Hocart's terms, "male on mother's side in her generation," but behavior is the heart of it, and consanguinity is not irrelevant, either.

Kinship, in systemic terms, is something that culture does to and with people. (Here we take the "culture does" stance, although you are aware that our system is a construct set up to help us understand the movement of people and things.) It invents from the behavior of those living and working together and apart culturally grouped and defined forms, analogous on the technological plane to the techniques by which energy and materials are extracted from habitat. In human terms, its end is security; in systems terms, efficient and adaptive organization. In its terminological aspect, it provides labels for the statuses and groups that emerge in cultural society.

Well, you might say, there are other statuses and groups, too, and they are named. Take shaman, chief, canoe maker, king, congressman, priest, or judge. Service (1971a: 101-4) makes an important distinction: Shamans and priests are shamans and priests to everyone in any society of which they are part; the names for them "refer to social positions in the society itself, not to a relationship with another person." And the names are not those commonly applied by family members to each other. That is, the terms are *sociocentric* and *nonfamilistic*. Kinship terms, on the other hand, are always relative, depending on the individual using them; they shift as Ego shifts. One Ego's father is another Ego's brother, another's husband, another's son. Furthermore, the terms are of the sort found in that last sentence: they are commonly found in families, households, and like domestic groups. Thus kinship terms are *egocentric,* not sociocentric, and *familistic,* not nonfamilistic. Summing it up in a definition, kinship terms are "egocentric-familistic status terms." Please note that in using the word *familistic* we do not need to endorse the view that the family is the fountain of all kinship behavior nor that the words used need have started there. The larger circle of kin *share* the terms with family, and family *shares* with them.

Now that we have dutifully made an effort to cope with what has been called kinship, let me append some unprofessional misgivings about it. An answer to the question What do kin terms label? perhaps should be prefaced by a cautious statement: We don't quite know. To me, there is some support for an answer like that often given to the question What is psychology? Psychology is what psychologists do. Kinship is what anthropologists have done, or overdone, in interpreting relationships. One can find sympathy for the tart remark of Jack Goody (1972: 5): "There has been much discussion about the 'meaning of kinship,' i.e., how kin terms are to be identified and interpreted. Some of this seems rather pointless since in practice observers have little difficulty in making the identification." There could be some ethnocentrism in that, in the sense that observers are identifying (and evaluating or interpreting) things from their own cultural (and professional subcultural) experience. Kinship, one might say, then, is a folk conceptualization of relationships.

Because of the circumstances mentioned in the first paragraph of this section, about the apparent importance of behavior labelled "kinship" in folk and professional wisdom, there has been what might be judged overkill, particularly in preoccupation with terminologies. Big categories such as *classificatory* and *descriptive* match major evolutionary categories of society, but smaller categories do not fit kinds of societies very precisely. To paraphrase a remark by the biological taxonomist George Gaylord Simpson about evolutionary categories, we have put the chart before the horse. Possibly Morgan (1964: 13-14) hit upon the core of primitive society when he defined it as "founded upon persons, and upon relations purely personal." Culture, in systems terms, netted these interpersonal behaviors, shaped them, and built more social culture on them, but kinship was only one of the ways in which it did so, and perhaps too much has been called kinship. Morgan was bemused by descent, but as Fried (1967: 124) has said, "the basic formula for the band egalitarian society...is 'we are probably close relatives because we live together.'" The system makes its relationships out of residence, as well as begats and many other behaviors.

Human Social Organization as an Aspect of Culture

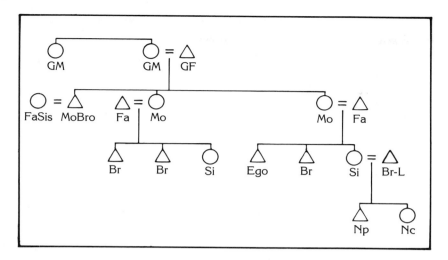

Relationships to male Cheyenne Ego in his natal camp. Note the consistent generational pattern of consanguineal and affinal terms. (After Anderson 1951.)

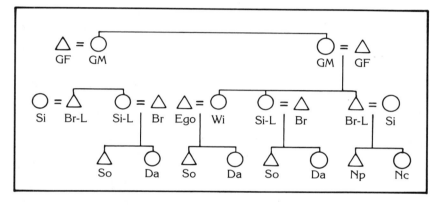

Relationships to male Cheyenne Ego in the camp into which he moves when he marries. Again, there is a consistent generational pattern among affines as well as consanguines, except that parents-in-law are raised a generation and called grandmother and grandfather. Note that all Ego's brothers' children are son and daughter to him and all the children of the women Ego calls sister are nephew and niece to him. (After Anderson 1951.)

There is said to be a convention in the field reports of archeologists that they end more often than not with the sentence "More work needs to be done." More needs to be done in categorizing and explaining cultural relationships in their social aspect, too, not necessarily beginning with more fieldwork but with a rethinking of what has been observed—and perhaps obscured—under kinship terminologies.

On the other hand, although I have stressed only a few big issues with regard to them, I decidedly do not intend to suggest that terminologies are something that can be swept under the rug by anthropology students. In the first place, they offer one way to put oneself into an individual's social universe in a primitive culture, to take a stand with Ego and get a sense of the relationships around him or her. And in the second place, how can one decide what weight should be given to terminologies and look for their causes if one doesn't know something about them?

Kinship terms
and social groups

Egocentric-familistic status terms that might be applied to people in two imaginary Cheyenne camps are arranged in the diagrams above. All would be employed by a male Ego, first in his natal camp and then in the one into which he moves when he marries. In relation to male Ego, the other seventeen people in the first camp and twenty-one in the second fall into fifteen statuses, seven of them being found in both groups. A Cheyenne male would find kin to whom he would apply the terms in many camps and bands; he would not be related to everybody, but to a large number of people. He could roam among his *kindred* (an anthropological term for a circle of relatives calculated from Ego, usually restricted to those he would meet in ordinary daily life or could call upon in emergencies or for aid in performance of social rituals).

This is a **cognatic descent** or **bilateral kinship** pattern, in which Ego finds no separate statuses peculiar either to father's or mother's side. Ego looks to the left and looks to the right, and lo, kinship is uniform. It is also a generational pattern, because sets of terms are generally restricted to a single generation in relation to Ego's. Statically, the whole resembles a ladder, with the single exception in this example that of parents-in-law, who share a status with grandparents. Our own pattern, in spite of its descriptive rather than classificatory character, also is cognatic and generational.

What possible factors were back of this arrangement of kin terms? The brunt of hunting and raiding fell upon a middle generation of active males, who cooperated with each other and depended on each other. Older males gradually withdrew from more active life when they had sons to replace them, and youngsters were not yet ready for full participation. Members of the active generation married one another's sisters and shared brother-in-law status; behaviorally, they were brothers, and brothers and brothers-in-law together might be translated "males of my generation." Sexual distinctions between siblings were reflected in the terms applied by brothers and sisters to each other's children, it might be noted. Male Ego called his brother's children, like his own, son and daughter and his sister's children the equivalent of nephew and niece. Female Ego called her brother's children nephew and niece and her sister's children, like her own, son and daughter.

Probably relevant also was the absence of a countervailing factor. Cheyenne camps and bands, as mounted hunters on the High Plains, could not settle down in one place and accumulate property and rights to specific resources that they could transmit vertically in descent lines. Ordinarily when groups do settle down and accumulate property, **corporate groups**—such as lineages or clans which hold title to the use of land—emerge, and there is some tendency for sets of statuses to be formed which emphasize the vertical line separations. Perhaps the Cheyenne were in such a situation when they lived on the Missouri tributaries, but, if so, life on the High Plains reversed it. Interestingly, all of the migrant tribes were tending toward this generational organization in the nineteenth century, no matter what their previous arrangements (Eggan 1955, Oliver 1962). However, let us not link bilaterality too glibly with nomadism. Settled Polynesian farmers and fishermen went even farther than Plains hunters in their generational pattern.

Lineal patterns differentiate kin linked through mothers and fathers and tend to push status terms up and down vertically, bundling some whole collateral descent lines into as few as two statuses in relation to Ego. The Hopi provide an example of lineality.

Human Social Organization as an Aspect of Culture

The Hopi live in uxorilocal-matrilocal households within their mesa-top villages. The structure of a household in its kinship aspect includes a woman, her daughters and their children, her unmarried sons, and the spouses of the women. It is much like a Cheyenne camp, but striking differences in Hopi as compared with Cheyenne kinship terms appear when it is looked at in a different perspective, as in the diagrams on p. 206.

None of the four diagrams represents an actual household, but each is an idealized lineage, a conceptualized **descent group**, viewed by Ego male or female, the lineages stemming from female founders. Titiev defines a Hopi lineage as "an exogamic, unilateral group of matrilineal kindred, demonstrably descended from a common ancestress" (1944: 58). There is no need to repeat verbally what the diagrams demonstrate; I recommend you explore each of them, starting with Ego. It may appear that in this exercise we are returning to the Morgan mode, climbing up and down descent lines without reference to anything else, but there is some relation with residence. Although the diagrams do not represent actual households, lineage members tend to live together, so that a Hopi would find households with cores of relatives roughly corresponding with the statuses represented in the diagrams.

But among the Hopi there are larger groupings, too—about thirty clans, each comprised of linked lineages, and about nine **phratries**, consisting of linked clans. Classically, *clan* is defined as a unilineal, exogamous kinship group with a name (White 1959: 155), a group whose members assume they are descended from a common ancestor or ancestress. Hopi clans are land-holding units, enter into political life (the Bear clan head, for instance, is village chief at Oraibi), and are important in ritual organization. In its principal house, each clan has one or more *wuya*, objects which are clan symbols and which may be the nucleus of one or another ritual (Titiev 1944: 58).

How did lineages, clans, and phratries get started and grow? Titiev (1944: 57-58) has hypothesized that "an original household may start out as the equivalent of one matrilineal lineage and clan, and that if it expands in size it may then become segmented into two households which later develop into two apparently distinct lineages within the same clan. . . .At a later stage each of the recently separated lineages is apt to acquire a new *wuya*, or a new name, or both. When this happens each lineage may properly be spoken of as a matrilineal clan. . . ." Later, as such clans increase in number and ties between them weaken, they form a phratry of two or more clans.

Robin Fox (1967: 86-92) has fleshed out the hypothesis in an ecological framework. It runs like this: Once the Hopi were hunters and gatherers, like their linguistic relatives, the Shoshone and Paiute, roaming the semidesert Great Basin, living in small, self-sufficient households centered by nuclear families, cooperating with other families on occasion and exchanging mates with them. Later, they became marginal farmers; the women, who had been the seed and root gatherers, had major responsibility for gardening and transmitted their knowledge and techniques to their daughters, the daughters' hunting husbands joining their wives in uxorilocal-matrilocal households. Farming supported slow increases in population, but the household settlements were scattered.

Terms applied by Hopi to relatives in particular lineages. Note especially the fourth diagram, in which all kin in mother's father's matrilineal lineage are grandmother and grandfather to Ego (both male and female). Generational or age distinctions are overborne by the lineal principle. (Reprinted from *Social organization of the western Pueblos* by Fred Eggan by permission of the University of Chicago Press. Copyright 1950 by the University of Chicago. All rights reserved.)

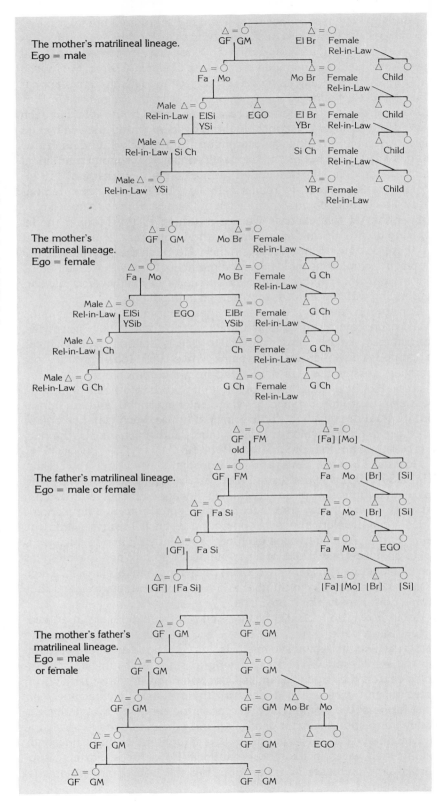

The mother's matrilineal lineage. Ego = male

The mother's matrilineal lineage. Ego = female

The father's matrilineal lineage. Ego = male or female

The mother's father's matrilineal lineage. Ego = male or female

When the Hopi moved into villages for a complex of reasons that included defense, the matrilocal households were retained, and they farmed small plots of land scattered below the mesas. Now, however, the males, who previously had moved away from their exogamous natal households and lost close contact, remained near at hand; they visited frequently, took part in household rituals and management of family affairs. Thus, Fox suggests, there arose recognized groups of males and females related by descent—**matrilineages**.

A key point is the place of *wuya* and rituals in maintaining ties between those people who stayed in an original household and those who moved away when it became too large and when farming plots were insufficient. Possibly as far back as the marginal farming days each house kept a religious object—an animal or bird skin or a bag of seeds— used in various humble rites. The house and its members became associated with the object and its name, as Bears, Parrots, Pumpkins, or Tobaccos. When, in the village phase of Hopi adaptation, or even earlier, segments of lineage groups in the households moved away, they retained the house name and became a dispersed clan. Later, as clans increased in size and people moved about, they, too, segmented. Even if the segments adopted new names and *wuya*, they retained their traditions of common origin. A phratry would consist of the parts of an original clan, each grown to clan size. Elman Service, who calls dispersed lineages, clans, and phratries kin *sodalities* (associations), points out that it is a general rule that "cultural inventions such as a name, ceremony, mythology, insignia of membership, and so on are. . .much more common in sodalities than in face-to-face residential groups—they are much more necessary" (1971b: 13).

As is sometimes the case, Hopi adaptation in the social aspect, here the formation and deployment of unilineal descent groups, was not wholly successful. In Titiev's view (1944: 98, 99), ". . .while the material culture of the Pueblos gradually became adjusted to an enlarged scale, their social organization failed to keep pace with it . . . the preservation of powerful clan ties prevented the development of strong, central village administrations; and the fact that the lesser social units successfully retained their integrity is ample proof that the pueblos were never welded into homogeneous wholes." Through their history, they have often been broken by factional strife. It suggests that while kinship, a complex cultural invention, may have been a mainstay through long ages of human history it has its limitations.

Two other kinds of groups related to kinship, segmentary lineages and conical or cognatic clans, will be discussed later in the context of political organization.

Associations as extracted parts

Although the statuses, groups, and rules of technologically primitive cultures can be put into kinship and residence contexts in part, some relationships exist that are more or less separable from them. That is, non-kin and those not living together act together. We shall call them **associations** in preference to other designations such as *clubs* and *sodalities*, because the term is not confining. It allows us to include a range from dyads (friends and partners) to large-scale groups (like organized **age-sets**), and from temporary ones with limited objectives (such as informal work parties) to long-lasting organizations that do a variety of tasks.

The adjective *voluntary*, which often accompanies the term *association*, is out of place in a "culture does" orientation. Associations provide additional alternatives above and beyond kinship and residence for participation in organized behavior, but, if we assume that any association is an extracted part in a symboling-dependent, energy-transforming system, then voluntariness on the part of any individual is an irrelevancy. *Association* is not an ideal term either, because kinship also depends on residence and other interpersonal behaviors. That is, kin associate. And non-kin often end up in relationships that are remarkably kinlike. But rather than invent a new term, we shall find some situations in which to apply the old one.

Copper Eskimo men formed partnerships, variously engaging in the free and easy behavior called "joking," dancing together, exchanging wives, and sharing harpooned seals. According to David Damas (1969: 127), "Social structuring within the band was based largely on partnerships which seemed for the most part to operate independently of existing kinship ties," and the dyadic relations cross-cut band membership. In New Guinea and its fringing islands, trading friends or partners formed extensive networks that linked culture to culture (Harding 1970: 96), and in the Philippines similar partnerships were the model for the peace pact "initiated by two individuals from different regions...," each of whom "holds the peace pact for his particular kinship group, although its provisions are binding on the whole region" (Dozier 1967: 84). Thus, non-kin dyads can be looked at as occupying one end of the association spectrum.

Some groups are formed to assist in economic production. When men assemble for farm work in northern Nigeria, they are rewarded with food or drink, a custom called the "field of beer." The group may become organized and persist and get a name. In one of the Kofyar villages studied by Netting (1968: 138-43) there were four groups of ten to thirteen members, the groups being roughly graded according to the ages of their members, from most junior to most senior; they had regular leaders and remained together as they grew older.

A spectrum from informality to formality is found in associations in the context of ritual. Among the Nootka, what Drucker (1951: 399) calls "age-grade clubs"—"rather amorphous informally made-up groupings, nominally based on age and sex lines..."—performed ceremonial dances. Small groups of Tsembaga young men who assumed during the ceremony a particular ritual headdress and who could call each other "brother" are regarded by Rappaport (1967a: 204) as having the ingredients of "supralocal age classes." People of the Hopi Pueblos, on the other hand, had several societies which were charged with the conduct of a single ceremony in its season and acted as curing groups; they were "open to all who [were] of the proper sex and age" (Titiev 1944: 103, 106). While in times past membership may have belonged to the particular clan which had charge of that society and its ritual, later it was drawn from any clan.

Human Social Organization as an Aspect of Culture

Like other East African peoples, the Nuer are known for their age-set organization in which boys of fourteen to sixteen years of age are initiated into the lowest group on the categorical ladder, to be joined in a number of succeeding years by others until a *ric*, or age-set, is completed. After a four-year interval, another *ric* is begun, and the groups move upward through the succession of generations. Unlike those of some other East Africans, Nuer age sets are not related to military or political activities (Evans-Pritchard 1940: 249-54).

The dyads and groups we are calling associations, then, form on the basis of the same characteristics as do kin statuses and groups—age, sex, residence, cooperation and sharing in cultural work. They cross-cut kinship and residence groups. With regard to internal structure, what any association lacks in comparison with kinship groups is the complement of statuses usually if not always found in the residential household. Associations usually stress age or sex or particular occupations and are more specialized than kin groups.

Association behaviors resemble kinship in some ways. For instance, a Nuer does not marry the daughter of an age mate because he is regarded as one of her fathers, nor does a Cheyenne military society member marry one of the girls who is an aid and "sister" to the group. The problem of separating association and kinship might go away if we returned to the old limiting definition of kinship as "relations of descent and marriage," but that would leave a great deal out of kinship and we would lose much in our understanding of it.

There appears to be an order in appearance and importance of associations in general evolutionary perspective, not a straight-line burgeoning nor a decline after an initial heyday, but successive ups and downs. After a survey of historical materials and theoretical statements about them, Robert T. Anderson (1971) concluded that "voluntary associations," which he defined as "formally constituted groups bound primarily by ties of shared interest rather than kinship or coresidence," have been rare among the mobile hunters and gatherers. They have been abundant among village cultivators ("when such villages are not integrated into complex political and economic systems") and much less in evidence in preindustrial states based on advanced agriculture and trade (from about 3000 B.C. until the Industrial Revolution). From that point on, they increased again in numbers and importance. It suggests that associations are variably adaptive at different cultural levels, depending on the comparative efficiency of statuses and groups in other contexts and their capacity to do what is not being done or not being done well.

Suggested Readings

Eggan, Fred, ed. 1955. *Social anthropology of North American tribes*. 2nd ed. Chicago: University of Chicago Press.*

Evans-Pritchard, E. E., and others. 1956. *The institutions of primitive society: A series of broadcast talks*. Oxford, England: Basil Blackwell.

Fox, Robin. 1967. *Kinship and marriage: An anthropological perspective*. Baltimore: Penguin Books.*

Kummer, Hans. 1971. *Primate societies: Group techniques of ecological adaptation*. Chicago: Aldine-Atherton.*

Lee, Richard B., and Irven DeVore, eds. 1968. *Man the hunter*. Chicago: Aldine.*

Marshall, Lorna. 1965. "The !Kung Bushmen of the Kalahari Desert." In *Peoples of Africa*. James L. Gibbs, Jr., ed. New York: Holt, Rinehart and Winston.

Quiatt, Duane D., ed. 1972. *Primates on primates: Approaches to the analysis of nonhuman primate social behavior*. Minneapolis: Burgess.*

Radcliffe-Brown, A. R. 1952. *Structure and function in primitive society*. Glencoe, Ill.: Free Press.*

Schusky, Ernest L. 1974. *Variation in kinship*. New York: Holt, Rinehart and Winston.*

Service, Elman R. 1966. *The hunters*. Englewood Cliffs, N.J.: Prentice-Hall.*

———. 1971. *Primitive social organization: An evolutionary perspective*. 2nd ed. New York: Random House.

Spiro, Melford E. 1970. *Kibbutz: Venture in utopia*. New York: Schocken Books.*

Steward, Julian H. 1955. *Theory of culture change: The methodology of multilinear evolution*. Urbana: University of Illinois Press.

Turnbull, Colin M. 1965. "The Mbuti Pygmies of the Congo." In *Peoples of Africa*. James L. Gibbs, Jr., ed. New York: Holt, Rinehart and Winston.

Van der Post, Laurens. 1958. *The lost world of the Kalahari*. New York: William Morrow and Company.*

Economics, defined as the social organization of production, distribution, and consumption of material goods and services, is the most important and consequential aspect of the social sphere of culture. By *consequential*, we mean that in the long run economics has a greater effect upon the other aspects of social life than they have upon it, although of course economic activity is conditioned by politics and other social relationships. This we would be led to expect from our systems orientation. When we call culture an energy-transforming system, conceptualizing its capture of environmental energies and its import of materials as the technological process, and call the social relations involved in the production and allocation of those energies and goods economics—it is logical to put this aspect on the forward social line.

Aspects and levels again

Once again, let us emphasize aspect, which is defined by the cultural tasks performed. Groups, statuses, and rules, whatever else they may do, have an economic aspect or side when they are involved in the organized producing, distributing, and consuming of the goods and services in any culture. The topics we shall meet presently—the organization of work, the ownership relation, and kinds of

Chapter Nine
The Economic
Aspect of Social
Organization

211

exchange—will point that up. Some social relations may be seen as primarily economic and others not; we needn't expect one aspect to wholly cannibalize the content of another, important as it may be.

It will be useful from the start to link varieties of economic behavior with levels of organization and integration reached in the social aspect of cultures as a whole. Although the evolutionary levels we are adopting—**egalitarian**, **rank**, **stratified**, and **state societies**—were devised by Morton Fried (1967) in the context of politics, they are relatable to economics, and here we emphasize that aspect of them, leaving the political to the following chapter.

Egalitarian and rank levels bracket primitive society. In both, division of labor rests primarily on age and sex, and all households have equal access to the basic resources necessary to maintain life—whether they are hunting-and-gathering areas, farm land, or fishing spots for subsistence or places where materials can be gotten for shelters, tools, weapons, containers, and the like. And human labor, as a resource, is equally free and available; a person works primarily for self and household and calls upon others for aid when needed but is not bound to work for someone else who has the right peremptorily to take a share of the produce. In rank society, there is some specialization of crafts beyond simple age and sex lines; there may be circumstances in which there is a partial and temporary restriction on the use of resources, and a status or group here and there may benefit in a material way from privilege, but these circumstances are exceptional, and there is little lessening of the basically egalitarian situation. Examples of egalitarian societies are Eskimo, Bushmen, Mbuti, and other hunter-gatherers; simple farming-and-herding cultures also retain strong egalitarian flavor. Instances of rank societies are Nootka and Trobrianders.

It is in modes of exchange that differences appear. As we shall see, a form called **redistribution** (a channeling of some goods and services to an acknowledged leader and a return to the producers in gifts and feasts) is added to the earlier-appearing but continuing egalitarian mode called **reciprocity**. Reciprocity is a more general giving and taking between statuses and groups.

Stratified and state levels are postprimitive. In Fried's definition (1967: 186), "A stratified society is one in which members of the same sex and equivalent age status do not have equal access to the basic resources that maintain life." Impairment of access may take the form of outright denial to some individuals or groups, as when land is not redistributed periodically or the redistribution is confined to some and excludes others, or through labor exploitation, as when have-nots are required to buy their subsistence with their labor or to turn over a portion of what they produce on the haves' land. Such a system, standing by itself and unsupported, Fried sees as unstable and short-lived, and there probably have been no indigenous developments of it in 2,000 years. That is, in that time there have not been instances in which stratification arose free from pressure or takeover by stronger systems in contact with the unstratified ones. Stratification will not work without a means to enforce it, and that means is the state—"the complex of institutions by means of which the power of the society is organized on a basis superior to kinship" (Fried 1967: 229).

Human Social Organization as an Aspect of Culture

One of the useful things about this set of concepts is that the terms can be used to indicate motion or movement as well as different kinds of groups and statuses. The nouns convert nicely into verbs, to point out what cultural systems in their general social, economic, and political aspects *do* at different energy levels. In regard to social relationships, they equalize, they rank, they stratify, and they maintain a state of stratification. This is word play, of course, but, nonetheless, devices that imply process as well as structure are preferable to alternatives that emphasize only structural parts (as, say, band, tribe, chiefdom, primitive state, and empire). So the terms are suited to identifying in a flexible way the adaptive or integrational states in the social aspect of cultural systems—states which represent an accommodation and balance between accumulated heritage and environments.

Division and organization of work

In egalitarian hunting-and-gathering cultures, the predominant division of work is along sex and age lines. Culture, in the instance of sex, may have netted a state of affairs in early *sapiens* environment, regularized it, and built upon it. *Homo sapiens* is an omnivorous animal, nature supplies both animal and vegetable foods, and "in the beginning" the sexes were unequally equipped to hunt. Women were burdened by pregnancies, menstrual periods, childbirth, and the care of infants and had less strength to muster in the emergencies hunting calls forth. (I add that last point because it is traditional to do so; more important is that the hunter had to be where the game was and when it was there, and a woman couldn't chase animals with a baby on her

Division of work. Guahibo men of the Orinoco River in Colombia construct the frames and thatch the houses. They also do most of the work in the swiddens. (Courtesy Nancy and Robert V. Morey.)

Food preparation is the work of the Guahibo women. Here is the first step in production of cassava from manioc tubers. The tubers are scraped, washed, grated, and then squeezed in an elongated basketry press like the one at lower left. (Courtesy Donald J. Metzger.)

back.) Women were efficiently the suppliers of plant foods and of smaller animals that could be trapped and clubbed, as well as collectors of shellfish and the like; men hunted bigger game. And together a man and woman could do about everything that needed to be done.

Dobe women gather *veldkos*, including the important mongongo nuts; men accompany them to the farther groves and help carry the burdens home, but men alone are hunters of game animals. Among Mbuti net-hunters, it is the men and boys who hold the nets and spear the game, although women and girls drive it into the nets; arrow-hunter men wield the bows and arrows. Copper Eskimo men stalk and kill seal and caribou; women fish, but their primary tasks are in the lamp-centered igloo or skin shelter. Cheyenne equestrian hunters were males; women collected berries and roots. Specialized fishing and whaling cultures like the Nootka (who had advanced socially to a ranking level of society) assigned the technology of those two pursuits to men; women collected shellfish and plants. Thus the households were fed. The technology of defense also was in the hands of men, for the same reasons that men were the hunters.

Consistent with their home-centered duties, women more often than not erected the shelters—the huts of the Bushmen and Pygmies, the tipis of the Cheyenne—for which males provided the material. But Eskimo men, skilled at providing quick shelter for themselves on hunting trips, cut the snow blocks and did most of the igloo construction, and Nootka carpenters who built the plank houses were men, for the technology of woodworking was theirs.

With the more sedentary life accompanying farming and mixed farming and herding, allocation of tasks along sex lines continues; both sexes work at food production, but there are divisions within it. Tsembaga women work harder than men in cultivation; they help with the first burning of the swiddens and are responsible for the second

Human Social Organization as an Aspect of Culture

burning; they plant the tubers and greens, do most of the harvesting and weeding with some help from the men, and care for the pigs (Rappaport 1967a: 43). On the other hand, among the Kuikuru, "virtually all horticultural work is done by men, including clearing, burning, planting, weeding, and fencing the plots. Women only dig up the tubers and carry them back to the village" (Carneiro 1961: 48). In Hopi labor, "there is marked sex dichotomy. Generally speaking, women fetch water, chop wood, prepare meals, tend the children, wash clothes, keep the house in repair, make plaques or baskets, and cultivate small gardens which are situated near springs. The men do the farming, herd sheep, haul wood, weave blankets, rugs and wearing apparel, and make moccasins" (Titiev 1944: 16). Nuer males drive the cattle, although milking is done by women and girls (and uninitiated boys, who

As another step in making cassava, the lumps of manioc, which bear the shape of the basketry press in which they were squeezed, are pounded in a mortar carved from a tree trunk. Following the pounding, the manioc is sifted into the pan at left. (Courtesy Donald J. Metzger.)

Then comes the baking of the sifted manioc flour. It is stirred continuously to prevent formation of the cassava cake. The shredded product is mixed with water to form either a drink or a kind of gruel. (Courtesy Donald J. Metzger.)

do not yet have adult male status); men, in fact, are forbidden to do milking, unless, as on journeys or in war, there are no women or boys around (Evans-Pritchard 1940: 22). Both sexes share equally in cultivation, but only men hunt; men and boys do most of the fishing, and women collect wild fruits and roots and prepare the food (Evans-Pritchard 1951: 129-30).

There is an aspect of sexual division of labor that hasn't received so much attention from anthropologists as the sheer fact of the division, and that is: Who works harder and contributes more to subsistence, man or woman? A conventional response is that women work more continuously and that drudgery is their lot while men conserve themselves for the more satisfying hunt, raid, and ritual. That is too simple, and I don't think we know enough to generalize. As with other

Human Social Organization as an Aspect of Culture

Women are the major burden carriers among the Binumarien, gardeners in highland New Guinea. When there is much to carry, men lend a hand. The mat-walled, thatched house is widespread in Oceania. Its form diffused to the highlands from the coast. (Courtesy Kristen Hawkes.)

facets of the general problem of labor allocation, measurement has only recently begun, and no doubt there will be surprises with respect to the sexual division and organization of labor as there have been with age.

You will recall from Chapter Five that 35 percent of Lee's Dobe Bushmen, both old and young, did not work at all. But how old is old enough to work? "Young people are not expected to provide food regularly until they are married. Girls typically marry between the ages of fifteen and twenty, and boys about five years later, so that it is not unusual to find healthy, active teenagers visiting from camp to camp while their older relatives provide food for them" (Lee and DeVore 1968: 36). Sahlins (1972: 51) cites the Dobe, as well as the farming Lele and Bemba of Africa, as instances into which late entry into productive activity contributes to the "underuse of labor-power," which we will note again shortly.

The Lele (Douglas 1965) are worth pursuing. These people, living in a park and savannah country south of the Congo rain forest, are, in comparison with their neighbors, the Bushong, inefficient hunters, fishermen, housebuilders, and farmers. They work intensively at farming only about six weeks, during the dry season, while the Bushong labor continuously throughout the year. Whereas Bushong men began farm work at the age of twenty and were productively employed into their sixties, Lele began in their thirties and retired in their mid-fifties. In the traditional culture (it is changing now), older men were polygynous and all men married late. "Boys would be boys, until their middle thirties. They led the good life, of weaving, drinking, and following the manly sports of hunting and warfare, without continuous agricultural responsibility" (Douglas 1965: 203). There is a complex of reasons for the prolonged bachelorhood, nonproductivity, and early retirement, but the point to be made here is that there is no easy answer to that amplified question relating to division of labor by age, How old is old enough to work, and how old is too old? Dobe, Lele, and other cases dispel our folk notion that in all simpler cultures every hand is required to work as soon as it can grasp a spear or hoe.

In primitive cultures, associations with economic tasks and the craft specializations that occur here and there also follow sex lines. Skilled Cheyenne arrow makers or quillers or Nootka canoe makers devoted more time to their crafts than did their household mates; they did not, however, specialize to the exclusion of the ordinary work required of every adult who did work. Specialization increases in rank societies, but the craftsmen remain involved in food production. When, in the course of social evolution, craftsmen become full-time specialists, a new kind of economic system is coming into being—one based primarily on production for exchange, not on production for household use. This point will be elaborated in an historical example later.

Why is there division of labor at all, why not an undifferentiated undertaking of tasks? Reasons can be found in both technological and social contexts. In technology, because an all-purpose tool is employed in different tasks it tends to be improved along the direction required in more specialized work and to break into specialized forms. As White (1959: 187) points out, and as we have seen in Chapter Five, Lower Paleolithic all-purpose choppers evolved into Upper Paleolithic scrapers, hammers, axes, and so on. Energy is expended more efficiently (that is, with greater relative return) with a specialized tool, and human skill is the analog of tool improvement. But this has a social correlate. Groups and statuses doing different tasks, producing different goods and services, are bound together, and social solidarity is thereby increased.

If sexual division of labor (and secondarily assignment of tasks on the basis of age) represents the basis of organization along two lines, the household in primitive cultures is the unit that brings them together and coordinates them. It centers what Marshall Sahlins, following the economic historian Karl Polanyi, calls the "domestic mode of production." "The household is...charged with production, with the deploy-

Human Social Organization as an Aspect of Culture

ment and use of labor-power, with the determination of the economic objective. Its own inner relations, as between husband and wife, parent and child, are the principal relations of production in society....How labor is to be expended, the terms and the products of its activity, are in the main domestic decisions..." (Sahlins 1972: 76-77). It is this group and its statuses and rules that set the level and limitations of its economics, comparable to the manor in medieval times or the corporation in modern capitalism.

We have seen that hunters and gatherers, farmers and herders did not overextend themselves on the food quest. In economic terms there is "underuse of labor-power." Available muscle could be directed to producing more, but it is not. And an interesting and important facet of the situation is that even within undemanding standards of work, not all households pull their weight in relation to others. "A fair percentage of domestic groups persistently fail to produce their own livelihood, although organized to do so" (Sahlins 1972: 69). They do not starve, because the margin between what they produce and what is required to maintain life is provided through the extensive give-and-take behaviors of kinship. A household which has an abundance at one time may be in want at another, and the primitive insurance system operates. But even so, some households chronically fail to measure up to others and to a comfortable standard.

It will not do to ascribe this to sheer laziness or cantankerousness; that is a surrender to a biological "human nature" assumption that will get us nowhere in our understanding of differences between cultures. If there is any validity at all in the cultural point of view, it rests on the contrary assumption that humans are differently motivated by the cultures that impinge on them. There is something in the domestic mode of production itself that limits deployment of available labor power and exploitation of available resources, whether it moves hunting-gathering Bushmen or farming-herding Nuer. That something lies in its nature, not man's and woman's. It is the organization of production for use and not for exchange. Production for exchange makes humans work harder and longer, while production for use induces them to slack off when their basic needs are satisfied.

The point of differential production probably was obscured by earlier anthropologists who found it necessary to redress the picture Europeans had about "lazy savages" who refused to work. As Malinowski (1950: 62) reported, "The Trobriander works in a roundabout way, to a large extent for the sake of the work itself, and puts a great deal of aesthetic polish on the arrangement and general appearance of his garden. He is not guided primarily by the desire to satisfy his wants, but by a very complex set of traditional forces, duties and obligations, beliefs in magic, social ambitions and vanities. He wants, if he is a *man*, to achieve social distinction as a *good gardener* and a good worker in general."

That might well be, but Malinowski fell into the same trap in presenting *the* Trobriander as did the European denigrators of "*the* savage." Later investigators of several cultures, particularly those who tried to quantify production, came up with evidence that "*the* native" and the household varied a good deal within and across societies.

The ownership relation

Ownership is a relation which culture establishes between resources and the things extracted and made from them, on the one hand, and groups and statuses on the other. The heart of the **ownership relation** is accessibility or availability; that which is available to group or status is owned, and what is owned is *property*. The behavioral content of the owner-property relationship runs from exclusive possession (all others keep out, hands off) to communal (everybody welcome), covering many degrees of variation in between.

In egalitarian hunting-gathering cultures, basic resources of land and water, plants and animals, and human labor are available and accessible to everyone. Humans become spaced out and organized in relation to resources, but the relationship is hardly ever (given the fluid membership of the groups, we might safely say never) found at the exclusive end of the spectrum of ownership. The six-mile radius around a water hole which a Dobe Bushman camp exploits so long as it is in that place and the section of forest over which a Mbuti camp collects and hunts are not closed to others. "These areas are not territories in the zoological sense," Lee (Lee and DeVore 1968: 31) says about the Dobe, "since they are not defended against outsiders." The bands which Lorna Marshall found among the !Kung varied in size, because "a band that owned comparatively good resources would tend to attract more members than a band with scant *veldkos*....When the semipermanent water holes go dry, the bands who own them may break up temporarily and the families may go to live with relatives who are at permanent water holes, or they may go as whole bands to another water hole where they have relatives" (1965: 251).

In human terms, that behavior is rational and, in cultural terms, adaptive. Land itself has no value except for the resources on it, and these fluctuate with the seasons and years and the intensity of their exploitation. When labor has been expended on a resource, the ownership relation shifts slightly toward the restrictive side of the spectrum—never far in regard to game caught and plants gathered, a bit more with cooked food, and more yet with things like tools, weapons, and implements. The !Kung hunter who brings down an antelope after stalking it for days does not own it outright by virtue of his labor. It is divided first among all the hunters in the party and the giver or lender of the effective arrow, if the hunter has not made it himself. Those who receive the first portions then distribute pieces to others. Nonconsumable artifacts are not regarded as wealth to be hoarded, and for good reasons. Materials are there for the taking, and people can make what they need; more than one of an object would be a nuisance to carry, and, indeed, it is as convenient to borrow an item as it is to possess one (Marshall 1965: 257-58).

This is not to say that an individual is to be left empty-handed or that kinship closeness or distance is wholly disregarded among hunters. M. J. Meggitt, ethnographer of the Walbiri in the Northern Territory of Australia, relates that fathers and sons who are "countrymen" (that is, who live in one of the four major divisions of the territory) borrow from each other freely. "The requests should, however, be kept within rea-

sonable limits. Thus, a man who has several spears parts with some of them willingly; but, should he have only one, his son or father should not ask for it. If he is asked, the man usually gives the single article to an actual or close father or son, but he refuses distant 'fathers' and 'sons' " (Meggitt 1965: 120).

When culture moves to firmer and less intermittent control over a given resource, as when land is brought into cultivation and animals are domesticated, firmer attachments grow up. Investment of labor (culture's channeling of human muscle power) in things as widely different as permanent fish weirs and dams and irrigation ditches are illustrations. Going along with progressive attachment to resources is a segmentation of society into more firmly bounded kin and residence groups. Production still centers in households, but rights in resources tend to derive from membership in, for instance, lineages and clans. The old principle of the hunters, all kin welcome, is not wholly abandoned, only modified, circumscribed. Within such groups all members are assured land to farm, or cattle to graze and pastures to graze them on, or a share of impounded fish.

A Kuikuru villager had within a four-mile radius 13,500 acres of forest he could cut and prepare for cultivation; he was limited not by prior ownership rights of others but by the distance he was willing to walk (Carneiro 1961: 48). In Oraibi, land worked by members of a matrilocal household was held in the name of the matrilineal clan. A Tsembaga might hunt, trap, and forage in any part of his tribal territory,

In egalitarian society, land which has been cleared and brought into cultivation enters temporarily into the ownership relation with social groups and statuses. But basic resources are available to all. Guahibo manioc swidden, Orinoco River, Colombia. (Courtesy Nancy and Robert V. Morey.)

The Economic Aspect of Social Organization

but his gardening rights were restricted to a subterritory held by his patrilineal clan and subclan. He could claim a particular garden plot by inheritance or by clearing virgin forest, but if he didn't have enough he asked a better-supplied relative in his subclan for more and was never refused. And if a subclan was short, individuals in it or the group as a whole asked for and received tracts from another subclan (Rappaport 1967a: 19).

The Nuer place cattle ownership in families (effectively, households), and the household head has disposal rights over them—including that of apportioning animals to sons of marriageable age for transfer to wives' people as "bride price." Adult sons, however, have rights in the herds they help tend; at the elder's death they inherit, each taking his portion when at last the herd is—reluctantly—broken up. Pasture and water supplies are held by sections of tribes, but effective use lies with households associated with particular lineages and clans. No continuing claims are made to specific cultivable plots, and one may plant wherever there is unused land conveniently near the kraal (Evans-Pritchard 1940: 17, 77).

The Kofyar illustrate neatly the effect of labor investment combined with pressure of population on available land. "The Kofyar insist that every square inch of arable soil, both village and bush, has an owner, a single person to whom the land belongs and who alone may decide on its use" (Netting 1968: 159). But this applies to the right of occupation and use, not to the right of transfer outside of a man's patrilineage. Only the lineage itself has that right. The holder may build and occupy a house on it, loan, lease, or share it with a tenant or anyone else, and pass it on to his heirs, but his holding stops short of the right to sell it from under his kin.

There is not much difference between the Kofyar and other farmers, or even hunters, in availability of materials for making tools, shelters, and other household needs (which everyone has the skill to make). Movable structures are the maker's alone, but permanent ones become part of the improved land and go with its transfer. However, the Kofyar farmers are on the threshold of that state of affairs in which land itself becomes a value, a thing to be bought and sold, not an inalienable resource open to the whole community, as among Kuikuru, nor to be allocated to descent groups, as among Hopi and Tsembaga. It is still relatively easy for a householder, by making a small payment to its owner, to obtain use of land, but tenancy itself is a toe in the door of the inegalitarian economy, where resources are exclusive possessions and a landless man can sell only his labor.

Reciprocity, redistribution, and market

Reciprocity, redistribution, and market are ways cultures in their economic aspect distribute goods and services.

Reciprocity, characteristic of egalitarian social organization, entails the obligation to share with others and to receive from others. One must give and assist generously and respond to gifts and aid in return—not at the time of the original favor but at any time thereafter when one has something to give. The term reciprocity is often linked in anthro-

Human Social Organization as an Aspect of Culture

pological theory with Marcel Mauss, nephew, student, and colleague of Emile Durkheim, who spoke of "prestations," gifts and the obligation to return gifts. It is Malinowski, however, who "drew to the surface, as it were, and introduced overtly into anthropological literature, the concept of reciprocity" (Firth 1957: 218).

Coming to the fore in rank societies, redistribution involves a flow of goods and services to "redistributive chiefs" and a more or less delayed return to the givers, either in the form of direct gifts or as feasts or in conjunction with other community activities. It is a kind of centralized pooling that goes beyond the sort associated with household heads in egalitarian societies, and it supports more complex political arrangements. Meaning of the term was clarified by the economic historian Karl Polanyi, and arrangement of the triad of reciprocity, redistribution, and market is associated with him (Dalton 1968: xiv).

Reciprocity and redistribution are the kinds of exchange found in the traditional cultures we have centered upon so far; market is not unknown in some of them, but it takes place in between-culture contexts, not internally. Here are some examples from the cultures with which we are familiar.

A !Kung Bushman hunter, as noted in the discussion of ownership, divides the game he has killed among others in his party and gives a portion to the donor or lender of the arrow he used to make the kill. Lorna Marshall (1965: 253) adds some significant information: "!Kung society makes a great deal of giving and lending arrows. Women and old men, as well as men in their hunting prime, receive arrows as gifts and may give them or lend them to a hunter, asking him to shoot for them. A hunter cannot refuse an arrow—as a person cannot refuse any gift—without offending the giver. He accepts the arrow and with it an obligation, but he gives or lends arrows in return and involves others in obligation to him" (Marshall 1965: 253). That is reciprocity. It involves not only the obligation to give, but the obligation to accept and to repay.

Reciprocity operates not only in distribution of food and other goods but also in mutual help, as in building shelters or carrying burdens—or, in farming cultures, in cultivation and other work. This is what we meant when we said earlier that egalitarians have general access to labor as well as to material resources. Both sides of reciprocity persist in the ordinary daily life of rank societies and into those societies emerging into more complex relations. Thus, the Kofyar, who restrict most sharing to households and close kin, call upon neighbors informally and also organize groups to thatch houses, excavate corrals, and spread compost on fields; the neighbors "ask in return only similar aid in their own farming" (Netting 1968: 136). Whereas among hunters the person who lags behind in his obligations meets only silent disapproval and eventual withdrawal of cooperation, the Kofyar, as might be expected where ownership is more firmly organized, have a mechanism for inducing compliance. "If someone absents himself from neighborhood work without excellent reason he may be berated and made to pay a fine in beer to his neighbors" (Netting 1968: 137). So there are variations in behaving reciprocally in different cultures, but the basic principle is the same: Help others, and they will help you; give to others, and they will give to you. Again, the Kofyar example points up the fact that

reciprocity is not confined to egalitarian organizations but is a mode of exchange that continues in higher cultural levels. Redistribution and market are added as evolution proceeds, although redistribution has its roots in pooling of goods in the egalitarian household.

For a setting that illustrates redistribution as clearly as the !Kung illustrates reciprocity, consider the feasts and **potlatches** of the Nootka. The Nootka, as mentioned before, lived in big plank houses in winter and summer villages, each house being inhabited by a number of small households. Their naming of kin was bilateral, but they recognized patrilineal lineages which centered the status structures of houses and which were linked with lineages or segments of them in adjacent houses. A chief headed the lineage and managed the resources it

Human Social Organization as an Aspect of Culture

owned (in Nootka ideology, the chief was the owner, although he was in actuality only the steward) and held that status by virtue of primogeniture—as firstborn of the previous chief. All the people were ranked; one was either a "noble"—a chief or a member of his immediate family (excluding younger sons)—or a "commoner"—all the rest. Rank was assigned strictly according to genealogical distance from the chief and his direct antecedents, so that younger sons gained few or none of the chief's prerogatives: they might raise their descendants' rank by marriage to a higher-ranking mate, but they could not change their own.

The chief's privileges and authority, resting on this position in his kin group, included the holding of ritual names and the right to give particular rituals, but more importantly they were economic. As owners or stewards of salmon streams, the chiefs gave permission to set traps in them to kin and followers and claimed the entire first catch. Likewise, inlets, bays, and the bordering seas were marked off; no one might fish until the chief or an assigned party made the first one or two catches for him; later, he collected part of the catch of all who fished there. But mark well: "No definite amount was specified (for his later collections): it was left to each man to give what he would. Informants say, 'The fishermen gave all they could spare. They didn't mind giving, for they knew the chief would give a feast with his tribute' " (Drucker 1951:251).

"The chief would give a feast...." Here we have the other side of the chiefly coin. "Every time the chief got a lot of food of any kind, he gave a feast...to give it away to the people" (Drucker 1951: 370). Whether he got it by claiming the first catch of salmon, the first pick of berries in his patches, or a share of a stranded whale on his beach or

Hospitality is a form of reciprocity. These Bedouin have slaughtered a sheep and will roast it to honor a visitor with a feast. (Courtesy Joseph Ginat.)

The Economic Aspect of Social Organization

whether it was a gift, he gave it away—that and whatever his kin additionally assembled for him. The purpose of the giveaway might be to celebrate his child's first tooth, or weaning, or first hunt, but those were only occasions of social life that provided an appropriate and ceremonious setting for the return giving. Redistribution among the Nootka, then, was the collection of goods at a central point, by a particular status, and its dispersion, immediate or delayed, among those from whom it was collected.

We might stop with Nootka feasts, without reference to potlatches, because the same elements of chiefly redistribution were in both. For the potlatches, "the general principle was the same as that of the feasts: when a chief accumulated a quantity of property he gave it away" (Drucker 1951: 376). Overtly, the purpose of that elaborate giveaway ceremony, with its meticulous seating and serving of visitors by rank, was transfer of a chief's privileges to his children, and the occasions were the same as for ordinary feasts, such as stages in a life cycle. The property was likely to be things like blankets and house boards as well as food—and also ceremonial privileges.

The economic base of the potlatch was obscured for a long time among anthropologists because it was observed and recorded after the 1870s, when much of Northwest Coast culture had broken down, populations had been decimated, wealth gained from involvement in a market economy had flooded in, and titles and privileges had been torn loose from their old social matrix. The result was ostentatious and boasting competition, apparently unrelated to the workaday world. It was interpreted as a game of buying, selling, and lending at interest, played for its psychological value, a means to humble opponents and exalt the individual. (An example of this interpretation is Benedict 1946: 173-87.)

But Nootka potlatches, at least, were not competitive, and their economic underpinnings are clear. Recent studies (for instance, Suttles 1968) show convincingly that the aboriginal potlatch was a way in which imbalance of resources and their harvest among communities was ironed out. People in one community or tribal group gave to their chief. Arranging a potlatch, he gave the goods to another chief; that one, having collected his own wealth, later gave in return—and the people on both sides were the final receivers. Chiefly redistribution also was characteristic of Polynesia; in Melanesia, redistribution was more commonly in the hands of "big men" who did not inherit their status but achieved it through vigorous promotion of production by kin and followers and lavish giveaways. (Malinowski's Trobrianders were atypical of Melanesia in that they had chiefs rather than big men.)

Just as reciprocity did not end with the egalitarian hunters, redistribution neither began nor ended with rank societies of specialized fishermen and of farmers. For instance, clans of the reindeer-herding Tungus of northeastern Siberia had no hereditary chiefs nor "big men," only household heads acting as a council. Clans were in effect owners of the reindeer, and each summer they collected and reapportioned animals to households whose herds had been depleted by wolves or epidemics (Service 1971c: 99). At the other end of the spectrum, Polanyi (1957: 51-52) held that redistribution continued as a characteristic of "central-

Human Social Organization as an Aspect of Culture

ized despotisms of a bureaucratic type," such as Hammurabi's Babylon and the Egyptian New Kingdom, as well as in ancient China, the kingdoms of India, the Inca empire, and the feudal systems such as those of the European Middle Ages. What the producers received after redistribution did not in those cases match the shares of the Nootka, but the basic principle seemed to be present: up the status ladder from the bottom and down from the top. The cases are complicated, too, by existence of powerful state organizations.

Market exchange is a different kind of exchange altogether. Here it is not the prior status of the exchangers that governs transactions (kin to kin, commoner to chief, peasant to feudal lord) but the goods and services themselves (pots for taro, coconuts for pigs, all-purpose money for labor). Market should not be identified with *marketplace* but with a principle of exchange having three facets: exchange items bring the transactors together; there is a calculation of the relative values of the items based on such considerations as their scarcity and the amount of labor in their production; and each transactor tries to gain an advantage over the other, to receive more than he gives, to make a profit. In a system dominated by this kind of transaction, everything—land, labor, produce, artifacts—finally becomes a commodity that can be bought and sold, and bought and sold at profit.

The market principle is not unknown in egalitarian and rank societies, but it operates where kin and neighbor relations thin out and break, at the boundaries of cultural systems. !Kung trade tanned hides, ostrich eggshell beads, and red powder made from heartwood of a tree to the Bantus for tobacco, metal, pots, and European goods. "The little Bushmen find the bigger, more aggressive Bantu hard bargainers and are rather at their mercy" (Marshall 1965: 257). The proud and self-reliant Nuer have had little recourse to market exchange past or present, but they procure spears, hoes, fishhooks, ornaments, anvils, and grindstones from Arab traders, who take in return ox hides and oxen (Evans-Pritchard 1940: 88). Intergroup exchange among the Tsembaga involves pigs, axes, bushknives, salt, and other commodities (Rappaport 1968: 105). It is not accidental that we find these examples in the context of intercultural trade, because exchange between cultures was an early seedbed of the market exchange principle.

Another orientation for primitive exchange

It is practicable to regard all or most exchanges in primitive cultures, whether egalitarian or ranked, as instances of reciprocity if one adopts the generalization of that term as proposed by Marshall Sahlins (1965: 145-49). He has defined two ideal end points of reciprocity, "generalized" and "negative," with a "balanced" kind in the middle.

Generalized reciprocity is the kind we met with in the food-sharing, artifact-lending, helping-hand behavior of hunters, herders, and simple farmers, a giving with the knowledge that a return will be made eventually but without calculation of the value of the gift or the return. In the longer run, things even out, but the flow is never interrupted. In balanced reciprocity, on the other hand, there is a more direct exchange, this for that, with a more or less equal return on the spot or within a

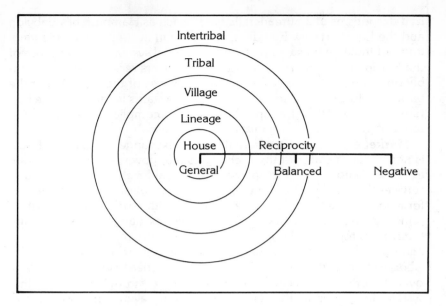

known and accepted period. "It is notable of the main run of generalized reciprocities that the material flow is sustained by the prevailing social relations; whereas, for the main run of balanced exchange, social relations hinge on the material flow" (Sahlins 1965: 148).

Finally, negative reciprocity "is the attempt to get something for nothing with impunity," and it runs from crafty and heated barter to theft and seizure.

The influence of household, kin, and neighbor relationships in the shaping of primitive exchange is suggested in the figure above, which Sahlins labels "reciprocity and kinship residential sectors" (1965: 152). Moving outward from household, generalized reciprocity gradually gives way to the balanced variety, and then reciprocity becomes increasingly negative. But the negative is almost always ameliorated by devices that overcome, for a time at least, the hostility that is associated with it—else there would be no trade, and raid and plunder might follow.

It should be understood that Sahlins's triad does not replace Polyani's reciprocity, redistribution, and market, which provides a useful perspective for all economies, primitive and modern. Sahlins proposed his elaboration of the notion of reciprocity as one way to understand better than before the exchanges in *primitive* societies which run from pure gift to barter and raid, and he encompasses along the way such behavior as chiefly redistribution. We have touched on his analysis because it has provoked a good deal of discussion in economic anthropology.

We shall now return to primitive trade as such, to see in what degree the market principle is present in some situations and how it is tempered.

Trade and market

Superorganic environments present special problems for people in egalitarian and rank societies. Technologies cope with their immediate habitats, and the social relationships that grow up achieve the distribution of materials and energies in a more or less efficient way within particular cultures. But social relations between households, bands, and villages progressively thin and break with distance; one who is not kin is a stranger and enemy. If goods are to be exchanged between systems, the kinlike relations must be extended or a wholly new basis for give and take must be set up. The first solution is a compromise: trade is carried on between partners and groups whose exchange behaviors have the quality of kinship reciprocity, but they are accompanied by other transactions which have a market orientation. In the course of evolutionary adaptation good-for-good progressively replaces the covering kin-to-kin partnership structure.

What trade in some prestate societies is like can be illustrated by Malinowski's Trobriand Islanders. The Trobrianders live on an archipelago off the eastern tip of New Guinea that includes Boyowa, an irregularly shaped island about thirty miles long, and a dozen much smaller ones. These Melanesians, who numbered over eight thousand at the time of Malinowski's two field trips between 1915 and 1918, were fishermen, pig raisers, and cultivators of yams, taro, sugarcane, and coconuts. Boyowa itself, a highly fertile tropical island supporting a relatively large population that lived in villages hardly a mile apart, had a fourth to a fifth of its land under cultivation. Malinowski estimated that the Trobrianders in a good year raised twice as many yams as they could eat; proud gardeners, they displayed their harvests and allowed the unused portions to rot. Interior villages consisted of two concentric rings of structures surrounding a dancing and ceremonial ground, the inner one of yam storage houses set on piles and boasting decorated fronts and platforms for lounging, the outer of smaller dwellings of nuclear family households. Coastal villages did not have that geometrical regularity.

Trobriand society, like that of the Nootka, was one in which there were ranked chiefs; they derived their authority partly from their positions as headmen of the leading villages but also (and more importantly) from their leadership positions in the four ranked matrilineal clans, whose members were dispersed throughout the villages and districts. Supplies of food and valued goods, which they used to organize tribal (as Malinowski called them) festivities and enterprises such as canoe building and to return gifts for various services, came to them primarily as obligatory gifts from relatives of their wives. They alone were entitled to engage in polygyny (marriage to more than one wife), and they chose as wives the sisters and daughters of headmen in the villages under their authority. Etiquette toward a chief marked off his status: in a chief's presence one squatted; when a chief sat, no one stood up. He had no means to enforce commands, however, save recourse to his sorcerer, whose machinations when they became known terrified errant commoners into compliance.

Of the Trobriand economy Malinowski wrote, italicizing his conclusion, *"The whole tribal life is permeated by a constant give and take,"* adding that "every ceremony, every legal and customary act is done to the accompaniment of material gift and counter gift . . . wealth, given and taken, is one of the main instruments of social organization, of the power of the chief, of the bonds of kinship, and of relationship in law" (1950: 167). You will recognize the reciprocity. And the chiefly redistri-

The Economic Aspect of Social Organization

bution: " . . . the higher the rank the greater the obligation. A chief will naturally be expected to give food to any stranger, visitor, or even loiterer from another end of the village . . ." (1950: 97).

Reciprocity in trade was the major focus of Malinowski's concern in his classic *Argonauts of the Western Pacific,* from which we have been quoting. He centered on the now widely known **kula**—"a form of exchange, of extensive inter-tribal character . . . carried on by communities inhabiting a wide ring of islands, which form a closed circuit" (1950: 81). Two kinds of objects figured principally in the *kula* trade—red shell necklaces, *soulava,* moving clockwise around the circuit, and white shell bracelets, *mwali,* moving counterclockwise, both included under the term *vaygu'a,* "valuables." Men had *kula* partners, commoners a few, the chiefs perhaps a hundred, with whom they exchanged *soulava* for *mwali* and vice versa, but never *soulava* for *soulava* or *mwali* for *mwali.* Partners might be near or distant, for the trade, carried in part by canoe fleets built and launched with ritual and drama, covered a triangle of islands whose longest side measured nearly 275 miles. No man knew its full extent nor understood it as a whole system; each sought only to get his hands on one of the valuables, keep it for a time, and then hand it on to one of his partners, from whom he would receive the opposite kind of valuable in return. In its major flow, the *kula* was external exchange and so fits a definition of trade, and its distribution mode was balanced reciprocity.

The Trobrianders had other kinds of trade, one of them dealing with food and one with utilitarian objects. In the first, called *wasi,* coastal fishing villages exchanged fish for yams with the inland farmers; amounts were not precisely calculated but roughly so, a bunch for a bunch, and the trading, again representing balanced reciprocity, was carried on only between established partners. The second, called *gimwali,* was barter pure and simple, a shift toward Sahlins's negative reciprocity. Trade was initiated by craftsmen of the interior, who carried wooden

A large, twin-masted trading canoe with outrigger, sailed by Siassi Islanders of Vitiaz Strait, between New Britain and New Guinea. The Siassi are one of three groups of overseas traders who link communities of the region in a great trading network. Outrigger of another canoe is visible in lower left foreground. (Courtesy Thomas G. Harding.)

Human Social Organization as an Aspect of Culture

A boar's tusk pendant, ornaments of dogs' teeth, a waistband of *tambu* shell and dogs' teeth, and a woven net bag also liberally decorated with dogs' teeth are worn by a Sio Islander, northeast New Guinea coast. Possession of shell and tooth valuables and ability to distribute pigs and other food mark a leading man in this area. (Courtesy Thomas G. Harding.)

dishes, baskets, combs, and lime pots to the farmers, fishermen, and sea traders and haggled for yams, coconuts, fish, and ornaments. Sometimes the others sought them out if they had a need for the artifacts, but in general Trobrianders looked down scornfully on this kind of transaction and contrasted it sharply with the balanced reciprocity of the *kula*. This exchange, negatively reciprocal barter, was carried on in connection with *kula* expeditions but never between *kula* partners themselves. The canoes carried large stores of food and artifacts and a lively barter took place on the beach some distance from the *kula* transactions.

It is not necessary to take sides on the matter in dispute among anthropologists as to whether food or artifacts were more important than *kula* objects or the other way around (Bohannan 1963: 237), but note the importance of the trading partner in external exchange. In primitive cultural contexts, distant communities, distant in both a geographical and a social sense, are hostile communities, areas of danger. Only when reciprocity is established near the balance point can goods flow freely, and this is done when partners set up kinlike or neighborlike associations. *Kula* partners, says Malinowski, "behave as friends." And

The Economic Aspect of Social Organization

Four boar's tusk pendants rest inside an unpainted bowl made by Tami Islanders, Huon Gulf, New Guinea. Tami produce the bowls used in bridewealth payments in other communities; they themselves require boar's tusks in marriage exchanges. (Courtesy Thomas G. Harding.)

"the overseas partner is. . .a host, patron and ally in a land of danger and insecurity" (1950: 91-92).

The same situation existed in another part of Melanesia a few hundred miles to the northwest, where three groups of islanders in Vitiaz Strait joined coastal and interior villages on New Guinea and New Britain in a trading network of several hundred communities (Harding 1970). Among interior groups, most goods flowed through channels of kinship and intermarriage; between coast villages and the interior, by way of trade friends and small marketplaces; and, at a greater distance spanned by island traders, again by trade partners. "Trade partnerships were enduring, heritable relationships, based usually on putative kinship, and were associated with a definite code that stipulates rules of hospitality and exchange between partners" (Harding 1970: 96). Although most of the villagers, with exception of the sea traders, were self-sufficient in subsistence, a vast amount of red ochre, obsidian, clay pots, palm wood bows, pandanus mats, woven net bags, bark fiber for fish nets, canoes, taro, fish, pigs, and sago changed hands. There was no single embracing system of exchange of *kula*-like objects, but there was a broad distribution of such things as dogs, pigs, dog tooth ornaments, and curved boar tusks; these went through partners, never markets.

Market as a principle or mode of exchange in Polanyi's sense, therefore, is not unknown between primitive cultures, but the negative reciprocity that is characteristic of our own land, labor, product, money, and capital markets is often subordinated to the generalized and balanced reciprocities rooted in the household economy and kin-based social relations. Neither are marketplaces unknown, as we have noted in passing, but they are, as economic anthropologists put it, "peripheral." That is, the people do not depend for their subsistence or livelihood on selling goods and services in a marketplace but rather exchange by barter only a small range of products that supplement what they raise and make (Bohannan and Dalton 1965: 4-5). Many prestate and preindustrial African cultures had and have now such

Human Social Organization as an Aspect of Culture

Pottery is offered for sale in this section of the market in Zacapoaxtla, Mexico. (Courtesy Nancy and Robert V. Morey.)

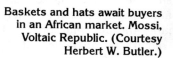

Baskets and hats await buyers in an African market. Mossi, Voltaic Republic. (Courtesy Herbert W. Butler.)

peripheral marketplaces, and they are particularly characteristic of Mesoamerica. When a culture moves into a full-fledged market principle system and marketplaces move from peripheral positions to increasingly substantial ones, the culture is no longer primitive but is a dependent segment of a higher-energy system. Peasant societies, to be discussed later, are all of that kind.

Money and multicentric economies

Money may or may not be the root of evil, but its etymological root has an interesting twist. When the goddess Juno's geese warned the Romans of an impending attack by the Gauls on Capitoline Hill, she earned the epithet (that is, the quality) of Moneta, The Warner. In her temple, coins were struck, and her epithet became transferred to the mint and the coinage process, hence the words *monetary* and *money* (Partridge 1958: 405). What came out of Juno's temple has become welded to the market. The process began in earnest in the first stratified and state systems in the third millennium B.C.

Conventionally defined, money is a medium of exchange (replacing inconvenient barter), a standard of value (everything has its price), a means of making deferred payments (buy now, pay later), and a way to store wealth. In addition, it should be durable, portable, divisible, and homogeneous. Wealth storage in money has become unfashionable

The Economic Aspect of Social Organization

and in post-Keynesian economics is bad economics, but the other characteristics remain. Go ye down to the marketplace, and anything can be bought with money—products, land, labor, and more money. (And, some say, power, authority, and prestige.)

There is no single thing like our **general-purpose money** in primitive cultures. Shells and woodpecker scalps in California, fiber blankets and beaten copper sheets on the North Pacific Coast, shells and feathers in Melanesia, all entered into economic transactions, but none was a general medium of exchange or a standard of value for all of the commodities or services distributed. They were forms of **special-purpose money.**

Recall the Trobriand *kula, wasi,* and *gimwali* exchanges, which were carried on separately and whose measures could be equated with difficulty if at all. The ordinary, daily flow of reciprocities and the chiefs' redistributions were not measured by a common scale, nor was the flow of goods in betrothals, marriages, bereavements, peace pacts, or payments to magicians, craftsmen, dancers, and so on. Within the Vitiaz Strait trading network, fifty or so kinds of goods were exchanged, some of which had rough barter equivalents between given commodities, but pigs, dog teeth, and boar tusks entered into marriage arrangements and into village and intervillage feasts that cemented peace pacts and raised the status of the organizers. Cattle were real wealth to the Nuer; marriage was always accompanied by a transfer of cattle from the groom's to the bride's kin, but it can't be said that the Nuer go to market to buy a wife—nor that cattle are bought and sold. In Swaziland, where as among the Nuer "cattle circulate primarily through marriage," Hilda Kuper (1963: 44-45) heard a telling remark by an educated man caught between the attitudes engendered by the old economy and the new: "I only like to sell cattle when I speak English." Traditionally, cattle transactions took place in a context outside market exchange.

An often-cited case of misreading of the primitive text to find all-purpose money in it is that of the economist W. E. Armstrong, who wrote that the Rossel Islanders, a thousand Melanesians living on a hundred-square-mile island southeast of New Guinea, carried on "mutual trafficking in pigs and concubines, in canoes and wives" (Armstrong 1967: 246) by means of a graded series of polished shell tokens which he said could be arranged in ascending value from 1 to 22. Armstrong gave little evidence as to how the shells entered into acquisition of daily subsistence, but, as the economic anthropologist George Dalton (1965: 52-58) has pointed out, shells 18 through 22 in the series had some strange, unmoneylike characteristics. They could not be acquired by any number of lower-class shells, and they were regarded as property peculiar to chiefs. Number 18 passed from one lineage to another as "payment" for wives shared by several men, for sponsoring pig or dog feasts, and for a feast on the launching of a particular kind of canoe. Number 20 was transferred to the relatives of a man who had had the honor of being murdered and eaten ritually!

There are two points of view, two solutions to the problem of orienting "primitive money." One is like that held by Leslie White, that "for the most part, primitive money is not employed in economic contexts at all, but in a game of social intercourse in which social values—status, prestige—are transferred or validated by such means" (1959: 258-59). White would restrict the term *money* to commercial, which is to say market, exchange. The other is like that advanced by Paul Bohannan, who distinguishes categories, sectors, or spheres in an economy, within each of which different sets of goods or services are found and which are linked for payment to particular kinds of commodities. He calls an economy with such spheres a **multicentric economy** (1963: 248) and illustrates it among the Tiv—whom he and his wife Laura Bohannan studied—a people numbering eight hundred thousand and who cultivate yams, millet, sorghum, and other crops on the north Nigerian plain.

In the subsistence sphere, which the Tiv call *yiagh*, farm produce and small livestock and household utensils, agricultural tools, and the materials they are made from were exchanged by gift in the manner of primitive societies and by barter in markets. In the prestige sphere, *shagba* in the Tiv language, were found slaves, cattle, a particular kind of white cloth, metal rods, medicines, and magical rites. They never entered the market and were exchanged only for each other—slaves for cows and brass rods, cattle and magical rites for brass rods and cloth, for instance (Bohannan 1963: 249-50). The third sphere was marriage, in which two men exchanged sisters or, in the absence of a sister, one man transferred another kinswoman, a "ward" to whom he was "guardian." "The only 'price' of one woman is another woman," writes Bohannan (1963: 250), suggesting by the quotation marks around the word *price* that it is hardly a market transaction.

The distinction between spheres was first drawn by the anthropologist Cora DuBois (1936), who found among the Tolowa-Tututni Indians of northern California a "subsistence economy" paralleled by a "prestige economy" in which dentalium shells and other valuables entered into prestige-building and prestige-maintaining exchanges. Although approving DuBois's conclusion that "subsistence economy is divorced from prestige, and money operates in the latter realm," White insists that "money in this culture is not money at all in our sense of the term; it is not a medium of exchange in commercial, i.e., economic, transactions, but an instrument employed in social ritual, a set of counters in a game of symbolic and psychologic values. It is unfortunate that the terms *money, economy* and *purchase* are used to describe such definitely noneconomic, noncommercial and nonfinancial culture processes" (1959: 259).

Current anthropological opinion, stemming from ecological studies, is that there is a heavy component of the economic in *kula*, potlatch, and other spheres and that tokens such as shell beads and necklaces and copper plates promote and enter into the flow of life-serving commodities and services. Andrew J. Vayda (1967), for instance, finds that trade feasts among the Pomo Indians of California, where beads were exchanged for food, had the effect of spreading out and equalizing goods among people who were unable to store temporary surpluses. Harding (1970) demonstrates that, while boar and dog tooth transactions centered trading partnership transactions in the Vitiaz Strait, in a broader context they went along with and promoted the distribution of pigs, bark cloth, bags, pottery, mats, and canoes. We indicated earlier that the potlatch evened out food supplies between Northwest

Coast communities whose resources varied in different years and seasons. Since we have defined economics as the social organization of production, distribution, and consumption of material goods and services, we have to admit *kula* and potlatch and their tokens into the economic context. The tokens may be called "money," but they are restricted to particular spheres of multicentric economies and are not the all-purpose root of evil of high-energy societies. There is also an historical and evolutionary restriction on them: they are found in primitive cultures which have some degree of ranking in their social aspect and in later and higher cultures which have moved only incompletely into market economics.

Suggested Readings

Bohannan, Paul, and George Dalton, eds. 1965. *Markets in Africa: Eight subsistence economies in transition.* Garden City, N.Y.: Doubleday and Company.*

Dalton, George, ed. 1968. *Primitive, archaic and modern economies: Essays of Karl Polanyi.* Garden City, N.Y.: Doubleday and Company, Anchor Books.*

Firth, Raymond. 1950. *Primitive Polynesian economy.* New York: Humanities Press.

———, ed. 1967. *Themes in economic anthropology.* Association of Social Anthropologists Monograph 6. London, England: Tavistock.

Helm, June, ed. 1965. *Essays in economic anthropology.* Proceedings of the 1965 annual spring meeting of the American Ethnological Society. Seattle: American Ethnological Society.*

LeClair, Edward, and Harold E. Schneider, eds. 1968. *Economic anthropology.* New York: Holt, Rinehart and Winston.

Malinowski, Bronislaw. 1950. *Argonauts of the western Pacific.* New York: E. P. Dutton and Company.*

Sahlins, Marshall D. 1968. *Tribesmen.* Englewood Cliffs, N.J.: Prentice-Hall.*

———. 1972. *Stone Age economics.* Chicago: Aldine-Atherton.*

Spooner, Brian. 1973. *The cultural ecology of pastoral nomads.* Modular Publications 45. Reading, Mass.: Addison-Wesley.*

Watanabe, Hitoshi. 1973. *The Ainu ecosystem: Environment and group structure.* American Ethnological Society Monograph 54. Seattle: University of Washington Press.

In politics, we are concerned with the social organization of **power, authority,** and **prestige.** *Power* and *authority* are threatening words if they are burdened with the connotations given them in our culture, linked as they are with the state and the majesty of the law, but they are definitely less so in the context of groups, statuses, and rules of prestate society.

Defining the political aspect of social organization

There are good precedents in the discipline of political science from John Locke onward for looking at power, a principal concept of politics, not primarily as a thing but as a relation (Friedrich 1963: 160). When leaders lead followers and followers follow leaders, it is power behavior. Obviously there is a great range in leader-follower situations, from the headman of a Bushman camp directing movement to a new site, to a Trobriand chief setting in motion craftsmen who build canoes and kin who collect goods for a *kula* expedition, to an Egyptian pharoah commanding that a pyramid be raised for his tomb, to the policy makers of an industrial state launching a Five-Year Plan or negotiating a treaty. At lower energy levels, political organization lies in the groups, statuses, and rules that accomplish the

Chapter Ten
Evolution
of Political
Organization

237

whole of the daily social work of culture; at higher levels, specialized ones grow up.

But there are situations in prestate societies as well as in those at the state level that present opportunity for "choice" and "decision," for "choosing" among alternatives that have consequences for public good or ill. Shall the band move to a new range and, if so, where and when? Shall the village hold a feast and invite neighbors, and how shall the quantities of food and other goods be assembled for it? What is to be done with the shirker or troublemaker, and, if anything is to be done, who will do it? Shall the group attack a neighbor, and, if it does, who will lead? These are situations in which alternative behaviors may appear, and the course followed begins with a status or group whose leadership capacity is by definition power, however humble and uncertain it may be. The leader may be a headman, elder, or chief, a clan or village council, or "the complex of institutions" of the state, whose power and authority may range from minimal to omnipotent. But it is the leading and following that mark the political aspect.

In speaking of choices and decisions we do not intend to place the motivations for behavior, nor the explanation of them, in the biological or psychological context. Other disciplines may properly do so, but for us they are acts interpretable by reference to the cultural system and are to be regarded as part of the chain of the system's behavior.

Authority refers to the supporting ideas and beliefs surrounding the leader-follower behavior. These ideas and beliefs motivate, exert force, help channel energy in certain directions. There is precedent for this definition, too, in political science, although we are lifting it out of a "people do" context to make a cultural restatement of it. Friedrich writes (1963: 218, 223), "Authority rests upon the ability to issue communications which are capable of reasoned elaboration. . . .The power handler shares with his followers all or part of (certain) values or beliefs, and therefore could, and at times will, explain to his following the reasons he acted in a certain way or more especially why he preferred them to act likewise."

In the examples given above for the power relation, the Bushman headman's leadership is backed by sentiments of the household and by respect for age and experience; the Trobriand chief's by the ideology of ranked kinship and **mana**, a supernaturalistic notion we shall encounter again later; the pharoah's by the belief that he was a god. Contemporary chiefs of state are backed by beliefs that a course of action will result in prosperity, security, national honor, or glory or an agreement that abiding by laws ensures order and is best for everyone in the long run. When authority weakens, the leader-follower relation may alter. Egalitarians can walk away, while a coercive state apparatus can suppress dissent.

It is often said that there may be power without authority and authority without power. I would agree with the first assertion, inasmuch as power may be supported by coercion or naked force to which the exploited may or may not effectively react. But if ideas and beliefs are not associated with the leader-follower relation, they are by definition not political. If power is absent, what is commonly called "authority" might better be labelled "prestige," a term with wider application.

Prestige is an evaluative term that can be applied to statuses, groups, and rules in culture, but it is not necessarily tied to power. If someone is looked up to, admired, or respected for certain qualities and accomplishments, he or she has prestige. Prestige is found so often outside of the active leader-follower relation that there is a temptation to rule it out of the political context altogether. It is retained because of its value in an evolutionary context, however, for much of the authority that backs up leader-follower behavior at lower cultural levels probably emerged from a background of prestige holding and giving. When power arises, prestige may be converted into authority. The word *prestige*, incidentally, derives from the Latin *praestigiae*, which means puzzlers' tricks; a talent for them may, metaphorically at least, be called into play even today by wielders of power and authority.

You may say that it is carrying the cultural systems point of view too far to ascribe power, authority, and prestige to rules as well as statuses and groups, but if so you have slipped into a people point of view rather than one that focuses on extracted behaviors and objects and makes culture out of them. Surely the Ten Commandments and the American Constitution, those clusters of symbols, those sets of rules, elicit following behavior in culture; they are buttressed by accompanying ideas and beliefs and are looked up to and respected.

Political anthropology has emerged as a specialization in the last few decades, although there was an early and continuing concern with government by ethnographers and theorists. The turn toward intensive comparative studies might be set with *African Political Systems,* edited by Meyer Fortes and E. E. Evans-Pritchard (1940), students of Radcliffe-Brown. In its preface, Radcliffe-Brown wrote (p. xiv), "In studying political organization, we have to deal with the maintenance or establishment of social order, within a territorial framework, by the organized exercise of coercive authority through the use, or the possibility of use, of physical force. . . . In dealing with political systems. . .we are dealing with law, on the one hand, and with war, on the other."

"Functions" of the political organization in maintaining internal order and regulating external relations of territorial groups continue to center most introductory discussions of politics. Sometimes that focus is useful, but when it becomes narrowed to law and warfare it is unnecessarily restrictive. We take the view that politics is only one aspect of internal social order and social control in general in human societies and that it is not the only regulator of external relations. And war, surely, is not the only way systems relate to each other.

One last point: Politics is only one way of looking at the adaptive responses of the whole cultural system in relation to its environments— and like the social aspect of which it is part those responses presumably are consistent with a culture's technology. It should not be given the position of prime mover in behavior of the cultural system.

Leader-follower relations
in egalitarian
and rank societies

The leader-follower relation in egalitarian hunting-gathering cultures is limited, shifting, impermanent. Individuals with particular qualities, abilities, and accomplishments—hunters, shamans, those with the wisdom of age—take the lead but usually in limited spheres such as hunting, ritual, and peacemaking. Leadership in one sphere does not necessarily mean precedence in another. Perhaps we can apply to these statuses the notion that Paul Bohannan (1963: 282) directed toward political groups within societies other than states—"multiple centers of power." Within their own households and kin and association circles, the egalitarians act out their mutual obligations and responsibilities without formal leadership statuses except for that of headman, itself a position with many limitations. And leadership, whether in statuses or groups, does not result in personal material gain or release from ordinary work.

The Bushman male who heads a band of several families takes no lead in organizing hunting, trading, craft making, or gift giving; any capable individuals act on their own. Nor does he judge or punish those who don't conform to expected behavior; public opinion takes care of that. He has the privilege of first choice of a site for his hut and fire. "He has no other rewards or prerogatives. He carries his own load and is as thin as the rest" (Marshall 1965: 267). When his vigor wanes, the young men cease to consult him.

For the Mbuti, Turnbull (1965: 302-3) reports, ". . . whether acting as bands or as segments, leadership of a sort exists, but it is divided into a number of different fields, in each of which several adults will jointly be recognized as deserving more of a hearing than others. Nearly every adult is accorded this respect in one or more fields, and every adult has the right to express himself in any field." Younger married men take the lead in hunting and in easing squabbles over division of game, and older widowers or neutral strangers become peacemakers in wider, noisier disputes. But the Pygmies are hostile to anyone who would become a leader, even if he is better fitted than others because of his ability.

"The Eskimo are intolerant of anything like restraint," according to Jenness (1922: 94). "Every man in his eyes has the same rights and the same privileges as every other man in the community. One may be a better hunter, or a more skilful dancer, or have a greater control over the spiritual world, but this does not make him more than one member of a group in which all are free and theoretically equal." As long as a man's energies and success last he may have some influence, "but when they fail his prestige and authority vanish" (1922: 93).

The example we will adduce for groups in a political context in an egalitarian society is in some respects a restricted one, inasmuch as the Nuer **segmentary lineage**, the kind of group in question, is probably found only in "tribal" societies which are expanding against competitors in areas to which they are ecologically adapted (Sahlins 1961). The Tiv, whom we encountered in our discussion of multicentric economies, also have segmentary lineages. Nonetheless, I think it illustrates the egalitarian principle that action is not directed from the top down in a permanent arrangement of dominant and subordinate groups but is coordinated among equals who join together or fight, depending on circumstances.

The Nuer household occupies a homestead, which contains a cattle

Human Social Organization as an Aspect of Culture

byre, an attached kraal, and separate huts for wives of its head. Clusters of homesteads make up the rainy season cultivating and cattle-tending villages. In the dry season, the villages become cattle camps, their households generally remaining in contact. Household and village are the principal economic units, and villages are largely autonomous and independent, both economically and politically.

Within a village there are found in kinship context several shallow patrilines three to five generations in depth, roughly corresponding, residentially, to households with wives and affines excluded, for although Nuer count kin on both mother's and father's side there is emphasis upon the latter in some respects. Clusters of lines in one or more villages trace genealogical relationships to a common ancestor, the agnatic kin connection between lineages (that traced through males) being spoken of as *buth*. This kind of descent reckoning can be pushed back to more remote common ancestors of collateral lines, embracing larger and larger numbers of kin so defined. Looked at from the point of higher-order joinings, smaller lineages are segments of larger ones, and the whole may be visualized, by Evans-Pritchard's scheme, as minimal, minor, major, and maximal segments, the last term referring to the parts into which a clan is divided (1940: 6).

Except for their effect in regulating marriage and in the transfer of cattle, the patrilines or lineages have little significance in ordinary daily affairs. Kin on both sides (mother's and father's) in household and village work and share together. But the lineage organization lurks in the background. Lineages and linked lineages can move into action and marshall people in separate villages and camping groups and larger territorial units into cooperative effort when broader cooperation is required. The more closely related lineages are, the more they are inclined to band together in the face of a threat to one of them and to confront in common cause an equivalent set of lineages in the struc-

Diagram of a segmentary lineage system, like that of the Nuer, based on descent through males. At the left, descendants of 1, a son of the clan founder, form one maximal segment, and the descendants of 2 another. All descendants of 3 and of 4, respectively, comprise major segments, and descendants of 7, 8, 9, and 10 taken separately form minor segments. Descendants of 15, 16, and so on form minimal segments. The situation would be the same on the right, in the maximal segment stemming from 2. A segment at any level may act independently in its own interests and in opposition to like segments but may combine with others at higher orders of joining if it is advantageous to do so.

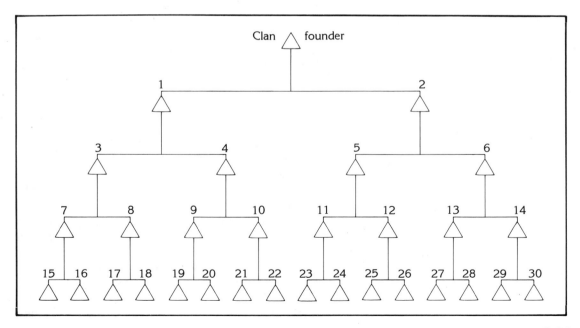

ture. They bring together not only agnatic kin but also cognatically linked relatives who live with them and are friendly with them. That the respective foes may be kin, viewed from the point of higher joinings in the lineage structure, does not matter; they ally with others and against others at appropriate levels, depending on the extent of the threat, crystallizing around "dominant" lineages that by custom take the lead. A whole Nuer subtribe may be marshalled for action by this means, particularly when the opponent is a non-Nuer group occupying desirable herding ranges or encroaching on Nuer territory.

Here is the important point: "Tiv-Nuer lineages do not come into existence except through the massing effect, in opposition to equivalent groups. They are not permanent, *absolute* social entities, but *relative* ones. Called into being by external circumstances, the level of organization achieved is in direct proportion to the social order of the opposition, and the lineage segment ceases to function as such when opposition is in abeyance. The lineage segment cannot stand alone but only stand 'against' " (Sahlins 1961: 333). This "structural relativity" is paralleled by "relativity of leadership," for there is no system of chiefs of higher segments. A qualified man leads only his own minor segment, and when it joins with another minor segment he may, by reason of his ability, speak for the paired group, and so it goes.

It should be added that the Nuer segmentary lineage and its related leadership has been effective as a social tool in expansion at the expense of neighbors, particularly the herding Dinka, whose component political units are not drawn together by a like system. Nuer and Dinka exploited the same savannah environment, but the Nuer lineages gave them a "superior military potential." Sahlins (1961: 339) suggests that Nuer expansion is "perhaps an outstanding instance of the Law of Cultural Dominance," one of the summations of systems behavior we encountered in Chapter Four.

Two kinds of native ranking systems arose in the Pacific Islands that provided kinds of leaders not characteristic of egalitarians. One, in Melanesia, centered on "big men," and the other, in Polynesia, focused upon chiefly status derived from inherited lineage rank (Sahlins 1963). Don't be disturbed that the Trobrianders were mentioned as having chiefs, because they are rather atypical of Melanesia. Chiefs and big men arose in other parts of the world (chiefs were encountered among the Nootka, remember), but it will be convenient to discuss them in the Pacific context.

Known variously as "man of importance," "man of renown," "generous rich man," or "center man," the Melanesian leader won power by gardening, magical, oratorical, or military prowess and attracted followers by assembling and giving away pigs, vegetable food, and valuables. He was a consummate wheeler-dealer, arranging marriages and advancing the goods required for them, sponsoring feasts and rituals. With his leadership established at home, he turned to a broader field, sponsoring intervillage feasts and potlatches, establishing peace by arranging compensation to those whose kin were killed in hostilities, employing any device afforded by the culture to stand out and to increase his power.

Generosity was essential for the big man, particularly in the beginning

Human Social Organization as an Aspect of Culture

Economic and political integration is fostered by reciprocal entertaining between communities. Here New Guinean Binumarien, both men and women, decorate themselves elaborately to receive visitors from another village. (Courtesy Kristen Hawkes.)

of his career, and he had to assemble surpluses to be generous. These at first came primarily by his inducing his own household members to work harder, his marrying more women to tend pigs, and his opening more gardens. Generous giving obligated recipients to respond to his initiative when a men's house was to be built and a feast was to be given, and so his power grew. And, although his personal interests appeared to be uppermost, what he did had broader political effects, uniting villages into a "supralocal organization" (Sahlins 1963: 292).

Whereas the Melanesian big man made his own position, and power did not outlast its holder, in Polynesia power "resided in the office; it was not made by demonstration of personal superiority" (Sahlins 1963:

Evolution of Political Organization

295). The Polynesian chief "owned" resources in the same sense as did the Nootkan; they came to him by right, and unlike the Melanesian big man he did not need to engage in initial maneuvers to obligate people to him. They were obligated already by his status. Additionally, he could *tabu* for a time exploitation of particular resources until he gave the word, so that those of lower rank had to turn temporarily to other places for their subsistence. This is not to say that he had no obligations to his followers, including the duty to be generous.

What the leader collected and the labor and services he commanded, most markedly in the advanced chiefdoms of Hawaii and Tahiti, went into maintenance of a court and armed retainers, wars with rivals, entertainment of visiting chiefs, support of craftsmen, and building of irrigation works and religious structures. At this end of the ranking scale, society moved close to stratification, for districts became impoverished if a chief made war upon them and levied tribute, but the Pacific Islands societies never established a full, state-supported system of stratification. The *state* is an organization based on principles other than kinship and is superior to and overrides kinship. As Sahlins puts it (1963: 297), "Chieftainship is never detached from kinship moorings and kinship economic ethics. Even the greatest Polynesian chiefs were conceived superior kinsmen to the masses, fathers of their people, and generosity was morally incumbent upon them." As members of a kinship-dominated society, followers fell away and rebelled if disparity in consumption became too great between themselves and their leader. So, indeed, have the oppressed in suprakinship states, but at their greater peril.

What is called the **conical clan** or ramage provides the kinship structure of Polynesian chiefdoms (it is also found in Africa and Asia and on the North Pacific Coast). It is a group based on lineal descent whose segments are ranked according to genealogical distance from the founder. There is a senior line running from the founder through first-

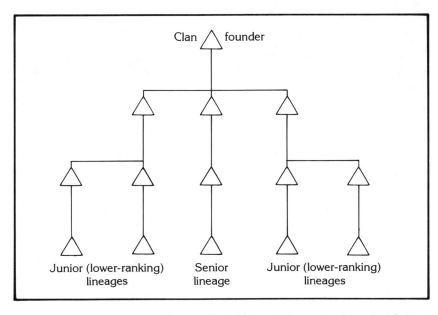

In contrast with the egalitarian segmentary lineage system, lineages of the conical clan or ramage are ranked according to genealogical distance from the founder. The senior or highest-ranking lineage represents direct descent through firstborn sons from the clan founder, and the junior, lower-ranked lines stem from younger sons. For all groups, in any generation, firstborn sons outrank the others.

Clan founder

Junior (lower-ranking) lineages   Senior lineage   Junior (lower-ranking) lineages

Human Social Organization as an Aspect of Culture

born sons, and junior or cadet lines descending from his younger sons. In any generation, the same principle is applied to members of all groups, the firstborn outranking the rest. A Polynesian community would be comprised of one or more lineages and affinal kin, with its local chief the firstborn of the leading lineage present. Over a cluster of communities, a district, there would be a paramount chief, again the ranking member of the lineage closest to the founder. The whole chiefdom would have at its head the highest paramount chief, firstborn of the founder's central line (Sahlins 1968: 24-25).

Thus a Polynesian chiefdom was a collection of ranked kin statuses and groups, held together economically by egalitarian reciprocity and chiefly redistribution and politically by leader-follower relations flowing through the ranks. As to the authority which backed the chief's power: "The position of the paramount chief is reinforced through deification of his ancestors, themselves former paramount chiefs, and through connecting this main line of descent to the important god or gods of the group. In consequence of divine descent, a certain sacredness and power (*mana*) is believed to be inherently a part of chieftainship" (Sahlins 1958: 142).

The capacity of the developed chiefdom to link in common enterprises communities in different ecological zones producing different foodstuffs and artifacts and to marshall labor for concerted action raised its economic and political level above that of the egalitarians. "To speak of the greater social scope and power of paramount chiefs does not completely document the advance," Sahlins (1968: 26) concludes. "What has been wrought is not just greater chiefs but a *system* of chieftainship, a hierarchy of major and minor authorities holding forth over major and minor subdivisions of the tribe: a chain of command linking paramount to middle-range and local-level leaders, and binding the hinterland hamlet to the strategic heights."

Most rank societies studied by ethnographers failed to reach the level of Polynesian society, and even among the Polynesians, as we have mentioned, power was tempered by competing motivations among followers. Speaking of ranking systems in general, Fried (1967: 133) asserts, "In rank society leaders can lead, but followers may not follow." The anthropologist Father John Cooper is said to have reported of those in the tropical regions of South America, "One word from the chief and everyone does as he pleases." (Carneiro 1961: 65). Chiefs may work as hard as anyone, and their position is dependent on the good will of their followers. Among the Nootka, for instance, "It was commonly recognized that the individual chief's ability to 'keep up his name,' that is, to live up to the reputation of his forebears in potlatching and feast-giving depended on the people...living in his house. 'That is the way with a chief,' explained an informant. 'If his "tenants" are good, helping him lots (working for him, giving him wealth), then he will get a good name, he can do much (i.e., potlatching). If they are no good or don't care for him, he can do nothing' " (Drucker 1951: 273).

Between the egalitarian bands on the one hand and the chiefdoms on the other, in that range of societies sometimes called "tribal," political leadership was limited. The Nuer, Evans-Pritchard (1940: 182) observed, "strut about like lords of the earth, which, indeed, they consider themselves to be. There is no master and no servant in their society, but only equals who regard themselves as God's noblest creation." In Nuerland, an elder is looked up to, but he "has no defined status, powers, or sphere of leadership" (1940: 179).

Hopi clan heads were called chiefs, but they were guides and advisors in limited kin groups. "A chief's word is respected and his opinion is usually sought on any vital matter, but there is virtually no provision for his active participation in government" (Titiev 1944: 65). A Hopi war chief, prestigeful through his daring wielding of a stone axe against enemies, sometimes took it upon himself to scold and thrash wrongdoers, but no strong and permanent power developed either in his status or in that of the Oraibi town chief, who headed the Bear clan. And Tsembaga big men, we are told, do not command obedience, nor is there "on the part of men in general any abdication, either expressed or tacit, of decision making in favor of big men" (Rappaport 1967a: 28). Egalitarianism yielded grudgingly in social evolution.

Social control
in evolutionary perspective

There are at least two things we might mean by *social control*. We might use the term to refer to the movement of the whole of the social aspect of a culture as it orders the interpersonal behaviors of people from cradle to grave, from the first steps in enculturation onward. That is control in the broad sense. Or we might mean something less—the ways in which a culture prevents interpersonal conflict and goes into action when social disorder occurs. To put it on the ground, if a Semai, a Kuikuru, or a middle-class American violates an important social rule and harms others, there are culturally prescribed ways to punish the violator or recompense the person wronged.

The narrower sense is the one we will follow, and we will use the plural of the term, *social controls,* because there are two distinct kinds of rules with evolutionary significance. There is **law**, characteristic only of state societies, and all the rest. The difference between them is what backs them up, the means by which the rules are enforced. Law is supported by organized application of force or coercion, while other rules have back of them the diffuse support of kinship and public opinion and the kind of retaliation that leads to feud. If any force enters into the reaction against breach of nonlaw rules, it comes from a variety of places, intermittently, not from a single, overriding focus of power which is the state.

Bushmen and Mbuti had a kind of practicality about social control that anticipated that of intelligent modern criminologists—remove the cause of possible conflict, rather than wait for conflict to happen. Rather than arouse envy by keeping a good knife, for instance, a Bushman gave it away. There was occasional violence and even murder among "the harmless people," as their ethnographer called them, but they deemed it better to let the aggressor go unpunished than to compound things into a feud. In a portrait of the even-tempered leader Toma, Elizabeth Marshall Thomas relates that at one camping place Toma's hut was placed beside that of his father's murderer—for "Toma was friendly even with him" (1959: 183). Complete harmony was not the lot of the Mbuti, either, but if a quarrel involved several people and threatened to disrupt a camp, a mediator would remind everyone that "a noisy camp is a hungry camp," which usually was enough to quiet the disputants. If it persisted, there might be a splitting up of the camp, one faction going one way, the other another (Turnbull 1965: 303). Better to walk away from trouble than endure it.

Violence was more common among the Copper Eskimo, and it was met either with counterviolence or simply accepted. "For minor offences—such as theft and abduction (of women), there is no remedy unless the victim takes the matter into his own hands and exacts compensation or vengeance....No man will commit a crime, save in the heat of passion, unless he believes that his kinsmen will support him against any attempt at revenge" (Jenness 1922: 94, 96). Although there are reports for other Eskimo groups of regulated physical combat and singing duels to bring public opinion to one's side and redress violence, Jenness found none among the Copper Eskimo, and in any event the effectiveness of such devices rests solidly upon the attitudes and sympathies of the community.

A Semai who fell into that uncomfortable state called *punan* because someone refused a request either endured it or asked compensation from the offender, sometimes calling on kin for support. It was possible to appeal further to the elders, but they were likely to be kin of the offender or offended and would take sides, and there was no way for them to enforce a judgment if they made one. "In brief, little violence occurs within Semai society. Violence, in fact, seems to terrify the Semai. A Semai does not meet force with force, but with passivity or flight. Yet, he has no institutionalized way of preventing violence—no social controls, no police or courts" (Dentan 1968: 59).

"In a strict sense Nuer have no law," in the judgment of Evans-Pritchard (1940: 162). "There are conventional compensations for damage, adultery, loss of limb, and so forth, but there is no authority with power to adjudicate on such matters or to enforce a verdict." The wronged individual calls on kin for support, and, if the parties cannot compromise or consent to a settlement, a feud may result. Mediators called leopard-skin chiefs may be called on to bring disputants and their elders together, but whatever force their decisions have rests upon their persuasiveness and the fact the parties agree to it (1940: 174).

Similarly, among the Hopi, it was kin organized in households and clans who kept order, disciplined their own, and stood against others for their customary rights. Earlier we noted that the only supraclan leaders at Oraibi were the village chief, head of the Bear clan, honored for his religious position, and the war chief, who, infrequently, acted as a policeman. To these might be added disciplinary *katcinas*, masked religious figures who urged on village work parties with a good deal of buffoonery and who wielded cactus whips—not, however, against miscreants whose misdeeds were the concern of kin. This involvement of the supernatural in social control is something we shall meet again later, and we give only one additional example here: The Kuikuru, among whom "formal leadership and authority are so weak. . .as scarcely to exist" (Dole 1966: 73), have recourse to **divination** and **sorcery** to discover wrongdoers and turn public opinion against them.

Trobriand social control Malinowski was inclined to interpret in legal terms, but it is clear that redress of serious wrongs came from subclan or clan pitted against subclan. Punishment for theft of food or valuables "would consist in the shame and ridicule which covers the culprit. . ." (Malinowski 1951: 118), so no physical force was involved. But killing, which occurred only rarely, was a matter to be settled between the subclans of aggressor and victim on the principle of an eye for an eye and a tooth for a tooth, or by the payment of "blood money," that is, transfer of property to the victim's kin to avoid feud. A chief could call only upon a sorcerer to frighten an offender against him. And, says Malinowski, there appear to be a few cases on record in which a chief called upon followers to kill someone who had offended him deeply. If it did occur, note that it was for an offense against the chief, punished by his followers at his instance. He did not punish theft or murder among the people: that was a matter for public opinion and for action by the wronged person's kin.

Among the Nootka, "the most common means of control was the counsel given a wayward person by his kinsmen. They sought to calm his wrath or mend his ways. . . . They appealed to his loyalty to the family 'to do right; not to do anything that will bring down our name. . .or involve us in trouble.' As a rule this sufficed. If it did not, the public reprimands would shame most people into conformance with conventional behavior" (Drucker 1951: 319). Kin feared taking revenge, for that could escalate into feud; tempers were allowed to cool, and eventually the wrong was forgotten.

And among the Cheyenne: Outright theft was rare, but if a man resented, say, use by another of his horse, he took direct action—perhaps with a club. If serious trouble threatened, the chiefs called the principals together and made a judgment, ordering one to pay something to the other. That was usually, but not always accepted. A quarrel might escalate to a killing, and one killing might lead to another. A murderer fled to escape vengeance from his victim's kin, while chiefs tried to induce the latter to accept blood payment. In any event, the miscreant "lost all standing" and "was obliged for a time to camp away from the main tribe, and often he went away from their camp and spent a year or more with some other tribe" (Grinnell 1923, I: 353-54). As we have mentioned, the chiefs during tribal encampments delegated policing tasks to the military societies, and it appears that in the late historical period the societies became more and more active on their own in punishing miscreants for theft or other offenses. If so, a control not so closely attached to kinship was arising. But considering the independence of camps and their leaders, it is doubtful that the chiefs' council or the societies held statelike power.

Political power in egalitarian and rank societies, it may be concluded, is multicentric and not unicentric. Custom and the weight of public opinion keep people in line and curb disorder and violence; but, if they occur, means for coercive redress either are lacking or they are wielded by separate clusters of kin. That being so, prestate societies have social controls, but they do not have law in the sense of the definition adopted.

It should be mentioned, however, that some anthropologists (e.g.,

Hoebel 1946, 1964, Pospisil 1972, White 1959) find law lower in the evolutionary scale of societies, for they do not set up the requirement of a central and paramount power for enforcement of rules.

How did ranking arise?

Rank, in current anthropological theory, represents the highest adaptive level in the social aspect of primitive culture. Or higher, one should say, because it emerged from only one underlying level, the egalitarian. All known rank societies are based on technologies of plant and animal domestication or on hunting-gathering-fishing in favored areas with concentrated resources, a circumstance that supports the generalization that availability of energy is a basic factor in culture building. But availability alone does not ensure advance. It is a necessary but not a sufficient condition. Goods and services that technologically supplied materials and energies represent must be produced and distributed in an organized and efficient way that does not inhibit the technology but on the contrary induces more production and more and broader-scaled social activity.

This is where the political aspect of rank meshes with the economic. It is the introduction of a leader-follower relationship by means of which the limitations of household production and distribution by reciprocity are in some measure overcome. As Sahlins (1972: 130) sees it, "In the course of primitive social evolution, main control over the domestic economy seems to pass from the formal solidarity of the kinship structure to its political aspect. As the structure is politicized, especially as it is centralized in ruling chiefs, the household economy is mobilized in a larger social cause." Some of the enterprises are direct and intensive investments of labor in technology—fish dams and weirs and irrigation ditches. These further build the energy base. Others contribute to community integration—feasts and rituals or the building of men's houses or religious structures—and intervillage ties through visiting and entertaining. Thus relationships become extensive, firmer, and more effective.

Underneath the rank system, there might not be much apparent change in the relationships of everyday life. An individual in it would still have direct access to resources of the habitat to feed self and household, sexual division of labor would still be prominent, and giving and receiving would follow largely the old principle of reciprocity. Relationships would be phrased in the ideology of kinship, and in the generality of those societies the individual would not be wholly bound to follow the commands of holders of rank. It is the economic and political potential of rank, the stratification that followed upon it in some cultures, that gives it evolutionary significance, rather than any overturn of primitive principles of organization. Whatever its own limitations, it fostered further central organization and control.

How did ranking originate? In rank societies, population densities within their territories are greater, and the people tend to be concentrated in villages which, although substantially independent, are linked with others by kinship, marriage, and exchange networks (Fried 1967: 112-16, 118-20). Villages are not exclusive to rank societies, but it is difficult to see how rank could have arisen without this organizational home base. Their territories are not greater in extent than those in egalitarian societies, but there is intensified work on the land immediately surrounding the villages.

Hunters, when their numbers increase, bud off from parent bands; so do farmers, herders, and sedentary fishing people from their villages, but when they move and settle down they tend to maintain a firmer connection with the home group. This connection is strengthened by the growth of kinship in a new direction from that of mobile hunters and gatherers: there is formalization of kinship groups along lineal and cognatic descent lines into which people are born or in which they acquire membership in other specific ways (Fried 1967: 120-28). Formation of such groups is fostered by association with specific areas and resources (the ownership relation), so that they become, as social anthropologists say, "corporate," holding property and other rights and privileges.

With these in being, there is a base for establishing priority of statuses and groups resting on genealogical distance from the founder and on the length of time the statuses or groups resided in the village. So rank, which adds order to the relations both of the residents of a village and people of the parent village and its offspring, becomes established. It is advantageous for people of lower rank to attach themselves to higher-ranking kin and for chiefs to keep and enlarge their followings. Rank motivates the movement and settling within the territory of such a society.

But rank as an ideology of priority is hollow without the linked economic behavior of redistribution. Gifts of goods and services flow to the redistributive chief and down again through the ranks. The difference between this emergent redistribution and the generalized reciprocity of the egalitarians is that in the process there is a temporary concentration of resources at one collection point, where it may be manipulated and channeled to support enterprises advantageous for the whole society as well as for the chief's prestige. Chiefly reciprocity does not represent a sharp break from reciprocity; it is a vitalized extension of it. As Sahlins (1972: 133) puts it, "Insofar as the society is committed socially to kin relationships, morally it is committed to generosity; whoever, therefore, is liberal automatically merits the general esteem." Generosity puts the receiver in debt to the giver. The chief, as the most generous giver of all, has the greater merit. It is the chief's liberality and exemplary effort that stimulates his own household and other households to accomplish what they ordinarily would not.

Rank societies as a class engage in external hostilities more often than do egalitarians, and when they do pressure on the land and competition is behind it. This might be expected to put forward prestigious political leaders and enhance the power of those who hold it already. But Fried, for one, lays lesser weight on war, which in rank societies is intermittent and often ritualized, as a builder of political organization. Although there is probably a correlation between population pressure on land and hostilities, he says, it is more frequently in activities such as feasts, ceremonies, and organized hospitality that the chief's status is raised and his effectiveness heightened. "It is in the conduct of such events that ranking reaches its apogee as the effective organizer of the population" (Fried 1967: 178).

Human Social Organization as an Aspect of Culture

A chief among the Mossi, Voltaic Republic. Royal, noble, and commoner lineages of the Mossi were ranked and stratified, with a hierarchical arrangement of power from kingdoms down through provinces, districts, and villages. The people paid taxes in grain and livestock. (Courtesy Herbert W. Butler.)

There is another facet to this organization of population that is important economically and politically. Whereas the territorial and residential parts of an egalitarian system are alike in their technological and economic orientation, exploiting the same kind of resources and producing the same things, rank systems incorporate diversity. There may be farming and fishing villages, for instance, and villages additionally specializing in particular crafts. ". . .[A] fully developed chiefdom is likely to have both regional specialization *and* individual division of labor tied into the redistribution" (Service 1971b: 138). Crafts such as making of pottery and baskets, weaving, and wood carving, as Service points out, are subsidized; specialization induces superior skill and product, and crafts become hereditary in family lines. Whether this specialization begins for regional or local exchange, one fosters the other, and the more efficient organization of production spreads into new areas.

The factors and the way they have been ordered for an explanation of the rise of ranking are tentative and hypothetical, as Fried and other anthropologists who have concerned themselves with the matter insist. Others would weight ecology, internal structure, population increase, pressure on the land, and external hostilities differently. Particularly is there dispute over population growth and food technology (does technology come first and increase the numbers of people, or does population growth come first and lead to intensified production?) and surpluses (do they arise automatically with more effective technology, or are they induced by more efficient organization?).

The state and early
urban society

The stratified society that followed ranking and preceded the state, one in which there are haves and have-nots and in which only the haves gain unrestricted access to basic resources, is, as indicated before, a hypothetical stage without current examples. A central power "superior to kinship" is required to maintain it, so that if a state apparatus does not emerge the society returns to ranking or egalitarianism—or it is incorporated into another, expanding state society.

The first states, so far as we know, arose in Southwest Asia, followed closely by Egypt and the Indus valley, and then China, Mesoamerica, and Peru. Gordon Childe, who coupled the phrase *food producing* with *Neolithic*, also coined the term *Urban Revolution* for the social outcome of domestication—by analogy with the way in which English villages grew into manufacturing towns following the Industrial Revolution. To him, *urban* meant both population concentrations and the presence of specialists—craftsmen, traders, and others—supported by surplus production of the farmers (1941: 142-43).

Childe's meaning is still the core in efforts to establish an analytical model for cities and their place in economics. "It is generally agreed that whatever else a city may be it is a unit of settlement which performs specialized functions in relationship to a broader hinterland. . . .Moreover, while numerous inhabitants of a city may engage in food production, it is agreed that the specialized functions of a city are not agricultural in nature" (Trigger 1972: 577). Although the first Southwest Asian states were city-states, city and state are not linked inseparably. There have been several historical paths to statehood.

Archeologists are reevaluating estimates of population in the first urban centers, particularly in Mesopotamia. For instance, whereas a British authority accepts earlier guesses of half a million people in each of its larger cities or towns at the peak of their expansion (Daniel 1968: 70), two Americans calculate for four partially excavated centers a modest average of seventeen thousand and a *total* population for lower Mesopotamia about the middle of the third millennium B.C. of three hundred fifty thousand to half a million (Braidwood and Reed 1957: 29). Organization and control of the occupational groups of the sort mentioned by Childe appear to have varied widely in Mesopotamia, Egypt, and Mesoamerica, as did the layout of the cities; but Mesopotamia will serve us as a context for the coming into being of the state. We will look first at some dramatic evidence of its existence and then go on to the events that led up to it.

Human Social Organization as an Aspect of Culture

Massive stone defense works, such as this hilltop fortress of Sacsahuaman near Cuzco, indicate the capacity of the Inca state to marshal labor. (Courtesy C. Melvin Aikens.)

The town of Machu Picchu was built by controlled labor in the service of the Inca during the so-called Late Period, which began about the middle of the fifteenth century. There were temples, plazas, complex waterworks, and paved walks and steps. Houses were built of dressed stone, plastered with mud, and had thatched roofs; they were built in compounds that probably represented kin units called *ayllu*. (Courtesy C. Melvin Aikens.)

In the middle of the third millennium B.C., in the small city-state of Lagash, one of the fifteen or twenty that had taken shape in the land of Sumer (lower Mesopotamia, between the Tigris and Euphrates), occurred what Samuel Noah Kramer (1959: 45-50) has called the first recorded case of social reform—plainly of reform of abuses by the state. Lagash was a walled town, centered by a temple whose administrators or priests held the land in trust for the town god, supervised communal projects, and collected and managed the distribution of food and goods. Besides the farmers, there were cattle breeders, boatmen, fishermen, many groups of craftsmen, and merchants who carried Lagash goods to neighboring states by land and water. With this specialization of occupations and crafts, the economy had gone beyond the simple domestic form and its reciprocal exchanges, although we can see a lingering redistribution rooted in the temple.

Now Lagash had a secular ruler, the *ishakku*, who was supported by his own armed retainers, administrators, tax collectors, and inspectors, as well as by the yield of his family land. In the twenty-fourth century B.C., the status was hereditary, held by the Ur-Nanshe dynasty, which had waged wars with other Sumerian states and had expanded its power and wealth at the expense of the temple administrators and the people. To raise and supply his army, and, of course, to maintain his

Evolution of Political Organization

palace and court, the *ishakku* taxed the citizens to extreme lengths and appropriated temple property for himself. (What had been a chiefly gift in rank society was now extracted by force.)

"From one end of the state to the other, our historian observes bitterly, 'There were tax collectors'" (Kramer 1959: 48). Every kind of wealth was taxed—cattle, fish, boats, the sheep at the shearing places. On the perfumer's preparation "the *ishakku* got five shekels, the vizier one shekel and the palace steward got another shekel." (Here we have an indication of all-purpose money—silver.) Kin who took their dead for burial at the town cemetery were taxed, and so were those who got divorced. "The oxen of the gods plowed the *ishakku's* onion patches; the onion and cucumber patches of the *ishakku* were located in the god's best fields" (Kramer 1959: 47-48)—until the ruler's lands and houses stretched across the domain.

But the citizens of Lagash, it is recorded, overthrew the Ur-Nanshe and chose from another family a new *ishakku* named Urukagina. He removed the old tax collectors and parasites, cleared the city of "usurers, thieves, and murderers," and stopped the exploitation of poor by rich. "Urukagina made a special covenant with Ningirsu, the god of Lagash, that he would not permit widows and orphans to be victimized by 'men of power'" (Kramer 1959: 49). So the *ishakku* laid down the law, and he had the force to back his commands; in all likelihood, it was a law that had arisen from custom before his time but had been abrogated by the greedy Ur-Nanshe. Alas, Urukagina held power only ten years, after which his city was overcome by the ruler of neighboring Umma.

The roots of this state-supported stratified society pictured by the

Sumerian temple complexes, such as this one at Khafājah from the Early Dynastic period (about 3000-2340 B.C.), are evidence of the rise of states. Khafājah was on the Diyala River, a tributary of the Tigris, in Iraq. (Courtesy Oriental Institute, University of Chicago.)

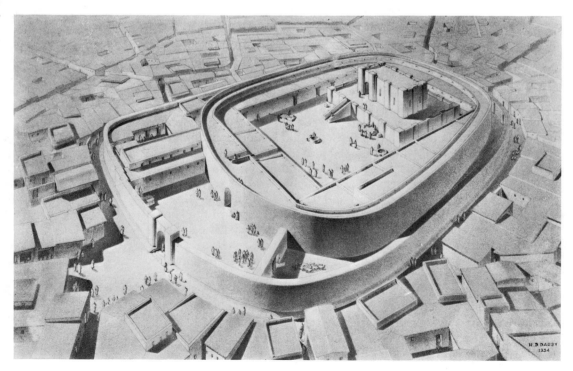

Human Social Organization as an Aspect of Culture

native historian go back at least as far as the first domesticators of wheat, barley, sheep, and goats, 3,000 to 5,000 years before in Iraq, Iran, Turkey, Syria, and Palestine. In the sixth millennium B.C., the lifeway represented at Jarmo (Chapter Six) became dominant on both sides of the highland crescent that runs from present-day Israel around northern Iraq and down the Zagros mountains of eastern Iran, and farmers gradually occupied the northern valleys of the Tigris and Euphrates. Archeologists identify two principal traditions, **Hassuna**, named for a site near modern Mosul on the Tigris, and **Halaf**, whose name comes from a site on the Syrian-Turkish border on a tributary of the Euphrates. Century after century, walls of the village houses, first of packed mud and later of unbaked clay bricks, were reared and leveled as the tells or mounds grew and dotted the northern Mesopotamian plain. From them, the people walked out to plant and harvest barley and wheat, to herd their flocks of sheep and goats (and later pigs and cattle), and to hunt with sling and spear.

There is not enough evidence of inequalities of wealth between households for us to assume that the societies represented were other than egalitarian or ranked. Surprisingly, the size of villages (about 150 to 200 people) and their spacing (two to three miles apart) appear not to have changed much in 7,000 years, at least in one sector of the region—the Zagros foothills of northern Iraq. Each village had then, as it has today, a little over five and a half square miles, including garden, pasture, and wasteland, for its sustenance (Braidwood and Reed 1957: 26-27). But obviously the Middle East has had towns and cities and nation-states for several thousand years; they arose first not at the edges of the crescent nor in northern Mesopotamia but in the southern part, in the land called Sumer, the biblical Shinar.

There, the overtaking and passing of the north occurred at least by the period called **Ubaid** (4500-3750 B.C.), when some villages of mud-plastered reed huts and sun-dried brick houses had become towns, supported by date-palm groves, fields within and without the walls in which barley and wheat were harvested with clay sickles, pastured sheep and goats (later, cattle and pigs also), and abundant catches of fish. Already the familiar Mesopotamian *ziggurat,* or stepped temple tower, was being built, and metallurgy appeared with the casting of copper axes in clay molds (later in the third millennium, tin was mixed with copper to produce bronze). Metallurgy, along with pottery turned on a free-spinning wheel that showed up in the following **Warka** (or Uruk) period, were among the technological inventions that furthered movement from the domestic to the craft division of labor (Braidwood 1967, Daniel 1968). Gordon Childe (1951: 148-60), who stressed technological accumulation and the rise of specialized crafts in the making of Sumerian civilization, posited a strong continuity between Mesopotamian beginnings and the southern flowering.

A cultural period that began with Warka, about 3750 B.C., and continued to the so-called **Early Dynastic**, about 3000 B.C., is designated the **Protoliterate** because of the growth of humankind's first system of writing. That was Sumerian cuneiform, a kind of formalized pictographic writing impressed by wood and reed styluses on wet clay tablets (producing marks which were wedge shaped, which is what *cuneiform*

	A	B	C	D	E
	Original pictograph	Pictograph in position of later cuneiform	Early Babylonian	Assyrian	Original or derived meaning
1					BIRD
2					FISH
3					DONKEY
4					OX
5					SUN
6					GRAIN
7					ORCHARD
8					PLOUGH
9					BOOMERANG
10					FOOT

means). It was employed first primarily in inventories of food, goods, and services contributed to and disbursed by the temples and in lists of signs for training scribes. Later cuneiform was used to record myths, epics, lists of rulers, land deeds, and royal records.

In its developed form in the later Assyrian period, cuneiform had about 600 signs that mostly indicated things, with only about 100 to 150 standing for syllables in common speech. As an illustration of how it worked, primary signs for *man* and *bread* could be coupled to indicate *eat*, and the sign for *mountain*, which also meant *foreign country*, could be paired with *man* to indicate *slave*. There were also diagrammatic signs, such as a semicircle for *one* and a circle for *10* and *totality*

Human Social Organization as an Aspect of Culture

and other devices to round out communication (cf. Gelb 1963). In their number system, the Sumerians enumerated up to 10, carried the count by tens to 60, and managed bigger aggregates as multiples of 60 (Menninger 1969: 162-66). Joined with evidence from archeology, cuneiform tables in the Protoliterate and Early Dynastic record the passage to stratification and the state.

Directional movement in Sumerian society

What follows concerns the processes discerned and conjectured in the Sumerian transition, drawn principally from Robert McC. Adams's book *The Evolution of Urban Society* (1966), which he based on a series of lectures delivered in honor of Lewis Henry Morgan. Adams believes it likely that the political base from which stratification emerged was represented by conical clans. Clans probably held title to land and redistributed it when necessary to their members; their segments and perhaps the clans themselves would have been ranked, and they were associated with particular villages and village clusters. Besides holding land and managing village affairs, the clans would contribute workers and fighters for community projects such as constructing buildings and irrigation dams and fielding a defensive force. Likely, leadership was provided by headmen of the villages and by clan councils composed of ranking chiefs.

Corporate clan groups may have diverged in occupational and craft specialization. Some remained farmers, but others, depending on their resources, became herders, leather workers, weavers, stone workers, carpenters, and so on—not exclusively, but differentiated enough so that each group depended on others for some goods and services. This would have led to dislocation of some corporate groups from their land holdings, particularly when craftsmen came to be concentrated in vil-

Group of statues from the Abu Temple at Tell Asmar (site of the walled town of Eshnunna) in the Early Dynastic period in Sumer. The god Abu (whose statue is about thirty inches in height) dominates the group, and the smaller figures are priests. (Courtesy Oriental Institute, University of Chicago.)

lages and towns; early on, this probably was accomplished by exchange and sale, only later by taxation and expropriation. Also, herders occupying fringe areas sometimes lost many of their animals during droughts and were forced into the towns and cultivated zone, where they would be directly dependent upon townspeople.

Focus of redistribution in the early Sumerian towns was the temple of the town god, managed by a group of priest-administrators who collected gifts and tithes, stored them (an important service in this region of unstable ecological conditions), and passed them out to groups that had varying needs. Into their hands passed the organization and management of labor and crafts; workers concentrated near the temple had to be supported by rations of bread, beer, fish, and clothing, and their dependence upon the economic mediation of the administrators increased over time. The temple also called upon labor gangs or corvées to plow its own fields, which existed alongside those held by kinship groups, and upon herders to care for its herds and flocks.

The priests themselves comprise perhaps the first discernible stratum in Sumerian society. Just what the circumstances were that led one group instead of another to become temple guardians and one village or another to take precedence as a redistributive center isn't known. But underlying the process as a whole, as Butzer (1971: 602-3) sums it up, was intensified agriculture based on irrigation of fertile soils, on improved sowing and harvesting, and on use of the animal-drawn plow; widespread trade that further induced craft specialization; an organization to ensure the flow of needed materials (stone and metal, for instance) to concentrations of craftsmen; and the rise of centers where foodstuffs and products were stored and exchanged. It is just a step further to visualizing that some villages would outstrip others because of favored locations and better resources. And remember that rank societies were already capable of managing different and specialized segments to some degree.

Although the early Sumerian leadership might be called theocratic, there was also, it is one of Adams's themes, a strong secular side to economics and politics, for along with concentration of power in the temples, large landed estates were growing up that were outside the temple organization and provided the base for another upper stratum. Instead of periodic distribution of land at need within the clans, it became concentrated in fewer households and individual statuses. (This is a point in Adams's interpretation that complements and corrects earlier preoccupation with the temple complex.) The development should not be viewed as starting with strong and tyrannical leaders who pushed their kin off the land, or who taxed them, but as the gradual rise of manors or "superhouseholds" which enlarged their holdings by purchase and built upon the customary duties and obligations owed the chiefs by lower-ranking kin. Within the estates there were the same kind of groups found in the temple precincts—farmers, herders, craftsmen, and attendants of the lord. Some tilled their old allotted lands; others were tenants or sharecroppers, and still others performed tasks for which they drew rations from the manor's stores.

And another factor contributed to the growth of secular upper-class

Human Social Organization as an Aspect of Culture

power. As towns grew in population and wealth, they pushed against their mutual boundaries and fought organized wars. In earlier times, temporary military forces were mustered by craft and clan groups under foremen, who perhaps were headmen, and there is evidence that at one time war leaders were elected. But later they profited by seizure of land and collection of tribute from the beaten foe; probably it is this turn that pushed one secular leader to the forefront and made him lord of the realm. A ruler, however, was still regarded as representative of the god, and booty enriched the temple as well as the manor. By Early Predynastic times, war equipment included copper axes, spears, daggers, and helmets, chariots were drawn by the domesticated ass, or onager, and soldiers fought in the phalanx, a massed and disciplined formation.

All along there had been freeholders who retained their old rights and lived in small communities of kin, both alongside and within the manors, although the land they held progressively declined in extent. Commoners were, then, a heterogeneous lot, freeholders with greater or lesser obligations to lords and priests; tenants and serfs; and landless craftsmen and laborers who subsisted both on the rations and favors of the rulers and what they got in exchange in the town markets.

And below rulers, priests, and commoners another class emerged— the slaves. Although egalitarian and rank societies may take captives, they dispose of them in one of two ways: they are killed, sometimes after torture, sometimes after being held for a short time as menials to be taunted for their loss of status, *or* they are adopted into the group that captured them, eventually with full status as kin. There is no pro-

Copper model of a chariot pulled by four onagers (wild asses) from Tell Agrab, Sumerian Early Dynastic period. The driver stands on treads over the axle and keeps his balance by gripping with his knees a wooden support covered with fleece. The animals are controlled by reins running to rings fixed in their upper lips. (Courtesy Oriental Institute, University of Chicago.)

ductive place in the domestic economy of egalitarian and rank societies for a human beast of burden or for a household servant or a full-time, specialized craftsman who must be constrained by force. Stratified society does have a place for slaves; they can be collected together, either as laborers or as craftsmen, managed by overseers, and fed with rations collected from the farmers. In Early Dynastic records there are mentions of female slaves (working as weavers, millers, brewers, cooks) and male slaves (working as gardeners).

What the cuneiform records portray is supported by the evidence of archeology. Small houses of commoners are packed together in the towns, but there are others four times their areal extent, built around courtyards and placed on the main roads, the larger ones having impressive furnishings and stores of wealth. And in the cemeteries small shafts, modest wooden coffins, and meager grave goods of the commoners contrast sharply with the great tombs of the royal leaders, accompanied in death by scores of servants and retainers sacrificed on the spot and by a hoard of wealth in precious metals and stone.

Placing the peasants

The Sumerian farmers of 4,000 or more years ago who fed the craftsmen, the priests, the merchants, and the rulers of the walled towns and the manors have something in common with many cultivators today in broad areas of India, China, Southeast Asia, Europe, the Soviet Union, Africa, South America, and Mesoamerica. They can be classified as a **peasant society**. Peasantries, particularly in their social aspect, are a creation and concomitant of stratified societies backed by the state, neither primitive peoples maintaining a marginal independence nor workers and managers in "factories in the fields."

Peasant culture, then, is not a general evolutionary category on the order of hunting-gathering-agriculture-industry, or egalitarian-ranked-stratified-state, but an integral and dependent part of state society. In the first states, they were egalitarian and ranked segments progressively pulled into the larger system, economically and politically. Migration, conquest, expropriation, exploitation, craft and regional specialization, and the growth both of local and extensive marketing systems have operated to produce them since.

When mechanization is predominant over hand labor and the animal-drawn plow in agriculture, peasants become a rural proletariat, selling only their labor. For it is no more possible to maintain large-scale mechanized farming with the family-centered household than it is to produce automobiles and refrigerators without full-time specialized craftsmen and assembly lines manned by a displaceable and mobile labor force. As individuals, of course, peasants throughout their history have moved from farm and pasture to cities and towns, replenishing the more slowly growing populations in them, and peasant farms have absorbed those leaving the populous centers. But the milieu from which they moved and to which they returned has represented a fairly stable and indispensable part of the state society.

In the analysis of Eric Wolf (1966: 4-10), peasants are like primitive cultivators in that they produce a **caloric minimum** in order to survive; a **replacement fund**, such as seed for the next planting, feed for ani-

mals, and repairs for houses and equipment, and also a social surplus he calls the **ceremonial fund**, which comprises contributions to religious and secular rituals related to births, marriages, illness and curing, funerals, the equipping of new families for a start in social life, and the support of cult activities. But peasants, unlike primitive cultivators, must also produce another social surplus that Wolf terms the **fund of rent**—payments in labor, produce, or money for landlords, tax collectors, and others representing statuses and groups in the stratified society that have "domain" over them.

Not all peasantries are alike. One difference arises from the technological adaptation—swiddening, irrigation, field agriculture, specialized gardening, cultivation of trees and vines, or concentration upon marketed crops like coffee, sugarcane, and cacao in the tropics. Another difference is the degree to which they are integrated into the larger market system—whether, for instance, they produce most of their own needs, buying a limited number of things in the market, or produce largely for the market and to what extent they sell their labor. A third difference rests upon the system of inheritance—whether land is transmitted undivided to a particular heir or divided up among survivors (Wolf 1966: *passim*).

Most important, however, is the manner in which power over peasants is exercised, through ownership and control of the land and its yield. Wolf (1966: 50-53) distinguishes three types of "domain," so defined: patrimonial, which is exercised by hereditary lords; prebendal,

House and maize gardens in Xochitepec, Mexico, the source of a peasant cultivator's four funds—caloric minimum, replacement, ceremonial, and rent. (Courtesy Nancy and Robert V. Morey.)

Saint's Day procession in Xochitepec, Mexico. Not only fiestas like this but also rituals of birth, marriage, illness and curing, and funerals are provided for out of the peasant's ceremonial fund. (Courtesy Nancy and Robert V. Morey.)

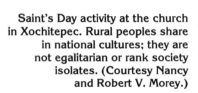

Saint's Day activity at the church in Xochitepec. Rural peoples share in national cultures; they are not egalitarian or rank society isolates. (Courtesy Nancy and Robert V. Morey.)

in which state officials are given estates to support them or a portion of tax revenues; and finally mercantile, in which the landowner is free to buy and sell it and extract his tribute as rent. The three practices may be mixed in any given system. As with all typologies, there may be modifications and revisions. Harris (1971: 255-58), for instance, speaks of feudal, prebendal, communist, and capitalist peasantries.

European folklorists have long been interested in detailing peasant customs, but peasantries became a focus of anthropological study as ethnographers in the 1930s began turning from their diminishing band and tribal societies, their "primitive isolates," to communities in India, Japan, Europe, Asia, and Africa that were by no means primitive or isolated. A theoretical pioneer in the movement, Robert Redfield (1953), called them **folk cultures** and societies, not clearly separable from the primitive and representing an ideal tradition-bound type to be posed against urban civilization—with particular communities undergoing change toward the dominant kind. Critics have held that Redfield's idealizations were distorted at both ends of the folk-urban spectrum of societies (Fried 1968: 497). In any event, neither the folklorists' interests nor the simple folk-urban continuum are characteristic of contemporary analyses, which are intended to grasp regional, national, and larger wholes and which try to understand the cultural processes in which peasantries are involved. The important point here is that peasantries are neither egalitarian nor rank societies but parts of the state-supported, stratified systems that brought them into being.

Human Social Organization as an Aspect of Culture

Caste and class

The rise of diverse occupational groups and of market exchange, viewed from the standpoint of economics, and the passage from egalitarian leader-follower relations through ranking to state-supported stratification, viewed from the standpoint of politics, underlie the evolution of **caste** and **class**. Caste and class are two lines along which economic and political integration of the segments of the new society proceeded. Caste linked occupations with descent groups, making them hereditary, a trend which had begun in rank systems. Now the kin-bounded occupational segments were stratified—differentially rewarded for their labor and talents in regard to wealth and power. Class did the same thing without primary reference to culturally defined descent groups.

In a lucid discussion of the basis of caste formation in preindustrial cultures, Harold A. Gould (1971: 7-8) points out that most people in them "continued to live in agricultural villages where they specialized in food production and in certain other occupations (carpentry, blacksmithing, pottery) that supported the activities of the farmers. Life in all three types of community among which populations were distributed—cities, towns, and villages— remained essentially on a modest level of complexity where in a majority of cases social identities could be determined by knowledge of one's forebears. The production of goods and services did not occur in factories but in families or other group settings that were modeled on kinship principles. . . .Men inherited their occupations from their fathers because occupations were regarded as another piece of property equivalent to all other objects, statuses, and obligations that were transmitted from one generation to the next." Drawn into the market context, then, occupations were property.

But sets of occupations that provided goods and services were ranked and stratified. At a minimum there were three groups: the power elites, who had political power because they controlled both basic resources and the producers; the technological implementers, or specialized craftsmen, who were rewarded for their skills; and the menials, who had neither resources nor skills. The groups were evaluated on the basis of what they contributed to the maintenance of the state itself, and rewards were calculated on a market basis, one against the other. Economics and politics, as always in the real world, joined.

Market was not the only factor. Warfare and conquest hastened stratification in some regions, and the social and religious ideology of rank and power at once confirmed the new dispensation and modified the way occupations were assorted into strata. Both took place in India, which we usually associate with a caste system.

An illustration of the linkage in caste of occupation and kinship—and the accompanying feature of the rule of endogamy, or marrying in—is provided by the south Indian village of Gopalpur, which had a population of something over five hundred when it was studied in 1959-60 by the anthropologist Alan R. Beals (1964). Its people lived in 113 households and were members of fifteen separate and endogamous jatis, or subcastes. "Ordinarily, people in Gopalpur conceive of a jati as a category of men thought to be related, to occupy a particular position within a hierarchy of jatis, to marry among themselves, and to follow particular practices and occupations" (Beals 1964: 25).

About three-fourths of the residents (eighty-three households) were members of three jatis—Salt Makers, Farmers, and Shepherds—which appeared roughly in the middle stratum. Above them were the Brahmins, a single household whose head was the Gauda, or village leader; the Lingayat Priests and the Lingayat Farmers (Lingayats are a sect worshipping the god Shiva); and the Carpenters and the Blacksmiths. Below them were the Barbers, the Muslim Priests, the Butchers and the Weavers (Gopalpur, of course is predominantly Hindu, but Muslims as well as Christians have been fitted into the caste structure), the Stoneworkers and the Basketweavers, and at the bottom a lone Leatherworker, an old woman who cleaned the Gauda's latrine. Traditional services not provided by the village jatis to each other were added by visiting jati members from other villages and districts, the Goldsmith, for instance, or the Deerhunters, or a Washerman qualified to clean clothing ritually, or a Singer to chant at rites.

Now, if we inspect the stratified groups, we can see that an expected

Positions of Gopalpur jatis in terms of ceremonial rank and economic status. Dietary practices detailed in the column at left establish a scale of purity and pollution. Access to land and occupational incomes determine economic status. Note that the middle class includes members of all jatis except the Brahmin at the top and Basketweaver and Leatherworker at the bottom. (From *Gopalpur: A south Indian village* by Alan R. Beals. Copyright © 1962 by Holt, Rinehart and Winston, Inc. Reprinted by permission of Holt, Rinehart and Winston.)

Ceremonial rank	Economic status		
	Landlord	*Middle class*	*Landless*
Vegetarian	Brahmin	Lingayat Priest	Lingayat Farmer
		Carpenter	
		Blacksmith	
Mutton, no beer		Salt Maker - - - - - - - - -	Salt Maker
Mutton and beer		Farmer - - - - - - - - - - -	Farmer
		Shepherd - - - - - - -	Shepherd
		Barber	
Beef, no pork		Muslim Priest	
		Muslim Butcher	
		Muslim Weaver	
Pork, no beef		Stoneworker - - - - -	Stoneworker
			Basketweaver
Beef and pork			Leatherworker

264   Human Social Organization as an Aspect of Culture

picture of elites, artisans, and menials emerges, but hardly in a clear-cut way. At and next to the top are the elite Brahmin Gauda and the Linga-yat Priest, and at the very bottom is the latrine cleaner (why she is a Leatherworker will be apparent in a moment). Artisans and food pro-ducers are ranged in between them in a middle class of "small farmers who can own and farm from about five to twenty acres of land, and specialists or professionals who happen to have a large or profitable clientele" (Beals 1964: 38-39). The middle class in Gopalpur has been entered by some members of every jati with exception of Basket-weavers and Leatherworkers.

But why, among the artisans, do Carpenter and Blacksmith take precedence over Weaver and Stoneworker? The answer is that position is based not only on market evaluations and social contributions, but also on ideas of dietary propriety and purity vs. pollution. "The notion of jati purity derives from the extent to which the traditional diet and occupation of a jati conforms to the ranking of things and actions along a scale of purity-pollution. Death is polluting and body wastes are polluting, but all products of the cow are pure. Occupations that in-volve killing things, or touching such polluted things as hair or dirty clothing, are ranked below occupations that involve the touching of pure things" (Beals 1964: 35).

Brahmins, the Lingayat jatis, the Carpenters, and the Blacksmiths are superior because they are vegetarians who live without taking animal life. Salt Makers, Farmers, and Shepherds are "pure meat eaters" who consume sheep, goats, chickens, and fish but who abstain from pork and beef. Below them are jatis which variously eat beef but *not* pork or beef *and* pork and finally the Leatherworker jati, which tra-ditionally removes dead animals from the village street, eats the meat, and works the leather. Within the categories there are gradations, too: Farmers rank above Shepherds because they do not "handle and cut the dead, and therefore unclean, wool of sheep," and Salt Makers rank above both "on the grounds that they drink only distilled liquor, not palm beer" (Beals 1964: 35). A concomitant of the purity-and-pollution beliefs is that members of one jati cannot accept certain foods from those below them. It should be understood that jatis do not occupy pre-cisely the same relative positions with respect to others in the whole of India and that there are exceptions to the rule of endogamy but that the same principles of ranking apply.

Conquest had an effect on Indian caste, although anthropologists in recent years have been more concerned with studying the working of the jati system than its early history. For instance, the Aryans or Indo-European speakers who invaded north India in the second millennium B.C. were described in the Hindu Vedic writings as stratifying into "the Kshatriyas or nobles, the Brahmins or priests, the Vaisyas or Aryan common people (peasants or artisans), and last the enslaved Shudras or non-Aryan blacks" (Noss 1949: 113). These are the *varnas*, or colors, that the West associates with the caste system, although **race** is today not an important factor. The jatis have had a more complicated eco-nomic and political base than that provided by conquest alone.

The ideology of caste should not be allowed to obscure that base even when it enters into the important relationship of patron and client, which should be noted briefly. The relationship between *jajmans* (patrons) and *purjans* or *kamins* (workers and suppliers of services) is a kinlike behavior that cuts across caste lines. It is obligatory for *jajmans* to supply grain to *purjans'* households and to assume a generally protecting role toward them and for *purjans* to yield freely their services and loyalty. In the performance of these services, *purjans* take on polluting tasks which their patrons could not do, and thus it is an accommodation both to economic necessity and ritual requirements.

But behind the purity-pollution beliefs and the rituals to which they are linked is the hard economic and political anatomy of the system of stratification. In village India, as Gould (1958: 429, 431) puts it, the basic distinction "is between the land-owning, cultivating castes, on the one hand, who dominate the social order, and the landless craft and menial castes, on the other, who are subordinate within it." Food and services are exchanged between "land-owning, wealth- and power-controlling high castes providing a structurally fixed share of their agricultural produce, along with numerous 'considerations,' in exchange for craft and menial services rendered by the mainly landless, impoverished, politically weak lower castes."

In a comparison of Indian caste and the stratified system of White-Black relations in the United States, Edward B. Harper (1968: 73-75) concludes that although the two have several things in common—including ideologies that rationalize economic and political inequalities, and at least partial endogamy—they differ in two important if obvious ways. They are, first, "race" in the United States and membership by birth in limited and bounded descent groups in India as the bases for assignment, and, second, the presence of only two groups in the United States as against a multiplicity of castes in India. "The multicaste system allows castes (*jati*) to be small and localized and thus to have a greater degree of uniformity of customs within a caste than would be likely in a dual-caste system" (Harper 1968: 73). And jati membership, being based on traceable descent in smaller groups, remains fixed and unambiguous.

In our own society, small local groups may grow up that are caste-like (we might think of northeastern Anglo-American families who assumed business and political leadership and who intermarried and southwestern Chicano and American Indian migrant workers, as well as Black communities), but economic and power positions shift over time, and individuals may with varying difficulty detach themselves from their localities and enter other ranked occupations. In spite of the hollow sound it may have to depressed ethnic groups (euphemistically called "the underprivileged"), the higher potential for individual mobility is characteristic of class as opposed to caste stratification. Industrial systems produce classes and overturn castes.

Suggested Readings

Adams, Robert McC. 1966. *The evolution of urban society: Early Mesopotamia and prehistoric Mexico.* Chicago: Aldine.*

Banton, Michael, ed. 1965. *Political systems and the distribution of power.* Association of Social Anthropologists Monograph 2. London, England: Tavistock.*

Human Social Organization as an Aspect of Culture

Barth, Fredrik. 1961. *Nomads of south Persia: The Basseri tribe of the Khamseh Confederacy.* Boston: Little, Brown and Company.*

Beals, Alan R. 1964. *Gopalpur: A south Indian village.* New York: Holt, Rinehart and Winston.*

Bohannan, Paul, ed. 1967. *Law and warfare: Studies in the anthropology of conflict.* Garden City, N.Y.: Natural History Press.*

Daniel, Glyn. 1968. *The first civilizations: The archaeology of their origins.* New York: Thomas Y. Crowell, Apollo Editions.*

Evans-Pritchard, E. E. 1940. *The Nuer: A description of the modes of livelihood and political institutions of a Nilotic people.* Oxford, England: Clarendon Press.*

Fried, Morton H. 1967. *The evolution of political society: An essay in political anthropology.* New York: Random House.*

Gould, Harold A. 1971. *Class and caste: A comparative view.* Modular Publications 11. Reading, Mass.: Addison-Wesley.*

Hoebel, E. Adamson. 1968. *The law of primitive man: A study in comparative legal dynamics.* New York: Atheneum.*

Kramer, Samuel Noah. 1959. *History begins at Sumer.* Garden City, N.Y.: Doubleday and Company, Anchor Books.*

Llewellyn, Karl N., and E. Adamson Hoebel. 1941. *The Cheyenne way: Conflict and case law in primitive jurisprudence.* Norman: University of Oklahoma Press.

Ray, Verne F., ed. 1958. *Systems of political control and bureaucracy in human societies.* Proceedings of the 1958 annual spring meeting of the American Ethnological Society. Seattle: American Ethnological Society.*

Sahlins, Marshall D. 1963. "Poor man, rich man, big-man, chief: Political types in Melanesia and Polynesia." *Comparative Studies in Society and History* 5: 288-303. Indianapolis: Ind.: Bobbs-Merrill reprints in the Social Sciences A-339.*

Shanin, Teodor, ed. 1971. *Peasants and peasant societies.* Baltimore: Penguin Books.*

Wolf, Eric R. 1966. *Peasants.* Englewood Cliffs, N.J.: Prentice-Hall.*

Wolf, Margary. 1968. *The house of Lim: A study of a Chinese farm family.* New York: Appleton-Century-Crofts.*

Yang, C. K. 1965. *Chinese Communist society: The family and the village.* Cambridge, Mass.: M.I.T. Press.*

Part Four
The
Ideological
Aspect of
Culture

Now that we have a grasp of technology and social organization in evolutionary perspective, we turn to our third and last major aspect of culture, ideology. Ideology was defined in Chapter Three as the totality of concepts and their relations in cultural systems, which might seem to be a cold and forbidding way to approach that most intimate of human activities, human thinking. At this point, it would be useful for you to review the earlier sections entitled "Thinking about technology" and "Categories of cultural behaviors" (which concerned the social aspect of culture). They explained the extraction of subject matters from the world we live in and the rationale for a "culture does" rather than a "people do" explanatory position in regard to human behavior. Yes, indeed, *humans* think. What we are trying to do is to set up a cultural model to orient the varieties of their thinking.

Thinking about ideology

Our orientation here will be consistent with the one we took in relation to technology and social organization. With reference to our paradigm—culture, *sapiens,* and habitat—we said that the raw materials and energies entering into any cultural tool or technique, or any group, status, or rule behavior, have their sources in culture's two environments. The

Chapter Eleven Cultural Orientation of Ideas, Beliefs, and Rituals

271

materials and behaviors (which are energy bundles) take on a cultural aspect in addition to whatever physical or biological properties they have as they cross, metaphorically, the symboling line into culture. Their shapes and behavioral variations from their entry time forward cannot be accounted for wholly in the language of the physical or biological sciences but require in addition the language of cultural analysis in order to be understood. That is the position we took in our study of technology and social organization and the position we take in regard to ideas, beliefs, and rituals.

Anthropologists ordinarily don't tangle with the *raw materials* of such notions as ancestral and **guardian spirits** and various kinds of forces in the fashion outlined here. Spirits and forces are usually taken as ethnographically recorded entities or behaviors and are correlated with the presence of particular social situations and forms. But the formation of concepts, if it is taken up, is usually cast in psychological terms as mental "projections" or affective "expressions," and that need not be the end of the matter. We can maintain a cultural orientation toward the invention of ideas and beliefs—an orientation involving the cultural system and its *sapiens* and habitat environments.

Well, then, concepts have noncultural and precultural source material in the same sense as axes or baskets or gestures with social meanings. What is the source material? It is human perceptions. Human perceptions are describable in physical and physiological terms, but when they are sorted out and bundled together and labelled with a word or other symbol they take their place in cultural systems. The symbol, the thing that stands for the perceptions, is essential in the making of this kind of cultural entity, but so are the perceptions themselves. They are as much a part of the concept as the symbol is. So we take as our definition of *concept* what we proposed early on: a bundle of perceptions with an attached symbol. We could also put it the other way around: a concept is a symbol with an attached bundle of perceptions.

For example, humans perceive and respond to light waves of different lengths. When one perceived segment of the spectrum is labelled "red" and another "blue," two concepts come into being. As we shall note later, all normal human beings presumably perceive the whole physical color spectrum, but their perceptions can be cut up and labelled in several ways—and, of course, they are in different cultures. Not all concepts are as simple as color perceptions and their categorical tags. *Witch* is not. *Life* is not. Neither is *culture*.

We need not assume that *all* human perceptions enter into cultural transformations, any more than all of the vocal sounds humans make become symbols of something and a part of language. We did not assume that all of a human being's actions and interactions with the habitat and with other humans required cultural analysis: only those that were symboling-dependent required such treatment. But when an array of perceptions *is* put together and linked with a symbol, it assumes a cultural aspect: it becomes understandable in the context of other cultural, symboling-dependent things. The word *witches* takes meaning in relation to other concepts in the ideological aspect of a culture and to cultural things in general. The concept *culture* does, too.

We cannot use the word *image* interchangeably with *perception,* because *image* calls up the idea of something simply mirrored or reflected. That would put us on a false path. A rock, a tree, an animal, or another human being do not automatically replicate or faithfully mirror themselves in the perceiver. Perceptions involve an active selection by the perceiver, depending in part upon his or her previous experience and learning. As a psychologist (Pronko 1969: 351) puts it, "... perception is not something naturally inherent in the stimulus object or guaranteed by it. Perception results from the organism-object interaction." Also, the word *image* is strongly linked in common understanding with the sense of sight, whereas perception involves not only seeing, but hearing, touching, smelling, and tasting. Concepts may incorporate perceptions gained through all five senses.

Once again: The making and using of concepts in the ideological aspect of culture can be likened to the behavior of technology, which captures materials and energies primarily from habitat and incorporates them into the cultural system. It also can be likened to the social aspect of culture, in which motions of humans in relation to one another and to things (as in the ownership relation) are shaped and incorporated in the regular, ongoing process of cultural sociality. Recall that, in connection with social organization, we said statuses could be viewed as named behavior bundles that are found, regularly and repetitively, in culture. Concepts are bundles, too—named bundles of perceptions.

As was the case with Ish's geologist's hammer and a great number of other things encountered in our study so far, we need not take concepts as immovably fixed in the ideological context. We noted, for instance, that conceptualized knowledge of the lay of the land and of the habits of game animals among the Netsilik Eskimo contributed so directly to the food quest that they might, if we wished, be looked at in their technological aspect. Social rules, which involve ideas and beliefs, and which Service (1971b: 17-18) viewed as "ideological determinants of social behavior," we designated as one of the three kinds of parts of social organization, the others being groups and statuses. So we can place concepts in technological and social organization contexts as well as in ideology in our efforts to understand them.

Nonetheless, it is useful for concepts as such to be provided with a context of their own, analytically separate from technology and social organization, in which they may find some meaning. One gain is that we are induced to look for the precultural sources of their raw materials, as we have just done. Another is that it helps us move toward a general evolutionary perspective. We need such perspective if we are going to try to discern and make judgments about directional movement in this kind of cultural behavior. Whether or not there has been a shift in preponderance of one general kind of concept to another kind in the movement from low-energy to high-energy systems is a legitimate question; to help answer it, we can put concepts into an aspect of their own. The last chapter takes up the problem of evolution.

Concepts and relations: Ideas and beliefs

So far, we have concentrated on concepts, the noncultural stuff from which they are made, and reasons for putting them into a separate context from time to time. But the word *relations* also appears in our definition of ideology. Simply put, we equate *concepts* with *ideas*, and *relations* with *beliefs*. Two or more concepts (or ideas) which are linked or associated form a belief; the linking is the relation. For example, *spirits* is one concept or idea, and the action word *live* is another. *Spirits live* is a belief.

Beliefs might also be called *propositions*, because they usually take the form of a sentence or can be put into sentences. Leslie White chooses to call propositions or beliefs (rather than concepts or ideas) the "components, the units of ideologies." He writes: "Experience is expressed in the form of propositions, declarative statements that say something about something: grass is green, fire is hot, I am hungry. These propositions are the components, the units, of ideologies. For want of a better term we may call them *beliefs*" (1959: 261).

You may get a bit restive at my own separation of ideas and beliefs as mere vocabulary play, but I think you can see that it is useful to have one word for smaller, rock-bottom entities (ideas) and another for complexes of them (beliefs) which are put together in varied ways. It provides a better way to catalog and describe concepts, which represent to us the first-order category of things relating to the ideological aspect of culture. You have a right to call for applications and illustrations in ethnographic contexts at this point, but I ask for patience until our own concepts are sketched out as economically as possible. We shall put these and other labels to work presently.

Along with ideas and beliefs, rituals also find meaning in ideological contexts. We shall postpone consideration of rituals until we have explored some categories of verbal concepts (concepts whose symbolic parts are words).

Naturalistic and supernaturalistic ideas and beliefs

An important thing about perceiving is that we humans respond not only to stimuli originating in the world outside of ourselves (the sun's rays, the wind, animals and plants, the movements of other humans) but to stimuli within ourselves. We perceive our beating heart and coursing blood, our breathing, and other actions of our bodies. We feel pleasure and pain, anger and fear, anxiety and confidence; we are drowsy or alert. We experience dreams, hallucinations, and trances, which are events internal to ourselves. Like perceptions of the external world, perceptions of events inside ourselves may become linked with symbols and so become conceptualized. They are bundled up, named, and joined arbitrarily with other perceptions and concepts, with other things and the behaviors of things that we perceive.

That the symboling process peculiar to culture casts its net over perceptions of internal stimuli as well as external ones has consequences in the formation of the concepts that go into ideologies. A symbol may point clearly and unambiguously to a stimulus, whether it is inside or outside the human animal, specifying just where the stimulus is and what its characteristics are. Or it may cloud the locus of a stimulus, interpreting it as outside of a particular human being when it is inside, or

The Ideological Aspect of Culture

vice versa, or it may jumble many perceptions together in a wondrous confusion.

As an example, take the word *quartz*, which in the English language refers to a common mineral, silicon dioxide. It is defined this way by a mineralogist (Loomis 1923: 100): "Occurs as hexagonal crystals, or in grains or masses; hardness 7; specific gravity 2.65; colorless when pure, luster vitreous; transparent on thin edges." The definition answers questions about the mineral, about its form, about what it can scratch (any substances softer than 7 on a given scale) and be scratched by (any substances harder than 7), about its weight in relation to other minerals, about its color, and so on. We call these characteristics properties of the thing itself, whose presence or absence can be verified by repeated observation and manipulation. We can assume with good reason that the thing "out there" has those properties.

But the mineral is found in other contexts of description than a mineralogist's handbook and in other contexts of use than ones that might be suggested by its physical properties. It may be an abrading or scratching tool or a hand-thrown missile, for instance. Our mineralogist himself touches on another use, outside of the context of mineralogy. In the European Middle Ages, pieces of clear quartz were shaped into crystal balls. "The gazing into the crystal ball was supposed to give some people supernatural vision. It seems to be a form of hypnotism, gazing at the bright reflecting surface tiring the eyes, and making possible visions, which are subjective rather than anything external" (Loomis 1923: 101-2). Whether or not hypnosis was the mechanism that produced the vision, Loomis has called attention to a kind of concept quite different from the scientist's concept of quartz. This kind of concept ascribes to things external to the observer properties which are derived from the experience or perception of internal processes and events.

In times past, the Cherokee of the Appalachian highlands also employed quartz crystals to foretell the future and to answer troubling questions. "There were five different sizes of divining stones used in ancient times. The largest was used in war divination; the next largest for feasts, purification, and divination concerning sickness; the next for hunting; the next for finding things lost or stolen; and the smallest for determining the time allotted for anyone to live. These curious stones were crystalline quartz and six-sided, coming to a point at one end like a diamond. They were called 'lights,' and were important in ritual" (Gilbert 1943: 345).

Now, a good deal more than immediate perception of the physical properties of quartz goes into a concept of that kind. We may hazard a guess that feelings of expectation and hope, fear and anxiety, the desire for psychological certainty, as well as memory of chance associations between the presence of crystals and happenings in the past, might be among the internally sensed events that make up the raw materials of a concept of crystal-that-foretells-the-future.

Following Leslie White (1959: 261), we shall call the kind of concept represented by the mineralogist's quartz a **naturalistic concept** and the kind exemplified by that of the people of the Middle Ages and the Cherokee a **supernaturalistic concept**. Any ideology is a mixed bag of naturalistic and supernaturalistic concepts and beliefs.

Cultural Orientation of Ideas, Beliefs, and Rituals

In his presentation of the terms, White (1959: 262) contrasts the meteorologist's explanation of a rain shower with the one that posits the existence of beings who make it rain: "The rain gods, witches, and devils of ideologies are merely the psyches of man projected into the external world without his knowledge or understanding of this fact, so that he believes they have an existence in the external world independently of himself. Supernaturalistic philosophies are the result of a failure to distinguish between the self and the not-self; naturalistic philosophies make this distinction."

White there draws upon a psychological process, projection, to make his point. He does not go on to orient concept making squarely with reference to an extracted cultural system which otherwise is implicit in his work. Logically, if we focus upon such a system, it is not *man* who projects rain gods, **witches**, and devils into the external world; it is *culture* that ensnares perceptions, bundles and names them, and so makes concepts of them. It gives perceptions a cultural existence in addition to a physiological and psychological one. Or, better, it produces variations in the behavior that call for cultural analysis.

Neither a psychological nor a cultural stance yields statements about perceptions and concepts more or less true than the other's. Each orientation is useful and appropriate in its own discipline. In suggesting this shift from the notion of projected psyches to culturally ensnared perceptions, I am only proposing a mechanism for concept formation that is consistent with the cultural model we have been working with.

Once we understand that a concept can have inside it perceptions of internal events as well as external ones, we will not be perplexed about the strange creatures that inhabit the jungles of some of the world's ideologies. Human imagination becomes a little more understandable. We can, if we wish, explore the content of a concept and sort out the stimuli that produce the perceptions that go into it.

But there is no need for us to analyze all concepts, one by one, to discover the whole range of their content and the origin of that content. We can take them at face value, in the way people talk about things. That is the way, for instance, that the anthropologist John Middleton (1967: 59) treats the witches of the East African Lugbara: "Witches do not exist in actuality, but are only figures of belief. Here I discuss them as the Lugbara do." If an Eskimo shaman says he is talking to his *tunraq*, so be it. If a Plains Indian asserts that a medicine bundle has mystical powers, we'll accept that, too. They are *cultural* facts. However, that they are cultural facts does not mean to us that witches, *tunraqs*, and mystical powers are less real than tools and human relationships and that they "do not exist in actuality." It means that, like tools and relationships, they are understandable in a cultural context and are products of cultural processes.

Naturalistic and *supernaturalistic* may not be the best terms that could be devised for kinds of ideas and beliefs when they are defined along the lines outlined above. We shall continue to use them because they are well established in anthropology, although their definitions and contexts of use are often different.

The anthropologist Edward Norbeck (1961: 11) presents a more common definition of *supernaturalism*: "By 'supernaturalism' we mean

The Ideological Aspect of Culture

to include all that is not natural, that which is regarded as extraordinary, not of the ordinary world, mysterious, and unexplained or unexplainable in ordinary terms." He adds that the supernatural may evoke or be associated with "awe, veneration, wonder, or fear" and a sense of "*apartness* from the mundane."

Being hard-nosed about concepts

How could one tell whether the perceptions a symbol wraps up into a concept are stimulated by objects and events outside of the perceiving human or by events in whole or part internal to the perceiver? Well, suppose an ethnographer is told that someone's death has been caused by a witch and that a community fears more deaths from witches. Traditionally defined, witches are persons who are inherently evil and who possess a power to harm others without physical contact or overt intervention. Sorcerers are evil, too, but they work their mischief through medicines and other physical substances and objects.

The ethnographer knows without doubt that *beliefs* in witchcraft and sorcery can dispose people to sicken and die. The victim who believes he has been bewitched or ensorceled is stricken with fear and slides physiologically into a state of shock; he or she has a lowered blood pressure, and the heart deteriorates due to a reduction of blood volume in the circulatory system as the blood plasma flows into body tissues (Cannon 1965). The physiological mechanism, then, is not at issue. Our question concerns the content of the concept *witch*, the source of perceptions which cluster under that particular symbol.

The ethnographer could explore the content of witch belief by finding out how the people describe witches—what their shapes and other

Rhythmic sound and motion and the internal experience called trance are some of the materials for ritual and belief in this curing dance of the !Kung Bushmen. The men are dancing and the women are seated in a circle clapping and singing. Note that one woman (second in the line) is dancing with the men; women dance only occasionally. (© 1976 by Laurence Marshall.)

!Kung Bushman curers ("medicine men") in trance. Two are in deep trance and are being held and cared for by others who are themselves in trance but not in the deepest state. The curer in right foreground holding the man directly in front of him is not in trance or is at most in a shallow state. (© 1976 by Laurence Marshall.)

characteristics are, under what circumstances they are said to appear, how they act on humans, and the reasons for their actions. The witch beliefs could be put into a social context, in which there would be noted the kinship and other relationships of accused witches and their victims, their respective statuses in economic and political affairs, and so on.

For example, take the witch concept of the Nyakyusa, who are herders and farmers in Tanganyika. The Nyakyusa, as described by the British social anthropologist Monica Hunter Wilson (1951: 308), "believe that witches exist as pythons in the bellies of certain individuals. They are something tangible, discoverable at an autopsy, and inherited." Lusting for milk and human flesh, witches suck the udders of cows and gnaw the insides of people and cause their death.

"All this happens in dreams," Wilson (1951: 308) writes. "Nightmares of being throttled, of being chased, of fighting, and of flying through the air are taken as evidence of an attack by witches; and, if a man wakes up suddenly at night in fear and sweating, he knows that 'they'—the witches—have come to throttle him. The witches are thought to fly by night on their pythons or 'on the wind'; they attack singly or in covins; and they feast on human flesh."

People accused of being witches, Wilson found, were people who were more successful than others and were not modest about it and who were stingy—all in all, bad neighbors. Charges were rarely laid against consanguineal kin but against non-kin villagers and co-workers and their own wives (who were not members of their husband's kin group).

We may conclude at this point that the word *witch* among the Nyakyusa has several referents. The referents include the accused persons,

The Ideological Aspect of Culture

the fantastic dreams, and feelings of envy, jealousy, fear, and hatred which arise from social strains in the village. The symbol *witch* embraces perceptions of all these things, and perhaps more, all jumbled together. Concepts of witches, then, are ideological things, on a par with concepts of milking stools and polygyny, and witches are as real as milking stools and polygyny. These traits are transmissible, stand in discernible relations with other traits, and have their uses in culture. In the case of witches, one use is as an explanatory device for bad dreams, sickness, and death.

Can we go further to establish the source materials of witch concepts and their loci, inside and outside perceivers? In addition to the verbal evidence of the victim's dreaming, we might add that gained from the techniques of sleep researchers, who have linked visible rapid eye movements (REM) with the phenomenon. Periods of REM are periods of dreaming. Vivid dreams also are accompanied by rapid breathing and a speeded-up pulse.

We might also strengthen our conclusion about the inside locus of some aspects of witches by falsifying or disproving an external locus. If Nyakyusa witches exist as humans transformed into pythons or as python riders who fly through the air and throttle their victims, they might be expected to make some noise, breathing heavily, for example, or growling, that could be picked up by acoustic devices. They should be substantial enough to be detectable by a light-sensitive photographic paper in a camera, to break a circuit between photoelectric cells, or to trip a wire to which tin cans are tied. Their body temperature should be capable of being recorded by a thermometer. If our instruments did not pick up physical signs of such an entity in an appropriate setting, we would have grounds to doubt that it exists *as described by witchbelievers*. It might be added that autopsies which are said to reveal witch stuff should be performed or attended by a cool and skeptical anatomist or coroner.

Although the procedures sketched might look like a parody of scientific investigation, it is necessary to grasp the point that however far removed we are from the developed physical and biological sciences, we can't leave the physical and biological levels of reality behind us. Symbols are physical things; if they were not, they would not be perceptible to us. Their referents, the things they stand for or point to, are physical things; if they were not, they would not be perceptible to us. Everything has a physical aspect; some things, like plants and animals, are additionally biological; and others, like harpoons and witches, are additionally cultural. Acceptance of this materiality points to ways in which we can establish the relationships between symbols and what they stand for. In the normal work of anthropology, researchers are not called upon to defend assignment of a concept and the purported relations between two or more concepts to a supernaturalistic or a naturalistic category. But hard-nosed confirmatory and falsifying procedures are available to back up a judgment.

There is less difficulty in picking out a naturalistic concept than a supernaturalistic one. The example of quartz indicates that. Any normally intelligent person can observe that an object called "quartz" is crystalline or grainy, what its weight is relative to other minerals, what it scratches and what it is scratched by, that it is glossy and that he or she can see through its thin edges. That person can be reasonably sure that the perceptions of weight, hardness, luster, and permeability to light are stimulated by the thing itself. Thus, the symbol attached to the cluster of perceptions—and hence to the object itself—is part of a naturalistic concept.

One organization of concepts: World view

Any culture, simple or complex, has many concepts. Aside from a naturalistic-supernaturalistic dichotomy, how can a culture's concepts be organized so that we can begin to understand them and their relations with other parts of culture? Possibilities lie in two directions: we can group them in established categories of anthropology or we can group them in what are purported to be the categories of the thinking, speaking natives themselves. We shall touch on native categories in Chapter Thirteen. Here we shall describe briefly an anthropological category, **world view**.

The notion of world view is so broad that almost any concept can be related to it, but in practice the number of its facets is limited by anthropologists who have defined and used it. Robert Redfield defined world view as "the way a people characteristically look outward upon the universe. If 'culture' suggests the way a people look to an anthropologist, 'world view' suggests how everything looks to a people.... But if there is an emphasized meaning in the phrase 'world view,' I think it is in the suggestion it carries of the structure of things as man is aware of them. It is in the way we see ourselves in relation to all else" (1953: 85-86).

Although world view may suggest "how everything looks to a people," it is the anthropologist who assembles the ideas and beliefs into a whole, and it is also the anthropologist who elicits and rounds out references to "the structure of things." Rarely, in a preliterate culture, can an individual present all of the elements in an ideology (nor, for that matter, can one in a literate culture).

But what are the parts of the structure that an anthropologist probes for? "It includes among other things recognition of the self and others; groupings of people, some intimate and near, others far and different; some usual ways of confronting the inevitable experiences of the human career; a confrontation of the Not-Man seen in some ordered relationships of component entities, this Not-Man including both observed features such as earth, sky, day, night, and also invisible beings, wills, and powers" (Redfield 1953: 94).

In reference to those elements, the Semai world view includes their self-image as a nonviolent people, their notion of *punan*, which forbids aggressive or selfish acts that make others unhappy, their division of a limited social universe into kin of the *jeg* and all others, who are *mai*. It is indicated by the "precautions," as Dentan (1968) phrases it, that they take during pregnancy and childbirth, and in sickness and death, precautions that take into account personal souls and spirits and harmful *nyani*. It embraces their classification of the natural world and the prescriptions and taboos related to them. And in it is one of the most

The Ideological Aspect of Culture

important attitudes of all, *patud*, "a feeling that there is a 'natural order,' that is, a way things should be and usually are" (Dentan 1968: 13).

The Mbuti see themselves as a people of the forest, separate and different from their neighbors, the Bantu villagers, who are wary of the forest and fear it. "The Forest is Mother and Father, because it gives us all the things we need . . . food, clothing, shelter, warmth . . . and affection. We are the children of the forest. When it dies, we die" (Turnbull 1965: 312). The major rites of the Mbuti, the *elima*, staged on a girl's arrival at puberty, and the *molimo*, held in times of bad hunting and upon a death, emphasize this relationship in their symbolism. Their resistance to restraint and their recognition of the wisdom of peace in the camps are other strands of their world view. The Pygmies do not see a world full of malevolent spirits as do some of their neighbors and do not practice sorcery and witchcraft.

In traditional Cheyenne culture, as interpreted by E. Adamson Hoebel (1960), the world of nature is viewed as a system of interrelated parts whose energies are used up or run down. To that degree, the outlook is mechanistic (although the Cheyenne would not use that word to describe the world they experience, and we can't credit them with a scientific vocabulary).

In Cheyenne view, parts of the world are governed by spiritual beings, such as spirits of the four directions, spirits above and below, and so on, who have the knowledge to make things run right. This knowledge the spirits imparted to the **culture heroes** of the past and to living persons, in the form of rules for right behavior and in the form of rituals. The rituals, if performed properly, would act upon the natural world to renew its resources and restore its vigor. Humans themselves do not control nature; it is ritual knowledge, transmitted by the supernaturals and taught by initiates to novices, that repairs breakdown in an essentially helping and friendly nature.

Cheyenne beliefs about the wider world are congruent with those of the social sphere. For instance, killing of a Cheyenne by a Cheyenne is looked upon as a very serious disturbance indeed, which has to be redressed not only by temporary banishment of the murderer but by renewal of the Sacred Arrows that symbolize tribal unity.

These references to Semai, Mbuti, and Cheyenne of the past embody only a small part of the ideas and beliefs in their ideologies, of course. But they illustrate the components that go into the making of the anthropological constructs called world views, which are attempts, as Redfield said, to suggest "how everything looks to a people." To portray that outlook, anthropologists may employ a people's own metaphors, as Turnbull did in reporting that the Mbuti say, "The Forest is Mother and Father." Or they may turn to metaphors of our own culture, as Hoebel did in presenting Cheyenne ideas and beliefs as both a mechanistic and spiritual system.

There is another facet of Redfield's quoted remarks that should not pass unnoticed: " . . . if there is an emphasized meaning in the phrase 'world view,' I think it is in the suggestion of the structure of things as man is aware of them" (1953). There is a reminder there that by and large the world of nature is orderly and that ideas and beliefs represent

The Sun Dance is a world renewal ceremony in traditional Cheyenne culture. In addition, the supernaturals respond to individual petitions of participants. Here the Sun Dance lodge is being constructed. The pledger, in white paint, is seated at the right. (Photograph by the author.)

The dance to greet the rising sun is part of the Cheyenne Dance (also called the Willow Dance). Dancers fast and abstain from water for four days and nights. Around their necks the dancers wear feathered whistles which are blown to mimic eagles' cries. (Photograph by the author.)

that order as people perceive it. That is true whether the concepts are classifiable as naturalistic or supernaturalistic.

In conclusion, world view contains the ideas and beliefs embodied in a culture's rules for behaving, its classifications of nature and human beings and the way they are used, and the elements of its legends and tales.

Another organization of concepts: Myth

When we turn from world view to **myth**, we reduce the scope and number of ideas and beliefs extracted from an ideology. Myths account for the natural and social landscape. They are stories of the creation of the world and the humans, animals, and plants on it, the origin of the stars, and the beginnings of peoples and their customs. A connotation of the word *myth* in ordinary language as an imaginary or fanciful story, unproven or unprovable, is not followed in anthropology. A myth's truth or falsity in that sense is irrelevant. Conceptualizations in

The Ideological Aspect of Culture

myth fall on the supernaturalistic side of the ideology spectrum more often than not, but that is not a judgment of inherent truth or falsity.

In the opinion of the anthropologists William A. Lessa and Evon Z. Vogt (1972: 249), "The term 'myth' at best serves as a unifying concept which enables anthropologists to talk about etiological narratives and other forms which, for the society involved, make up a body of 'assumed knowledge' about the universe, the natural and supernatural world, and man's place in the totality." "Etiological narratives" refers to stories of origin and cause.

Preliterate peoples often lack distinctive and unitary **creation myths** but share a cluster of tales with their neighbors. In one Cheyenne story, a human floating in a universal sea called upon water birds to dive beneath the surface to find some earth, a task at which a small blue duck finally succeeded. From a bit of earth brought up on the duck's bill, the man created the lands of the earth. A creator (who is not credited with creation of the sea nor of the earth) then made the first man and woman from his own ribs, one from the left side and one from the right. The bison, however, was first brought to the people by a female culture hero, Yellow-haired Woman. Following a period of disappearance of the bison, it was returned to the Cheyenne, along with domesticated corn, by the culture heroes Sweet Medicine and Erect Horns (Grinnell 1923, II: 337-39).

Although the Nuer ascribe the origins of all things, earth and heaven, plants and animals, themselves and their customs, to a creative spirit or first cause (which Evans-Pritchard translates as God), they lack specific stories about the process. The closest approach to a creation myth among the people relates that " . . . the tamarind tree, called Lic, was itself the mother of men who, according to one account, emerged from a hole at its foot or, according to another account, dropped off its branches like ripe fruits" (Evans-Pritchard 1956: 6).

Ritual as patterned behavior and symbol

Like the verbal symbols that are part of concepts, rituals also stand for or represent something, and therefore they are closely related to a culture's ideology. Conceivably, a ritual could stand alone as symbol, but it usually requires associated word-concepts to put it into context that gives it meaning.

Like many other words in the English language, *ritual* may be found in use as a substantive, or noun, and as an adjective, a descriptive term or modifier (e.g., the ritual began, and ritual [that is, ritualized] singing continued through the night). The first use indicates a segment or string of behavior, the second some qualities or characteristics of the behaving: it is repetitive, stereotyped, formal, standardized, patterned. *Ceremony* and *ceremonious* are near synonyms, except that a ceremony is commonly thought of as an extended event consisting of many rituals.

As an example of the repetitive and patterned nature of ritual, take a very small segment of the Cheyenne Buffalo Men ceremony, which occupied an evening and the day following and which in earlier times was directed to magically calling the bison and in later times to healing. It required a pledger, or principal performer, an instructor, their wives,

The sightless eyes of a buffalo skull on its low mound watch over the frame of a Plains Indian sweat lodge. (Photograph by the author.)

and several assistants. The following small segment deals only with the transfer of objects from the ground outside into the lodge that had been constructed for the ceremony.

"The instructor, placing a bit of root in his mouth, blew first on the right palm of the instructor's wife, twice to the right, twice to the left, and once to the center, and repeated on her left hand. She grasped [a medicine] bundle in two hands, and after making four ritual feints raised it and carried it into the lodge. The pledger similarly picked up and proceeded with [a] pipe after his hands had been medicined.

"Pipe and bundle were laid, with ritual feints, immediately southeast of a shallow circular pit about twenty-four inches in diameter, the earth from which had been removed in a bison skin and taken to the mound on which [a bison skull] was to rest. . ." (Anderson 1956: 96).

If we were to regard repetitiveness, patterning, and so on, as the only marks of ritual, we would find it not only in ceremonies like the Buffalo Men ceremony but in such mundane activities as hunting and gardening and behaving toward kin and friends, because doing things over and over again in the same way is efficient and economical of energy. In ideological context, however, rituals should be taken to mean not only observable behaviors that have those characteristics but those which, in addition, have symbolic meaning, that is, stand for something else. In that sense, they are like verbal concepts.

Let's carry this distinction forward a bit. Technologically, the meaning in a Kofyar's wielding of an axe lies in its delivering energy along a cutting edge, a habitat-facing action that, as we said before, is one of a complex of subsistence-shelter-defense motions of a culture. An axe is a symboling-dependent thing which required symboling-dependent culture to bring it into being, but in a technological context it does not of itself stand as a symbol. An axe *may* itself become a symbol, as was

The Ideological Aspect of Culture

the fate of Old Ish's geologist's hammer, but technologically it is a hewing and chopping tool, and that's the end of the matter. Efficiency is increased if it is wielded in a repetitive, patterned way, but the patterning has no meaning outside of the tool context.

Similarly, the nurturing and enculturating behavior of a Mbuti mother or the following of followers after leaders among the Nootka we assign to the primarily *sapiens*-facing social aspect. The relationships of mother-child and follower-leader are the behavioral content of what is summed up in status terms. Mothers nurture and leaders lead. True, a drive toward efficiency may result in repetitive and patterned ways of nurturing and leading in specific situations. And, like an axe, nurturing and following motions *may* become arbitrary symbols of something else, but in their narrowly social context that is not their first task. It is permissible to speak of social rituals, but when we use that term we have already lifted it into an ideological context, that part of the ideology in this case which makes symbolic statements about social behaviors and groups.

Like the referents of a vocal symbol, a ritual's referents are bundles of human perceptions of objects, events, or processes that we assume can all be located either inside humans or in the world outside of humanity. Since the most characteristic and frequent kind of symboling is vocal language, it is probable that most instances of ritual are enacted in relation to vocal symbols that already have done some summing up of experience. Thus, what the ritual stands for, what it symbols, can usually be elicited or explained in the language of the culture in which the ritual is found. Indeed, speech behavior itself takes on a ritual aspect when segments of it become repetitive and stereotyped, as in magical spells and prayers to the gods or the chanting of a myth.

A Cheyenne priest qualified to conduct a Buffalo Men ceremony was this honored man, Old Bull. He also was a sacred leader at many Sun Dances. (Photograph by the author.)

Cultural Orientation of Ideas, Beliefs, and Rituals

Given this linkage of vocal concepts and nonvocal symbols, we can make do with the same classification device for both, the naturalistic-supernaturalistic dichotomy. If a ritual as symbol clearly and forthrightly points to objects or events that motivate perceptions, whether they are internal or external to humans involved in the perceiving, the task they are doing might be called naturalistic. If there is ambiguity or confusion, we would have to label it supernaturalistic. Individuals may clasp hands as a symbol of friendly feeling and intentions, or one may clasp the hand of another to direct into himself or herself a mystical force the other is believed to have a lot of. Which would be interpreted as naturalistic and which supernaturalistic? And on what grounds?

Among the Cheyenne, a common ritualized behavior was the offering of a tobacco-filled pipe to someone being asked an important favor. Whether the favor asked was the loan of a horse for a raid or the use of a ritual object in a ceremony, the offering was symbolic only of the fact that the matter was an important and solemn one to the petitioner. The context was naturalistic. When, however, a pipe was offered to one of the conceptualized beings in the Cheyenne pantheon, we would have to place it within the supernatural context to understand it, no matter how much the act resembled the earthy and earthly behavior between the Cheyenne petitioner and the fellow Cheyenne who was being asked a favor. A feather in a war bonnet that indicated only a coup by its wearer we would interpret differently from a feather placed in a medicine bundle at the direction of a spirit seen in a vision.

You may become restive at this iteration of the matter of contexts, but maybe there is no better place to drive home the point than in ritual and ceremony. No extended, organized set of ritual behaviors needs to be regarded wholly as naturalistic or supernaturalistic, even though, as a whole, it is directed toward one end of the spectrum or the other. Some effective ideological statement of human-to-human, human-to-culture or human-to-habitat relations is likely to be present, no matter how many rain gods, witches, or devils are otherwise involved. And, on the other hand, a secular ceremony, one involving an athletic event or a Woodstock-like celebration, say, is likely to have in it concepts and rituals which on inspection are found to be squarely supernaturalistic, as we have defined the term.

Rituals related to technology and social organization

Rituals, as organized behaviors, arise out of the ordinary business of living. Take Trobriand yam and taro gardening, for instance (Malinowski 1935, I). It calls for rational choice of fields to be planted in a given year, for cutting and burning the underbrush, working the soil, planting the cuttings, training and protecting the growing plants, weeding, and harvesting. Phases in the cycle are initiated and directed by the *towosi*, or garden magician, who is an expert farmer and works as hard as anyone on the practical side. In addition, he knows the rites and spells required, in Trobriand view, to ensure success. For example, at the beginning of the farming year, the *towosi* cuts down a sapling in a garden, recites a spell over it, and tosses it out of the area to be cultivated. A

The Ideological Aspect of Culture

Harvesting yams is a technological ritual among the Binumarien of New Guinea. One day a year is chosen by the old men of the village, and all yams are harvested at once. (Courtesy Kristen Hawkes.)

second sapling that he cuts is inserted, again with an incantation, into the ground. Individuals then follow suit in their own plots.

It is apparent that the first act, without its trimmings, is no more than what is appropriate to starting gardening. A plot, after all, must be cleared of undergrowth. But cutting of the first sapling takes on an additional meaning. Tossed into the uncut jungle, it represents the removal of evil influences from the garden. The second act, pushing a cut sapling back into the ground, might appear to be irrational, but its meaning is clear from the spell which is uttered. It describes how the garden will grow exhuberantly, clearly an act of **imitative magic** in which the planted sapling represents the total crop.

We might adduce other examples of ritual connected with technological pursuits—of subsistence, shelter, and defense—but Trobriand gardening illustrates sufficiently the point that ritual behaviors tend to rise out of ordinary activity, activity which assumes additional meanings in the context of the culture's stock of concepts. That is also true for rituals related to social behaviors. Giving and receiving, leading and following, as indicated before, are the real content of social relations, but they can also stand for the relationships themselves or for analogous relations posited between men and supernatural powers and beings.

Ritualization may appear at any place in a cultural system, but we would like to know where and when it is most likely to occur. For a suggestion about the social aspect, we can do no better than reach back to the work of the Flemish anthropologist Arnold Van Gennep, whose pioneering book on the **rites of passage** (1960) was first published in 1909.

The lives of individuals in society, as Van Gennep observed, are punctuated by passages from one status to another, from newborn to social infant to child, to initiated and married adult, to the world of the mourned and remembered dead. The passages resemble the move-

On the day the yams are harvested, they are displayed in front of a yam house before they are stored away. Binumarien yam houses, located in the gardens, resemble the dwellings the people used to build. (Courtesy Kristen Hawkes.)

ment across one's own society's territory to another or into a sacred place such as a temple or grove. Indeed, spatial passage provided the metaphorical framework for his discussion of status passages. As Van Gennep phrased it (1960: 26), "A society is similar to a house divided into rooms and corridors. The more the society resembles ours in its form of civilization, the thinner are its internal partitions and the wider and more open are its doors of communication. In a semi-civilized society, on the other hand, sections are carefully isolated, and passage from one to another must be made through formalities and ceremonies which show extensive parallels to the rites of territorial passage...." Rituals mark the severance of an individual from an old status, entry into and temporary containment in a marginal state between the old and new, and finally full assumption of the new. The three phases he called rites of separation, transition, and reintegration or incorporation.

Van Gennep's book influenced ethnographers to collect and organize observations of customs clustering around pregnancy and childbirth, initiation, betrothal and marriage, and dying and disposal of the dead, but theoretical extension of his discovery was relatively neglected. One who has further explored the matter is Max Gluckman (1962), a leader of the so-called Manchester school of social anthropology.

Durkheim and others, as well as Van Gennep, Gluckman points out, remarked that tribal (what we have called egalitarian and rank) societies display more ritualization in social relationships than do advanced (stratified, state, urban) societies. Such ritualizing, Gluckman suggests, arises from the fact that people living in simple societies play out their various roles—father, mother, household head, village leader, craftsman, and so on—within small groups, cheek by jowl, as it were. There is little physical or spatial separation of stages on which the roles are played, and one person is continually stepping from one social position with its appropriate tasks (what we have labelled in its totality as status) to another and back again, all within a relatively confined space. In contrast, in urban societies, "the various roles of most individuals are segregated from one another since they are played on different stages"

The Ideological Aspect of Culture

Social ritual: Part of a marriage ceremony of the Binumarien. The bride is being decked with numerous grass skirts by her own female kin. She will be ladened with dowry objects and will walk in a procession to the place of the groom's kin. (Courtesy Kristen Hawkes.)

Interring a corpse, East Semai. The body, wrapped in sarongs, has been taken to the grave on a carrying pole. (Courtesy Robert K. Dentan.)

(Gluckman 1962: 35). Home, job, market, politics, religious observance we can visualize as spatially and socially separate one from another. So Gluckman proposes (1962: 34) that "(a) the greater the secular differentiation of role, the less the ritual; and the greater the secular differentiation, the less mystical is the ceremonial of etiquette; (b) the greater the multiplicity of undifferentiated and overlapping roles, the more the ritual to separate them."

That is not to say that every time a person assumes a role or takes up a task he or she performs a ritual to announce it. It is only that culture has defined a status and produces a dramatization of it when someone enters it for the first time. Gluckman, too, finds ritual behavior arising out of ordinary life, remarking that ". . .ritualization in tribes. . .isolates roles largely by exaggerating the prescribed behavior appropriate to each role involved" (1962: 42).

There is some resemblance between rites of passage and technological rituals of the Trobriand gardening sort. As an initiation rite, say, serves to put boundaries around a status and signals an individual's entry into it in the course of the life cycle, planting and harvest rites

Cultural Orientation of Ideas, Beliefs, and Rituals

mark phases of the annual round and initiate and marshal efforts to carry out the basic work of the cultural system. (Ritualization is not confined to agricultural systems; the Eskimo, for instance, ritualize a young man's assumption of hunter status and separate ritually the segments of the annual round dependent on sea-mammal and land-animal hunting.) The important thing is that both kinds of ritual occur at points of change in the direction of cultural activity related either to social status or to technological pursuits.

Can we relate this to the cultural processes discussed previously? Both integration and adaptation are involved. If ritual makes parts of systems such as statuses and groups stand clear and sorts out and labels their tasks, that means some specialization, and hence efficiency in their performance. Efficiency promotes the conservation of energy, which is derived from environmental sources. Further, if ritual signals the beginning of a new activity or course of action and the end of an old one, a kind of coordination is achieved—that internal adjustment and accommodation of parts and processes we called integration.

Extending the adaptational point of view

The adaptive process, you will recall, is the movements and reactions by which a culture maintains a balance or equilibrium state and redresses an imbalance. It involves two-way exchanges and adjustments between a culture and its environments, habitat and *sapiens*, as well as the superorganic environment represented by competing cultural systems. We might find it hard to believe that rituals with a supernaturalistic orientation would have any real effect in the extraction of energies and materials or defense of the culture. It appears, however, that rituals may be strong auxiliaries in adaptation.

The Naskapi hunters of northeastern Canada, like some other peoples in North America, Siberia, and early China, practiced **scapulimancy**, or divination with the use of animal shoulder blades. Divination, which we encountered in Cherokee scrying, or crystal gazing, is a general term for attempts to predict future events or to answer questions by supernatural means. In the Labrador Peninsula, where the Naskapi lived, shoulder blades were used to indicate the direction hunters should take to locate game. The bone (from a caribou if caribou was the quarry) was cleaned, dried, attached to a split-stick handle, and oriented to serve as a sort of map of the hunting territory. When it was held over the hot coals of a fire, cracks and burned spots appeared on the flat bone, and these were interpreted as signs of places where game would be found.

We would have to grant that as far as we know there is no discernible relationship in reality between cracks and spots on singed shoulder blades and the location and movement of caribou and other animals. Experience, rather than this kind of magic, ought to provide a surer guide to the hunter: where he has found game before, he should find it again. But that is where rational decisions might put things awry. A device that would randomize men's behavior, take it out of its rut, so to speak, might send the hunter to where the game was.

Omar Khayyam Moore, who called attention to the Naskapi case and

Looking west from the Tsembagas' dance ground. Before the *kaiko* and the planting of stakes at the territorial boundary, people of the Tsembaga hamlets settle around a traditional dance ground. Some producing gardens can be seen in the middle distance. (Courtesy Roy A. Rappaport.)

In the rituals at the uprooting of the *rumbim*, a Tsembaga dances on hot stones. In his left hand he holds a pandanus fruit, which he will pierce symbolically with a cassowary bone. (Courtesy Roy A. Rappaport.)

An old Tsembaga addresses his ancestors before the arrival of visitors for a *kaiko* entertainment. After the ancestors and allies have been provided with sacrificed pig, warfare can be resumed. (Courtesy Roy A. Rappaport.)

whose interpretation we are following here, suggests that it is precisely that randomizing effect on behavior in choosing directions to go out after game that made scapulimancy useful and thus persistent in the culture. He writes (1957: 73): "Certainly the apparent irrelevance of such techniques is no guarantee of their inutility. On the contrary, if shoulder-blade augury. . .has any worth as a viable part of the life-supporting hunt, then it is because it is in essence a very crude way of randomizing human behavior under conditions where avoiding fixed patterns of activity may be an advantage. . . ." The explanation, he reminds us, has not been put to observational test, and so the question must remain open.

In a more complex case, the cyclical rituals of the Tsembaga, those New Guinean gardeners and pig raisers whose technology was described in Chapter Six, have been interpreted by their ethnographer Roy A. Rappaport (1967a, 1967b) as regulating relationships of the people to the habitat and to groups with which they are in contact. As noted before, domesticated pigs are killed and eaten only at times of illness, injury, fighting, and death, all occasions when high-grade protein is required to offset physiological stress (something, of course, of which the Tsembaga are unaware). Since their numbers are not kept in check by regular use for food, the pigs, which are fed on sweet potatoes, tend to increase until they become a burden to the gardeners and a source of dissension in the community. And because sweet potatoes are the important human staple, humans and pigs in effect are competing for food.

The Tsembaga and their neighbors fight, and we have no reason to think that the basic cause of fighting is other than the culture's drive for resources and security. But they have ritualized the competition and the economic behaviors entering into it. As Rappaport (1967b: 28-29) sums it up, ". . .the operation of ritual among the Tsembaga and other Maring helps to maintain an undegraded environment, limits fighting to frequencies which do not endanger the existence of the regional population, adjusts man-land ratios, facilitates trade, distributes local surpluses of pigs throughout the regional population in the form of pork, and assures people of high quality protein when they are most in need of it." When he speaks of maintaining "an undegraded environment," Rappaport is referring to the reduction in the number of pigs before they play too much havoc in gardens, although up to a point they are useful in keeping the soil stirred up and preventing unwanted saplings from growing.

When fighting breaks out, it continues for several weeks and ends either in one group destroying the gardens and houses of the other and driving it from its territory, or, more frequently, in stalemate and truce. The land cannot be occupied immediately by a winner, however, because it is thought that the ancestral ghosts which inhabit it are a danger to outsiders. The group which keeps its territory then performs the important ritual of planting the *rumbim*, in which all the males place their hands on a cordyline plant as it is placed in the ground and a vow is made to their own ancestors to raise and offer to them many pigs. Most of the community's pigs are then slaughtered and eaten by the people and their allies.

The Ideological Aspect of Culture

Like the Tsembaga, the Binumarien of New Guinea prize the flesh of pigs, but unlike the Tsembaga they do not have an elaborate ten-year cycle of sacrifice and feasting. Here stones of an earth oven are being heated to cook the trussed animal. (Courtesy Kristen Hawkes.)

After about a decade (during which fighting is taboo and the truce can be broken only after the *rumbim* has been ritually uprooted), the pig population increases to the nuisance point, a circumstance which paves the way for a year-long **kaiko**, or pig festival. Just before that, stakes are placed at the territorial boundary. If the adjacent enemy has abandoned its land, the stakes are extended to encompass it, for it is thought that by that time the enemy ancestor ghosts have left the land, too. The migrants have gone to another available territory or have moved in with kin or allies. (When the defeated group plant the *rumbim* in their new home, it is an indication that they have given up the old. If a defeated group plant *rumbim* in the old territory, it means they still lay claim to it.)

Then, during the *kaiko*, the host group entertains allies at feasts and dances, repaying obligations and obligating other people, cementing social ties, and providing a place for trading. At its conclusion, there is a sacrifice of most of the host group's remaining pigs and distribution of the meat to the guests. Then the people are free to resume warfare, because, in Tsembaga ideology, the ancestors and allies have been provided with sacrificed pigs, and they can be called upon for assistance in hostilities.

It is evident that the ritual cycle does space out warfare and ensures periods of peace, at the same time allowing a redistribution of people and land over an extended period. Interestingly, it is the burdensome pig surplus (induced by taboos on ordinary consumption) and the necessity to dispose of it in the interest of land conservation and social harmony that triggers the cycle.

So, in two quite different situations, Naskapi use of shoulder-blade divination to regulate their search for game and Tsembaga planting and uprooting of the *rumbim* and sacrifice of pigs to regulate warfare and redistribution of people and wealth, ritual appears to have adaptive

Cultural Orientation of Ideas, Beliefs, and Rituals

consequences in the technological and social aspects of the cultural systems. The rituals can be placed within the ideological aspect because they are patently symbolic, but they are not "merely" symbolic in their effects.

The categories *religion* and *magic*

Here we shall look at some traditional meanings of the terms *religion* and *magic* and give them a place in the study of cultures. Both involve concepts and rituals.

In *Primitive Culture*, Tylor devoted more than a third of his chapters to **animism**, "the belief in Spiritual Beings," which, he said, would serve as a "minimum definition of Religion" (1958, II: 8). The belief, in his view, was a device contrived by humans to explain troubling experiences. "It seems as though thinking men, as yet at a low level of culture, were deeply impressed by two groups of biological problems. In the first place, what is it that makes a difference between a living body and a dead one; what causes waking, sleep, trance, disease, death? In the second place, what are those human shapes which appear in dreams and visions?" Since both were phenomena closely connected with the body as well as separable from it, they were combined in a conception of apparitional-soul or ghost-soul, to be found in the forms of soul or spirit among all peoples (Tylor 1958, II: 12-14).

Tylor posited that the concept was extended progressively to animals (which, like humans, live) and nonliving things (which, after all, appear in the dreams of humans), to the dead who continued to maintain relations with the living, and to nature in general as animated by spirits, giving rise to belief in many gods, or **polytheism**. **Monotheism**, belief in one spirit or god, was the end of the evolutionary process. Thus, spiritual *beings*, separate, discrete, and personalized, characterized Tylor's view of religion.

Tylor's singling out of an intellectually derived belief in spiritual beings as one strand in religion is often joined with Sir James Frazer's view that **religion** is "a propitiation or conciliation of powers superior to man which are believed to direct and control the course of nature and of human life" (Frazer 1929, I: 50).

Tylor's younger contemporary, R. R. Marett, stressed the affective or emotional side of behavior rather than the intellectual (as Tylor did) and asserted that the earliest form of religion must have been derived from feelings about power present in persons and things. He called his conception of a nonpersonalized force, a thing in itself, **animatism**. (One of Marett's major ethnographic sources for his concept was the *mana* of the Melanesians, which he wrongly interpreted as an independent, free-floating force that might enter into persons or things.)

Most influential of early views on **magic** was Frazer's. Magic, in Frazer's scheme, is not particularly concerned with personalized spirits, as is religion, but with mechanical and coercive use of things believed to have inherent supernatural powers. Ascription of a thing's power to act upon other things, Frazer held, rested on two wrong-headed principles of thought: "first, that like produces like, or that an effect resembles its cause; and, second, that things which have once been in contact continue to act on each other at a distance after the physical contact has been severed" (1929, I: 11). The principles underlie imitative or homeopathic magic on the one hand and **contagious** magic on the other. The first may be illustrated in a person's making an image of an enemy and piercing or destroying it to cause the enemy's illness or death; the second, by a person's working upon a bit of the victim's hair, fingernails, or clothing, with the expectation the effect would be felt by the victim.

Conceptual separation of religion from magic also was a concern of the functionalists. For instance, Emile Durkheim's often-quoted definition of religion is this: "... a unified system of beliefs and practices relative to sacred things, that is to say, things set apart and forbidden—beliefs and practices which unite into one single moral community called a Church, all those who adhere to them" (1947: 47). On the other hand, magical beliefs do not unify people into a cohesive group or moral community, in Durkheim's view. "*There is no Church of magic*" (1947: 44). To Malinowski, both religion and magic "arise and function in situations of emotional stress," but religion, which is characterized by belief in ghosts, spirits, and the like, is "a body of self-contained acts being themselves the fulfillment of their purpose." Magic, on the other hand, tries to *get* something; it is "a practical art consisting of acts which are only means to a definite end expected to follow later on" (1948: 67-68).

Perhaps there was a compulsion in these scholars to distinguish religion from magic in the primitive world; they took words ready-made in their own culture and tried to find applications for them in the ethnographic and historical record. Anthropologists generally avoid the issue today by speaking of the magico-religious. This may or may not be an improvement, but it recognizes that subservient-propitiatory behavior toward supernatural beings, on the one hand, and manipulative acts, on the other, are both present in many rituals. Participants in the Buffalo Men ceremony, for example, offered prayers to the spirits, but they also believed that correct and undeviating performance of ritual acts would have a direct effect upon nature.

Because of the prominence of religious doctrines and movements in the history of our own culture, we might expect the category *religion* to be useful in the study of ideologies and social organizations of egalitarian and rank peoples. But elements which might go into it are just as well left to world view (Semai natural order, Cheyenne spirits of the four directions), adaptations in hunting (Naskapi divination) or gardening (Tsembaga *kaiko*), medicine (Eskimo shamans, Kalinga mediums), and so on. And some would find a home in myth.

The problem of describing "a religion" in simpler cultures is like the problem of finding politics there. We tried to solve the latter by fixing on the characteristic of leading and following and pursuing examples of it. Is there a kind of behavior on the order of political leading and following which can be labelled "religious"?

Anthony F. C. Wallace (1966: 107) defines religion as "*a set of rituals, rationalized by myth, which mobilizes supernatural powers for the purpose of achieving or preventing transformations of state in man and nature.*" (Transformations of state in *sapiens* would be illustrated by a man's becoming a shaman, a healer's making a sick person well, or a girl's becoming an adult; in nature, by a good harvest or by prevention of a calamity.) Another, and broader, definition is Norbeck's (1961: 11): " . . . we shall define religion as ideas, attitudes, creeds, and acts of supernaturalism." (You will recall that Norbeck defined supernaturalism as things and events regarded as out of the ordinary and mysterious and associated with feelings of fear, wonder, and awe.)

Both definitions unequivocally place supernaturalism as a differentiator between religion and nonreligion, although Wallace begins with rituals and ends with their human goals. My own preference is to emphasize rituals, as Wallace does, but admit naturalistic concepts as well as supernaturalistic ones into a definition, like this: A religion is an organized set of rituals and related concepts, at least some of which are definable as supernaturalistic. There is a good deal in the ideological and social complex of religion as commonly understood that is not supernaturalistic, as the term has been defined in this chapter, and supernaturalism is present in a far broader field and operates in many more contexts than religion. Religion and magic I would leave with their commonsense or folk meanings and would not use as analytical or technical terms.

Suggested Readings

Agar, Michael. 1974. *Ethnography and cognition.* Minneapolis: Burgess.

Banton, Michael, ed. 1966. *Anthropological approaches to the study of religion.* Association of Social Anthropologists Monograph 3. London, England: Tavistock.*

Evans-Pritchard, E. E. 1956. *Nuer religion.* London, England: Clarendon Press.*

Forde, Daryll, ed. 1963. *African worlds: Studies in the cosmological ideas and social values of African peoples.* London, England: Oxford University Press.*

Lessa, William A., and Evon Z. Vogt. 1972. *Reader in comparative religion: An anthropological approach.* 3rd ed. New York: Harper and Row.*

Malinowski, Bronislaw. 1948. *Magic, science and religion and other essays.* Glencoe, Ill.: Free Press.*

Middleton, John, ed. 1967a. *Gods and rituals: Readings in religious beliefs and practices.* Garden City, N.Y.: Natural History Press.*

———, ed. 1967b. *Magic, witchcraft, and curing.* Garden City, N.Y.: Natural History Press.*

———, ed. 1967c. *Myth and cosmos: Readings in mythology and symbolism.* Garden City, N.Y.: Natural History Press.*

Norbeck, Edward. 1974. *Religion in human life: Anthropological views.* New York: Holt, Rinehart and Winston.*

Rappaport, Roy A. 1967. *Pigs for the ancestors: Ritual in the ecology of a New Guinea people.* New Haven, Conn: Yale University Press.

Redfield, Robert. 1953. *The primitive world and its transformations.* Ithaca, N.Y.: Cornell University Press, Great Seal Books.*

Tyler, Stephen A., ed. 1969. *Cognitive anthropology.* New York: Holt, Rinehart and Winston.

Tylor, Edward Burnett. 1958. *Primitive culture.* Published as part I, *The origins of culture,* and part II, *Religion in primitive culture.* New York: Harper and Brothers, Torchbooks.*

Wallace, Anthony F. C. 1966. *Religion: An anthropological view.* New York: Random House.

One of the characteristics of ideology is that it can be heard. Concepts are words and sentences, or they can be translated into words and sentences if they take the form of symbolic objects or gestures such as a flag or a handshake. For that reason, we need to pay some attention to human language and how it structures sounds. Language might have been introduced earlier in our study, because the sounds humans make enter into social and technological contexts as well as ideology, but it has been sufficient for our purposes so far to refer only to the symboling process in general, which, along with energy transformation, is the mark of culture. In this chapter, we consider sounds as symbols in the specific context of language.

Nonhuman primate communication

To use the device of contrast, which helped us understand technology and social organization, we first look back at language's analog in the communication systems of lower primates. We then take up the characteristics of human language, some variations in the ways it accomplishes its work in different cultures, how it changes, and in what sense it evolves.

Nonhuman primates are in general noisy animals, but the sounds they make carry far less in the way

Chapter Twelve
Language as Cultural Mechanism and Content

297

of specific information than do human vocal messages. The sounds themselves do not directly stand for things and happenings in the environment. Rather, the sounds indicate an animal's emotional state, which itself has come about in response to events in the environment. The animal's repertoire of sounds is limited, loosely structured, and has to be supplemented by nonvocal signals.

As the primatologist Jane B. Lancaster (1968: 439-40) comments, "Man is so accustomed to sounds having definite, restricted meanings that the first question asked on hearing a monkey sound is, 'What does it mean?' In our experience it takes some time for a student to lose this human bias and to understand the sounds in the context of normal monkey behavior. Man expects sounds alone to carry meaning, but in nonhuman communication sounds usually carry only part of the meaning; facial expressions, gestures, and postures are essential in conveying the full message." Students call that kind of transmission of messages **multimodal communication,** or composite communication.

Not only does nonhuman primate communication employ several modalities—"visual, auditory, tactile, and sometimes olfactory," as Marler (1965: 583) enumerates them—but it greatly enlarges the context of message sending and receiving. Meanings of messages are not carried adequately even by the composite signals but depend on the ongoing social behavior of the group, the customary parts individual animals play in it, and other environmental factors. A juvenile, for instance, may send out a threatening display. If it is apart from the other animals, it may be ignored, or it may be threatened in return. If it is near an attentive mother, the animal to whom the threat is made may respond quite differently (Lancaster 1968: 442).

In a multimodal system of this kind, heavily dependent on social context, messages are far from specific. They do not stand apart; they blend and merge. About the only way that meanings can be sharpened is through intensity: an animal can threaten, say, in a minimum or maximum way, using the same set of signals but varying the vigor of its acts.

To illustrate multimodality, dependence on social context, and use of intensity, we may turn to Jane Goodall's Gombe Stream chimpanzees, to whom reference was made in discussions of noncultural technology and social organization. Goodall (Van Lawick-Goodall 1972: 30-33) found seven situations in which her chimps uttered distinguishable calls that were combined with bodily acts. They included feeding, relaxed recognitions between individuals, active physical contacts and interchanges without aggressive intentions, situations in which the animals were anxious or frustrated, and encounters involving aggressive behaviors on the one hand and submissive ones on the other.

Messages in the seven social situations were carried in part by some two dozen vocal signals in all—grunts, barks, pants, laughs, screams, whimpers, cries, and so on—accompanied by appropriate gestures, facial expressions, and postures, all capable of being varied in intensity. For instance, while lying passively in its nest or nonaggressively responding to another's approach, a chimpanzee might, in Dr. Goodall's words, utter a "quiet 'huu,' " or a "series of 'panting hoots and calls' " rising or falling in pitch. The chimpanzee pushed out its lips slightly in connection with the first vocalization, but in the second it formed its lips into a trumpet. During excited melees in which the chimps charged up and down and drummed upon trees, there were "panting hoots with shrieks and roars," mouths were open, and teeth were sometimes showing.

And what do nonhuman primates communicate? Their own emotional states. As Jarvis Bastian (1965: 598) puts it, "The information transmitted to the receiver refers primarily to the current emotional disposition of the signaler. The consequences of effective reception are largely modifications of the emotional dispositions of the receivers." This means that there is virtually none of the message sending so characteristic of humans—direct information about the environment which can be responded to directly by the receiver.

That is not to say that nonhuman primates can't communicate environmental information at all. It is just that it is not done by vocal signals that properly can be called language. For instance, as Kummer (1971: 42) reports about the hamadryas baboon (whose social organization was discussed previously), ". . . the discovery of a small water hole by one baboon is immediately communicated to his neighbors by the unique posture of the drinking animal: head low, rump and tail in the air."

Vocalizations might be among the signals that send an animal to a water or food source, but they are only indirect signals: the first and primary communication is the sender's motivational state—excitement, fear, contentment, or whatever. A nonhuman primate does not signal vocally, "There is a tiger in the bush" or "There are lots of nuts in this tree," but rather, "I am excited and afraid" or "I am very gratified," and it is up to the receiver to fill in from the sender's behavior (to which the vocables have only called attention) what the whole situation is. Among primates, what are sometimes referred to as food calls or warning calls are not specific about a food or threat, but only point to the level of excitement of the animal making it. Others have to look at the animal to see what is causing its excitement. They do not respond to words, names, or sentences.

Lancaster concludes (1968: 440): "The ability to use names allows man to refer to the environment and to communicate information about his environment as opposed to the ability to express only his own motivational state. Object-naming is the simplest form of environmental reference. It is an ability that is unique to man. In itself it is not language, but without it human language cannot exist."

Naming, she makes clear, refers not only to nouns but also to actions and qualities. "For example, 'table' is a name, but so too is 'running,' 'soft,' 'red,' and 'loud' " (1968: 452).

With these judgments in hand, we can deny that our closest living relatives have vocal languages, and when we refer to language henceforth we shall be referring to the vocal language of human beings.

Characteristics of language

The most important structural characteristic of language itself is its **duality of patterning.** The linguist Charles F. Hockett and his colleague Robert Ascher (1964: 139) explain it this way: "The utterances of a language consist wholly of arrangements of elementary signaling units called *phonemes* (or *phonological components,* to be exact), which in themselves have no meanings but merely serve to keep meaningful utterances apart. Thus, an utterance has both a structure in terms of these meaningless but differentiating elements, and also a structure in terms of the minimum meaningful elements." (*Utterance* refers to any uninterrupted segment of speech.)

Take the English word *cat.* It is made up of three sounds, written here with slashes separating them to indicate that they are **phonemes**: /k/, /ae/, /t/. By itself, separately and independently, any one of the sounds stands for nothing, and in that sense it is meaningless. Each is only one of the thirty-two sounds in what the noted linguist Leonard Bloomfield (1933: 90) referred to as "Standard English, as spoken in Chicago." But together the three sounds, arranged as they are, point to you know what. Rearranging the three otherwise meaningless sounds produces two other meaningful clusters: /ae/, /k/, and /t/ (*act*), and /t/, /ae/, and /k/ (*tack*). So language presents two aspects: the phonological, whose elements, the phonemes, are in themselves meaningless, and the morphological, consisting of words or **morphemes** that have referential meaning, that do stand for something. **Morphology** is the beginning of grammar, which also deals with phrase and sentence construction.

That the linguist's phonemic notation is different from the conventional written forms of the words should be noted in passing. The visual signs of a culture's writing system may stand only imperfectly for the vocal signs of the spoken language, so the linguist devises new ones to avoid ambiguity. In written English, the conventional alphabetic sign *a* stands for all three of the central sounds in *cat, late,* and *calm,* all pronounced differently, so new symbols are made to represent those three different pronunciations—correspondingly /ae/, /e/, and /a/. The /e/ stands for the vowel sound in words like *late* and *hate;* because /e/ was preempted for *that* purpose, another symbol was devised to stand for the vowel in *bet* and *get*—/e/.

To return to Hockett's statement that the phonological components "merely serve to keep meaningful utterances apart," suppose that you, a visitor speaking another language, heard one of Bloomfield's Chicagoans say at one time, "You cat, you," and at another, "You cad, you." The speaker would tell you, if you questioned him, that *cat* and *cad* do not mean the same thing, so you would conclude that differences in meaning of the two messages hinge on differences between the two sounds /t/ and /d/. Ergo, meaningless in themselves, /t/ and /d/ "keep meaningful utterances apart."

Without the phoneme, human language could not have become the highly flexible and efficient symboling mechanism or instrument that it is, possessed of the other characteristics we will come to shortly. It might have remained more like nonhuman primate communication systems, whose messages cannot be broken down into smaller components. Accenting this position, Edward Sapir wrote, ". . .the essential point is that through the unconscious selection of sounds as phonemes, definite psychological barriers are erected between various phonetic stations, so that speech ceases to be an expressive flow of sound and becomes a symbolic composition with limited materials or units" (Mandelbaum 1949: 8). The term *expressive* in that statement is applicable to the sounds by which the lower primates signal their agitation and satisfaction; the sounds arise from and are part of their bodily states. The "phonetic stations" to which Sapir refers are positions of the tongue in relation to other parts of the mouth that interrupt and shape the column of sound that arises from the voice box.

Every language has in the course of its history selected from the range of sounds humans are capable of making the definite sets of sounds that are its first-level building blocks. The number of languages known is on the order of 4,000 to 5,000; the number of phonemes from one language to another ranges from about ten to seventy. Even ten is an adequate number, because, as the linguist Joseph H. Greenberg (1968: 10) points out, " . . . only 10 phonemic units, themselves meaningless, will provide 10,000 different sequences of length 4 (i.e., 10^4)"—and that doesn't take into account other manageable unit lengths.

Once a body of utterances is collected and the phonemes of a language are teased out, it becomes apparent that there is order and predictability, not only in the fact that a given set of sounds (and no others) will be used for coding a message but also in the permissible ways in which sounds can be compounded into morphemes or words. Morphemes are word parts of two kinds; some are "free," (i.e., capable of standing alone, like *man*), while others are "bound" (i.e., not capable of standing alone, like *ly*). The morphemes in that illustration would comprise the word *manly*. Morphology, or word building, is one aspect of grammar. The other is syntax, or phrase and sentence building. Grammar (morphology and syntax) is concerned with meaning—referential meaning. We shall touch on it in the next section.

In addition to its duality of patterning (meaningless phonemes and meaningful grammar), language has four other important characteristics—arbitrariness, productivity or openness, semantic universality, and capacity for displacement. They are a closely related set.

Arbitrariness has been met with before in discussions of symboling. It means that there are no inherent physical or biological relationships between the symbol (be it a word or a grammatical sentence) and whatever it stands for. The symbol does not mirror or duplicate its referent physically; it is not, to use a precise word, iconic, like a picture or a diagram is in reference to what it portrays.

With regard to productivity or openness, Hockett and Ascher (1964: 139) explain, " . . . we freely emit utterances we have never said nor heard before, and are usually understood, neither speaker nor hearer being aware of their novelty." A language has no finite set of sentences that its users learn (nor a finite set of words, either); the linguistic forms permit an open-ended and creative addition and rearrangement of reference, action, and relationing words, old or borrowed or newly coined.

Semantic universality means that language is restricted to no domain in its reference (as nonhuman primate communication is practically restricted to communication of motivational states), that no domain is closed to it. We can talk about ourselves, about our environment, or about language itself—as we are doing now. Any message sent in one language can be translated into another; even a message sent in a non-language system is convertible into language form, as when we interpret the dance message of bees returning to the hive which informs other bees of the direction and distance of a source of honey (Greenberg 1968: 14). Needless to say, neither bees nor nonhuman primates can convert a linguistic message so precisely into another form.

Actually an aspect of universality, but deserving of a separate place for emphasis, is the characteristic called displacement. It means that "we speak freely of things that are out of sight or are in the past or future—or even nonexistent" (Hockett and Ascher 1964: 139). We are not bound to the here and now, to the world immediately within range of our senses at a particular time.

Labelling perceptions with words and sentences

In a passage that is often quoted, Franz Boas (1911: 21-22) pointed out that whereas in English there is a basic word for snow, and different kinds or conditions of snow are described by qualifying words and phrases—snow on the ground, falling snow, drifting snow, snowdrift—the Eskimo language has separate, single words for each of those states of the crystalline stuff but lacks a general word for it. (The Eskimo words, in relation to the foregoing English translations, are *aput, qana, piqsirpoq,* and *qimuqsuq*). With regard to seals, although like us Eskimo do have a general word for the animal, there is a separate word for a seal basking in the sun, one for a seal floating on a piece of ice, and others for seals of different ages and sexes.

Words that bundle up and label perceptions may have separate origins or may be modifications of one basic word or root. Boas noted that English employs different root words for a set of actions—to grip, to kick, to bind, to bite—while Dakota, spoken by native Americans on the Plains, modifies a single root to form them. In Dakota, the basic word *xtaka* means "to grip." "To kick" is *naxta'ka,* "to bind" (in bundles) is *paxta'ka,* "to bite" is *yaxta'ka,* "to be near to" is *ic'a'xtaka,* and "to pound" is *boxta'ka.*

Do Eskimo and English speakers perceive snow and seals differently, and do Dakota and English speakers experience actions differently? It is not necessary to make that assumption about preconceptualized perceptions. The same reality "out there" that impinges on human senses is managed appropriately by separate root words, by modifications of a single root, or by phrases. Linguistic forms, however, may classify perceptions differently by singling out and emphasizing some features of the experience, by combining some, and by ignoring or excluding others. Within their settings, within the experience of their speakers, all languages in their morphological and syntactical (that is, word-building and sentence) aspects have equal potential as differentiators, bundlers, and classifiers. All are capable of dealing with the specific and the general.

That does not mean that all languages have equally large lexicons (vocabularies, dictionaries). Some cultures have segregated and ex-

The Ideological Aspect of Culture

plored domains that others have not and have invented appropriate tags for additional and augmented experiences. An Eskimo living the traditional hunting life could not be expected to discuss atomic physics adequately with a traditional Eskimo vocabulary. But we assume that the structure of the Eskimo language could manage new perceptual demands over a period of time, whatever they were.

Perceptions (and by way of perceptions the things in the world around us) are classified in language not only by single words and phrases but by the larger constructions called sentences. In spite of their brevity, the sentences "John runs" and "The girl hit the ball" label as wholes larger segments of experience and perception than each of their component words does if spoken separately. The two sentences are of a kind particularly characteristic of English and some other Indo-European languages—the actor-action form, which Bloomfield (1933: 172) called a "favorite sentence form." There is nothing inevitable about the actor-action orientation. What is referred to as "John runs" might just as well be "John-running" or "running-John" to represent the slice of reality reflected by perception.

There is another feature in those two sentences that illustrates different selections from and presentations of perceptions. *Runs* and *hit* are in English tense forms, representing *present* and *past* time, respectively. Time, after all, derives from perceptions of things and events and their places relative to each other. But there are other ways of handling temporal relations than with a simple past, present, and future paradigm, and sometimes features are tacked onto them that English would exclude or report separately.

In the Hopi language, for instance, a variation of a verb form combines our past *and* present by permitting a speaker to report a real or specific situation which is happening now *or* which happened in the past (in our terms). By another form, the speaker states that he *expects* something to happen. That would seem to correspond to our future tense, but it does not do so precisely and exclusively, because it can be projected back into an account of the past—a situation we might translate into English as "was going to" or "began to." (That might shake an English speaker, because "began to" in his view refers to past time only and certainly not to the future.) A third form of Hopi verb does not refer to a single piece of action but asserts something held to be generally valid and true, such as "Rain comes from clouds."

The linguist Benjamin Lee Whorf labelled those three forms "validity forms" or "assertion categories" of three kinds—"reportive," "expective," and "nomic," respectively, having nothing to do with time as such (Carroll 1956: 113). Nonetheless, Hockett (1958: 237) is inclined to put them into a paradigm of tense, albeit a paradigm different from ours—". . .one [form] used in statements of general timeless truth ('Mountains are high'), a second used in reports of known or presumably known happenings ('I saw him yesterday,' 'I'm on my way there right now'), and a third used of events still in the realm of uncertainty, hence often where we would think of the events in the speaker's future ('He's coming tomorrow')."

Obviously, English can cope with the distinctions that the Hopi language has systematized in its verb forms (the English translations indicate that), but it does so in paraphrase, in larger constructions. On the other hand, to indicate simple past, present, and future alone, Hopi would present what to English speakers would be circumlocutions.

There is no sharp and unbridgeable gap between word and sentence. The word is the smallest construction that can stand alone and have meaning in a language, but that which can be labelled by a word in one language may require a sentence (two or more words joined by conventional devices and rules) in another. What utterances, long or short, point to may be simple objects extracted from environment (seals, snow), objects along with their behaviors and qualities (basking seals, drifting snow), or larger segments of experience and perception (stories about historical events, statements about what it is to be a man or a woman, creation myths). And that aspect of things that we may call their static, physical materiality need not be what is extracted for prime attention. It may be an action in itself, with the actor or agent subordinate or not involved at all. Thus, as lightning fills the sky, the Hopi says not "It is lightning" but "Flashes."

The open question
of creativity

The arbitrariness of symboling in language, as we have seen, does not at all imply disorder. Language is a rule-bound domain, which means that regularities within it, both phonological and grammatical, can be perceived and conceptualized.

Still another aspect of language, the **semantic aspect**, dealing with meaning as such, can be conceptualized separately. Meaning, of course, permeates the grammatical level in one sense, in that rearranging the elements of "The dog bit the man" to "The man bit the dog" produces an altered meaning according to the rule of order in English of subject, verb, and object. But the things and events and their relations, to which linguistic forms point or correspond and which give the latter referential meaning, lie outside of the language itself. Then how do particular, patterned sound sequences get attached to perceptions, and especially how do they do so in such an open and creative way?

A strictly behaviorist position relying on situational or social learning fails to account for it. The child beginning to speak at around eighteen months of age does not stumble from situation to situation, picking up words and other speech forms wholly by trial and error. And social learning implies a model, a completely crafted speech segment, to be learned from. A child's sentences for which there are no precedents cannot be said to be copies of existing models.

We bypassed this problem in our discussions of symboling by asserting that we need not be concerned with how the linkages come about but can accept them as an accomplished fact, place the associations as observed and inferred within our cultural constructs, and assess their relations with one another and their effect on human behavior. What is in the brain and how the brain works are beyond our competence; there must be a division of labor in our attempts to understand the facets of human behavior. In any event, we asserted, culture appears to be learned and passed on in a fashion not accounted for by situational and social learning, and we are content to call that residual kind of learning *sym-*

The Ideological Aspect of Culture

bolic. But if we can't offer solutions to linguistic creativity from within culturology, we can at least indicate two positions of linguists.

First, a speaker's creative use of language might be compared to the operationalist's use of analogies as explanations (Chapter Four). As Hockett sees it (1973: 108), "Openness in human language is made possible largely because human beings *analogize.*" Utterances that are heard for the first time serve as models within which variations can be inserted. If successful, they are repeated and persist; if not, they disappear. On the individual level, " . . . analogies which are ready to function, singly or by blending, in a speaker's production of new linguistic forms constitute his grammar," and, on the collective level, "the kind of book we customarily call a 'grammar' concentrates on the analogies that are the most productive and hence the most pervasive. . ." (Hockett 1973: 111).

A second point of view is that of the *transformational* or *generative* grammarians, led by Noam Chomsky (e.g., 1967). The focus of generative grammar is not on how small constituents get built up into meaningful sentences but, on the other side of the coin, how ideas, which represent the semantic level, get expressed in sound. Chomsky will have nothing to do with stimulus-response or analogies. "The idea that a person has a 'verbal repertoire'—a stock of utterances that he produces by 'habit' on an appropriate occasion—is a myth, totally at variance with the observed use of language. Nor is it possible to attach any substance to the view that the speaker has a stock of 'patterns' in which he inserts words or morphemes. Such conceptions may apply to greetings, a few cliches, and so on, but they completely misrepresent the normal use of language . . . " (1967: 400).

Generative grammarians look to cognitive anthropologists to help them find out what governs the forms of speech. However, Chomsky stresses that all languages have similar underlying principles called "invariant properties," "linguistic universals," or "universal grammar." He says these principles may be genetically determined, or innate, although he is not unalterably committed to innateness. A human being uses these principles to express thoughts and interpret the world in novel ways. What he or she knows about language comes about by interaction of innate mental structures, maturation in early childhood, and the environment (particularly the language environment provided by parents and others). This knowledge is called **language competence**—"the knowledge he must have in order to produce grammatically correct sentences or in order to interpret others' speech" (Gumperz 1973: 752)—a knowledge that enables a person to say grammatically what no one else has said or heard before and to understand what has not been heard before.

The means by which vocal symbols get attached to their referents is still an open problem. In the history of linguistics, meaning was not always considered an important concern. As Dell Hymes (1971: viii) sums it up, study first was centered narrowly on **phonology**, then successively on morphology, on syntax, and finally on semantics. Concern with meaning was inevitably broadened from a focus on language itself (*la langue*, as the nineteenth-century French linguist DeSaussure called it) to language in use, to speech, or *la parole.* That led to investigations in a field called sociolinguistics, concerned with the relations of speech acts to other behaviors in the social aspect of culture.

Linguistic change and relations of languages

Each of the twenty or so cultures we have discussed at one time or another to illustrate technological and social adaptations has a separate language. The language usually bears the same label as the culture, as Cheyenne, Nootka, Hopi, Nuer, Karimojong, and Kofyar, to cite some North American and African instances. Like cultures and culture areas, languages do not always have clear spatial boundaries. Neither do they have clear temporal ones, for the language as spoken at one point in time is not identical with its state a decade, century, or millennium before or after.

Languages change in their phonological, grammatical, and semantic aspects at a pace imperceptible to their speakers, and segments of language communities tend to drift apart if cultural or geographical barriers inhibit the free flow of speech among their members. Whether two communities are said to speak the same language depends squarely on their mutual intelligibility. If there are many resemblances between the two and an insufficient number of differences to markedly slow or prevent communication, the gap is dialectical. Linguistic forms in different languages that demonstrate descent from common, earlier forms are called *cognates,* a key notion in historical studies.

Cheyenne and Arapaho, for instance, neighbors and allies on the Plains in the nineteenth century, spoke languages descended from a common ancestor called Proto-Algonkian; the ancestors of the contemporary Ojibwa, Menominee, Fox, and Cree also spoke dialects of that reconstructed form (Hockett 1973: 302). In widening relations, other tribes in eastern Canada, the Great Lakes region, the Ohio valley, and the Atlantic coast are joined under the Algonkian label, the implication being that in the past they were a single speech community or a group of communities speaking closely related dialects. And Algonkian as a whole is tied to languages in the Northwest called Wakashan (including the Nootka).

Changes are not haphazard but regular. Whole series of patterned sound shifts turn up in parent and daughter languages sharing particular phonemes in particular sound environments. Take the Latin words *cantāre* ("sing"), *carbō* ("charcoal"), *campus* ("field"), *cārus* ("dear"), *capillus* ("hair"), and *caballus* ("horse"), the *c* in each case being pronounced as *k*. Compare the corresponding French *chanter, charbon, champ, cher, cheveu,* and *cheval,* which uniformly replace *k* with *ch,* pronounced *sh.* With evidence of such correspondences, it is possible to phrase a phonetic law: Latin *c* (*k*) before *a,* long or short, becomes modern French *ch* (*sh*). On the other hand, Latin *c* (*k*) before *e* or *i,* whether long or short, becomes *c* (pronounced *s*) in French: *centum* ("hundred") to *cent, cervus* ("stag") to *cerf, cēra* ("wax") to *cire,* and so on (Sturtevant 1947: 67).

Sometimes new words are created not by patterned sound shifts but by alteration of old materials by analogy with other linguistic forms that are present. Harry Hoijer (1971: 284) illustrates with a change from

The Ideological Aspect of Culture

Old to Modern English: in Old English, the word for cow was cū and its plural was cȳ (pronounced to rhyme with French *rue*). Plurals of many other words were formed by suffixing -*as* to the singular, as stān ("stone," the *a* pronounced as in *calm*), stān-*as*. In the course of time, -*as* was added to cū to form its plural, and the form cȳ was dropped.

Besides patterned phonemic change and analogy, borrowing is a mechanism that changes a language's content. Borrowing is readily evident to us English speakers in French derivatives such as *mirage*, *garage*, and *gourmet*, still too recently adopted to have been forced into the more usual English phonemic patterns. As turnabout, the French have taken from us *le besbol, le futbol,* and *le biftek.*

Discovery of the genetic relationships between languages through the comparative method leads to historical models such as those in the figures below. The family tree is a convenient way of visualizing connections, although it may tend to suggest that languages break apart as wholes, within a short time. The linguist Morris Swadesh (1971: 33)

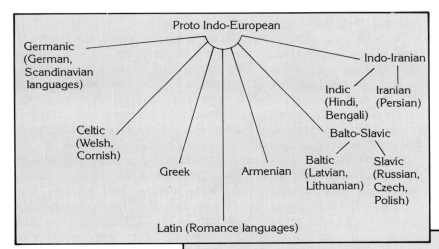

One kind of historical model, a tree representation of some languages stemming from Proto Indo-European. Languages in parentheses are contemporary examples in their groups.

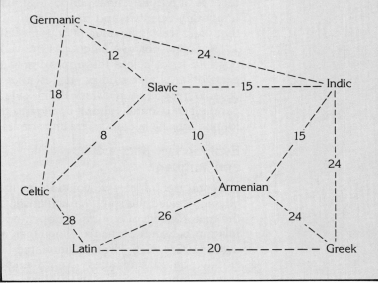

The net, another model of genetic connections between languages, makes it possible to suggest minimum centuries of divergence between contemporary tongues in the same family. Glottochronology is used to establish divergences. (After Swadesh 1971.)

notes that "nowadays linguistic genealogists are generally too sophisticated to believe that languages always divide by abrupt splits. They therefore accept the model of gradual dialect formation, but claim that in the long run, when intermediate variants have been lost, it is the same as if there had been a sharp split." (This would be true, Swadesh adds, in cases in which a few language communities are socially and geographically separated but are equally divergent linguistically from one another, or when only two subgroups of a larger entity exist.) A net (as represented in the figure at the bottom of p. 307) may present divergences more realistically.

Correspondences in sound shifts can indicate connections and establish relative times of the breaks between speech communities. They tell us, for instance, that Swedish, Danish, Norwegian, and Icelandic diverged from a preceding Old Norse, which then was one of the branches of Proto-German, coexisting along with Old English, Old Saxon, and Old High German. "Lexicostatistic glottochronology," invented by the linguist Morris Swadesh, is a method leading to specific dating of the breaks.

Glottochronology is "the sequence in which stages in the history of a language have appeared or the history of the separation of a language into local dialects, and the differentiation of these in a more or less gradual fashion into distinct languages. . . .[The method] is lexicostatistic because it is based on the counting of similar words among vocabularies of related languages, according to the following criterion: Under similar conditions, the lower the number of agreements, the longer the dialects have been separated" (Swadesh 1971: 271).

The words which are counted are a basic list of one hundred terms that includes body parts, activities, quantities, sizes, colors, pronouns, and so on, "universal and simple things, qualities, and activities, which depend to the least degree possible on the particular environment and cultural state of the group" (Swadesh 1971: 275). Swadesh found by counting cognates in related languages for which there were written records at different time periods (for instance, classical Latin and contemporary Spanish, and English at the time of King Alfred and today) that there was an average retention of 86 percent of the basic words in 1,000 years. For two languages derived from a common parent, it is possible to calculate the approximate date of their separation from each other. Later studies suggest that the retention rates may have broader ranges than Swadesh indicated and that they are not independent of general cultural change to the degree he believed, but the foundations he laid down are important in historical studies.

Evolutionary perspective and language

In the period of antievolutionism that followed the pioneers, language received the same particularistic and relativistic treatment given the major facets of culture. It appeared evident that there was no correlation between particular languages and lifeways. As Edward Sapir wrote (1921: 213), "Totally unrelated languages share in one culture, closely related languages—even a single language—belong to distinct culture spheres." So, even if some kind of scaling of cultures was possible (and that was grudgingly admitted only with regard to technology, if at all), languages did not evolve along with them. Furthermore, it was held impracticable to rank languages, because all were adequate to their tasks, utterances in one tongue were translatable into any other, and all had equal potential for expansion and elaboration. In a statement often quoted, Sapir (1921: 219) asserted: "Both simple and complex types of language of an indefinite number of varieties may be found spoken at any desired level of cultural advance. When it comes to linguistic form, Plato walks with the Macedonian swineherd, Confucius with the head-hunting savage of Assam."

With the return to evolutionism, anthropological linguists have reassessed the matter. One of them, Dell Hymes (1961), holds that, while languages are perhaps structurally equivalent, all of them are not now functionally so. That is, some languages do in fact have more tasks and do more, and some have fewer and do less, because of the simple fact that the cultures of which they are part are simple or advanced. His position is that languages have evolved and are evolving in response to technological and social changes.

To understand the evolutionary process in language, Hymes suggests, it is necessary to enlarge the context from one of language regarded only as a code to one of total speech behavior, which involves more than language structure. The actual *use* of language can be seen, for instance, in relation to what he calls **routines**, which "range from reciting the alphabet, counting, and greeting, to the sonnet form, the marriage ceremony, and the direction of a buffalo hunt" (1961: 58). With social complexity, numbers and varieties of routines increase, and variations in their control by individuals increase as well. Speech patterns become related to the playing out of roles in different settings (compare for yourself playgrounds, politics, churches, markets, laboratories, and scientists' conferences) and to the attitudes that reflect cultural differences in group, status, class, and so on.

So a human population encompasses groups with different speech habits that are subject to selection pressures from the cultural and natural environment. Some are prestigious, some are not; some are adaptive, some are not. The speech habits of a dependent minority, for example, while functionally adequate within the community, might be at a disadvantage in competition with the patterns of the socially dominant. If selection operates, the speech of the community changes, and this you will recognize as specific evolution.

With regard to the general evolution of language, Hymes posits three levels to the present: primitive or proto-languages of the distant past which did not have full language status (and which are not recoverable), full languages, a status shared by all known tongues, and advanced languages represented by world languages such as English, Russian, Chinese, French, Spanish, German, and perhaps a few others. The vocabularies of the advanced languages in their extent and development are analogous, Hymes suggests, to the technologies in the cultures of which they are part, showing "increase in range and variety of adjustments to environment in comparison to dialects or regional or minority languages, where these are not supported by a standard language outside the situation" (1961: 72).

Language as Cultural Mechanism and Content

The advanced languages' dominance in science, in particular, marks their practical precedence over others and gives them a continuing selective advantage. Are other languages potentially able to accommodate advances? Yes, says Hymes, as "...any set of speech habits is capable of expanding in content and functions sufficiently to serve a complex civilization and its associated systems of thought. Yes, of course, *potentially* it can so serve; but we must distinguish between potential and actual development, recognizing that some languages are actually of the more advanced type while others are not" (1961: 73-74).

Morris Swadesh (1971: 44-45) also distinguished, for the last 10,000 years, three levels: local, classic, and world languages. Like Hymes, he discerned an adaptive factor: "When we discount the profusion of synonyms for stylistic reasons, the size of vocabularies is a fair index of how far languages have developed. Another touchstone is the extent to which they are used in higher education and all forms of advanced research. By this measure, perhaps the only true giants of our time are English, Russian, French, German, Italian, and Japanese" (1971: 51).

A case can be made, then, that language evolves along with the rest of culture. Confirmatory evidence from a small semantic domain—basic color terms—has been discovered by Brent Berlin and Paul Kay (Berlin 1970). Basic color terms are words like *red* and *green* (not *reddish* or *greenish*) which are not included under any other terms (as *scarlet* would be) and are not limited in their application (as *blonde* would be). They are words that come to attention as soon as colors begin to be discussed with informants.

Berlin reports (1970: 5-6), "We found that while different languages may encode different numbers of basic color terms, there nevertheless exists universally a total inventory of just eleven basic color categories from which the color terms of any given language are always drawn. These categories are black, white, red, green, yellow, blue, brown, pink, purple, orange and gray." Furthermore, there is an order—an evolutionary order—in the selection of the eleven basic terms. All languages (a judgment based on a sample of more than one hundred) have words for black and white, which comprise one category. Red is the next category to be added; either yellow or green takes the third position; in fourth position is either yellow or green, depending on which of the two was selected previously; the fifth category is blue; the sixth is brown; and the final category consists of gray, orange, pink, or purple (Berlin 1970: 8). There are, in all, seven categories arrived at in temporal order—"evolutionary stages in the development of basic color terms" (Berlin 1970: 9). Those cultures with the smallest number of terms are the most primitive technologically and economically, and those with the largest number are the advanced ones.

If you should wonder how people in some simple cultures make do with only black and white, those all-inclusive terms indicate something like "dull" or "dark" and "brilliant" or "light." But the point is that these *are* the basic terms, and there are only two. That apparently is sufficient, so far as basics go. In specific situations, where finer distinctions are required, there may be recourse to devices like those we employ when we say something is "cherry colored" or "like an orange." But basic color terms are not dependent on analogies and metaphors; they stand by themselves as reference points.

If evolution is anywhere, it is everywhere, said E. B. Tylor. He would have been gratified with this demonstration.

Suggested Readings

Burling, Robbins. 1970. *Man's many voices: Language in its cultural context.* New York: Holt, Rinehart and Winston.

Crystal, David. 1971. *Linguistics.* Baltimore: Penguin Books.*

Greenberg, Joseph H. 1968. *Anthropological linguistics: An introduction.* New York: Random House.*

Hymes, Dell. 1964. *Language in culture and society.* New York: Harper and Row.

Langacker, Ronald W. 1973. *Language and its structure: Some fundamental linguistic concepts.* 2nd ed. New York: Harcourt Brace Jovanovich.*

Waterman, John T. 1963. *Perspectives in linguistics.* Chicago: University of Chicago Press, Phoenix Books.*

After our examination of language, which is both a cultural mechanism and a body of content of particular importance for ideologies, we turn in this last chapter to the question of the evolution of ideology itself. We have seen that languages behave and change in ways describable as regular and lawlike and that contemporary linguists are returning to the evolutionary point of view in their studies after a period of relative neglect.

Chapter 13
Evolution
in Ideas and
Beliefs

Looking for directional change

Can directional movements be discerned in ideology, as they can in technology and social organization? An answer to that question depends in part on whether one takes a specific or a general evolutionary stance. No particular culture is impelled to transform itself from a hunting-gathering base to domestication, or from egalitarianism to ranking or stratification, unless environmental relations are altered or there are internal crises. It will remain as comfortably secure and successful as it can in its own environments—*sapiens*, habitat, and superorganic—and change just so much as it has to if it is to persist. Its ideology will promote technological and social conservatism so long as the culture's posture is secure. On the other hand, if alterations in culture-environment relations are followed by important changes in technology and social organization, ideology follows along to rationalize the new equilibrium and to do its part in maintaining and increasing the efficiency of the system.

So we do not assume an inevitable displacement of supernaturalism by naturalism, everywhere and anywhere. The Cheyenne, for example, turned from farming to hunting, and their social organization shifted to one appropriate for a nomadic life. We have no reason to believe there was less supernaturalism in their philosophy as a whole when they were sedentary farmers than when they became hunters. We admit that we don't know much directly about their ideas and beliefs during the farming phase of their history, but we could make some good deductions by referring to reports about those who held to the farming adaptation along the Missouri and its tributaries in historic times.

To repeat, then, persistence and success in environments are what we look for first in particular cultures, rather than an inevitable progress in relation to a scale drawn by general evolution. Given cultures have their ups and downs.

As we have seen, there is good reason to conclude that even when belief and ritual face toward the supernaturalistic side of the ideology spectrum they have adaptive effects for the culture. On the other hand, things and events do have physical and biological properties as well as cultural ones. Recall a statement by Robert Redfield (1953: 86) that we quoted: " . . . if there is an emphasized meaning in the phrase 'world view,' I think it is in the suggestion it carries of the structure of things as man is aware of them." Nature has a structure, and natural things have properties. Human perceptions of properties and structures are conceptualized differently from culture to culture. We assume that if a culture conceptualizes naturalistically and wields things directly and effectively in terms of those properties its adaptational capacity ought to be superior to one that relies more heavily on supernaturalism and the indirect effects of ritual.

Now, although given cultures have their ups and downs, new adaptations sometimes rise to a new level of energy capture and efficiency, as when domestication became established in the Middle East and elsewhere, and ranking social systems marshalled larger numbers of humans and fostered specializations in their work. At the new level, the cultures represent dominant types, and they spread at the expense of the older ones. Has there been a replacement of supernaturalism by naturalism in this perspective? A case can be made for the position that there has—not total replacement, obviously, but an expansion of naturalism in some segments of ideology.

In a way, the situation in ideology resembles the social one, in which impersonal factors became dominant over personal ones in the ordering of human lives. Whereas kinship in egalitarian societies enwrapped all of the people in the community, setting the tone of economics and politics and all other aspects of relationing, kinship in the political state shrank effectively to household and family. Property relationships are characteristic now of all spheres except the domestic one. Of course, they have intruded there as well (witness the legal quarrels of family members over disposition of wills, and the familiar purchase of good

The Ideological Aspect of Culture

behavior: "Be a good boy, and I'll put a quarter in your piggy bank"). But it seems safe to say that only in home and hearth (and perhaps within a few other areas such as social clubs and religious communities) are personal, and not property, relations dominant in human behavior in the state society.

In another respect, however, the analogy does not hold. Supernaturalism could not have dominated the ideological aspect of primitive cultures to the degree that kinship bloomed in the social. Some areas of action, some domains of discourse, might have been dominated by supernaturalism, but a hard core of naturalism would have been necessary for coping effectively with the recalcitrant properties of the physical and biological world. Evidence from some simpler cultures today seems to support that.

In this chapter, we will look at some classification systems in the ideologies of low-energy cultures which pertain to things in immediate habitats. Classifications, after all, are organizations of concepts. With evidence in hand for the naturalistic treatment of things vital for maintenance of cultures, we will then make a leap to some concepts of broader extension which make up cosmologies—ideas and beliefs relating to the origin and structure of the world and the universe and humankind's place in it. In that area, we will find some marked differences between simple and complex cultures and will try to draw a lesson from the contrast. Along the way, we will take note of a kind of universal structure in ideologies. Finally, we will look at a kind of concept making that properly can be called neither naturalistic nor supernaturalistic but is a sort of compromise between them. That is art.

Discovering native concepts

Before we proceed with conceptual organizations, a word is needed about ethnographic sources. One criticism directed at world views and other organizations of concepts such as myths and religions is that they are *our* categories, not those of the people being observed, so that they distort ideas and their relationships. A relatively new orientation, **cognitive anthropology**, assumes that "each people has a unique system for perceiving and organizing material phenomena—things, events, behavior, and emotions . . ." and "focuses on *discovering* how different peoples organize and use their cultures" (Tyler 1969: 3). Cognitive anthropologists elicit the names for classes of objects as they are understood by the speakers of native languages and the relations of the classes as they are arranged in levels of hierarchies to form taxonomic schemes. To take a simple example from our own system, end tables and dining tables are contrasting kinds of tables and tables as a whole contrast with chairs, sofas, and desks, but all are included under the category *furniture* (Tyler 1969: 7). And so it goes with organizations of plants, animals, tools, kin, and everything else perceived by people: all are taxonomies which may or may not have a hierarchical structure.

Plants, animals, tools, kin—each group comprises what the cognitive anthropologist calls a **semantic domain**—"a class of objects all of which share at least one feature in common which differentiates them from other semantic domains" (Tyler 1969: 8). It is the task of the

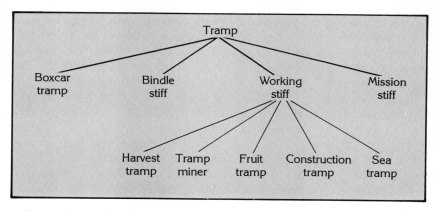

Branching diagram, an organizing device in cognitive anthropology. *Tramp* in this example is a semantic domain which is broken into categories, and one of the categories is further subdivided. The ethnographer recorded eight kinds of tramps at the second categorical level, but for simplicity only four are given here. (After *The cultural experience,* James P. Spradley and David W. McCurdy, Chicago: Science Research Associates, 1972.)

anthropologist, by this view, to *discover* semantic domains and their characteristics rather than to impose them from the outside.

There are other facets to cognitive anthropology than its methods for eliciting semantic domains, one of them being a commitment (on the part of some of its practitioners) to a definition of culture as only what is in human heads—not houses, gardens, tools, clans, and states but perceptions of those entities and the organization of perceptions into conceptual categories. That is, what is ideology in our terms is culture under the orientation of not a few cognitivists. But, as Marvin Harris puts it, and any materialist would agree, "cultures are more than codes" (1968: 601). It is hardly possible to account for massive accumulations of technology and social organization and their evolution by reference only to the way people perceive and conceptualize them. That does not mean that discoveries made with the techniques of cognitive anthropology have no relevance for evolutionary anthropology.

Useful names for environmental resources

The Fore are a linguistic group in the eastern New Guinean highlands consisting of about ten thousand people who subsist on sweet potatoes and other root crops and on pig raising. Wild plants and animals supplement the diet and are used extensively for decoration and for utilitarian purposes in the culture. Like other highland peoples, the Fore possess a classification system for the resources in their habitat—names for plants, animals, and materials exploited—which are strongly naturalistic and utilitarian. As a matter of fact, they parallel, in the basis for their distinctions, those found in the scientific taxonomies of zoologists and botanists in the Western world.

For example, Jared M. Diamond (1966) found that all birds in the Fore tribal territory had been given names, that they had been grouped into "big name" or higher-level categories and subdivided into units called "small names," the latter corresponding remarkably well with the species designations of Western scientists. Our ornithologists sorted birds in the region into 120 species; the Fore sorted them into 110 "small name" categories, and there was a one-to-one correspondence between them in 93 cases. Patently, the Fore are acute observers of real and objective differences between birds—differences in form, plumage, calls and other behavior, habitat choices, and so on.

316

The investigator suggests that the bird classifications are highly utilitarian and basically economic (and so are the Fore categorizations of wild plants and animals). In the past, birds were economically even more important than they are today, and correctly identifying and naming them was essential to Fore fowlers. If the hunters were looking for a fat-breasted bird for meat or brilliant feathers for a ritual costume, distinct names to which were attached perceptions of those characteristics as well as perceptions of bird calls and customary habitats would make their individual and cooperative efforts efficient.

Native peoples do not always score so high in relation to Western scientific naming categories as the Fore. For instance, Ralph Bulmer (1970) found that among another New Guinean people, the Karam, about 60 percent of the lower-order groupings of vertebrate animals corresponded with zoologists' named species. However, and this is the important point, where they did not correspond, the *basis* on which the native classification was made was a set of clearly marked features—again, form, behavior, and habitat. One is reminded here of Anatol Rapoport's definition of "empirical investigation": "An investigation which begins with a recording of observations . . . " (1954: 93). Putting the matter in people terms, the Fore and Karam made empirical investigations, recorded not in laboratory notes and manuals but in the workaday vocabulary of their languages. They are acute observers, and they are clear about what part of their perceptions their concepts point to.

What the Karam classification clearly specifies, in Bulmer's view, is "objective discontinuities in nature," which is the same focus as that of

How the Shoshone Indians classify birds. This is an illustrative segment of an ethnoornithological system in which ninety to a hundred birds are classified and is part of a larger ethnozoological system. It demonstrates, among other things, the taxonomic structure of native categories, that is, a structure of class inclusion or transitivity, and the mapping of native onto scientific categories. The symbol " in Shoshone words indicates a glottal stop. (After " 'Eagle' = 'Bird': A note on the structure and evolution of Shoshone ethnoornithological nomenclature," Per Hage and Wick R. Miller, *American Ethnologist,* Special Issue on Folk Biology, 1976, in press.)

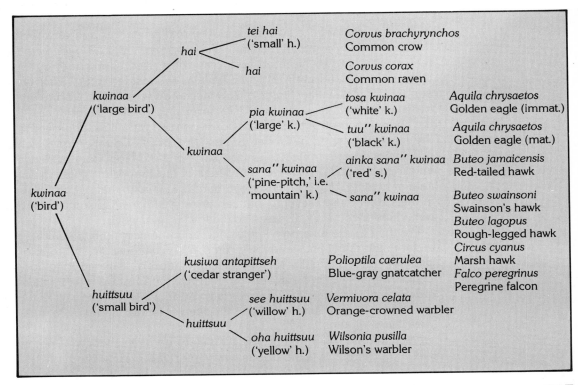

the Western scientist who sets up species in the living world and kinds of things in the nonliving. He writes (1970: 1,081-82), "...as far as *wild* fauna is concerned (and I think this goes for wild flora too), they are not only applying units which are in the logical sense 'species,' but they are concerned with, and to a large extent aware of, the discontinuities which define biological species, even where their folk taxa do not correspond one-to-one to these." Their criteria, in other words, are those included in Western practice.

Generalizing, Bulmer writes (1970: 1,082), "I would further chance my arm and argue that any human population which gets its living by direct exploitation of natural resources, whether by hunting and gathering, agriculture, fishing or pastoralism, is forced to meet nature on its own terms and to categorise those aspects of the natural environment which are relevant to it in a biologically realistic way."

There we have it. In our terms, a culture must cope with its habitat, and effective coping is furthered by naturalistic concept making. We have called symboling arbitrary, but what is arbitrary about it in habitat naming is the choice of symbol, such as a sound cluster or other object to label the symbol's referents. What is not wholly arbitrary but orderly, selective, and adaptive is the bundling of resemblances and the recognition of significant differences between things perceived—at least in those domains that are matters of life and death for a culture. Given our assertion that technology—provisioning, sheltering, defending—is the most important and consequential aspect of culture, we would expect that the natural resources from which it extracts materials and energies would receive reasonably clear delineation in ideology and language. Supernaturalism would be a shaky reed as a guide to the crucial properties of habitat.

Another example of awareness of the real properties and effects of things is native American medicine. An historian, Virgil J. Vogel, found that more than two hundred botanical drugs used aboriginally by Indians in North and Latin America have been included in the *Pharmacopoeia of the United States of America* and the *National Formulary,* two standard guides, and that "in a surprising number of instances... the aboriginal uses of these drugs corresponded with those approved in the *Dispensatory of the United States*" (1970: 6)—a publication which accepts or rejects remedies on the basis of hard laboratory evidence and clinical experience. And knowledge of the American Indian in the field of healing, Vogel suggests, compares solidly with that of Europeans in the sixteenth and seventeenth centuries. If Indians had some bizarre remedies for common diseases, so did the civilized world.

Pointing to the extensive knowledge of human and animal anatomy of the native Aleutian Islanders, Eskimo, and Siberians, the anthropologist William S. Laughlin suggests accumulation of it began long ago. "Ancient man was a carnivore who had to hunt in order to eat and in order to utilize animal products for fabricational purposes as well as for food. Knowledge of anatomy has thus been of immediate value in making a living" (Laughlin 1961: 171).

Laughlin asserts further, "The consistent underestimation of primitives' knowledge is a notorious and unfortunate fact, although the reasons are not difficult to assay. Apparently without exception, every

The Ideological Aspect of Culture

fieldworker who has included such an investigation in his schedule has remarked that he was unable to exhaust the native's knowledge because of too little time or because he himself lacked the necessary knowledge to record those things that the native informant wished to tell or show him" (1961: 166).

There is evidence and expert opinion, then, that, in the immediate confrontation of primitive cultures and their habitats, at least the lower-level concepts for managing biological phenomena were forthrightly naturalistic and practical. (And considering the efficient selection of materials for tools and other devices, so were those of the impinging physical world.) It is likely that much naturalistic thinking has been obscured not only by the incapacity of ethnographers to keep up with their informants' knowledge but also by the accompanying presence of supernatural belief and ritual that ethnographers painstakingly recorded.

Extensions of primitive ideas and beliefs

If naturalistic concept making is characteristic of much of a primitive culture's confrontation with things in the immediate habitat that it must use for survival, the situation does not hold for the broadest extensions of ideas and beliefs, those explaining origins and causes.

The Fore themselves explain the social and cultural world as having been instituted by two creative beings, Jugushimanta and Morufonu, who emerged from the earth. Jugushimanta gave birth to a female and then to a male child, whose human appearance and spirit was the work of the wind, and the two creators then went about the country, peopling the region with its different social groups, planting gardens, and introducing animals and plants useful to the people (Berndt 1962: 41-47).

"The earth was the original element," Asen Balikci (1970: 209) begins his summary account of the creation myths of the Netsilik Eskimo. "It is the one thing that has always existed. At first there was darkness or a kind of twilight all around, and when man first appeared, he lived without sunlight. There were no animals to hunt then; man did not have to suffer for his livelihood, but there were no pleasures either."

It was an orphan girl who became a goddess, Nuliajuk, who created the animals of the earth and who prompted men to hunt for them. For a time animals and men spoke the same language, in which words had strange and magical powers that could be employed to transport people through the air. And it was a womanless world, for it was not until after a great flood that girls were born, part of the progeny of two surviving men, shamans, who copulated together. People who rose into the sky became stars (Balikci 1970: 209-12).

According to the !Kung, there lived in the eastern sky a god who first created and named himself and then successively brought into being the lesser god of the western sky and wives for both of them, and " . . . the earth and the water holes, the sky and the rain, the sun and the wind and the things that grow on the earth, and the animals with their stripes and colors . . . " (Marshall 1965: 269). He created man and woman and commanded them to breathe. And he gave them their tools and weapons and their knowledge of how to live as Bushmen.

A Hopi myth describes an emergence of the people from an Under-world. It was cold and dark on the surface of the earth, but a distant light led them to a field in which corn, watermelon, and beans were growing, and the deity Masau'u gave them the gift of fire and assigned land to their clans. The dead still return to the Underworld, where they live lives duplicating those on earth, sometimes emerging as katcinas, the spiritual beings impersonated in masked dances, and as clouds which bring rain (Titiev 1944).

Each culture has myths of varying scope, some of them purporting to explain the whole visible world, some of them neglecting it, but all accounting for parts of nature and human social life and customs. Thus the Nootka, who lacked a unitary myth of creation, postulated an Un-dersea-world off Vancouver Island where lived in human form the Sal-mon-people and the Herring-people, who donned their scaly skins when they left the great house they shared. The many rituals and privi-leges of the separate lineages were related to supernatural experiences of the ancestors (Drucker 1951).

The contrast of contemporary cosmology

The examples were introduced to illustrate that product of ideology called cosmology, concepts and beliefs relating to the origin and struc-ture of the universe and humankind's relation to it. It is in cosmology that we find the sharpest contrast between the ideology of science in industrial cultures and the mythical representations of primitive ones. In the primitive world, as the Africanist Daryll Forde (1954: x) has written, "Gods, spirits, and magical forces beyond the community, together with witches and sorcerers within it, are postulated in explana-tion of the workings of the universe, of the incidence of benefits and misfortunes, and of the strains of life in society." They are absent from the scientific cosmology. Matter, energy, space, and time are the elements.

The sun and its planets, according to one contemporary summary (Jastrow 1968), took shape out of a cloud of hydrogen gas and debris from earlier stars about 4,500,000,000 years ago—the sun at the dense and fiery center of the cloud, the planets on the cooler, less dense margins. The earth began to look something like it does today after a long period of condensation of the gases into a ball of rock and iron. Formation of the continents came about through the rising of masses of lighter rocks above the heavier ocean floors, which gradually filled with water from the earth's interior. Not until 1,500,000,000 years after the earth's birth did life appear, and life's molecular building blocks have now been put together by scientists in laboratories which duplicate the environmental conditions of that distant time. And, from single-celled organisms, paleontologists and geologists have traced the evolution of the complex plants and animals we see about us today.

Our universe, in which the sun and planets came into being, itself began as a mass of hydrogen gas and the dust of exploded stars, more than 10,000,000,000 years ago. All of its component stars were formed by the same process—from clouds of gas whose atoms fell with increas-ing speed and energy toward their centers, raising temperatures sufficiently to ignite nuclear reactions in the hydrogen. Like other suns, ours will burn until its hydrogen is exhausted, signaling its impending end by swelling to a "red giant" that will vaporize its planets and then collapse and dwindle away as a "white dwarf." The biggest stars end their careers in gigantic explosions that blow their materials into space, where, mixed with primordial hydrogen, they form into new stars.

No doubt you have already learned something about this story in your science classes, although you may not have thought of it as a cosmology. It is never presented as final and detailed truth, but there is at least one thing about it that moves it out of the realm of myths of origin: the accumulation and integration of the knowledge in it has depended upon the observational and experimental methods of the special sciences, sciences backed up by an intricate technology, an elaborate social organization, and naturalistic concept making.

Where we, as cultural anthropologists, take our places in the story building is properly at that point at which the expanding primate brain produced symboling behavior, with its crucial consequences in the accumulation of human experience and its evolution evaluation. Culture is part of the structure of our universe, and we have traced its ascending forms on earth. Our part, I trust, shares the naturalistic character of the rest of the contemporary story, a character which appeared long ago in the naming of birds and animals of the forest, now extended into origins and causes.

A common structure
in ideologies

Although supernaturalistic concepts dominate the creation myths of low-energy cultures and naturalistic concepts dominate the scientific cosmologies of advanced cultures, there is a way in which ideologies tend to be like one another, no matter what the level of culture they are part of. They share a hierarchical structure of concepts. In the terms introduced in Chapter Two, ideologies and their segments consist of ideas and beliefs of lesser and broader extension which can be arranged in levels from the more specific to the more general and inclusive.

Primitive cultures vary in the attention they pay to systematizing ideas and beliefs, and their structure is not readily apparent either to the people or to an outside observer. But in all likelihood one is there, and it can be elicited or constructed by the observer. Also, in primitive cultures, ideas and beliefs in one domain can often be related directly or indirectly to other parts of the culture, for which they stand as symbols, aside from having their own content.

An example is the spirits of the Nuer, which Evans-Pritchard (1953) categorizes as spirits of the above and of the below. In the first class are Spirit who is in the sky, spirits of the air, and souls of those who have been killed by lightning. In the second are totemic spirits, nature sprites, and fetishes. Each, Evans-Pritchard says, is in a sense a different conception, but again they are alike, because all are refractions of Spirit (also translatable as God), which is to say they are Spirit in different mediums or localities. We might call them aspects of a single concept, with different qualities or characteristics singled out in different contexts.

Evolution in Ideas and Beliefs

The spirits bear some relation to the society as a whole and to its parts at different levels. As aspects of Spirit, the lesser spirits, for instance, stand in tutelary (guardian or protector) relationships to individuals, lineages, villages, and larger political groups. "Just as ... two lineages are distinct and opposed groups in relation to one another at one level of segmentation and are a single unit at a higher level of segmentation, so spirit as conceived in relation to these segments must be divided at the lower level and undivided at the higher level. It is intelligible, therefore, that in its relation to the segmentary social order the conception of Spirit is broken up into diverse refractions, while in relation to nature and man in general the many become again the one" (1953: 209).

The structure of the Nuer spiritual order resembles in some ways our conception of energy, which we touched on in Chapters Two and Seven. Defined as "the capacity to do work," energy takes such forms as motion, light, heat, and electricity. Energy is never created or destroyed but changed from one form to others, most often the more to the less highly organized. In a structural sense, energy as a totality is the analog of the Nuer's Spirit who is in the sky; it is the broadest category that incorporates variant forms.

As another example, take the Kalabari, a fishing and trading people who live in villages located on raised areas of mud in the mangrove swamps of the Niger delta (Horton 1962). Each village is comprised of a number of land-holding lineages whose members trace descent from the founding fathers, both consanguineally and affinally. Strictly lineage affairs are handled within the lineages. Village affairs as a whole are in the hands of a headman and a council, the latter drawn from the age sets.

As Horton reconstructs it, there are four levels or worlds: the "place of the people," of humans, animals, plants, and physical objects; the level of spirits of various kinds; the level of many specific "creators" and "destinies"; and finally a level of Creator and Destiny as two unities.

Every living and nonliving thing has a personal spirit that animates it and gives it direction. But there are also three classes of "free spirits": the ancestors of the lineages, who look to the welfare of their descendants; the village heroes, who supervise the interests of the village as a whole; and the water people, who are linked with the struggle against unruly nature and against the deviant and disorderly in society (such as the wealthy and powerful, those who fail to live up to family obligations, and idiots and morons). The spirit worlds, then, relate to individual, to lineage, to village, and to deviance from expected behavior.

The next two levels in Kalabari world view, the levels of the individual and generalized creators and destinies, are particularly interesting. Although everybody has a spirit, the joining of spirit and individual in the womb is the work of a *tamuno*, or creator. Everyone also has a *so*, or destiny. A person's destiny is disclosed by his or her spirit to his or her creator before individual and spirit are joined; from that point on, the person's life course is laid down. Neither lineages nor villages as such have creators, it being held that those social entities are only the sum of the individuals in them. But both kinds of groups have destinies which shape their courses.

The Ideological Aspect of Culture

The final concepts, at the highest level of the hierarchy, are Great Creator, spoken of as female and as the creator of all things out of mud, and the generalized and overriding *so*, which refers to the behavior of everything created, translatable, again, as destiny.

I think you will recognize the hierarchy of concepts involved here. There is a progression from the more concrete and specific to the more generalized, from individual spirits and from creators and destinies of the individual to the collectivity. Along the way, they take account of the behavior of individual, lineage, village, and immediate environment, and finally of the world. As the concepts become more general, and more broadly inclusive of observations in several directions, they tend to become "dematerialized," as Horton phrases it. They are more difficult to apply to intimate and ordinary daily life and observations about it.

Horton compares the Kalabari world view with Western scientists' conceptualization of the submicroscopic world, with its atoms and smaller particles arranged in hierarchies, a model based originally on the planetary system. Some concepts describe the world as ordinarily perceived, with properties of color, temperature, mass, and extension. At the atomic level, color and temperature are ignored. At another level, writes Horton (1962: 211), the scientist "even drops the category of spatial extension in the ordinary sense. As we ascend from level to level, fewer and fewer of the categories appropriate to the description of observable reality apply; until, as the physicists often like to emphasize, their highest-order models are not really material at all. This dematerialization of successive levels of reality is a consequence of one of the basic functions of explanation—that of unifying apparent diversity. . . ."

Inclined as we are to a materialist position, we would not put the matter as a loss of materiality. The procedure is that, in our selective extraction of characteristics of things for higher-level concepts, we ignore some properties and retain others. There may be some rephrasing in the process, but we think that concepts always refer to *something* —never to *nothing*. It is, however, only one point of view about the matter.

Here, then, is warrant for the statement that we can find a universal structure within ideologies. Does this mean that differences between primitive world views and scientific models of reality are lacking or trivial? Of course not. Whatever their similarities in hierarchical arrangements and in "dematerialization" of higher-order concepts (in Horton's sense), the Kalabari ideas and beliefs discussed here are describable as supernaturalistic and the scientist's as naturalistic. The gap between them is the result of a long history of conscious and controlled testing of the purported relationship between concept and observation. The structure remained similar, but the content changed.

Facets of the evolutionary problem

Why is not the same kind of concept making that often characterizes a primitive culture's confrontation with immediate environment, particularly in relation to technology, not carried into the matters of origins and causes of things? And why does naturalism characterize conceptions of origins and causes in high-energy cultures?

For one thing, ideas and beliefs about origins and causes are not subject to natural verification procedures, as are those about the characteristics of things immediately useful in daily subsistence, shelter, and defense. Nor can they be, in the absence of technology and experience appropriate to the testing. How can one judge between an Eskimo orphan goddess and a !Kung god of the eastern sky as creators of animals? Cultural anthropology finds the Eskimo and !Kung ideas and beliefs interesting and themselves worthy of explanation. But, like other sciences, it does not depend on them to explain physical or biological reality—nor to explain cultural reality. It is possible to judge between the merits of **vitalism** and **spontaneous creation** on the one hand and biological evolution on the other because of the systematic accumulation of observations and the actual manipulation of the building blocks of living things. The gap from nonliving to living is not completely bridged yet, but we can have some confidence that it will be.

Recall that the manioc in South American gardens is good to eat. But one species is sweet, another bitter. The bitter manioc is edible, too, if a poisonous substance is removed by squeezing and heating the plant. Accurate distinction between species is vital, and violating procedural guidance in the preparation of the bitter manioc produces quick penalties. The technology of verification is well within the capacity of the culture; it is in the technological aspect of daily life.

Technology, then, is the first ally of naturalism, and its expansion into many domains takes with it the procedures first evidenced in the planting and the chase. Cultures technologically dominant carry with them, like their languages in which science is encapsulated, their procedures for concept making, expanded not only in new geographical regions but in new human concerns.

Another side to the evolution of ideology is its relation to social organization. With the increase in numbers of specialized groups and statuses, many of them resting upon occupations and crafts (as noted in our discussion of castes and classes), knowledge accumulated along particular lines, a process hastened by the invention of writing and record keeping. Scientific disciplines, of course, are highly specialized. And with the concentration of wealth and power under the state, resources were diverted to organized groups engaged in knowledge accumulation and its interpretation.

It is possible, then, to view the evolution of ideology as an adaptive response to the development of the other two major aspects of culture.

Art in the context of cultural process

Among the "varied and extraordinary" ways of humankind are its arts—painting, sculpture, music, literature oral and written, drama and the dance, and several more. They deserve a comparative look such as that given technology and social organization, but for lack of space we shall confine ourselves to orienting art in the context of cultural process.

The reason we place art within a discussion of ideology is that its stylistic elements resemble concepts. They are perceptible things and they have referents—things they point to and bring together—located inside human beings (emotional states) and outside of them (a clay pot, a fiber mat, or another human being in motion, for instance). Furthermore, artistic behavior seems to represent a compromise between naturalism on the one hand and supernaturalism on the other as a way of interpreting experience. All this makes little sense, of course, unless we keep in mind our focus on culture as a system.

Are we picking wings from butterflies? Art, it is so often said, is a matter of individual expression of affect or emotion, of an esthetic impulse, and to inject into it in an intellectualist way the notions of energy and symbol risks the kind of scorn Wordsworth directed against the scientist who would botanize upon his mother's grave.

However, let's take artists first, from a "people do" view. They manipulate a medium (themselves in the dance, their voices in song, brush and pigment in painting, a chisel and wood or stone in sculpture) and produce an object (a dance, a song, a painting, a sculptured figure). Inside artists, there is an affective or emotional state, a pleasurable one. The artist *feels*, and what is produced has the capacity to evoke roughly similar feelings in the beholder or auditor. That occurs particularly if the latter has been conditioned by exposure to similar works whose characteristics or formal properties have been labelled in the culture as pleasing, beautiful, good, exciting. All cultures have such canons or judgments, such evaluative concepts.

Technological activity is one source of art. Art arises, as Franz Boas said, from technical virtuosity, from mastery by the crafter of material

Sio woman decorating a pot. Pottery, made at only a few localities in northeastern New Guinea, is highly valued and widely traded. Beyond the technological and social aspects, however, pot making and decorating can be put into the context of artistic activity. (Courtesy Thomas G. Harding.)

Evolution in Ideas and Beliefs

and techniques. "Artistic productivity and skill are closely correlated. Productive artists are found among those who have mastered a technique, among men when the industries are in their hands, among women when they are devoted to industrial activities" (1955: 19). A large proportion of plastic and graphic arts are by-products of or had their origin in the utilitarian manufacture of tools, weapons, containers, clothing, habitations.

But the crafter proceeds beyond utilitarian necessity; he or she shapes, balances, embellishes, using repetitive and traditional elements which have the potential to evoke pleasure in the beholder. The elements are simple enough: proportions of parts (as in a clay pot, a carved wooden spoon, the framing of a house or shrine), or smoothed or roughened surfaces, or repeated straight or wavy lines, and so on.

Social behaviors are also initiators of art. The relationing behaviors of speech, song, dance, pageantry, drama, rituals of daily intercourse are shaped, balanced, embellished, and presented in the mold of formal design, in a manner that arouses pleasurable emotion in the artistic doer and the passive participant alike. There are esthetic ways to eat and drink, to serve kava (as among Polynesians) or tea (as among Japanese), to present and receive a gift, and to acknowledge the presence of a leader or the obligations of a follower.

And, finally, ideological behavior often displays an esthetic quality in its presentation of ideas and beliefs, whether in the recitation of a creation myth or a scientific cosmology. You have encountered, no doubt, the judgment of specialists that this or that theory or solution to a problem is "elegant" in its logic, simplicity, and economy, in its formal perfection. So scientists experience esthetic emotion, not only or necessarily in playing the violin or manipulating water colors or oils in their leisure time.

Now, to return to the diagrammatic embrace of our extracted cultural system and its environments, whether or not you take esthetic

Art and ritual combine in the Deer Dance of the Santa Clara Pueblo Indians. Santa Clara is a Tewa-speaking pueblo on the west bank of the Rio Grande north of Santa Fe. Animal or game dances once were confined to the winter season. (Courtesy Jane Hawkins.)

The Ideological Aspect of Culture

pleasure in it, it should be apparent that the artistic behaviors and products we have mentioned, no less than the unadorned hunt or harvest, the giving or receiving of gifts, or buying or selling, are vehicles of energy flow, in White's phrase "energy transformations by symbolic means." Art is work, and what it produces takes the form the culture has established. But it involves the energy of ordinary work *plus* what is required in rounding out the task with disciplined emotion.

Technologically speaking, a house is complete without its carved lintel; sociologically a ritual may be accomplished without the grace notes of elaborate speech or gesture; ideologically a stick without embellishment may serve as the repository of a spirit. But transformation of energy and material proceeds beyond the utilitarian when the artist is moved by the artistic symbol—**style**.

So we may call style that aspect of behaviors and productions represented by patterned and repetitive parts, forms, and shapes and qualities of texture, color, and sound that evoke esthetic pleasure. And esthetic pleasure is the pleasurable emotion in a style context. Physiologically it is indistinguishable from any other emotion, but it finds new and additional meaning in this particular cultural context.

And it may not be utilitarian, in the ordinary sense, but it has utility: it captures energies that might otherwise remain outside of or escape the cultural process, and it locks them into forms that have their own identity and a capacity for guiding this kind of behavior of *Homo sapiens* (emoting, or expressing emotion) into cultural channels. You might say, anthropomorphically, that culture is an insatiable cannibal of available energies; it cannot let well enough alone but strives to net even emotions into its own symboling-dependent forms. Also, style crosscuts all kinds of behaviors and productions and impresses a unity on them. So it has an integrating effect and promotes the efficiency of the system as a whole.

Like the Deer Dance, the Buffalo Dance at Santa Clara is presented in costume that includes dresses, shirts and kilts, leggings, moccasins, and belts, the dancers holding staffs, rattles, and fans. Steps and patterns of the dance are stylized elements. (Courtesy Jane Hawkins.)

Evolution in Ideas and Beliefs

Flute player, Fulbe, Voltaic Republic.
(Courtesy Herbert W. Butler.)

Young Semai man playing a nose flute.
(Courtesy Robert K. Dentan.)

Whether art evolves in general perspective is an old problem in anthropology. An opinion representative of the negative position is that of A. L. Kroeber, who contrasted art with technology and science. "On the whole ... the scientific-technological process is an accumulative one. Each generation or new society can begin where others left off ... [the arts] progress independently, in different directions; whereas science and the mechanical arts progress on the whole in a direction determined by nature as it exists prior to man" (Kroeber 1952: 155).

One thing that has made it hard to see evolution in art is the fact that

The Ideological Aspect of Culture

human emotional states are one of its components. The capacity for physiological creation of these states has not changed, so far as we know, since *Homo sapiens* emerged—and likely since long before that in our predecessors. What the prehistoric Magdalenian *felt* is probably *felt* by the contemporary artist, primitive or literate. What the Magdalenian culture could draw into association with style was raw, precultural emotion. Contemporary cultural process works with the same stuff.

When we assert that art has not evolved at all from the Upper Paleolithic to the present, we say this: Paleolithic paintings arouse in *me* esthetic appreciation comparable to that aroused by a Picasso; therefore, there is no substantial difference in the two arts. But this is a confusion of the esthetic sentiment with the whole of art and its setting. One might as well say (to draw an analogy from the social context) that because mothers in primitive cultures love their children, as do mothers in contemporary cultures, in no respect has social organization evolved.

It is perhaps safe to say that the range of emotional states within a single species like our own has definable limits. But compare the habitat with the limited emotional resources of *sapiens*. Habitat is immensely variable, absolutely and relatively. In the course of the evolution of culture, the properties of habitat are progressively explored, unlocked, harnessed by accumulation and evolution of tools and techniques. *This* part of the evolution of art we can see—art in ochre, art in metal. *This* part changes.

By the principle of specific evolution, we expect that art will develop adaptively in relation to the content, emphases, environments, and energy level of a given culture. Emotion will be ensnared by style in the making of baskets or the production of a steel-frame skyscraper. Since a culture is heir to its past, our art encompasses baskets *and* skyscrapers. And we should add, in order to note social relations, probably it is not the steelworker who experiences esthetic emotion (although it may be) but the architect who planned the whole.

In order to understand art in a general evolutionary context, we require an orientation similar to that used in regard to language. In the contemporary world, both have intruded into new domains along with the dominant cultures which carry them. We learn something by looking at them in isolation but not enough that we can find their evolutionary path.

Culturation evolution as ideology

Unlike the fictional M. Jourdain, a character in Molière's play *Le bourgeois gentilhomme,* who was surprised to learn that he had been speaking prose all along, you are aware that we have been speaking an ideology, not only in these last chapters but throughout this introduction to cultural anthropology. More accurately, we have been presenting a segment of an ideology. It is an organization of concepts that are part of our own language and culture, and it is intended to represent observations (about Bushman food gathering, Nootka chiefly behavior, Trobriand ritual, for instance) and to explain them. Explanations rested on arrangements of ethnographic statements placed in relation to one another and on concepts of broad extension which are extractions of characteristics of the objects and events observed. The key concepts included *culture, symboling, energy transformation, evolution,* and *systems* and their *environments.*

The word *science* was on the whole used sparingly. Science in the first place is highly organized naturalism, and we would be content to have reached a naturalistic explanation of human behaviors (a matter of placing observations against clearly specified contexts). While hypothesis, theory, and law are procedures and goals of science, the emphasis has not been on that aspect of sciencing (one of Leslie White's terms) but on establishing an orientation, a culturological (in that it focuses on extracted cultural systems) and evolutionary one. With one orientation in hand, and with some awareness of others, students can proceed to more austere realms of quantified observations and verification of theories.

If one had to choose a set of the most important marks of an educated person in our society, surely there would be included in it the trait of self-consciousness and alert awareness of the separability of the self and the not-self, entities and their posited relations which Robert Redfield incorporated into the idea of world view. The sun, the earth, and its other planets, all of nature, are objects of which we are aware and which we conceptualize. We are also aware of the things we have called "culture," of course, but there tends to be a widespread naiveté with respect to their relationships with the self. We are aware of history, and some of us are willing to admit that we respond every day of our lives to an accumulation of human historical experience. But there is abroad in the land little useful understanding of how that accumulation has in effect shaped itself in orderly ways.

Surely we have not reduced the stature of humanity nor given it a subordinate position in the animal kingdom by orienting it analytically in a system that places the aggregate of human experience as the focus of study. The whole purpose has been to provide a context for some understanding of a few of humanity's wondrously varied customs in different times and places. If you should state to a friend as a matter of fact that "*sapiens* is an environment of culture," you would have missed the point of our study altogether—and I trust you have not done that. Culture is a presentation of humanity's behavior that affords in itself the possibility of devising answers to important questions about the similarities and differences—continuities and discontinuities—in that behavior.

Conformably with our orientation and the demands of space, we have presented a minimum about the evolution of humanity and its predecessors and the human traits which are interpretable in a biological context. That evolution has set *sapiens* apart behaviorally has been emphasized by some references to our closest contemporary relatives, the higher primates. The principal motif in our study has been the evolution of culture in its major aspects, with reference to such categories as hunting-gathering-fishing, farming-and-herding, and industrial technologies; egalitarian, ranked, stratified, and state societies; and (less clearly defined) supernatural and natural ideologies. Process has been given equal attention with taxonomies.

Ideology, like other aspects of culture, will continue to evolve, both adaptively within particular cultures and in a general sense as that dominant cultural type, the industrial state, reinterprets old domains and ventures into new ones. One movement should be visible to you now. Firmly rooted in the Western intellectual tradition for the last few centuries has been the theme of mastery of *sapiens* over nature. It was hardly questioned that technological progress would continue without foreseeable end, producing new security and comforts for more and more humans from the inexhaustible storehouse of the planet. Now, in a manner of speaking, nature has asserted itself against the never-satisfied demands of human populations (demands originating in and motivated by industrial culture), and ideology has moved, feebly but perceptibly. The ecological philosophy has been raised against that of the developer, the idea of zero population growth against that of unlimited human breeding.

Our cultural model with its environments offers orientation and insight into this and like problems—those of rapacious technology reaching for materials and energies, of human relationships arising to manage it and being shattered and reshaped as a result of the confrontation of technology and habitat, and of human perceptions of events being incorporated into concepts which themselves will have weight in future movements of culture.

Culturology itself as a variety of Western ideology dealing with human behavior is a product of advanced technology and social organization. It is consistent, as I see it, with that dramatic evolutionary turn in human relationships from the personal to the impersonal, which was discerned so clearly by Lewis Henry Morgan. A person-centered, "people-do" intellectual posture would seem to be furthered by a society with a fixation upon personal relations. Perhaps I am wrong about that, but at any rate a comparative science of humanity would not have been possible without collection in a few places of massive bodies of information about many peoples from many times and places and studies of that information by specialists. And that followed from Western dominance and incursion into the far places of the world, whatever other costs it entailed.

Now that you have become acquainted with this orientation toward the varieties of human behavior, I hope you will make use of it. Perhaps a rereading of the cultural sketches which began our study would offer a small test. You should understand the peoples described in them a little better than you did before. But a bigger and more substantial test would come in its application to our nation and others and to the problems we face together.

Suggested Readings

Borgstrom, Georg. 1973. *The food and people dilemma.* North Scituate, Mass.: Duxbury Press.*

Calder, Nigel. 1971. *Technopolis: Social control of the uses of science.* New York: Simon and Schuster, Clarion Books.*

Childe, V. G. 1956. *Society and knowledge.* New York: Harper and Brothers.

Commoner, Barry. 1972. *The closing circle: Nature, man, and technology.* New York: Alfred A. Knopf.

Hoyle, Fred. 1956. *Man and materialism.* New York: Harper and Brothers.

Russell, Bertrand. 1962. *The scientific outlook.* New York: W. W. Norton and Company.*

Turk, Amos, Jonathan Turk, and Janet T. Wittes. 1972. *Ecology, pollution, environment.* Philadelphia: W. B. Saunders.*

Waddington, C. B. 1960. *The ethical animal.* Chicago: University of Chicago Press, Phoenix Books.*

White, Lynn, Jr. 1968. *Machina ex deo: Essays in the dynamism of Western culture.* Cambridge, Mass.: M.I.T. Press.

References

Adams, Richard N. 1960. "An inquiry into the nature of the family." In *Essays in the science of culture in honor of Leslie A. White*. Gertrude E. Dole and Robert L. Carneiro, eds. New York: Thomas Y. Crowell.

Adams, Robert McC. 1966. *The evolution of urban society: Early Mesopotamia and prehispanic Mexico*. Chicago: Aldine.

Anderson, Robert. 1951. "A study of Cheyenne culture history, with special reference to the northern Cheyenne." Ph.D. dissertation, University of Michigan, Ann Arbor.

———. 1956. "The Buffalo Men, a ceremony of petition deriving from the Sutaio." *Southwestern Journal of Anthropology* 12: 92-104.

———. 1960. "Reduction of variants as a measure of cultural integration." In *Essays in the Science of culture in honor of Leslie A. White*. Gertrude E. Dole and Robert L. Carneiro, eds. New York: Thomas Y. Crowell.

Anderson, Robert T. 1971. "Voluntary associations in history." *American Anthropologist* 73: 209-22.

Arensberg, Conrad M. 1963. "The Old World peoples." *Anthropological Quarterly* 36: 75-99.

Armstrong, W. E. 1967. "Rossel Island money: A unique monetary system." In *Tribal and peasant economies: Readings in economic anthropology*. George Dalton, ed. Garden City, N.Y.: Natural History Press. (Originally published 1924.)

Balikci, Asen. 1963. "Shamanistic behavior among the Netsilik Eskimos." *Southwestern Journal of Anthropology* 19: 380-96.

333

———. 1970. *The Netsilik Eskimo*. Garden City, N.Y.: Natural History Press.

Barrau, Jacques. 1968. "L'humide et le sec: An essay on ethnobiological adaptation to contrastive environments in the Indo-Pacific area." In *Peoples and cultures of the Pacific: An anthropological reader*. Andrew P. Vayda, ed. Garden City, N.Y.: Natural History Press.

Barton, R. F. 1949. *The Kalingas: Their institutions and custom law*. Chicago: University of Chicago Press.

Bastian, Jarvis. 1965. "Primate signaling systems and human languages." In *Primate behavior: Field studies of monkeys and apes*. Irven DeVore, ed. New York: Holt, Rinehart and Winston.

Beals, Alan R. 1964. *Gopalpur: A south Indian village*. New York: Holt, Rinehart and Winston.

Beattie, John. 1964. *Other cultures: Aims, methods and achievements in social anthropology*. London, England: Cohen and West.

Benedict, Ruth. 1946. *Patterns of culture*. New York: Penguin Books. (Originally published 1934.)

Berlin, Brent. 1970. "A universalist-evolutionary approach in ethnographic semantics." In *Current directions in anthropology*. Ann Fischer, ed. Bulletins of the American Anthropological Association, vol. 3, no. 3, part 2, pp. 3-18.

Berndt, Ronald M. 1962. *Excess and restraint: Social control among a New Guinea mountain people*. Chicago: University of Chicago Press.

Bertalanffy, Ludwig von. 1968. *General system theory: Foundations, development, applications*. New York: George Braziller.

Bloomfield, Leonard. 1933. *Language*. New York: Henry Holt and Company.

Boas, Franz. 1911. Introduction to *Handbook of American Indian languages*. Washington, D.C.: Smithsonian Institution, Bureau of American Ethnology Bulletin 40, part I, pp. 1-83.

———. 1955. *Primitive art*. New York: Dover. (Originally published 1927.)

Bohannan, Paul. 1963. *Social anthropology*. New York: Holt, Rinehart and Winston.

———, and George Dalton. 1965. Introduction to *Markets in Africa: Eight subsistence economies in transition*. Paul Bohannan and George Dalton, eds. Garden City, N.Y.: Doubleday and Company, Anchor Books.

Bordaz, Jacques. 1970. *Tools of the Old and New Stone Age*. Garden City, N.Y.: Natural History Press.

Boulding, Kenneth. 1956. "General systems theory: The skeleton of science." In *The Society for the Advancement of General Systems Theory, General systems yearbook* 1: 11-17. L. von Bertalanffy and A. Rapoport, eds. Washington, D.C.: Society for General Systems Research.

Bowman, Isaiah. 1934. *Geography in relation to the social sciences*. New York: Scribner and Sons.

Brace, C. Loring. 1967. *The stages of human evolution: Human and cultural origins*. Englewood Cliffs, N.J.: Prentice-Hall.

Braidwood, Robert J. 1975. *Prehistoric men*. 8th ed. Glenview, Ill.: Scott, Foresman and Company.

———, and Charles A. Reed. 1957. *The achievement and early consequences of food-production: A consideration of the archeological and natural-historical evidence*. Cold Spring Harbor Symposia on Quantitative Biology 22, 19-31. Indianapolis, Ind.: Bobbs-Merrill reprint series in the Social Sciences A-23.

Bronowski, J. n.d. *The common sense of science*. New York: Random House, Vintage Books. (Originally published 1951.)

Buckley, Walter. 1967. *Sociology and modern systems theory*. Englewood Cliffs, N.J.: Prentice-Hall.

Buettner-Janusch, John. 1966. *Origins of man*. New York: John Wiley and Sons.

334

Bulmer, Ralph. 1970. "Which came first, the chicken or the egg-head?" In *Echanges et communications, Mélanges offert à Claude Lévi-Strauss à l'occasion de son 60ème anniversaire.* Jean Pouillon and Pierre Maranda, eds. The Hague, Netherlands: Mouton.

Burling, Robbins. 1965. *Hill farms and padi fields: Life in mainland Southeast Asia.* Englewood Cliffs, N.J.: Prentice-Hall, Spectrum Books.

———. 1970. *Man's many voices: Language in its cultural context.* New York: Holt, Rinehart and Winston.

Butzer, Karl W. 1971. *Environment and archeology.* 2nd ed. Chicago: Aldine-Atherton.

Cannon, Walter B. 1965. " 'Voodoo' death." In *Reader in comparative religion: An anthropological approach.* 3rd ed. William A. Lessa and Evon Z. Vogt. New York: Harper and Row. (Originally published 1942.)

Carneiro, Robert L. 1960. "The culture process." In *Essays in the science of culture in honor of Leslie A. White.* Gertrude E. Dole and Robert L. Carneiro, eds. New York: Thomas Y. Crowell.

———. 1961. "Slash and burn cultivation among the Kuikuru and its implications for cultural development in the Amazon basin." In *The evolution of horticultural systems in native South America: Causes and consequences— A symposium.* Johannes Wilbert, ed. Caracas, Venezuela: Supplementary Publication Antropologica 2, pp. 47-67.

———. 1973. "The four faces of evolution: Unilinear, universal, multilinear, and differential." In *Handbook of social and cultural anthropology.* John J. Honigmann, ed. Chicago: Rand McNally and Company.

Carroll, John B., ed. 1956. *Language, thought, and reality: Selected writings of Benjamin Lee Whorf.* Boston and New York: Technology Press of Massachusetts Institute of Technology and John Wiley and Sons.

Chang, Kwang-chih. 1962. "China." In *Courses toward urban life.* Robert J. Braidwood and Gordon R. Willey, eds. Viking Fund Publications in Anthropology 32. New York: Wenner-Gren Foundation for Anthropological Research.

———. 1965. "Relative chronologies of China to the end of Chou." In *Chronologies in Old World Archaeology.* Robert W. Ehrich, ed. Chicago: University of Chicago Press.

Childe, V. Gordon. 1941. *Man makes himself.* London, England: Watts and Company. (Originally published 1936.)

———. 1951. *Social evolution.* London, England: Watts and Company.

Chomsky, Noam. 1967. "The formal nature of language." In *Biological foundations of language.* Eric H. Lenneberg. New York: John Wiley and Sons.

Cipolla, Carlo M. 1962. *The economic history of world population.* Baltimore: Penguin Books.

Clark, Grahame. 1967. *The Stone Age hunters.* New York: McGraw-Hill.

———. 1971. *World prehistory: A new outline.* Cambridge, England: Cambridge University Press.

Cohen, Ronald. 1970. "Generalizations in ethnology." In *A handbook of method in cultural anthropology.* Raoul Naroll and Ronald Cohen, eds. Garden City, N.Y.: Natural History Press.

Conklin, Harold C. 1969. "An ethnoecological approach to shifting agriculture." In *Environment and cultural behavior: Ecological studies in cultural anthropology.* Andrew P. Vayda, ed. Garden City, N.Y.: Natural History Press.

Cook, Earl. 1971. "The flow of energy in an industrial society." *Scientific American* 225: 134-44.

Cottrell, Fred. 1955. *Energy and society: The relation between energy, social change, and economic development.* New York: McGraw-Hill.

Dalton, George. 1965. "Primitive money." *American Anthropologist* 67: 44-65.

———. 1968. Introduction to *Primitive, archaic, and modern economies: Essays* of *Karl Polanyi.* George Dalton, ed. Garden City, N.Y.: Doubleday and Company, Anchor Books.

Damas, David. 1969. "Characteristics of Central Eskimo band structure." In *Contributions to anthropology: Band societies.* David Damas, ed. Ottawa, Canada: National Museums of Canada Bulletin 228, Anthropological series 84, pp. 116-38.

Daniel, Glyn. 1968. *The first civilizations: The archaeology of their origins.* New York: Thomas Y. Crowell, Apollo Editions.

Deloria, Vine, Jr. 1969. *Custer died for your sins: An Indian manifesto.* New York: Macmillan.

Dentan, Robert Knox. 1968. *The Semai: A nonviolent people of Malaya.* New York: Holt, Rinehart and Winston.

Diamond, Jared M. 1966. "Zoological classification system of a primitive people." *Science* 151: 1,102-4.

Dole, Gertrude E. 1966. "Anarchy without chaos: Alternatives to political authority among the Kuikuru." In *Political anthropology.* Marc J. Swartz, Victor W. Turner, and Arthur Tuden, eds. Chicago: Aldine.

———. 1973. "Foundations of contemporary evolutionism." In *Main currents in cultural anthropology.* Raoul Naroll and Frada Naroll, eds. Englewood Cliffs, N.J.: Prentice-Hall.

Douglas, Mary. 1965. "The Lele—Resistance to change." In *Markets in Africa.* Paul Bohannan and George Dalton, eds. Garden City, N.Y.: Doubleday and Company.

Dozier, Edward P. 1967. *The Kalinga of northern Luzon, Philippines.* New York: Holt, Rinehart and Winston.

Driver, Harold E. 1961. *Indians of North America.* Chicago: University of Chicago Press.

Dröscher, Vitus B. 1971. *The friendly beast.* Translated from the German by Richard and Clara Winston. New York: E. P. Dutton and Company.

Drucker, Philip. 1951. *The northern and central Nootkan tribes.* Washington, D.C.: Smithsonian Institution, Bureau of American Ethnology Bulletin 144.

DuBois, Cora. 1936. "The wealth concept as an integrative factor in Tolowa-Tututni culture." In *Essays in anthropology presented to A. L. Kroeber.* Berkeley: University of California Press.

Durkheim, Emile. 1947. *The elementary forms of the religious life: A study in religious sociology.* Glencoe, Ill.: Free Press. (Originally published 1915.)

Dyson-Hudson, Rada, and Neville Dyson-Hudson. 1969. "Subsistence herding in Uganda." *Scientific American* 220: 76-89.

Eggan, Fred. 1950. *Social organization of the western Pueblos.* Chicago: University of Chicago Press.

———. 1955. "The Cheyenne and Arapaho kinship system." In *Social anthropology of North American tribes.* 2nd ed. Fred Eggan, ed. Chicago: University of Chicago Press.

Evans-Pritchard, E. E. 1940. *The Nuer: A description of the modes of livelihood and political institutions of a Nilotic people.* Oxford, England: Clarendon Press.

———. 1951. *Kinship and marriage among the Nuer.* Oxford, England: Clarendon Press.

———. 1953. "The Nuer conception of spirit in its relation to the social order." *American Anthropologist* 55: 201-14.

———. 1956. *Nuer religion.* Oxford, England: Clarendon Press.

———. 1965. *Theories of primitive religion.* Oxford, England: Clarendon Press.

Firth, Raymond. 1957. "The place of Malinowski in the history of economic anthropology." In *Man and culture: An evaluation of the work of Bronislaw*

Malinowski. Raymond Firth, ed. London, England: Routledge and Kegan Paul.

Flannery, Kent V. 1969. "The ecology of early food production in Mesopotamia." In *Environment and cultural behavior: Ecological studies in cultural anthropology*. Andrew P. Vayda, ed. Garden City, N.Y.: Natural History Press.

Forde, C. Daryll. 1950. *Habitat, economy and society: A geographical introduction to ethnology*. London, England: Methuen and Company. (Originally published 1934.)

———. 1954. Introduction to *African worlds: Studies in the cosmological ideas and social values of African peoples*. Daryll Forde, ed. London, England: Oxford University Press.

Fortes, M., and E. E. Evans-Pritchard, eds. 1940. *African political systems*. London, England: Oxford University Press.

Fox, Robin. 1967. *Kinship and marriage*. Baltimore: Penguin Books.

Frazer, James George. 1929. *The golden bough: A study in magic and religion*. 2 vols. New York: Book League of America.

Fried, Morton H. 1967. *The evolution of political society: An essay in political anthropology*. New York: Random House.

———, ed. 1968. *Readings in anthropology*. 2nd ed. Vol. II, *Cultural anthropology*. New York: Thomas Y. Crowell.

Friedrich, Carl Joachim. 1963. *Man and his government: An empirical theory of politics*. New York: McGraw-Hill.

Gates, David M. 1971. "The flow of energy in the biosphere." *Scientific American* 225: 88-100.

Geertz, Clifford. 1963. *Agricultural involution: The process of ecological change in Indonesia*. Berkeley: University of California Press.

———. 1964. "The transition to humanity." In *Horizons of anthropology*. Sol Tax, ed. Chicago: Aldine.

———. 1969. "Two types of ecosystems." In *Environment and cultural behavior: Ecological studies in cultural anthropology*. Andrew P. Vayda, ed. Garden City, N.Y.: Natural History Press.

Gelb, I. J. 1963. *A study of writing*. Rev. ed. Chicago: University of Chicago Press, Phoenix Books.

Gilbert, William Harlen, Jr. 1943. *The eastern Cherokees*. Washington, D.C.: Smithsonian Institution, Bureau of American Ethnology Bulletin 133, Anthropological Papers 23.

Gluckman, Max. 1962. "Les rites de passage." In *Essays on the ritual of social relations*. Max Gluckman, ed. Manchester, England: Manchester University Press.

Goldstein, Leon J. 1957. "The logic of explanation in Malinowskian anthropology." *Philosophy of Science* 24: 156-66.

Gonzales, Nancie L. Solien. 1969. *Black Carib household structure: A study of migration and modernization*. American Ethnological Society Monograph 48. Seattle: University of Washington Press.

Goody, Jack. 1972. *Domestic groups*. Modular Publications 28. Reading, Mass.: Addison-Wesley.

Gough, E. Kathleen. 1959. "The Nayars and the definition of marriage." *Journal of the Royal Anthropological Institute of Great Britain and Ireland* 89: 23-34. Indianapolis, Ind.: Bobbs-Merrill reprint series in the Social Sciences A-378.

Gould, Harold A. 1958. "The Hindu Jajmani system: A case of economic particularism." *Southwestern Journal of Anthropology* 14: 428-37.

———. 1971. *Caste and class: A comparative view*. Modular Publications 11. Reading, Mass.: Addison-Wesley.

Greenberg, Joseph. 1968. *Anthropological linguistics: An introduction*. New York: Random House.

Griaule, Marcel, and Germain Dieterlen. 1954. "The Dogon of the French Sudan." In *African worlds: Studies in the cosmological ideas and social values of African peoples.* Daryll Forde, ed. London, England: Oxford University Press.

Grinnell, George Bird. 1923. *The Cheyenne Indians.* 2 vols. New Haven, Conn.: Yale University Press.

———. 1956. *The fighting Cheyennes.* Norman: University of Oklahoma Press. (Originally published 1915.)

Gumperz, John J. 1973. "Language and communication." In *Explorations in anthropology.* Morton H. Fried, ed. New York: Thomas Y. Crowell.

Haddon, Alfred C. 1934. *History of anthropology.* London, England: Watts and Company.

Harding, Thomas G. 1960. "Adaptation and stability." In *Evolution and culture.* Marshall D. Sahlins and Elman R. Service, eds. Ann Arbor: University of Michigan Press.

———. 1970. "Trading in northeast New Guinea." In *Cultures of the Pacific: Selected readings.* Thomas G. Harding and Ben J. Wallace, eds. New York: Free Press.

Harper, Edward B. 1968. "A comparative analysis of caste: The United States and India." In *Structure and change in Indian society.* Milton Singer and Bernard S. Cohn, eds. Viking Fund Publications in Anthropology 47. New York: Wenner-Gren Foundation for Anthropological Research.

Harris, Marvin. 1968. *The rise of anthropological theory.* New York: Thomas Y. Crowell.

———. 1971. *Culture, man, and nature.* New York: Thomas Y. Crowell.

———. 1972. "One man's food is another man's whitewash." *Natural History* 81: 12-14.

Harsanyi, John C. 1968. "Explanation and comparative dynamics in social science." In *Theory in anthropology: A sourcebook.* Robert A. Manners and David Kaplan, eds. Chicago: Aldine.

Hempel, Carl G. 1959. "The logic of functional analysis." In *Sociological theory: Inquiries and paradigms.* Llewellyn Gross, ed. Evanston, Ill.: Row, Peterson and Company.

Hocart, A. M. 1972. "Kinship systems." In *Readings in anthropology.* 3rd ed. Jesse D. Jennings and E. Adamson Hoebel, eds. New York: McGraw-Hill.

Hockett, Charles F. 1958. *A course in modern linguistics.* New York: Macmillan.

———. 1973. *Man's place in nature.* New York: McGraw-Hill.

———, and Robert Ascher. 1964. "The human revolution." *Current Anthropology* 5: 135-68.

Hoebel, E. Adamson. 1946. "Law and anthropology." *Virginia Law Review* 32: 835-54. Indianapolis, Ind.: Bobbs-Merrill reprint series in the Social Sciences A-117.

———. 1960. *The Cheyennes: Indians of the Great Plains.* New York: Holt, Rinehart and Winston.

———. 1964. *The law of primitive man: A study in comparative legal dynamics.* Cambridge, Mass.: Harvard University Press. (Originally published 1954.)

Hoijer, Harry. 1971. "Language and writing." In *Man, culture, and society.* Rev. ed. Harry L. Shapiro, ed. London, England: Oxford University Press.

Holder, Preston. 1970. *The hoe and the horse on the Plains: A study of cultural development among North American Indians.* Lincoln: University of Nebraska Press.

Holmberg, Allan R. 1960. *Nomads of the long bow.* Chicago: University of Chicago Press. (Originally published 1950.)

Horton, Robin. 1962. "The Kalabari world-view: An outline and interpretation." *Africa* 32: 197-220.

Hubbert, M. King. 1971. "The energy resources of the earth." *Scientific American* 225: 60-70.

Hulse, F. S. 1971. *The human species.* 2nd ed. New York: Random House.

Hymes, Dell H. 1961. "Functions of speech: An evolutionary approach." In *Anthropology and education.* Frederick C. Gruber, ed. Philadelphia: University of Pennsylvania Press. Indianapolis, Ind.: Bobbs-Merrill reprint series in the Social Sciences A-124.

———. 1971. Foreword to *The origin and diversification of language.* Morris Swadesh. Chicago: Aldine-Atherton.

Jarvie, I. C. 1969. *The revolution in anthropology.* Chicago: Henry Regnery.

———. 1973. *Functionalism.* Minneapolis: Burgess.

Jastrow, Robert. 1968. "Cosmic evolution." *Natural History* 72: 34-38.

Jenness, Diamond. 1922. *The life of the Copper Eskimo. Report of the Canadian Arctic Expedition 1913-1918,* Vol. 12. Ottawa, Canada: King's Printer.

———. 1959. *The people of the twilight.* Chicago: University of Chicago Press, Phoenix Books. (Originally published 1928.)

Joynt, Carey B., and Nicholas Rescher. 1961. "The problem of uniqueness in history." *History and Theory, Studies in the Philosophy of History* 1: 150-62.

Kaplan, Abraham. 1964. *The conduct of inquiry: Methodology for behavioral science.* San Francisco: Chandler.

Kaplan, David. 1960. "The law of cultural dominance." In *Evolution and culture.* Marshall D. Sahlins and Elman R. Service, eds. Ann Arbor: University of Michigan Press.

———. 1965. "The superorganic: Science or metaphysics?" *American Anthropologist* 67: 958-76.

Kemp, William B. 1971. "The flow of energy in a hunting society." *Scientific American* 225: 104-15.

Klein, Richard G. 1969. *Man and culture in the Late Pleistocene: A case study.* San Francisco: Chandler.

Kramer, Samuel Noah. 1959. *History begins at Sumer.* Garden City, N.Y.: Doubleday and Company.

Kroeber, A. L. 1944. *Configurations of culture growth.* Berkeley: University of California Press.

———. 1947. *Cultural and natural areas of native North America.* Berkeley: University of California Press.

———. 1948. *Anthropology.* Rev. ed. New York: Harcourt, Brace and Company.

———. 1952. *The nature of culture.* Chicago: University of Chicago Press.

———, and Clyde Kluckhohn. 1952. *Culture, a critical review of concepts and definitions.* Cambridge, Mass.: Papers of the Peabody Museum of American Archaeology and Ethnology 47, 1.

Kummer, Hans. 1971. *Primate societies.* Chicago: Aldine-Atherton.

Kuper, Hilda. 1963. *The Swazi: A South African kingdom.* New York: Holt, Rinehart and Winston.

LaBarre, Weston. 1949. "The cultural basis of emotions and gestures." In *Personal character and cultural milieu.* Rev. ed. Douglas G. Haring, ed. Syracuse, N.Y.: Syracuse University Press.

Lancaster, Jane B. 1968. "Primate communication systems and the emergence of human language." In *Primates: Studies in adaptation and variability.* Phyllis C. Jay, ed. New York: Holt, Rinehart and Winston.

Lanning, Edward P. 1967. *Peru before the Incas.* Englewood Cliffs, N.J.: Prentice-Hall.

Laughlin, William S. 1961. "Acquisition of anatomical information by ancient man." In *Social life of early man.* Sherwood L. Washburn, ed. Viking Fund Publications in Anthropology 31. New York: Wenner-Gren Foundation for Anthropological Research.

Lee, Richard B. 1969. "!Kung Bushman subsistence: An input-output analysis." In *Environment and cultural behavior: Ecological studies in cultural anthropology.* Andrew P. Vayda, ed. Garden City, N.Y.: Natural History Press.

———. 1972. "Work effort, group structure and land-use in contemporary hunter-gatherers." In *Man, settlement and urbanism.* Peter J. Ucko, Ruth Tringham, and G. W. Dimbleby, eds. London, England: Gerald Duckworth and Company.

———, and Irven DeVore, eds. 1968. *Man the hunter.* Chicago: Aldine.

Lessa, William A., and Evon Z. Vogt. 1972. *Reader in comparative religion: An anthropological approach.* 3rd ed. New York: Harper and Row.

Linton, Ralph. 1936. *The study of man: An introduction.* New York: Appleton-Century.

Llewellyn, Karl N., and E. Adamson Hoebel. 1941. *The Cheyenne way: Conflict and case law in primitive jurisprudence.* Norman: University of Oklahoma Press.

Loomis, Frederick Brewster. 1923. *Field book of common rocks and minerals.* New York: G. P. Putnam's Sons.

Lowie, Robert H. 1937. *The history of ethnological theory.* New York: Farrar and Rinehart.

MacNeish, Richard S. 1964a. "The origins of New World civilization." *Scientific American* 211: 29-37.

———. 1964b. "Ancient Mesoamerican civilization." *Science* 143: 531-37.

Malinowski, Bronislaw. 1935. *Coral gardens and their magic.* 2 vols. New York: American Book Company.

———. 1939. "The group and the individual in functional analysis." *American Journal of Sociology* 44: 938-64. Indianapolis, Ind.: Bobbs-Merrill reprint series in the Social Sciences S-183.

———. 1948. *Magic, science and religion and other essays.* Glencoe, Ill.: Free Press.

———. 1950. *Argonauts of the western Pacific.* New York: E. P. Dutton and Company. (Originally published 1922.)

———. 1951. *Crime and custom in savage society.* New York: Humanities Press. (Originally published 1926.)

———. 1960. *A scientific theory of culture and other essays.* New York: Oxford University Press, Galaxy Books. (Originally published 1944.)

Mandelbaum, David G., ed. 1949. *Selected writings of Edward Sapir in language, culture, and personality.* Berkeley: University of California Press.

Manners, Robert A., ed. 1964. *Process and pattern in culture: Essays in honor of Julian H. Steward.* Chicago: Aldine.

Marler, Peter. 1965. "Communication in monkeys and apes." In *Primate behavior: Field studies of monkeys and apes.* Irven DeVore, ed. New York: Holt, Rinehart and Winston.

Marshall, Lorna. 1965. "The !Kung Bushmen of the Kalahari Desert." In *Peoples of Africa.* James L. Gibbs, Jr., ed. New York: Holt, Rinehart and Winston.

Mason, Otis T. 1907. "Environment." In *Handbook of American Indians north of Mexico.* Frederick Webb Hodge, ed. Washington, D.C.: Smithsonian Institution, Bureau of American Ethnology Bulletin 30, part 1, pp. 427-30.

Mauss, Marcel. 1954. *The gift: Forms and functions of exchange in archaic societies.* Translated by Ian Cunnison. London, England: Cohen and West.

Mayhall, Mildred P. 1962. *The Kiowas.* Norman: University of Oklahoma Press.

Meggitt, M. J. 1965. *Desert people: A study of the Walbiri Aborigines of central Australia.* Chicago: University of Chicago Press.

Menninger, Karl. 1969. *Number words and number symbols: A cultural history of numbers.* Translated by Paul Broneer from the revised German edition. Cambridge, Mass.: M.I.T. Press. (Originally published 1958.)

Middleton, John. 1965. *The Lugbara of Uganda.* New York: Holt, Rinehart and Winston.

———. 1967. "The concept of 'bewitching' in Lugbara." In *Magic, witchcraft, and curing.* John Middleton, ed. Garden City, N.Y.: Natural History Press. (Originally published 1955.)

Miller, James G. 1956. "Toward a general theory for the behavioral sciences." In *The state of the social sciences.* Leonard D. White, ed. Chicago: University of Chicago Press.

Moore, Omar Khayyam. 1957. "Divination—A new perspective." *American Anthropologist* 59: 69-74.

Morgan, Lewis H. 1871. *Systems of consanguinity and affinity of the human family.* Smithsonian Contributions to Knowledge, 218. Washington, D.C.: Smithsonian Institution.

———. 1964. *Ancient society.* Leslie A. White, ed. Cambridge, Mass.: Harvard University Press, Belknap Press. (Originally published 1877.)

Murdock, George Peter. 1945. "The common denominator of cultures." In *The science of man in the world crisis.* Ralph Linton, ed. New York: Columbia University Press.

———. 1949. *Social structure.* New York: Macmillan.

———. 1957. "World ethnographic sample." *American Anthropologist* 59: 664-87.

———. 1959. *Africa: Its peoples and their culture history.* New York: McGraw-Hill.

———. 1968. "The current status of the world's hunting and gathering peoples." In *Man the hunter.* Richard B. Lee and Irven DeVore, eds. Chicago: Aldine.

Nagel, Ernest. 1952. "Some issues in the logic of historical analysis." *The Scientific Monthly* 74: 162-69.

Netting, Robert McC. 1968. *Hill farmers of Nigeria: Cultural ecology of the Kofyar of the Jos Plateau.* American Ethnological Society Monograph 46. Seattle: University of Washington Press.

———. 1971. *The ecological approach in cultural study.* Modular Publications. Reading, Mass.: Addison-Wesley.

Newman, Philip L. 1965. *Knowing the Gururumba.* New York: Holt, Rinehart and Winston.

Norbeck, Edward. 1961. *Religion in primitive society.* New York: Harper and Brothers.

Noss, John B. 1949. *Man's religions.* New York: Macmillan.

Oakley, Kenneth. 1957. "Tools makyth man." *Antiquity* 31: 199-209.

Odum, Eugene P. 1971. *Fundamentals of ecology.* 3rd ed. Philadelphia: W. B. Saunders.

Oliver, Symmes C. 1962. *Ecology and cultural continuity as contributing factors in the social organization of the Plains Indians.* Berkeley: University of California Publications in American Archaeology and Ethnology 48, 1.

Partridge, Eric. 1958. *Origins: A short etymological dictionary of modern English.* New York: Macmillan.

Piddington, Ralph. 1950. *An introduction to social anthropology.* Vol. 1. New York: Frederick A. Praeger.

Polanyi, Karl. 1957. *The great transformation.* Boston: Beacon Press. (Originally published 1944.)

Pospisil, Leopold. 1972. *The ethnology of law.* Modular Publications 12. Reading, Mass.: Addison-Wesley.

Pronko, N. H. 1969. *Panorama of psychology.* Monterey, Calif.: Brooks/Cole.

Radcliffe-Brown, A. R. 1940. Preface to *African political systems.* M. Fortes and E. E. Evans-Pritchard, eds. London, England: Oxford University Press.

———. 1952. *Structure and function in primitive society.* Glencoe, Ill.: Free Press.

References

Rapoport, Anatol. 1954. *Operational philosophy: Integrating knowledge and action*. New York: Harper and Brothers.

Rappaport, Roy A. 1967a. *Pigs for the ancestors: Ritual in the ecology of a New Guinea people*. New Haven, Conn.: Yale University Press.

———. 1967b. "Ritual regulation of environmental relations among a New Guinea people." *Ethnology* 6: 17-30.

———. 1971. "The flow of energy in an agricultural society." *Scientific American* 225: 116-32.

Redfield, Robert. 1953. *The primitive world and its transformations*. Ithaca, N.Y.: Cornell University Press.

Reed, Charles A. 1959. "Animal domestication in the prehistoric Near East." *Science* 130: 1,629-39.

Reynolds, Vernon. 1967. *The apes*. New York: E. P. Dutton and Company.

———. 1972. "Open groups in hominid evolution." In *Primates on primates*. Duane Quiatt, ed. Minneapolis: Burgess.

———, and Frances Reynolds. 1965. "Chimpanzees of the Budongo Forest." In *Primate behavior: Field studies of monkeys and apes*. Irven DeVore, ed. New York: Holt, Rinehart and Winston.

Sahlins, Marshall D. 1958. *Social stratification in Polynesia*. American Ethnological Society Monograph. Seattle: University of Washington Press.

———. 1961. "The segmentary lineage: An instrument of predatory expansion." *American Anthropologist* 62: 322-45.

———. 1963. "Poor man, rich man, big-man, chief: Political types in Melanesia and Polynesia." *Comparative Studies in Society and History* 5: 285-303. Indianapolis, Ind.: Bobbs-Merrill reprint series in the Social Sciences A-339.

———. 1965. "On the sociology of primitive exchange." In *The relevance of models for social anthropology*. Michael Banton, ed. Association of Social Anthropologists Monograph 1. London, England: Tavistock; New York: Frederick A. Praeger.

———. 1968. *Tribesmen*. Englewood Cliffs, N.J.: Prentice-Hall.

———. 1972. *Stone Age economics*. Chicago: Aldine-Atherton.

———, and Elman R. Service, eds. 1960. *Evolution and culture*. Ann Arbor: University of Michigan Press.

Sapir, Edward. 1921. *Language*. New York: Harcourt, Brace and Company, Harvest Books.

Service, Elman R. 1966. *The hunters*. Englewood Cliffs, N.J.: Prentice-Hall.

———. 1968. "The prime-mover of cultural evolution." *Southwestern Journal of Anthropology* 24: 396-409.

———. 1971a. *Cultural evolutionism: Theory in practice*. New York: Holt, Rinehart and Winston.

———. 1971b. *Primitive social organization: An evolutionary perspective*. 2nd ed. New York: Random House.

———. 1971c. *Profiles in ethnology*. Rev. ed. New York: Harper and Row.

Sharp, Lauriston. 1970. "Steel axes for Stone-Age Australians." In *Cultures of the Pacific: Selected readings*. Thomas G. Harding and Ben J. Wallace, eds. New York: Free Press. (Originally published 1953.)

Spencer, Herbert. n.d. *First principles*. New York: Lovell, Coryell and Company. (Originally published 1862.)

Spencer, Robert F. 1971. "The social composition of the north Alaskan whaling crew." In *Alliance in Eskimo society*. Lee Guemple, ed. Proceedings of the American Ethnological Society, Supplement, 1971: 110-20.

Spier, Robert F. G. 1970. *From the hand of man: Primitive and pre-industrial technologies*. Boston: Houghton Mifflin.

Spiro, Melford E. 1970. *Kibbutz: Venture in utopia*. New York: Schocken Books. (Originally published 1956.)

Starr, Chauncey. 1971. "Energy and power." *Scientific American* 225: 36-49.

Steward, Julian H. 1936. "The economic and social basis of primitive bands." In *Essays in anthropology in honor of Alfred Louis Kroeber.* Berkeley: University of California Press.

———. 1955. *Theory of culture change: The methodology of multilinear evolution.* Urbana: University of Illinois Press.

Stewart, George R. 1949. *Earth abides.* New York: Random House.

Stocking, George W., Jr. 1968. *Race, culture, and evolution: Essays in the history of anthropology.* New York: Free Press.

Sturtevant, Edgar H. 1947. *An introduction to linguistic science.* New Haven, Conn.: Yale University Press.

Summers, Claude M. 1971. "The conversion of energy." *Scientific American* 225: 148-60.

Suttles, Wayne. 1968. "Variation in habitat and culture on the Northwest Coast." In *Man in adaptation, the cultural present.* Yehudi A. Cohen, ed. Chicago: Aldine.

Swadesh, Morris. 1971. *The origin and diversification of language.* Joel Sherzer, ed. Chicago: Aldine-Atherton.

Sweet, Louise. 1965a. "Camel pastoralism in north Arabia and the minimal camping unit." In *Man, culture, and animals: The role of animals in human ecological adjustments.* Anthony Leeds and Andrew P. Vayda, eds. Washington, D.C.: American Association for the Advancement of Science.

———. 1965b. "Camel raiding of north Arabian Bedouin: A mechanism of ecological adaptation." *American Anthropologist* 67: 1,132-50.

Thirring, Hans. 1962. *Energy for man: From windmills to nuclear power.* New York: Harper and Row, Torchbooks.

Thomas, Elizabeth Marshall. 1959. *The harmless people.* New York: Alfred A. Knopf.

Thurber, James. 1945. *The Thurber carnival.* New York: Harper and Brothers.

Titiev, Mischa. 1943. "The influence of common residence on the unilateral classification of kindred." *American Anthropologist* 45: 511-30.

———. 1944. *Old Oraibi: A study of the Hopi Indians of Third Mesa.* Cambridge, Mass.: Papers of the Peabody Museum of American Archaeology and Ethnology 22, 1.

Tobias, Phillip V. 1965. "New discoveries in Tanganyika: Their bearing on hominid evolution." *Current Anthropology* 6: 391-411.

Trigger, Bruce. 1972. "Determinants of urban growth in pre-industrial societies." In *Man, settlement and urbanism.* Peter J. Ucko, Ruth Tringham, and G. W. Dimbleby, eds. London, England: Gerald Duckworth and Company.

Turnbull, Colin M. 1961. *The forest people.* New York: Simon and Schuster.

———. 1963. "The lesson of the Pygmies." *Scientific American* 208: 26-37.

———. 1965. "The Mbuti Pygmies of the Congo." In *Peoples of Africa.* James L. Gibbs, Jr., ed. New York: Holt, Rinehart and Winston.

———. 1968. "The importance of flux in two hunting societies." In *Man the hunter.* Richard B. Lee and Irven DeVore, eds. Chicago: Aldine.

Tyler, Stephen A., ed. 1969. *Cognitive anthropology.* New York: Holt, Rinehart and Winston.

Tylor, Edward B. 1916. *Anthropology.* New York: D. Appleton and Company. (Originally published 1881.)

———. 1958. *Primitive culture.* Published as part I, *The origins of culture,* and part II, *Religion in primitive culture.* New York: Harper and Brothers. (Originally published 1871.)

Ubbelohde, A. R. 1955. *Man and energy.* New York: George Braziller.

Van Gennep, Arnold. 1960. *The rites of passage.* Translated by Monika B. Vizedom and Gabrielle L. Caffee. Chicago: University of Chicago Press, Phoenix Books. (Originally published 1909.)

Van Lawick-Goodall, Jane. 1967. *My friends the wild chimpanzees.* Washington, D.C.: National Geographic Society.

———. 1972. "A preliminary report on expressive movements and communication in the Gombe Stream chimpanzees." In *Primate patterns.* Phyllis Dohlinow, ed. New York: Holt, Rinehart and Winston.

Vansina, Jan. 1970. "Cultures through time." In *A handbook of method in cultural anthropology.* Raoul Naroll and Ronald Cohen, eds. Garden City, N.Y.: Natural History Press.

Vayda, Andrew P. 1967. "Pomo trade feasts." In *Tribal and peasant economies: Readings in economic anthropology.* George Dalton, ed. Garden City, N.Y.: Natural History Press.

Vogel, Virgil J. 1970. *American Indian medicine.* Norman: University of Oklahoma Press.

Wallace, Anthony F. C. 1966. *Religion: An anthropological view.* New York: Random House.

Washburn, S. L., and Irven DeVore. 1961. "Social behavior of baboons and early man." In *Social life of early man.* Sherwood L. Washburn, ed. Viking Fund Publications in Anthropology 31. New York: Wenner-Gren Foundation for Anthropological Research.

White, Leslie A. 1945. "History, evolutionism, and functionalism: Three types of interpretation of culture." *Southwestern Journal of Anthropology* 1: 221-48.

———. 1948. "Lewis Henry Morgan: Pioneer in the theory of social evolution." In *An introduction to the history of sociology.* Harry Elmer Barnes, ed. Chicago: University of Chicago Press.

———. 1949. *The science of culture: A study of man and civilization.* New York: Farrar, Straus and Company.

———. 1957. *How Morgan came to write systems of consanguinity and affinity.* Ann Arbor: Papers of the Michigan Academy of Science, Arts, and Letters 42: 257-68.

———. 1959. *The evolution of culture: The development of civilization to the fall of Rome.* New York: McGraw-Hill.

———. 1964. Introduction to *Ancient society.* Lewis H. Morgan. Leslie A. White, ed. Cambridge, Mass.: Harvard University Press, Belknap Press.

———. 1966. *The social organization of ethnological theory.* Houston: Monograph in Cultural Anthropology, Rice University Studies 52, 4.

———, with Beth Dillingham. 1973. *The concept of culture.* Minneapolis: Burgess.

Wiener, Norbert. 1948. *Cybernetics.* New York: John Wiley and Sons.

Williams, Thomas Rhys. 1972. *Introduction to socialization.* Saint Louis: C. V. Mosby.

Wilson, Monica Hunter. 1951. "Witch beliefs and social structure." *American Journal of Sociology* 56: 307-13. Indianapolis, Ind.: Bobbs-Merrill reprint series in the Social Sciences A-243.

Wisdom, J. O. 1956. "The hypotheses of cybernetics." In *The Society for the Advancement of General Systems Theory, General systems yearbook* 1: 111-22. L. von Bertalanffy and A. Rapoport, eds. Washington, D.C.: Society for General Systems Research.

Wissler, Clark. 1923. *Man and culture.* New York: Thomas Y. Crowell.

———. 1941. *Indians of the United States.* New York: Doubleday, Doran and Company.

———. 1950. *The American Indian.* New York: Peter Smith. (Originally published 1917.)

Wolf, Eric R. 1966. *Peasants.* Englewood Cliffs, N.J.: Prentice-Hall.

Wylie, Laurence. 1974. *Village in the Vaucluse.* 3rd ed. Cambridge, Mass.: Harvard University Press. (Originally published 1957.)

Glossary

Acheulian: A term referring to Lower Paleolithic stone tools, associated with *Homo erectus,* which include biface cleavers and hand-axes and flakes struck from cores.

adaptation: A state of equilibrium or balance between cultural systems and their environments, or the process by which the state is achieved. Also applicable in biological contexts, as the process by which organic systems become fitted for survival and success in their environments.

affinal kin, affines: Social statuses and groups established or linked by marriage.

age set: One of a number of formal groups whose criterion for membership is age or generation.

animate energy: Physiological energy, maintained by food intake. Contrasts with inanimate or physical energy, derived from fuel, wind, flowing water, the atom, and so on.

animatism: The belief in an impersonal or nonpersonalized force residing in persons and things.

animism: The belief in supernatural beings, such as souls and spirits.

Apollonian: A term derived from the philosopher Nietzche by Ruth Benedict and applied to Southwestern Indian cultures to mean distrust of individualism and of disruptive extremes of behavior, and commitment to a calm, traditional "middle way."

345

ascendant: In kinship context, a forebear or ancestor.

aspect: The way a thing looks or the interpretation we make of it from a particular point of view. Human behavior, for instance, has biological and cultural aspects, and culture has technological and other aspects.

associations: Groups such as partnerships, work parties, age sets, and clubs, whose membership is separable from kinship and residence contexts, and which usually are oriented toward specific and limited tasks or objectives.

Australopithecus: A tool-making ape, chronologically the earliest and developmentally the most primitive genus in the three grades or levels of the hominid family.

authority: Ideas and beliefs surrounding and supporting leader-follower, or power, behavior.

band: One of the basic residential or territorial groups among hunters and gatherers (the other is the household), variable in size and composition but most often composed of from twenty-five to fifty persons.

big man: A leader in rank societies who acquires his power not through descent, as does a chief, but through his generosity, personal effort, and sponsoring of social events.

bilateral kinship: A pattern of kinship which is uniform and equal on mother's and father's sides.

caloric minimum: The number of calories required to sustain the average working adult in a given culture and natural environment.

caste: An endogamous, ranked, and stratified social group based upon descent and hereditary occupation.

ceremonial fund: Expenditures for social rituals accompanying birth, marriage, death, and like events, as well as community festivals and entertainments.

clan: An exogamous and named social group which includes several lineages and whose members claim descent from a common ancestor.

class: One of a number of stratified groups in a state society which have unequal access to economic resources and political power.

classificatory kinship terminology: A pattern of naming kin in which lineal and collateral relatives are grouped together under primary terms (such as *father, mother, daughter*) at some points.

cognatic descent: Descent calculated through antecedents of both sexes rather than one.

cognitive anthropology: A specialized branch of cultural anthropology directed toward eliciting and interpreting native classification systems.

collateral relatives: Consanguineal kin not in one's direct line of descent, as uncles, aunts, and cousins.

concept: In the context of this book's orientation, a bundle of perceptions with an attached symbol, such as a word, or a symbol and its attached perceptions. Commonly, an idea.

conical clan: A descent group whose component lines are ranked according to genealogical distance from the clan founder.

contagious magic: In Frazer's terms, magic based on the inference

346

that whatever one does to a material object will affect the person who was in contact with it. Thus, one can harm enemies by working on bits of their hair, on their fingernails, or on discarded pieces of their clothing.

context: A background or setting that gives meaning to an object or event. The setting may be the whole existing one or a selected set of surrounding circumstances extracted and named according to some particular point of view and labelled with terms of broad extension.

corporate group: A social anthropological term for continuing groups that hold and manage some kind of property or other rights.

creation myth: A more or less connected set of stories of a supernaturalistic sort concerning the origin of the world and the things and beings in it.

Cro-Magnon: A variety of *Homo sapiens* who lived in Europe in Upper Paleolithic times.

cross-cousin: The relationship of Ego to any offspring of his or her mother's brothers or father's sisters.

cultural dominance: The principle that a cultural system which exploits the energy resources of its environment most effectively will tend to spread at the expense of less effective ones in that environment.

cultural evolution: In a general sense, the progression of kinds of cultural adaptations as a whole from low-energy to high-energy organizations. In a specific sense, the transformation of a culture's adaptation to its environments from one kind to another.

cultural pattern: A descriptive summary of customs or sequences of cultural behavior.

cultural process: The dynamics or movements of cultural systems, summed up in terms of broad extension, such as *discovery, invention, adaptation,* and the like.

culture: In common terms, customs, or traditional customs. In the context of this book's orientation, a symboling-dependent, energy-transforming system of objects and events.

culture area: A geographical region in which separate cultures are more or less similar to one another and different from cultures in other regions. One of the family of "middle-ground" or pattern descriptions.

culture hero: The bringer or inventor of customs or lifeways, usually employed in a supernaturalistic context.

culturological: An adjective for a mode of interpretation of human behavior in terms of culture rather than sociology or psychology.

descendant: One's offspring and their offspring, *ad infinitum.*

descent group: A culturally defined social group whose members are descended from a common ancestor.

descriptive kinship terminology: A pattern of naming kin in which lineal relatives are clearly separated from collateral relatives.

diffusion: A culture process involving the movement of elements from one cultural system to another.

discovery: A culture process in which things move into culture from environments because of the particular, useful properties they have—

as the cutting ability of flint. To put it psychologically, humans become aware of those properties.

divination: A forecasting or finding out by supernatural means.

dominance: The superior or superordinate end of ranking relationships among lower primates who establish a sort of pecking order in a group.

duality of patterning: The characteristic of human language by which elementary signaling units, or phonemes, have no meaning of themselves but combine to form units with referential meaning, such as words or sentences.

dyad: A set of relationships between only two statuses, as mother-daughter, father-son, husband-wife.

Early Dynastic: The period in Sumerian history beginning a century or two after 3000 B.C. and ending about 2400 B.C., when Sargon of Akkad conquered the land.

ecology: The relations between populations of organisms and their habitats, or the branch of biological science dealing with the study of those relationships. By extension, the term is applicable to relations of cultural systems and their habitats.

economy: A measure of the units of energy required to make a tool or machine or other cultural device.

efficiency: A measure of the energy a tool or machine or other device converts, transmits, delivers, or stores in relation to the energy it consumes or expends in the task.

egalitarian society: A kin-based primitive society in which households have roughly equal access to basic resources, division of labor rests primarily on sex and age, reciprocity dominates distribution of goods and services, and leader-follower relationships are limited, shifting, and relatively impermanent.

Ego: The selected individual or status, the focal point in calculation of kin relationships. You are Ego when you label your relatives with kin terms.

empirical: Depending on observation or experience.

enculturation: A process by which human individuals and groups are enwrapped in and their behavior is programmed by a culture.

endogamy: The rule or practice of a person's marrying within a culturally defined and prescribed group of which he or she is a member.

energy: In physics and engineering, the physical capacity or ability to do work. Work is done when a body is moved.

equifinality: The principle applying to the behavior of open systems, such as culture, in which a final or given state may be reached from different initial conditions and by different paths.

ethnocentrism: The setting up of one's own customs as the standard for evaluation; the belief that one's own customs are superior and those of other people inferior.

ethnographic present: The time at which an ethnographer made his or her observations, spoken of later as if it were the present.

etiquette: A part of the prescribed behavior between statuses and groups which mark off one from another. It is one means of social control.

exogamy: The rule or practice of marrying out, which requires that a member of a culturally defined group must marry outside of that group.

extended family: A kin group consisting of two or more nuclear families—either siblings and their spouses and children, or a married pair and their children and children's spouses and offspring.

extraction: The selection and removal of an object or a characteristic of an object from its surroundings in order to place it in new contexts for understanding. We use the term *extraction* in preference to *abstraction* because of the unfortunate common connotation of the latter as something wholly imaginary or unreal.

folk cultures: Redfield's term for cultures lying toward the opposite end of a spectrum from urban and civilized; substantially, peasant cultures, but not clearly separable from primitive ones. In Redfield's view, folk cultures tend to move from traditional, kin- and religion-oriented lifeways toward the secular, market-centered, urban type.

function: A social anthropological term which means variously what a thing does, what it contributes to the maintenance of a society, or what its relations are with other things in the society.

functional alternatives: Different social or cultural forms which do the same tasks or make the same kind of contributions to the whole.

functionalism: A name for the doctrines of one of the principal schools of anthropological theory, particularly associated with Radcliffe-Brown and Malinowski. In addition to its emphasis on function, the school is largely nonhistorical and nonevolutionary.

fund of rent: A charge against the production of a peasant made by a landlord or someone else with power.

general evolution: A temporal succession of forms in the physical, biological, or cultural domains as wholes.

general-purpose money: A medium of exchange, a standard of value, and a means of making deferred payments for goods and services.

genetic: Transmitted through biological heredity.

genetic mutation: A change in the structure and effect of a gene, the mechanism by which biological characteristics are transmitted from generation to generation.

geographical determinism: The notion that differences in human lifeways are produced largely by differences in climate, landforms, and like factors.

guardian spirit: A supernatural being who serves as protector and helper to a person, most usually, as in Plains Indian culture, acquired during a vision.

habitat: Ordinarily, the natural setting of a plant or animal population. In our orientation, an alternate term for natural environment—which is to say, everything that isn't culture or people and which impinges on them.

Halaf: One of the two earliest farming traditions in northern Mesopotamia, possibly beginning early in the sixth millennium B.C.

Hassuna: An early village farming culture in northern Mesopotamia, sixth millennium B.C., considered by some archeologists the earliest in the valley proper, as opposed to the upland flanks. Roughly contemporary with Halaf but ended before the latter.

historicism: A kind of historical interpretation directed to understanding past events by placing them in their own, immediate, contemporaneous context.

history: A kind of interpretation of events which emphasizes time relations and tends to be particularistic rather than generalizing or nomothetic.

hoe farming: A kind of nonmechanized cultivation in relatively permanent fields in which the water supply comes from rains, flooding streams, or springs.

Holocene: The present geological epoch, which began about 10,000 years ago, following the Pleistocene.

hominid: The zoological classificatory family which includes the genus *Homo* and forms immediately ancestral to it, such as the Australopithecines.

hominoid: The classificatory superfamily which includes the hominids plus contemporary and fossil apes, but not monkeys or prosimians or their fossil forms.

Homo erectus: A grade or evolutionary level in the hominids; a species of our genus which evolved from *Australopithecus* and preceded our own species, *Homo sapiens.*

"Homo habilis": The fossil hominid which most classifiers label as an Australopithecine variety but which some place in the genus *Homo* because of certain progressive characteristics.

Homo sapiens: The biological species to which all contemporary humans belong. Technically, we are *Homo sapiens sapiens,* and the Neanderthals were *Homo sapiens neanderthalensis.*

household: A basic domestic or residential group whose cooperating members live together in one or a few closely connected dwellings. It usually, but not always, has an internal structure based on kinship.

hybridization: A crossing of genetic strains that produces an altered plant or animal.

hypothesis: A proposed explanation for a set of observations or facts, from which one can make more or less successful predictions.

ideology: The totality of concepts and their relations in a cultural system, or, more simply, ideas and beliefs.

imitative magic: Magic based on the principle that an effect can be produced by imitation of that effect. For instance, one can work harm on enemies by making images of them and piercing or destroying them.

inanimate energy: Energy derived from fuel, water, wind, and other physical, nonliving sources.

incest: Forbidden sexual relations within a degree of kin relations defined by a culture.

integration: A cultural process that involves the accommodation or fitting together of parts.

invention: A new cultural device that controls and combines discoveries and extends their previous uses; also a culture process.

involution: State-restoring movements in a culture which intensify the use of old means to conserve or preserve the structure; contrasts with *revolution.*

irrigated terracing: A kind of cultivation that involves control of water supply through earth- and water-retaining structures.

kaiko: The pig festival of the Tsembaga Maring of highland New Guinea.

kinship: Social relationships that involve descent and marriage.

kraal: An enclosure of brush or other material for cattle; also, East and South African household areas, with their dwellings, cattle pens and barns, and granaries.

kula: The trading network in the Trobriand Islands characterized by circulation of valued shell armbands and necklaces.

language competence: The knowledge one must have to speak grammatically correct sentences and understand others' speech in a particular speech community.

law: A form of social control, rules backed by application or threat of force by the state.

Levallois: A term referring to a technique for striking flakes from prepared flint cores which appeared first in Lower Paleolithic industries.

lineage: A social group whose members count descent from a common known ancestor, either through males or through females. Clans are composed of several related lineages.

lineal: An adjective describing a kinship principle, pattern, or terminology which emphasizes vertical descent relationships as opposed to horizontal or generational ones.

magic: In Frazer's terms, the mechanical and coercive use of things believed to have supernatural powers. Most definitions emphasize the manipulative character of magic as opposed to the subservient-propitiatory character of religion.

maize: *Zea mays,* Indian corn, an American Indian domesticate.

mana: A supernatural force, transferable by contact, often to the peril of the receiver, from one person or thing to another. The term comes from Malayo-Polynesian languages. In Pacific cultures *mana* is associated particularly with chiefs.

manioc: An edible, starchy tuber, also known as manihot, mandioca, cassava, and yuca, domesticated by South American Indians; the source of tapioca. There are two kinds—a bitter, which must be processed to expel the poison, and a sweet.

market exchange: A kind of exchange in which the values of goods and services themselves, rather than the social relationships of the exchangers, govern the transaction.

marriage: A culturally established and refined relationship between a male and a female which includes sanctioned sexual relations and social recognition of children born to them. Marriage establishes ties between groups, and its principal goal is mutual aid.

Massaum: A ceremony of the Cheyenne which continued for four days and nights and centered upon preparation of a wolf skin worn by the principal participant, called the pledger, and included animal mimetic dances by several cult groups. It is also called the Contrary Dance, because the Contrary Warriors, who ritually reversed normal behaviors, were active in it.

matrilineage: A social group whose members count descent through females from a common female ancestor. Matrilineal clans are composed of a number of matrilineages.

meaning: The place or position of a thing in a context. The context may be an actual one, including the observed objects and events preceding and surrounding the thing, or a theoretical one, in which major aspects of the complex are extracted and generalized.

Mesolithic: The period in which there was an adaptation to forests, bogs, and beaches rather than tundra, and which represents a transition between the Upper Paleolithic and Neolithic lifeways. Temporally, it lay in the beginning of the Holocene or Recent geological epoch.

metabolic apparatus: The organs involved in metabolism, in which there is a conversion of food into protoplasm and transformation of energy into living processes.

methodological superorganicism: The principle that cultural events are explained best in terms of other cultural events and that individuals' psychological motives and drives can be regarded as constants and do not explain cultural variations.

Miocene: The geological epoch which began about 28,000,000 years ago and ended about 12,000,000 years ago, and during which the hominoids divided into ancestors of the hominids on the one hand and ancestors of contemporary apes on the other.

monotheism: The belief that only one God exists.

morpheme: The minimal unit or form in a language that has referential meaning; it is composed of one or more phonemes.

morphology: The formal aspects of language at the first level of meaning rather than the purely phonological or sound level. Morphology as a study deals with morphemes and with words built out of them. Above morphology is syntax, which is the way words are put into phrases and sentences.

mortar and pestle: Respectively, the container in which grain and other things are crushed and pounded and the object used for pounding them.

Mousterian: A term referring to the Middle Old Stone Age culture characterized particularly by flake tools and associated with Neanderthals.

multicentric economy: An economy with several sectors or spheres in which different sets of goods or services are found, each set being linked for payment to particular commodities or special-purpose money.

multilinear evolution: The term Steward used to characterize his methodological position, which assumes that cultural types recur when conditions are similar but that there is no widespread, regular sequence of development of them.

multimodal communication: Systems like that of nonhuman primates in which postures, gestures, and facial expressions, not sound alone, carry a large part of the message so that more senses than hearing are called upon to receive them.

myth: A traditional story that accounts for the origin or existence of the world, the things in it, and lifeways; explanations in myth lie toward the supernaturalistic side of the ideological spectrum.

naturalistic concept: A concept in which perceptions of events that are internal to the perceiver are clearly separated from and not confused with perceptions of events that are external to the perceiver; the two classes of perceptions are clearly and unambiguously labelled.

natural selection: The mechanism of evolution in which some characteristic of plants or animals is selected for survival by reason that the trait meets environmental requirements; because the organisms in a population which have the trait have a higher survival rate than those which do not have it, they pass on the trait to their offspring, and the population changes. Natural selection was a discovery of Charles Darwin.

Neanderthal: A rugged variety of *Homo sapiens* which preceded humans of contemporary type at the beginning of the Upper Pleistocene epoch.

Neolithic: An older archeological designation for a period characterized by ground or polished tools, as opposed to chipped or flaked ones, which succeeded the Microlithic in the Holocene epoch. The meaning has shifted to designate the earliest farming lifeways, rather than a tool-making technique.

Neothermal: The warmer climatic conditions in the Holocene or Recent epoch that followed the glacial age.

nomothetic: Directed toward the discovery of regularities or general laws in nature.

nuclear family: A married man and woman and their offspring; also called the elementary or conjugal family.

Oldowan: A term referring to chopper tools, made from crudely chipped pebbles, found in Basal and Lower Pleistocene formations in East Africa.

ownership relation: The behavior of statuses and groups directed toward property, ranging from communal sharing to exclusive possession.

padi: A rice field.

Paleolithic: The Old Stone Age, beginning with the first tools made by symboling humans and continuing through the end of the Pleistocene epoch; it is divided into Lower, Middle, and Upper (or Advanced) periods.

paradigm: A pattern or model we follow when we do anthropological or other explanatory work, as when we say that humans, natural environment, and culture are three domains we study. It provides places to put observations and shows how the parts of the whole we are talking about can be arranged. The term is often used by grammarians, who mean by it a model for the inflection of a class of words.

parallel cousin: The relationship of Ego to mother's sister's son and daughter and to father's brother's son and daughter.

peasant society: An agriculturally based segment of a state society, particularly a preindustrial one, which maintains a traditional lifeway but which is dominated economically and politically by the upper strata of the state.

perception: A process in which the organism responds to stimuli—selecting, organizing, and interpreting information gained through the five senses; also any organized unit of such responses.

phoneme: The minimal sound unit, the building block of language.

phonology: The sound aspect of language, without reference to meaning; the study of language at the phonemic level.

phratry: A social group composed of two or more linked clans.

Pithecanthropus: The so-called Java man, a Lower Pleistocene hominid classified as *Homo erectus*.

Pleistocene: A geological epoch 3,000,000 years in duration, ending about 10,000 B.C., divided into Basal, Lower, Middle, and Upper segments. Popularly known as the Ice Age.

polygamy: A marriage in which a man has two or more wives at the same time (polygyny) or a woman has two or more husbands (polyandry).

polytheism: The belief in the existence of more than one god.

potlatch: A social ritual, particularly among Northwest Coast Indians, in which property is given away or destroyed, raising the prestige of chiefs and their groups.

power: Empirically, the leader-follower relationship.

presentism: A kind of historical interpretation which involves "a study of the past for the sake of the present," in which events are taken out of their own contemporaneous contexts and arranged to show a progressive movement.

prestige: Approval, admiration, or respect accorded certain persons and things.

primitive: A term which can be applied to low-energy cultures based technologically on hunting, gathering, and fishing or on simple farming in which kinship dominates social relations. It also means "early" or "original" in a temporal sense.

probabilistic statement: A statistical generalization; one that applies to the likelihood or nonlikelihood of something occurring in a class of events, given a certain set of circumstances. Probabilities are often stated as odds or measured on some scale.

Protoliterate: The cultural period in lower Mesopotamia during which the first writing system developed, roughly 3750 to 3000 B.C.

quinoa: Chenopodium, or goosefoot, a plant with edible seeds, an American Indian domesticate.

race: A human population or regional aggregate which differs from other human populations in some of its genetically inherited variable traits. As a way to grasp human variation, defining and trying to distinguish races has more disabilities than advantages.

ranked society: A social system based, like that of egalitarian society, on kinship and locality but characterized by increasing importance of redistribution over reciprocity as a mode of exchange and by more permanent and firmly established leadership.

reciprocity: A mode of exchange, or of distribution of goods and services, in which there is an obligation to give and receive.

redistribution: A channeling of goods and services to an acknowledged leader and a return to the givers and producers in gifts and feasts, characteristic of ranked societies or chiefdoms.

redistributive chief: The key status in an exchange system dominated by redistribution, exemplified by Nootka and Trobrianders. Kin and followers contribute to the chief's stores, and the chief is obligated to make generous returns.

relativism: The point of view that customs are to be understood only in the context of the particular culture of which they are part.

religion: In relation to a cultural systems point of view, an organized set of rituals and related concepts, at least some of which are definable as supernaturalistic.

replacement fund: One of the surpluses the cultivator must produce above basic subsistence needs, this one including seeds for planting, food for cattle, and maintenance or renewal of equipment and shelter.

residence rules: Requirements or preferences as to the domicile of a married pair in relation to kin groups: with the husband's (virilocal), with the wife's (uxorilocal), with either, without significant preference (ambilocal), and apart from both (neolocal). Rules also relate to the place children are reared: with father's group (patrilocal), with mother's (matrilocal), and with mother's brother's (avunculocal).

rites of passage: Rituals that mark an individual's assumption of status, such as birth, marriage, and death.

ritual: Repetitive, stereotyped, patterned behavior. In an ideological context, ritual is additionally symbolic.

routines: The patterns of language in use, associated with particular cultural activities; examples are utterances customary in directing a hunt, in taking part in a ritual, in political oratory, in learning in a classroom, or in writing a scientific report.

Sacred Arrows: Four revered objects of the Cheyenne, brought to them by their culture hero, Sweet Medicine, and kept in a bundle in the care of a priest. They are the center of a major ceremony, the Arrow Renewal.

Sacred Hat: A ritual object analogous to the Sacred Arrows, in the care of a priest of the Suhtai group among the Cheyenne.

scapulimancy: Divination with the use of animal shoulder blades, practiced natively in northern Asia and northern North America.

segmentary lineage: A descent group of a kind which splits into lineal segments retaining connections with each other in higher-order groupings that can be marshaled for common action.

semantic aspect: As part of linguistics, an aspect concerning the rules for relating vocal symbols to their referents. In a broad sense, it is language looked at with meaning itself, rather than phonology or grammar alone, as the important focus. How to account for creativity in language is a semantic problem.

semantic domain: A class of objects distinguished in a culture that share at least one characteristic in common.

shaman: A part-time specialist in supernatural rituals in primitive cultures. Traditionally in anthropology, a shaman's powers are said in native belief to be derived from confrontation with supernatural beings.

Sinanthropus: Peking man, a Lower Pleistocene hominid classified as *Homo erectus.*

slash-and-burn: A kind of farming which involves burning of forest cover and planting of seeds or cuttings in ash-covered fields and gardens; also called swiddening.

social relationships: The behavior of people toward one another, individually and in groups.

social structure: The parts of a culture in its social aspect and their arrangement.

sorcery: Supernatural rituals with an evil goal. Commonly, a sorcerer is said to use medicines or other harmful substances and objects to sicken or kill people or otherwise work mischief.

special-purpose money: Objects which serve as media of exchange and payment, in limited spheres of an economy, for specific classes of goods and services rather than as general standards of value.

specific evolution: A transformation or shift in the mode of adaptation of a particular cultural system and changes following it.

spontaneous creation: The doctrine that something can come suddenly from nothing. A variety of the view is abiogenesis, or spontaneous generation, a notion in prescientific biology which had it that plant and animal species sprang into being without living antecedents.

state society: A stratified society whose specialized organizations of government are based on property rather than kinship relations.

stratified society: A post-primitive society in which there are inequalities between statuses and groups in regard to access to basic resources.

structure: The parts of any system and their arrangement, regarded in a static rather than a dynamic sense.

style: A symbolic element in art consisting of patterned forms and qualities of actions and material productions which evokes the kind of pleasure we call esthetic.

Sun Dance: The major ceremony of Plains Indians that derives its name from a gazing-at-the-sun dance among the Dakota; the Cheyenne called their variant of the ceremony the Medicine Lodge or Willow Dance.

supernaturalistic concept: A concept that combines and confuses under one symbol perceptions of events internal and external to the perceiver.

superorganic: A synonym for *culture* or *cultural.*

swidden: A field or garden in slash-and-burn cultivation.

symbiotic relationship: A mutually beneficial and dependent relation between adjacent cultures different in some important respects, as between farmers and herders in Southwest Asia and between Bantu farmers and Pygmy hunters in Africa.

symbol: An object or event that stands for other objects or events, the association being arbitrary in the sense that there are no physical or biological reasons for the linkage. We call the process in which the arbitrary linkages are made *symboling.*

system: A structure regarded additionally in its dynamic aspect, its parts moving in relation to each other and interacting with environments.

taboo, *tabu:* A prohibition against some kind of act because of assumed supernatural danger to the violator. The term is derived from Malayo-Polynesian languages.

taro: An edible, starchy tuber of the arum family, a staple among Southeast Asian and Pacific Island cultivators.

technology: The tools and techniques for subsistence, shelter, and defense; the aspect of culture through which the major portion of its energies and materials is extracted from habitat.

territoriality: An animal behavior which consists of occupying and defending a tract of land, water, or vegetation against intruders.

theory: A general statement which explains regularities in the behavior of some part of nature and leads to new investigations. There is no rigid line between hypothesis and theory, although popularly the first is regarded as a preliminary stage of the second.

thermodynamics, first law of: The law of the conservation of energy, which states that energy is conserved in any transformation of matter, or that energy is neither created nor destroyed, only transformed. For example, mechanical energy when dissipated reappears as heat.

thermodynamics, second law of: The law that applies limitations to energy as heat, stating that heat never flows of itself from a colder to a hotter body.

tradition: Something handed down from generation to generation, whether as limited as a story or as broad as a lifeway.

Ubaid: A southern Mesopotamian historical period and culture dated about 4500-3750 B.C. The people of Ubaid were villagers and townspeople supported by wheat and barley cultivation, sheep and goat raising, and fishing.

understanding: The grasping of meaning, which is to say, the apprehension of the place of a thing in a context.

universals: A term referring not to specific traits but to general categories of things found in all cultures. Our basic universals are technology, social organization, and ideology.

vitalism: The doctrine in prescientific biology that a living thing has a principle or property separate and distinct from physical or biological properties or forces and that it lives because of this separate entity.

Warka: The Arabic name for the site of Uruk or Erech in southern

Mesopotamia, applied to a cultural phase or period following Ubaid and included in the Protoliterate period. The culture was at its height around 3500 B.C.

wattle-and-daub: A kind of construction in which mud or clay is plastered over interlaced branches on a pole frame.

witch: Conventionally defined, a person with inherent or inborn power to harm others without physical contact or overt intervention.

world view: The aspect of ideology directed toward the description and interpretation of the world surrounding humanity and humanity's place in it. In Redfield's terms, it is "the way a people characteristically look outward upon the universe."

Index

kinship among, 204-7
myth among, 320
Households:
  band societies and, 187-89
  Black Carib, 191-92
  Israeli kibbutz, 192-93
  Nayar, 190-91
Human Relations Area Files, 51, 57
Hunters and gatherers:
  adaptability of, 124-25
  as affluent societies, 124
  distribution of, 119
  social organization of, 184-88
  technology of, 119-28
Hunting, gathering, and fishing
      adaptations. *See* Adaptations,
      hunting, gathering, and fishing

Ideology:
  defined, 55, 271, 297
  evolution of, 313-15, 323-24, 331-32
  structure of, 321-23
Idiographic interpretation, 74
Inanimate energy, 162
Incas of Peru, 253
Incest taboo, 195
Industrial Revolution, 129, 165-69
Integration, 58, 60-61, 181, 290
Internal combustion engine, 166
Invention, 58-59
Irrigated terrace farming, 130, 142-44

Japan, 95, 143
Jarmo, 152-53
Jenness, Diamond, 4

Kalabari of Africa, 322-23
Kalinga of the Philippines, 16-21, 208
  adaptations of, 144
  headhunting pattern of, 84
Kaplan, Abraham, 36
Kaplan, David:
  on cultural dominance, 90
  on methodological
      superorganicism, 93-96
  on traditions, 39-40
Karam of New Guinea, 317-18
Kawai, Masao, 110
Kemp, William B., 135
Kibbutz, Israeli, 192-93
Kinship groups, types of:
  clans, 206-7, 257
  conical (cognate) clan, 244-45, 257
  lineages, 206-7
  phratries, 206-7
  segmentary lineages, 240-42

Kinship terms, 197-203
  classificatory, 197-99
  cognatic, 204
  descriptive, 196-97
  lineal, 204-6
  as status terms, 202
Kofyar of Nigeria:
  calorie production of, 140
  farming calendar of, 138
  social organization of, 208,
      222, 223
  technological adaptations of,
      137-40
Kostenki culture, 116-17, 151
Kroeber, Alfred L., 77-78
  on culture, 39
  on culture areas, 85, 88
  on diffusion, 60
  on pattern, 84
Kuikuru of Brazil:
  division of labor among, 215
  ownership among, 221
  technological adjustment of, 134-36
!Kung Bushmen:
  annual round of, 123
  bands and households of, 186-88
  division of labor among, 214
  myth among, 319
  ownership among, 220
  reciprocity among, 223
  trade among, 227
  trance among, 277-78
Kwakiutl Indians, 127

Lagash, city-state of, 253-54
Language:
  change, 306-8
  characteristics, 299-302
  creativity in, 304-5
  evolution of, 308-11
  morphemes in, 301
  morphology and, 302-4
  and perception, 302-4
  phonemes in, 300-301
  semantic aspect of, 304
Laughlin, William S., on primitive
      knowledge of anatomy, 318-19
Law (as social control), 246-49, 254
Leakey, Louis S. B., 110-13
Learning, kinds of, 36
Lee, Richard B., 119
  on bands, 220
  and index of subsistence effort, 122
Lele of Africa, 218
Levallois technique, 116
Lévi-Strauss, Claude, 78